TO A
ARE A DEAR

SOUND.

Justin Roberts

Slavery and the Enlightenment in the British Atlantic, 1750–1807

This book examines the daily details of slave work routines and plantation agriculture in the eighteenth-century British Atlantic, focusing on case studies of large plantations in Barbados, Jamaica, and Virginia. Work was the most important factor in the slaves' experience of the institution. Slaves' day-to-day work routines were shaped by plantation management strategies that drew on broader pan-Atlantic intellectual and cultural principles. Although scholars often associate the late eighteenth-century Enlightenment with the rise of notions of liberty and human rights and the dismantling of slavery, this book explores the dark side of the Enlightenment for plantation slaves. Many planters increased their slaves' workloads and employed supervisory technologies to increase labor discipline in ways that were consistent with the process of industrialization in Europe. British planters offered alternative visions of progress by embracing restrictions on freedom and seeing increasing labor discipline as central to the project of moral and economic improvement.

Justin Roberts is an assistant professor at Dalhousie University in Halifax, Nova Scotia, where he specializes in the study of slavery and the Atlantic World. He is the recipient of multiple fellowships, including awards from the Huntington Library, John D. Rockefeller Library, John Carter Brown Library, Virginia Historical Society, Library Company of Philadelphia, and the Robert H. Smith International Center for Jefferson Studies. Professor Roberts has published articles on slavery in the *William and Mary Quarterly*, *Slavery and Abolition*, and *Historical Geography*. He received his Ph.D. from Johns Hopkins University.

Slavery and the Enlightenment in the British Atlantic, 1750–1807

JUSTIN ROBERTS
Dalhousie University, Nova Scotia

CAMBRIDGE UNIVERSITY PRESS
Cambridge, New York, Melbourne, Madrid, Cape Town,
Singapore, São Paulo, Delhi, Mexico City

Cambridge University Press
32 Avenue of the Americas, New York, NY 10013-2473, USA

www.cambridge.org
Information on this title: www.cambridge.org/9781107025851

© Justin Roberts 2013

This publication is in copyright. Subject to statutory exception
and to the provisions of relevant collective licensing agreements,
no reproduction of any part may take place without the written
permission of Cambridge University Press.

First published 2013

Printed in the United States of America

A catalog record for this publication is available from the British Library.

Library of Congress Cataloging in Publication Data
Roberts, Justin, 1975–
Slavery and the Enlightenment in the British Atlantic, 1750–1807 / Justin Roberts,
Dalhousie University, Nova Scotia.
 pages cm
Includes bibliographical references.
ISBN 978-1-107-02585-1 (hardback)
1. Slavery – Great Britain – Colonies – History – 18th century. 2. Slavery – Atlantic Ocean
Region – History – 18th century. 3. Slaves – Great Britain – Colonies – History – 18th
century. 4. Enlightenment – Great Britain – Colonies. I. Title.
HT1165.R63   2014
306.3'62094109033–dc23   2012043740

ISBN 978-1-107-02585-1 Hardback

Cambridge University Press has no responsibility for the persistence or
accuracy of URLs for external or third-party Internet Web sites referred to
in this publication and does not guarantee that any content on such
Web sites is, or will remain, accurate or appropriate.

For my father

Contents

List of tables	*page* viii
List of figures	x
Acknowledgments	xiii
Introduction	1
1. Clock Work: Time, Quantification, Amelioration, and the Enlightenment	26
2. Sunup to Sundown: Agricultural Diversity and Seasonal Patterns of Work	80
3. Lockstep and Line: Gang Work and the Division of Labor	131
4. Negotiating Sickness: Health, Work, and Seasonality	161
5. Labor and Industry: Skilled and Unskilled Work	202
6. Working Lives: Occupations and Families in the Slave Community	238
Conclusion	279
Appendix A	293
Appendix B	297
Bibliography	323
Index	345

Tables

A1.	Most-Labor-Intensive Tasks Performed by Field Workers Each Month on Barbadian Plantations	*page* 297
A2.	Most-Labor-Intensive Tasks Performed by Field Workers Each Month on Jamaican Plantations, Part 1	298
A3.	Most-Labor-Intensive Tasks Performed by Field Workers Each Month on Jamaican Plantations, Part 2	299
A4.	Most-Labor-Intensive Tasks Performed by Field Workers Each Month of the Year at Mount Vernon (Combined Totals), 1797, Part 1	300
A5.	Most-Labor-Intensive Tasks Performed by Field Workers Each Month of the Year at Mount Vernon (Combined Totals), 1797, Part 2	301
A6.	Average Number of Annual Working and Nonworking Days per Field Worker at Mount Vernon, 1797	302
A7.	Average Number of Annual Working and Nonworking Days per Slave at Newton and Seawell from 1796 to 1798	303
A8.	Average Number of Annual Working and Nonworking Days per Slave at Prospect in 1787 and 1791	304
A9.	Labor Activities of Field Workers on the Outlying Mount Vernon Farms in 1797, Part 1	305
A10.	Labor Activities of Field Workers on the Outlying Mount Vernon Farms in 1797, Part 2	306
A11.	Labor Activities of Field Workers at Prospect Estate in 1785	307
A12.	Total Labor Activities of First Two Gangs at Prospect in 1787 and 1791, Part 1	308
A13.	Total Labor Activities of First Two Gangs at Prospect in 1787 and 1791, Part 2	309

A14.	Labor Activities of First Two Gangs at Newton, 1796–1798, Part 1	310
A15.	Labor Activities of First Two Gangs at Newton, 1796–1798, Part 2	311
A16.	Labor Activities of First Two Gangs at Seawell, 1796–1797, Part 1	312
A17.	Labor Activities of First Two Gangs at Seawell, 1796–1797, Part 2	313
A18.	Frequency Distribution of Sick Days for Newton Field Workers, 1796–1797	314
A19.	Frequency Distribution of Sick Days for Mount Vernon Field Workers, 1797	314
A20.	Labor Activities of Ditchers at Mount Vernon in 1797	315
A21.	Labor Activities of Spinners and Knitters at Mount Vernon, 1797	315
A22.	Combined Work Days of Craftsmen at Newton and Seawell, 1796–1798	316
A23.	Carpenter Activities at Mount Vernon in 1797	317
A24.	Labor Activities of Coopers at Mount Vernon in 1797	318
A25.	Labor Activities of Masons (Brick Layers) at Mount Vernon, 1797	319
A26.	Duration of Absences at Newton and Seawell, 1796–1798	320
A27.	Number of Slaves Away during Each Absence at Newton and Seawell, 1796–1798	321

Figures

1.1. Work log entry, Somerset Vale, October 13 to November 9, 1776. *page* 62
1.2. Work log entry, Seawell, May 3, 1796. 63
1.3. Work log entry, Newton, July 4, 1798. 64
1.4. Work log entry, Mount Vernon, August 4–10, 1793. 65
1.5. Work log entry, Prospect, February 23–28, 1789. 66
2.1. Average number of days worked each year by field hands at Prospect (1787 and 1791), Mount Vernon (1797), Newton (1796–1797), and Seawell (1796–1797). 84
2.2. Annual number of hours worked per field hand at Newton, Prospect, and Mount Vernon. 86
2.3. Average number of hours worked each month by field hands at Prospect, Mount Vernon, and Newton. 88
2.4. Seasonal wheat and corn labor allocation at Mount Vernon. 93
2.5. Seasonal cash crop labor allocation at Prospect (1787 and 1791 combined). 94
2.6. Percentage of first-gang labors spent on cash crops each month at Newton and Seawell, 1796–1798. 96
2.7. Share of total revenue from cotton at Seawell, 1788–1801. 100
2.8. Cash crop production as a percentage of total work days. 104
2.9. Number of days each month the primary mill was operating at Newton and Seawell (Barbados) in 1796–1798. 121
2.10. Number of days each month the primary mill was operating at Pleasant Hill in 1786 and 1789–1790 and at Somerset Vale in 1776–1777. 122
2.11. Number of days each month the primary mill was operating at Prospect (Jamaica) in 1787 and 1791. 122

2.12.	Average daily production totals from the York Plantation boiling house (Jamaica) for the crop of 1791.	124
2.13.	Days of the week in which the Newton Mill was in operation for the crop of 1798.	125
2.14.	Total number of cash crop harvesting days each year in Barbados, Jamaica, and Virginia.	128
4.1.	Monthly sickness rates for field hands at Newton and Seawell, 1796–1798.	173
4.2.	Monthly sickness rates for Prospect slaves, 1787.	174
4.3.	Seasonal mortality rates on Caribbean sugar plantations, 1779–1809.	176
4.4.	Seasonal mortality by sex on Jamaican plantations, 1779–1798.	177
4.5.	Monthly sickness rates for Mount Vernon field hands, 1797–1798.	178
4.6.	Seasonal birth rates on Jamaican sugar plantations, 1779–1809.	185
4.7.	Average annual sick days by age category among first-gang slaves at Newton, 1796–1797.	188
4.8.	Average annual sick days by age category among field hands at Mount Vernon, 1797.	189
5.1.	Labor activities of all Newton and Seawell tradesmen, 1796–1798.	225
5.2.	Labor activities of all Mount Vernon tradesmen, 1797.	226
6.1.	Day of the work week on which absences occurred.	267
6.2.	Total days of absence at Newton and Seawell, 1796–1798.	268

Acknowledgments

This book, which was born of a dissertation I wrote at Johns Hopkins University, would not have been possible without the guidance and support of a broad community of scholars, friends, and family. I owe more debts of gratitude than I can ever adequately repay or even acknowledge. Philip D. Morgan, my doctoral adviser, deserves my greatest thanks for his remarkable generosity with his time, his constant guidance through the labyrinth that is the early career of a professional historian, and his insistence on deep empirical research. David Eltis set me down the path to becoming a historian, and this book's themes have been powerfully shaped by my memory of his graduate seminar at Queen's University. Phil and David will be role models throughout my career. Many colleagues have offered me the friendship and the intellectual stimulation to help see me through this project. I cannot thank them enough for their careful and constructive criticism and their thorough reading of chapter drafts. I owe the most to Lorena Walsh, Ashleigh Androsoff, Eric Otremba, Peter Coclanis, Michael P. Johnson, Eric Crahan, and the late John Russell-Wood. They all read the entire manuscript at least once and gave me the encouragement and suggestions I needed to keep improving this book. I'd also like to thank, in no particular order, Jerry Bannister, Paddy Riley, Jack Crowley, Simon Newman, Trevor Burnard, Max Edelson, Daniel Hopkins, Claire Gherini, Jessica Roney, Jessica Stern, Taylor Stoermer, Ian Beamish, James Roberts, Molly Warsh, Melissa Grafe, Eran Shalev, Jack P. Greene, David Schley, Toby Ditz, Greg O'Malley, Kate Murphy, Catherine Molineux, Jonathan Gienapp, Cole Jones, Stephanie Gamble, Steffi Cerato, Joseph Adelman, Craig Hollander, Katie Gray, Leonard Rosenband, Jerome Handler, Michael Smith, and Anya Zilberstein for their helpful insights and support with portions of this work at its various stages.

This project required extensive research in archives in the United States, Caribbean, and United Kingdom, and such research would never have been possible without monetary support from several institutions, including an Andrew W. Mellon Fellowship at the Huntington Library, a Gilder-Lehrman Fellowship at the Robert H. Smith International Center for Jefferson Studies, a scholarship from the National Society of the Colonial Dames of America, a Center for New World Comparative Studies Fellowship at the John Carter Brown Library, a Gilder-Lehrman Fellowship at the John D. Rockefeller Jr. Library, a Betty Sams Christian Fellowship in Business History at the Virginia Historical Society, a Program in Early American Economy and Society Fellowship at the Library Company of Philadelphia, an Albert J. Beveridge Grant from the American Historical Association, and a doctoral award from the Canadian Social Sciences and Humanities Research Council.

An early version of this project was published in the *William and Mary Quarterly* as "Working between the Lines: Labor and Agriculture on Two Barbadian Sugar Plantations, 1796–97" (see *William and Mary Quarterly*, 63.3 [July 2006]: 551–586). That article has been adapted and revised, but fragments of it still appear in several chapters. I would like to thank the editors of the *Quarterly* for granting me permission to incorporate it into this book.

Introduction

The great majority of slaves in the British Americas began their work days with the rising sun and ended them sometime after sundown. Work was the *raison d'etre* of the system of slavery. In the eighteenth century, an improvement movement swept through the British Americas, changing how planters conceptualized and managed their plantations. The working world of the plantation was transformed by new management theories, which were in turn shaped by broader Atlantic discourses about moral reform and scientific and agricultural improvement. The Enlightenment conviction that moral and economic progress were compatible led planters to believe that increasing productivity could accompany benevolent management.

The new work routines and management systems had a considerable impact on the day-to- day lives of slaves. Work influenced the formation of slaves' families, their community hierarchies and dynamics, and their morbidity, fertility, and mortality rates. Given the critical role that work played in shaping the lives slaves led, it is striking how often slavery scholars have overlooked the details of slave labor, focusing instead on other aspects of the institution and the lives of the people within it.[1] The vast majority of a plantation slave's waking hours were spent working, and new forms of labor discipline and supervision in the eighteenth century enabled planters to extract more working hours and greater physical efforts on a wider variety of tasks from their slaves.

In the last half of the twentieth century, slavery scholars were at the forefront of a paradigm shift in historical studies that made agency and

---

[1] Ira Berlin and Philip D. Morgan, "Labor and the Shaping of Slave Life in the Americas" in Berlin and Morgan, eds., *Cultivation and Culture: Labor and the Shaping of Slave Life in the Americas.* (Charlottesville: University of Virginia Press, 1993) 1-48.

resistance central themes in the study of subalterns.[2] They began to focus on what slaves did on their own time rather than under the eyes of the master.[3] The resistance paradigm helped to dismantle the racist conceptual apparatus that enabled slavery to be described as a benevolent institution.[4] It also made it clear that slaves were never simply passive victims or complicit actors in their own tragedy. Nevertheless, a growing number of critics have pointed out that the emphasis on autonomous and successfully resistant slaves and slave cultures has gone too far. In the 1990s, Sidney Mintz was one of many scholars calling for a new approach to studying the lived experience of slavery because, as he explained, on sugar plantations, "only a tiny fraction of daily life consisted of open resistance. Instead most of life then, like most of life now, was spent living."[5] To appreciate the lived experience of enslaved peoples, we need to know more about what kind of work they did and when and how it changed.

In the twenty-first century, the resistance paradigm continues to be entrenched in slave studies because it is so intricately interwoven with a particular set of beliefs that scholars have held about the nature of the institution.[6] The tendency in the literature on slavery is to stress the chattel principle of slavery and to cast slavery as the polar opposite of freedom;

---

[2] For a prominent example see Michael Mullin, *Africa in America: Slave Acculturation and Resistance in the American South and the British Caribbean, 1736–1831* (Chicago: University of Illinois Press, 1992); for historiographical overviews see Robert William Fogel, *Without Consent or Contract: The Rise of American Slavery* (New York: Norton, 1989), 154–198, and Robert L. Paquette, "Social History Update: Slave Resistance and Social History, "*Journal of Social History* 24.3 (Spring 1991), 681–685.

[3] Peter A. Coclanis, "The Captivity of a Generation." *William and Mary Quarterly* 61.3 (July 2004), 544–555.

[4] For examples of how some of the older literature casts slavery as a benevolent institution, see Ulrich Bonnel Phillips, *American Negro Slavery: A Survey of the Supply, Employment and Control of Negro Labor as Determined by the Plantation Regime*. (New York: D. Appleton & Company, 1952 [1918]; H. J. Eckenrode, "Negroes in Richmond in 1864," *Virginia Magazine of History and Biography* 46.3 (July 1938), 193–200.

[5] Sidney Mintz, "Slave Life on Caribbean Sugar Plantations: Some Unanswered Questions," in Stephen Palmie, ed., *Slave Cultures and the Cultures of Slavery* (Knoxville: University of Tennessee Press, 1995),13; Palmie, "Introduction," in Palmie, ed. *Slave Cultures*, xviii; Robert William Fogel and Stanley L. Engerman, "Changing Views of Slavery in the United States South: The Role of Eugene D. Genovese," in Robert Louis Paquette and Louis A. Ferleger, eds., *Slavery, Secession and Southern History* (Charlottesville: University Press of Virginia, 2000), 6; Fogel, *Without Consent or Contract*, 154–198.

[6] For recent examples of the continuing emphasis on resistance and cultural survivals as resistance see Eric Robert Taylor, *If We Must Die: Shipboard Insurrections in the Era of the Atlantic Slave Trade* (New Orleans: Louisiana State University Press, 2006); James H. Sweet, *Recreating Africa: Culture, Kinship, and Religion in the African-Portuguese World, 1441–1770* (Chapel Hill: University of North Carolina Press, 2003).

scholars depict the institution as being uniquely different from other forms of coerced labor.[7] Slavery has been fetishized as a subject; the institution has been cast as aberrant. By representing slavery as the absolute denial of freedom and as distinctly different from other forms of early modern labor, scholars are led to search for the ways in which slaves resisted total domination and struggled to obtain freedom from their bondage. Within this investigative framework, slaves become political actors more than laboring people, which constrains the kinds of inquiries historians are able to make about the day-to-day experiences of enslaved workers. In slave studies, the scholarly emphasis on resistance and on the quest for freedom makes it a highly politicized subject, given modern concerns with individual freedom, but it also makes the investigation transhistorical, because it fails to contextualize the ways in which either resistance or freedom were both defined and experienced at particular places and points in time. Freedom is an abstract and historically contingent concept. There are a wide range of social conditions and cultural boundaries at any given time that place restrictions on individual freedom, and the ways in which individuals and societies understand, value, and pursue freedom has changed over time.[8]

Slavery was a brutal and violent institution, and the chattel principle, in some ways, made it distinct from other forms of coerced labor (such as naval impressment or indentured servitude), but it was also one of many forms of dependency in the hierarchical world of the eighteenth-century Atlantic. Thus, the violence within slavery must be understood as part of a spectrum of violence in the early modern world.[9] In terms of the daily

---

[7] James Oakes, *Slavery and Freedom: An Interpretation of the Old South* (New York: W.W. Norton & Company, 1990), xiv-xv; David Brion Davis, *Inhuman Bondage: The Rise and Fall of Slavery in the New World* (New York: Oxford University Press, 2006), 29–35.

[8] Robert J. Steinfeld, *Coercion, Contract and Free Labor in the Nineteenth Century* (New York, Cambridge University Press, 2001); Matthew C. Pursell, "Changing Conceptions of Servitude in the British Atlantic, 1640–1780," Ph.D. Dissertation. (Brown University, May 2005); Robert J. Steinfeld, "Changing Legal Conceptions of Free Labor," in Stanley Engerman, ed., *Terms of Labor: Slavery, Serfdom, and Free Labor* (Stanford: Stanford University Press, 1999), 137–167; Stanley L. Engerman, "Slavery at Different Times and Places," *American Historical Review* 105.2 (2000), 480–484; Marcel van der Linden, "The Origins, Spread and Normalization of Free Wage Labour," in Tom Brass and Marcel van der Linden, eds. *Free and Unfree Labor: The Debate Continues* (New York: Peter Lang, 1997), 501–524; Robert. J. Steinfeld and Stanley Engerman, "Labor- Free or Coerced? A Historical Reassessment of Differences and Similarities," in Brass and van der Linden, eds., *Free and Unfree Labor*, 107–126.

[9] Kenneth Morgan, *Slavery and Servitude in Colonial North America: A Short History* (New York, New York University Press, 2001); Robert J. Steinfeld, *The Invention of Free Labor: the Employment Relation in English and American Law and Culture, 1350–1870* (Chapel Hill: University of North Carolina Press, 1991); Steinfeld, *Coercion, Contract and Free*

experience of the workers, slavery was not altogether different from other systems of forced labor. Freedom was attainable only by degrees for the vast majority of workers in the Atlantic. From apprentices to convict slaves, the early modern Atlantic was an unfree world. Most workers were dependent, bound, or coerced in some way, denied specific bundles of rights and freedoms. The difference between slavery and other forced labor systems is more a matter of degree than kind.

The scholarly emphasis on slavery as the complete denial of freedom and as a unique institution has distorted the kinds of questions we have asked about the lived experience of enslavement. By transforming slaves into resistant subalterns battling for freedom, we have made a caricature of them, undermining our ability to understand them as human actors living within a coerced labor system that placed severe constraints on their ability to exercise any kind of opposition to slavery or attain any significant autonomy. Agency is an inadequate concept in the study of plantation slavery. It is unsuitable for discussing forced labor scenarios in which there is a significant asymmetrical power imbalance between masters and slaves.[10]

What is needed in slave studies is a paradigm shift, a new set of questions altogether. We need to reimagine slaves as much more complex than just politicized actors engaged with their master in an endless contest for freedom. Historians have now long debated the degrees by which each party in this contest proved to be the victor or the vanquished. The history of slavery is more than a history of winners and losers. Thinking about slaves foremost as coerced laborers and about slavery as a kind of labor history allows us to ask questions about these peoples' experience of particular working worlds.[11] To reconceptualize slaves in this way, scholars must avoid fetishizing the violence within slavery or casting the system as unique. They need to recognize it as part of an early modern world in which most laborers (and whole groups of people, such as women or children) experienced some degree of coercion.

Labor; Pursell, "Changing Conceptions of Servitude"; Steinfeld, "Changing Legal Conceptions of Free Labor"; John Donoghue, "'Out of the Land of Bondage:' The English Revolution and the Atlantic Origins of Abolition," *The American Historical Review* 115.4 (2010), 943–974.

[10] Walter Johnson, "On Agency," *Journal of Social History* 37.1 (Fall 2003), 113–124.

[11] For examples of the work now being done on slavery as a kind of labor history, see Frederick C. Knight, *Working the Diaspora: The Impact of African Labor on the Anglo-American World, 1650–1850* (New York: New York University Press, 2010); Seth Rockman, *Scraping By: Wage Labor, Slavery, and Survival in Early Baltimore* (Baltimore: Johns Hopkins University Press, 2009); Stuart Schwartz, *Slaves, Peasants and Rebels: Reconsidering Brazilian Slavery* (Urbana: University of Illinois Press, 1992); Berlin and Morgan, eds., *Cultivation and Culture*.

In this sense, eighteenth-century slavery was neither aberrant nor peculiar. It was not distinct but rather part of a spectrum of laboring experiences. The story of eighteenth-century slavery in the British Atlantic is more complex than a simple contest between heroically resisting bondsmen and their evil oppressors. Instead, it is a far richer story of a particular group of early modern laborers and their complex and changing worlds.

By privileging freedom as an essential element in the transition to a modern and industrialized world, eighteenth-century antislavery activists and generations of subsequent scholars have mischaracterized slavery and underestimated the adaptability of forced labor systems. Since the eighteenth century, stage-based and whiggish theories of human development have represented slavery as a stage of development that was incompatible with progress, capitalism, technological innovation, industrialization, and with the rise of civilized and enlightened nations – indeed, with the rise of modernity.[12] Yet slavery is, in some ways, more suitable than most systems of labor for capitalist innovation. The extreme degree of coercion and control in slavery is part of what makes it suitable. Because slavery guarantees a captive labor force, which slaveholders can easily allocate to a variety of labors, the institution reduces the risks inherent in acquiring and maintaining labor. By reducing the risks in labor management, slavery offset the potential risks that came with technological innovation and change. Slavery is an immoral and dehumanizing labor system, but it is also highly adaptable, viable, and flexible, and it is fully consistent with economic progress. It is critical not to conflate arguments about the immorality of slavery with arguments about its efficiency or viability.[13]

In the eighteenth century, most of the managerial staff and the owners of large slave plantations were convinced that there was nothing backward about plantation slavery. In response to the growing critique of slavery and the slave trade, these planters offered an alternative vision of the relationship between slavery and human progress. They stressed the need to discipline the unenlightened, and they conceptualized work, forced or free, as an innate good because it contributed directly to economic progress and inculcated habits of industry that would be morally redemptive. They measured progress and improvement by the size of their crops and by how much labor

---

[12] Seymour Drescher, *The Mighty Experiment: Free Labour Versus Slavery in British Emancipation* (New York: Oxford University Press, 2002); Oakes, *Slavery and Freedom*, 53.

[13] Robert William Fogel, *The Slavery Debates: A Retrospective, 1952–1990* (Baton Rouge: Louisiana State University Press, 2003), 24–48.

they could extract from their human capital. Many scholars have stressed how Enlightenment principles of liberty and natural rights created revolutionary fervor throughout the Atlantic and pathways to freedom for slaves. Yet, certain sets of Enlightenment principles also helped to cultivate a series of darker outcomes for slaves, and scholars have underplayed those connections. Planters, driven by the Enlightenment commitment to progress and inspired by Newtonian universalism and Baconian empiricism, developed new management systems geared toward extracting more work from enslaved workers. The Enlightenment gave rise to a new set of moral sensibilities that reduced some of the physical barbarity within slavery and ended the slave trade, and it also advanced ideas about freedom and free labor that helped to dismantle the institution of slavery altogether. Yet, at the same time, there was also a ruthless rationalism to the Enlightenment and a pragmatism and expediency that helped foster industrialization, factory discipline, and, in the plantation Americas, more exhausting plantation work regimes in which planters strove to reduce the workers into depersonalized and interchangeable units of production.[14] This was the dark side of the Enlightenment.

On large plantations, there was a multilayered hierarchy of white managers. The highest authorities were the people who made long-term decisions about planting, such as the resident plantation owners and the plantation attorneys, who were legally empowered to make decisions for absentee owners. These attorneys were often resident plantation owners who also supervised one or more estates for absentee owners. Sometimes absentee owners were involved regularly in the operations of the plantation, and sometimes they left the management almost entirely to the managerial staff of the plantation. Beneath this executive class of plantation owners and attorneys was the chief overseer, who was sometimes called a manager,

---

[14] Roy Porter, *The Creation of the Modern World: The Untold Story of the British Enlightenment* (New York: W.W. Norton & Company, 2000); Joel. Mokyr, *The Enlightened Economy: An Economic History of Britain, 1700–1850* (New Haven: Yale University Press, 2009); Joel Mokyr, "The European Enlightenment and the Origins of Economic Growth," in Jeff Horn et al., eds., *Reconceptualizing the Industrial Revolution* (Cambridge: MIT Press, 2010), 65–86; Susan Manning and Frances D. Cogliano in "The Enlightenment and the Atlantic," Manning and Cogliano, eds., *Atlantic Enlightenments* (Burlington, VT: Ashgate, 2008), 1–18; Dorinda Outram, *The Enlightenment*, 2nd ed. (New York: Cambridge University Press, 2005), 61–77; Trevor Burnard, *Mastery, Tyranny and Desire: Thomas Thistlewood and His Slaves in the Anglo-Jamaican World* (Chapel Hill: University of North Carolina Press, 2004), 101–174; Lynn Avery Hunt, *Inventing Human Rights: A History* (New York: W.W. Norton & Company, 2007), 70–112, 146–175.

and below him was one or more overseers. These were the men who made day-to-day decisions about planting. In theory, they carried out the orders of their superiors, but this was not always the case and tensions between higher and lower levels of management were common. At the bottom rung among the white planting staff in the Caribbean were the bookkeepers, who served as assistants to the overseer. There were also white staff who were employed either permanently or intermittently on the plantation as doctors or tradesmen. This book uses "planters" as a collective term for the plantation owners and their white managerial staff, but it will draw distinctions between these planters whenever their perspectives or interests differed significantly. For the most part, the discussion of planters' approaches to plantation management will focus on those people who were involved in developing agricultural strategies or in supervising enslaved labor.[15]

Slavery and Enlightenment in the British Atlantic operates on three levels. It is a labor history of slaves on large eighteenth-century plantations, a business history of plantation management, and a cultural and intellectual history of the ways in which planters conceptualized the management of a plantation and its laborers. This book examines slaves' lived experience in detail, focusing on the activity that consumed most of their days: work. It identifies the precise kinds of chores slaves did day to day, the ways in which plantation work routines changed with the season of production, and the relationship between the working world and the slaves' health, their families, and the communities they formed. It also explores planters' ideas about work routines and about slaves' capacities for work, and the operation of those ideas in daily practice. It will argue that work was the key factor in shaping slaves' lives and their communities, and that work routines on the mainland and in the Caribbean were shaped by dynamic and evolving plantation management schemes that were heavily influenced by the same pan-Atlantic Enlightenment discourses.

The dictates of nationalist historiographies, the ways in which modern political divisions shape the boundaries that historians draw around their subjects, and lingering myths about American exceptionalism have encouraged scholars to think of Barbados and Jamaica as part of a Caribbean world that was distinctly different – especially after 1783 – from the thirteen colonies that formed the United States. The movement toward Atlantic history among early Americanists has led to a reconsideration of the discipline's traditional

---

[15] The best work on the managerial staff of large plantations is B. W. Higman, *Plantation Jamaica; Capital and Control in a Colonial Economy, 1750–1850* (Kingston, Jamaica: University of the West Indies Press, 2005).

regional divisions; it has also drawn more scholarly attention to the ways in which areas throughout the Anglo-American world continued to share certain historical trajectories after the American Revolution.

The three specific regions under investigation in this study – Virginia, Jamaica, and Barbados – varied significantly in their physical size, climate, and landscapes; their black-to-white and African-to-creole ratios, the demands and intensity of their labor regimes, the degree to which their slave populations were self-reproducing, the number of resident planters, the extent to which their production was diversified, and the proportion of land under cultivation. This study explores these contrasts and the similarities among all three regions, attempting – whenever the evidence allows – to avoid grouping the Caribbean into one region and characterizing it as the polar opposite of the Chesapeake.

The one area of mainland North America that most resembled the Caribbean sugar islands was the Lowcountry. Its massive rice and indigo plantations, its climate, its slave majority, and its poor rates of natural reproduction among the slaves make the Lowcountry a more obvious point of comparison with the Caribbean than does the Chesapeake. Yet a comparison of South Carolina, for example, and Jamaica would not reveal findings that would surprise scholars or advance the literature in as meaningful a way. In contrast, the Chesapeake was not a fully integrated part of a greater Caribbean world and, given the significant demographic differences and reproductive rates between enslaved populations in Virginia and most areas of the Caribbean, one would expect there to be sharp contrasts in plantation management and in the work routines of slaves. By using Virginia instead of South Carolina as a point of comparison with Barbados and Jamaica, *Slavery and Enlightenment in the British Atlantic* seeks to uncover significant and unexplored similarities in the ideas that drove plantation management on large plantations in places that, on a superficial level, appear so strikingly different.

Barbados, in the eastern Caribbean, is the oldest of the sugar islands in the British Caribbean. It is unique in the history of the British Caribbean. It is almost 100 miles east of the rest of the Windward Island chain. That distance helped ensure that the island was never invaded or seriously threatened by a foreign power. Without the constant threat of invasion, living and planting in Barbados was always less risky than in other sugar islands. The trade winds also kept the island slightly cooler than most of the Caribbean. By the late eighteenth century, Barbados had the largest proportion of resident planters and the highest proportion of white settlers among the major sugar islands. Many of the resident planters came from families that had been on the island since the sugar revolution of the seventeenth century. Despite the constant decline of the enslaved population until the end of the eighteenth century, there were a growing number of enslaved workers whose parents and grandparents were Barbadian-born. Enslaved family lineages began to develop on Barbadian plantations. Sugar planting became part of a family tradition for both whites and their black bondsmen. Resident planters understood well how to cultivate the crop, and Barbadians were the vanguard of the movement to improve sugar planting. Other planters in the sugar islands commonly pointed to the Barbadians as the most skilled and efficient of all planters.[16] The second plantation manual in the British Caribbean, published in 1755, was written by a Barbadian, and the first agricultural society devoted to sugar planting appeared in Barbados in 1804.[17]

There was far more uniformity in the geographical conditions on Barbados than in Jamaica. Barbados is a tiny island (166 square miles) and, compared to most of the other major sugar islands in the British Caribbean, the terrain is generally flat.[18] Throughout most of Barbados, the climate, terrain, and soils were ideal for growing sugar. The interior Scotland District is the most rugged and hilly region of Barbados. It comprised about 20 percent of the island but there is no significant elevation in the interior. Sugar cane is a tropical or subtropical grass, which grows best where it receives 1,500–1800 mm of rain a year, but it can tolerate more rain or slightly less.[19] Average annual rainfall in Barbados ranges from 1,000 mm on the southeast coast to 2,280 mm in the interior, making most of the island ideal for sugar cultivation. By the end of the seventeenth century, the forest cover had been almost entirely cleared, and sugar was being grown on every tillable square foot of the island.[20] The uniformity in climate and geographical conditions made Barbadian plantations excellent sites for experimentation, and it made it easier for planters to share ideas

---

[16] Patrick Kein, *An Essay upon Pen-Keeping and Plantership* (Kingston, Jamaica: His Majesty's Printing Office, 1796), 26; Samuel Martin, *Essay upon Plantership*, 4th ed. (London: Samuel Chapman, 1765), 7.
[17] William Belgrove, *A Treatise upon Husbandry or Planting* (Boston: D. Fowle, 1755). *Minutes of the Society for the Improvement of Plantership in the Island of Barbados* (Liverpool: Thomas Kaye, 1811).
[18] Richard B. Sheridan, *Sugar and Slavery: The Economic History of the British West Indies* (Baltimore: Johns Hopkins University Press 1974), 127.
[19] Michael Craton, *Searching for the Invisible Man: Slaves and Plantation Life in Jamaica* (Cambridge: Harvard University Press, 1978), 9.
[20] Russell Menard, *Sweet Negotiations: Sugar, Slavery, and Plantation Agriculture in Early Barbados* (Charlottesville: University of Virginia Press, 2006).

about agricultural improvement and compare their results – their plantations became laboratories. Without rugged terrain, the slave's field work on Barbadian estates was also less arduous than it was on the steeper and mountainous grounds found in many of Jamaica's parishes.

The seventeenth century was the golden age of Barbadian sugar production, but, by the eighteenth century, Barbadians had to grapple with significant cultivation issues and rising competition from other sugar frontiers. A sugar revolution in the late 1640s transformed Barbados, and it became by far the richest of the English colonies in the Americas – a position it held until the early eighteenth century.[21] Deforestation and intensive cane agriculture caused the soil quality to decline and created land and fuel shortages. By the second quarter of the eighteenth century, the Leeward Islands, led by Antigua, took over from Barbados as the primary sugar-producing region in the British Caribbean.[22] To maximize their dwindling resources and remain competitive, eighteenth-century Barbadians were forced to hone their skills and innovate. They adopted new methods of cane holing to prevent erosion; they addressed the fuel shortage by using cane trash instead of wood to stoke the fires in the boiling house; they revitalized the soils with extensive manuring.[23]

Jamaica in the Western Caribbean and Barbados in the Eastern Caribbean were not only more than 1,300 miles from each other, they were at opposite ends of a spectrum of sugar production in the British Caribbean. They had distinctly different histories and landscapes. In contrast to tiny Barbados, Jamaica, in the western Caribbean, was by far the largest of the British Caribbean sugar islands. At more than 4,400 square miles, it is about twenty-five times the size of Barbados.[24] Unlike Barbados, the terrain, forest cover, and climate vary greatly across Jamaica, and planters have distinctly different geographical concerns throughout the island. Whereas all of Barbados could be cultivated for sugar, some areas of Jamaica, such as the Blue Mountains, were too steep and rugged to be viable lands for sugar plantations. Remote and often impenetrable mountain terrain fostered the

---

[21] David Eltis, *The Rise of African Slavery in the Americas* (New York: Cambridge University Press, 2000), 202; B.W. Higman, "The Sugar Revolution," *Economic History Review* 53.2 (2000): 213–236.

[22] Eltis, *Rise of African Slavery*, 193–22.

[23] David Watts, "Origins of Barbadian Cane Hole Agriculture," *Journal of the Barbados Museum and Historical Society*, 32.3 (May 1968), 143–151; David Watts, *The West Indies: Patterns of Development, Culture, and Environmental Change Since 1492* (New York: Cambridge University Press, 1987), 382–447.

[24] Sheridan, *Sugar and Slavery*, 208.

development of maroon communities or made it easier for slaves to abscond from work for a period of time. The rough terrain also made the cultivation of sugar on some of the more accessible mountain grounds particularly demanding for the slaves and livestock. Rainfall ranges throughout Jamaica from an annual average of between 900 mm per year around Kingston (too dry to cultivate quality canes) to an average of more than 5,000 mm a year in the mountains of the northeast (so wet that it was difficult to cut and grind canes during the harvest). Eighteenth-century Jamaica may have been wetter than it is today.[25] Jamaican geographies and weather patterns created difficulties for planters in that island which Barbadians never faced.

If Barbados was king of sugar production in the British Caribbean in the seventeenth century, the eighteenth century belonged to Jamaica. Jamaica was wrested from the Spanish under Oliver Cromwell's "western design" plans in 1655, in the midst of a sugar revolution sweeping through the Eastern Caribbean, but it was slow to develop as a sugar island.[26] Jamaica came to dominate British sugar production at some point before the middle of the eighteenth century.[27] Transportation costs for shipping sugar from the island and slaves to it kept Jamaica beyond the frontier of profitable English sugar production until the 1720s, and piracy and buccaneering offered an alternative source of profits, with lower initial investment costs than sugar planting for most seventeenth-century Jamaicans.[28] In terms of total output, slaves resident in the colony, and forced immigration of slaves, the Jamaican economy was most fully developed from the 1780s until the end of the slave trade in 1807, but the most consistently high profits probably came in the last two decades before the American Revolution.[29] Despite Jamaica's position as the leading sugar producer in the British Caribbean, the land was never as fully cultivated as the land in Barbados.

---

[25] Amanda Thornton, "Coerced Care: Thomas Thistlewood's Account of Medical Care on Enslaved Populations in Colonial Jamaica, 1751–1786," *Slavery & Abolition* 32.4 (Fall 2011), 539.

[26] Richard B. Sheridan, "The Formation of Caribbean Plantation Society, 1689–1748," in P. J. Marshall, ed., *The Oxford History of the British Empire: The Eighteenth Century*, vol. II (New York: Oxford University Press, 2001), 395.

[27] Verene Shepherd, *Livestock, Sugar and Slavery: Contested Terrain in Colonial Jamaica* (Kingston, Jamaica: Ian Randle Publishers, 2009), 15–16.

[28] Eltis, *Rise of African Slavery*, 205–206.

[29] Roderick McDonald, *The Economy and Material Culture of Slaves: Goods and Chattel on the Sugar Plantations of Jamaica and Louisiana* (Baton Rouge: Louisiana State University Press, 1993), 2; Trevor Burnard, "Et in Arcadia Ergo: West Indian Planters in Glory, 1674–1784," *Atlantic Studies* 9.1 (March 2012), 19–40.

Whereas almost every acre in Barbados was under intensive cultivation when that island reached its peak in sugar production, less than a third of Jamaica was under cultivation by the turn of the nineteenth century.[30]

Sugar reigned in Jamaica but it was far from the only crop. Even at the apex of its sugar production, Jamaica was more economically diverse than Barbados. Livestock farms (or "pens"), often acting as satellite operations for the larger sugar plantations, were spread throughout the island, making Jamaica a land of both ranchers and sugar planters. Planters would send new slaves to the pens as part of the process of "seasoning," slowly acclimatizing them to the new environment in order to keep death rates at a minimum. Coffee took hold in the mountains of Jamaica at the end of the eighteenth century. In the nineteenth century, planters began to embrace coffee more fully in response to a depression in the sugar market and to the rising cost of slaves.[31] Coffee was less labor intensive, and Jamaican planters were chronically land-rich and labor-poor.

The acquisition of the Ceded Islands in 1763 brought a rapid expansion of the sugar frontier in the British Caribbean, but both Jamaica and Barbados continued to prosper. Jamaica continued to be the major sugar producer in the British Caribbean, and its own sugar frontiers in areas such as Westmoreland continued to expand in the eighteenth century. But the Barbadian economy had also experienced a renaissance by the end of the century.[32] In terms of total sugar production in the Caribbean, the French

---

[30] Gilbert Farquhar Mathison, *Notices Respecting Jamaica in 1808–1809–1810* (London: J. Stockdale, 1811), 55.

[31] Philip D. Morgan, "Slaves and Livestock in Eighteenth Century Jamaica: Vineyard Pen, 1750–1751," *William and Mary Quarterly* 52.1 (1995), 47–76; Verene A. Shepherd, "Livestock and Sugar: Aspects of Jamaica's Agricultural Development from the Late Seventeenth to the Early Nineteenth Century" *Historical Journal*, 34. 3 (September 1991), 627–643; S. D. Smith, "Sugar's Poor Relation: Coffee Planting in the British West Indies, 1720–1833," *Slavery & Abolition* 19.3 (December 1998), 68–89; Verene Shepherd, "Diversity in Caribbean Economy and Society from the Seventeenth to the Nineteenth Centuries," *Plantation Society in the Americas* 5.2-3 (1998), 175–187; Shepherd, *Livestock, Sugar and Slavery*.

[32] Otis Paul Starkey, *The Economic Geography of Barbados: A Study of the Relationships between Environmental Variations and Economic Development* (New York: Columbia University Press, 1939), 99–112; Menard, *Sweet Negotiations*, 89–90; B. W. Higman, "Economic and Social Development of the British West Indies from Settlement to ca. 1850," in *The Cambridge Economic History of the United States*, vol. 1, *The Colonial Era*, ed. Stanley L. Engerman and Robert E. Gallman, eds. (New York: Cambridge University Press, 1996), 317; Eltis, *Rise of African Slavery*, 197–204; J. R. Ward, *British West Indian Slavery, 1750–1834: The Process of Amelioration* (New York: Oxford University Press, 1988), 61–118; Karl Watson, *The Civilised Island, Barbados: A Social History, 1750–1816* (Ellerton, Barbados: Caribbean Graphic Production, 1979), 47.

colony of St. Domingue outstripped Jamaica by far in the 1780s, but the only successful slave revolt in the Americas ended sugar production in St. Domingue in 1791, significantly bolstering the profits of Jamaican and Barbadian sugar planters as they filled the vacuum.[33] The 1790s were boom years throughout the British sugar plantations.[34]

Despite this significant increase in profitability, both Barbadian and Jamaican planters faced considerable challenges to those profits in the last half of the eighteenth century, including competition from other islands for resources, the disruption of the Seven Years' War and the American Revolution, a series of severe hurricanes in the 1780s, declining sugar prices, currency inflation, rats, and plagues of other pests. With less woodland, less fertile soil, smaller plantations, smaller revenues, and less available land than Jamaicans, Barbadian planters had more difficulty contending with these challenges to production and profits. This difficulty forced them to become particularly innovative.[35] Sugar planters experimented in the late eighteenth century with the cultivation of other cash crops, particularly cotton in Barbados and coffee in Jamaica. Many planters adapted to economic challenges by producing more clayed sugar and rum, keeping more livestock for fertilizer, and becoming more self-sufficient (including growing more of their own provisions) to cut costs.[36] To a greater extent than their Jamaican counterparts, Barbadians focused on not only lowering the cost of maintaining their labor force (through amelioration and the growth of onsite provisions) but also on the production of refined sugars and by-products.[37]

With a shortage of land, the largest Barbadian estates were never as large as Jamaican estates, and, as a result, the slave population in Barbados was much smaller. Approximately 70 percent of all Barbadian bondsmen

---

[33] Laurent Dubois, *Avengers of the New World: The Story of the Haitian Revolution* (Cambridge: Belknap Press of Harvard University Press, 2004); see also Stanley L. Engerman, "France, Britain and the Economic Growth of Colonial North America," in John J. McCusker and Kenneth Morgan, eds., *The Early Modern Atlantic Economy* (New York: Cambridge University Press, 2000), 227–249.

[34] Burnard, "Et in Arcardia Ego," 33.

[35] John McCusker and Russell Menard, *The Economy of British America, 1607–1789* (Chapel Hill, NC: University of North Carolina Press, 1985), 166; Justin Roberts, "Uncertain Business: A Case Study of Barbadian Plantation Management, 1770–1793," *Slavery & Abolition* 32.2 (June 2011), 247–268.

[36] Starkey, *Economic Geography of Barbados*, 99–112; Ward, *British West Indian Slavery*, 61–64; and Eltis, *Rise of African Slavery*, 197–204.

[37] McCusker and Menard, *Economy of British America*, 165.

lived on sugar plantations.[38] In the late eighteenth century, an estate of 350 acres with 200 slaves was large by Barbadian standards. Only a handful of estates had more than 400 slaves.[39] Barbados always had a lower black-to-white ratio than the other major sugar islands and a larger share of resident planters. Even in the late eighteenth century, as many as two-thirds of planters were resident in Barbados. Between 1760 and 1790, in the midst of a Barbadian renaissance, the Barbadian slave population actually decreased from 87,000 slaves to 75,000 slaves.[40] Many of the largest and most successful plantations continued to grow in this era, but smaller and less successful plantations contracted or folded. The declining population was caused in part by a loss of life in the 1780 hurricane and by famine on some estates during the American Revolution (although the extent of this famine has been exaggerated by historians). In addition, many slaves were moved to new and more profitable plantation frontiers in the Ceded Islands.[41] By switching from cane to a less labor intensive crop, cotton, in the 1780s, some of the estates in Barbados were able to operate with slightly fewer slaves.[42] The Barbadian slave population became unique among the sugar islands around the turn of the nineteenth century. Whereas a natural and steady decline in the slave population was the norm on most Caribbean sugar islands, the Barbadian slave population, even though it was growing smaller in the late eighteenth century with outward migration, became self-reproducing in the last quarter to half century before emancipation. This one fact alone makes Barbados exceptional among the sugar islands.

There were far more slaves and more massive sugar plantations in Jamaica than there were in Barbados. Approximately 60 percent of late eighteenth-century Jamaican slaves lived on sugar plantations.[43] Large

---

[38] J.R. Ward, "The Profitability of Sugar Planting in the British West Indies, 1650–1834," *Economic History Review* 31.2 (May 1978), 207.

[39] Higman, "Economic and Social Development of the British West Indies," 297–336; Jerome Handler and Frederick W. Lange, *Plantation Slavery in Barbados: An Historical and Archaeological Investigation* (Cambridge: Harvard University Press, 1978), 38–40.

[40] John McCusker, "Economy of the British West Indies, 1763–1790: Growth, Stagnation or Decline," in J. McCusker, ed. *Essays in the Economic History of the Atlantic World* (London: Routledge, 1997), 312.

[41] Richard Sheridan, "The Crisis of Slave Subsistence in the British West Indies During and After the American Revolution," *William and Mary Quarterly* 33.4 (1976), 615–641; *British Sessional Papers, Commons, Accounts and Papers, 1789*, Part III, as quoted in Michael Craton, James Walvin, and David Wright, eds. *Slavery, Abolition and Emancipation* (London: Longman, 1976), 94.

[42] Starkey, *Economic Geography of Barbados*, 106; *British Sessional Papers, Commons, Accounts and Papers, 1789*, Part III, 90.

[43] Ward, "Profitability of Sugar Planting," 206.

estates in Jamaica tended to have between 400 and 500 slaves, but the largest had more than 1,000 slaves.[44] Unlike Barbados, which had a shrinking slave population, the Jamaican slave population was expanding in the late eighteenth century. New frontiers of the island were opening up, and the island became the leading point of disembarkation in the British Caribbean for slavers selling their cargoes. Between 1760 and 1790, the slave population grew from 173,000 to 276,000 slaves.[45] By 1808, immediately after the slave trade ended, the slave population peaked at 354,000, by far the largest slave population of any island in the British Caribbean.[46] The growth was due not to natural increase but to massive imports. Between 1750 and 1808, more than 605,000 slaves disembarked in Jamaica, but the population in the same period grew by only 151,000 slaves. Although many of the imported slaves were re-exported from Jamaica, the severity of the labor regime bore the brunt of the responsibility for the difficulties planters faced in maintaining the slave population.[47] The number of slaves disembarking in Jamaica was more than four times the number of slaves disembarking in Barbados. No other island in the Caribbean, British or otherwise, had more imports than Jamaica over the same period.[48] Whereas Barbados had the lowest black-to-white ratio among the sugar islands, the black-to-white ratio was always a concern in Jamaica, leading the island legislature to create deficiency laws to try to maintain enough whites on each plantation. Only about a third of Jamaican planters were resident.

Jamaica's economy became more diverse in the early nineteenth century and, although the number of slaves on the island was still rapidly expanding, the proportion of Jamaican bondsmen living and working on sugar plantations fell from 60 to 50 percent.[49] After the abolition of the slave trade, Jamaican sugar planters, always land-rich and labor-poor, suffered from increasingly severe labor shortages as the slave population continued

---

[44] Michael Craton, "Jamaican Slavery," in Stanley Engerman and Eugene Genovese, eds. *Race and Slavery in the Western Hemisphere: Quantitative Studies* (New Jersey: Princeton University Press, 1975), 249–284; Higman, "Economic and Social Development of the British West Indies.'"
[45] McCusker, "Economy of the British West Indies, 1763–1790," 312.
[46] B. W. Higman, *Slave Population and Economy in Jamaica, 1807–1834* (Kingston, Jamaica: Cambridge University Press, 1977), 61.
[47] Greg O'Malley, *Final Passages: The Intercolonial Slave Trade, 1619–1807* (Ph.D. Dissertation, Johns Hopkins University, 2006).
[48] David Eltis et al., *Voyages: Transatlantic Slave Trade Database* http://wilson.library.emory.edu:9090/tast/assessment/estimates.faces?yearFrom=1501&yearTo=1866
[49] Ward, "Profitability of Sugar Planting," 206n.

to decline. Whereas Jamaican planters had more difficulty than Barbadian planters maintaining an adequate labor-to-land ratio, they did not struggle with fuel and land shortages or soil fertility to the same extent.[50] Compared to Barbadian sugar plantations, Jamaican estates had a much greater share of their land devoted to pasturage, provision grounds, and woodlands.

Virginia, as a staple crop producer, was, with Barbados, the oldest of the major plantation colonies in British America. As a mainland colony, Virginia had ample land resources. In the late eighteenth century, Virginia was more than fifteen times the size of Jamaica and more than 400 times the size of Barbados. It was not nearly as densely cultivated as either of these sugar islands, nor was it as densely settled with slaves. The terrain is generally flat in the Virginian tidewater, with gently sloping hills rising up into the Piedmont. Unlike the Caribbean, which has a rainy season and a dry season each year, there are four distinct seasons in Virginia, and monthly precipitation is more consistent in Virginia, with the greatest amount of rain coming in July and August. Average monthly temperatures vary in the Chesapeake much more than they do in the islands, and the seasons more powerfully shaped the working environment in Virginia than they did in the sugar islands. Much like Jamaica, however, the climate varies significantly throughout Virginia.

Tobacco was king in Virginia in the seventeenth century and through much of the eighteenth century. Tobacco depleted the soil in six or seven years, and the land required a twenty-year fallow period to regenerate, which meant that planters "used up" the land rapidly.[51] Small tobacco plantations dotted the landscape. These were not capital-intensive properties, and they were transitory, which meant that planters moved their labor forces and their plantations to new lands often, clearing and cultivating an ever growing share of the backcountry. Tobacco was Virginia's main export crop throughout the colonial era but, by the 1730s, most planters had turned to more diversified production – producing more corn and wheat and investing more in animal husbandry. Some planters began this process as early as the 1680s, adopting the techniques of English farmers.[52]

---

[50] Craton, *Searching for the Invisible Man*, 1–50.
[51] Lorena S. Walsh, "Slave Life, Slave Society, and Tobacco Production in the Tidewater Chesapeake, 1620–1820," in Morgan and Berlin, eds., *Cultivation and Culture*, 173.
[52] Lorena S. Walsh, "Plantation Management in the Chesapeake, 1620–1820," *The Journal of Economic History* 49.2 (June 1989), 397; Lorena S. Walsh, *Motives of Honor, Pleasure and Profit: Plantation Management in the Colonial Chesapeake, 1607–1763* (Chapel Hill: University of North Carolina Press, 2010), 224.

After the mid-eighteenth century, more than half of the revenues on big Virginian plantations came from grains.[53] With the switch to grain, large planters had less need to move around. The cultivation of grains required new capital expenditures (livestock, plows, and grain mills), but it was less labor intensive (meaning smaller investments in labor). The new capital purchases were not easily moveable. The tobacco market was slumping and, like their Barbadian counterparts, Virginians were contending with declining soil quality. Diversifying production allowed large Virginian planters to address these problems. There was significant complementarity in the timing of wheat, corn, tobacco, and meat production, and diversification helped improve the total profits per laborer by avoiding downtime in the annual crop cycle.[54] After the mid-eighteenth century, the production of wheat and other grains expanded rapidly throughout the Chesapeake. Crop diversification and the expansion of animal husbandry that accompanied grain production made the landscape seem like a collection of farms rather than plantations.[55] The American Revolution had a deleterious impact on the Chesapeake economy.[56] With good tobacco prices, however, planters recovered quickly in the decade after the war, but, in the 1790s, another downturn in the price of tobacco caused Chesapeake planters to turn again more fully to the production of wheat and other grains.[57]

The slave population in Virginia, self-reproducing by the early eighteenth century, was the healthiest in the Americas. Slaves were reproducing rapidly and naturally. Between 1755 and 1782, the number of slaves in Virginia doubled, growing faster than the Jamaican population despite the fact that Jamaican planters were relying on fresh African imports and Chesapeake planters, by the last quarter of the eighteenth century, had stopped importing Africans.[58] In 1790, there were 293,000 slaves in

---

[53] Walsh, "Slave Life, Slave Society, and Tobacco Production," 180; Walsh, *Motives of Honor*, 601.
[54] James R. Irwin, "Slave Agriculture and Staple Crops in the Virginia Piedmont" (Ph.D. Dissertation, University of Rochester, 1986), v.
[55] Philip D. Morgan, *Slave Counterpoint: Black Culture in the Eighteenth-Century Chesapeake and Lowcountry*. (Chapel Hill: University of North Carolina Press, 1998), 28.
[56] Walsh, "Slave Life, Slave Society, and Tobacco Production," 187; John McCusker, "Economy of the British West Indies," 329.
[57] Walsh, "Slave Life, Slave Society, and Tobacco Production," 187–191.
[58] Richard Dunn, "After Tobacco: The Slave Labour Pattern on a Large Chesapeake Grain- and-Livestock Plantation in the Early Nineteenth Century," in Kenneth Morgan and John J. McCusker, eds., *The Early Modern Atlantic Economy* (New York: Cambridge University Press, 2000), 344–363, 345; Morgan, *Slave Counterpoint*, 61, 85.

Virginia alone – slightly fewer than there were in Jamaica at the same point and almost four times as many as there were in Barbados. Whereas there was a clear slave majority in Barbados and Jamaica, slaves in the Chesapeake comprised less than half the total population. By 1808, with continued population growth, the Virginian slave population had outgrown the Jamaican population, and Virginian planters began selling surplus slaves to the emerging cotton frontiers of the Deep South.[59]

In terms of the size of an individual estate's slave population, the vast majority of Virginian plantations were much smaller than Barbadian or Jamaican estates. Most grain and tobacco planters occupied small estates and worked the land with only a handful of slaves. The majority of Chesapeake plantations at the start of the American Revolution had fewer than twenty slaves and less than 300 acres.[60] Whereas Jamaica was an absentee society, virtually all Virginia planters were resident planters. Barbados fell somewhere between these extremes. The largest plantations in Virginia were divided into multiple quarters (smaller units of cultivation). With the switch to grain, more land was cleared and plowed for cultivation and for pasturage for the draft animals needed in grain cultivation. In terms of the size of the slave population, Virginian estates were smaller than sugar plantations, but, in terms of the landholdings, a few of the Virginian estates were much larger than even the largest Jamaican plantations.

This book attempts to triangulate Jamaica, Barbados, and Virginia by showing that, in some respects, Barbados shared as much with Virginia as it did with Jamaica. Scholars looking no further than the dominant export crop and the regional category of Caribbean often group Barbados and Jamaica in their analysis. Certainly, there are valid reasons for making generalizations about the two as Caribbean sugar islands. Sugar as a crop had a significant and determinative influence on the formation of a slave society – including everything from the size of plantations and their slave populations to the visual appearance of the landscape and the seasonal rhythms of life. The climate in Barbados is much more like Jamaica than it is like Virginia, and the sugar planters on both islands were equally subject to hurricanes and pests, to the same highs and lows in sugar prices, and to the same pressures from metropolitan abolitionists. Yet, the grouping of Barbados and Jamaica, by privileging the dominant crop as the defining characteristic of a plantation society, overlooks the often significant ways

[59] Morgan, *Slave Counterpoint*, 61, 95, 100–101.
[60] Ibid., 41, 44.

in which sugar islands differed. Kingston, Jamaica, is 1,350 miles from Richmond, Virginia. It is also 1,050 miles from Bridgetown, Barbados. Grouping them together as part of one region is artificial and arbitrary – a sign of the less developed scholarship addressing the Caribbean than the mainland. In many ways, Barbados can be positioned along a spectrum between Jamaica and Virginia, including the degree of diversification in daily production, demographics of the slave population, proportion of African-born slaves, ratio of whites to blacks, size of the average plantation, proportion of resident planters, severity of the work regime, and, of course, the reproductive performance of the slave population. Barbados was the only sugar island in which the slaves were reproducing by the late eighteenth century or early nineteenth century. After abolition, the Barbadian population grew slightly. Why were Barbadian and Virginian slaves naturally reproducing while the Jamaican slave population declined so rapidly?

Jamaica and Virginia were also similar to each other in some ways but less so than Barbados and Virginia. The slave population continued to expand in Jamaica and Virginia in the late eighteenth century, while the Barbadian population shrank. In terms of the available land, the size of the slave population, and the size of some of the largest estates, Jamaica was more like Virginia than Barbados. Given how much of the scholarly literature has tended to generalize about sugar islands while drawing stark contrasts between the Caribbean and the North American colonies, it is important to recognize that Barbadian plantations were, in some ways, more like Virginian than Jamaican plantations. Not only was there significant diversity among the sugar islands but even Jamaica and Virginia shared a few similarities in this era.

Detailed case studies of individual plantations – Newton and Seawell in southeastern Barbados, Prospect in northeastern Jamaica, and Mount Vernon in northern Virginia – form the core of *Slavery and Enlightenment in the British Atlantic*. I have chosen to focus on the estates from which detailed work logs have survived. Work logs offer a strong evidentiary base for the study. They offer richly detailed snapshots of plantation work regimes in the 1780s and 1790s, but this book also relies on a wide variety of other sources to sketch in the preceding and intervening periods. By splicing this material together, this book offers a meaningful moving picture that shows change over time while highlighting the rich data available for particular moments.

Although this book focuses on four specific estates in detail, it also draws on considerable supporting evidence from a variety of large plantations. For Jamaica, substantial supporting evidence is also drawn from several estates for which there are partial or less detailed work logs (Pleasant Hill and Phillipsfield, in St. Thomas in the east; Duckensfield, along the Plantain Garden River in St. Thomas in the east; and Somerset Vale, in St. Thomas in the east) and from the correspondence of Simon Taylor, the most prominent attorney in the island at the end of the eighteenth century, who managed several large plantations in St. Thomas in the east. For Barbados, supporting evidence has been drawn from a richly documented estate (Turner's Hall) in the interior Scotland District, from the minutes of the Barbadian Society for the Improvement of Plantership, and from the correspondence among owners, attorneys, and overseers on the two Codrington estates in St. John parish in the center of the island. For Virginia, the focus is overwhelmingly on Mount Vernon. Comparable records for large Virginian estates are unavailable – in part because there were fewer large plantations than there were in the sugar islands and in part because there were fewer absentee planters for which records had to be made. Wherever possible, supporting evidence has been drawn from Monticello, in Albemarle County in the central Virginia piedmont, and from Mount Airy in Richmond County, and Sabine Hall in Lancaster County – both in the tidewater in the Northern Neck – and from some smaller estates. Overall, this book's evidence is weighted toward eastern Jamaica and toward northern Virginia but, because it is a small island with largely uniform terrain and climate, plantations from almost all regions of Barbados are represented in this study.

Newton and Seawell were in Christ Church Parish, on flat and low-lying terrain in southeastern Barbados. In the last quarter of the eighteenth century, they were closely linked estates. In the 1790s, they shared the same manager, Sampson Wood, and the same absentee owners, John and Thomas Lane. The manager compared the two plantations in his reports and explained agricultural techniques at Seawell by referring to Newton. The estates exchanged provisions, distilling equipment, and skilled slaves in times of need and were close enough – less than five miles apart – that the manager, who lived at Newton, traveled back and forth on many mornings. Although closely connected, Newton and Seawell were different units. At 459 acres and 255 slaves, Newton was one of the largest sugar plantations in late eighteenth-century Barbados. It was also one of the oldest. By 1796, when the first work logs were created for the estate, Newton had been operating for a century and a half (it is still a sugar plantation today, in the same basic location). Canes had also been cultivated at Seawell for more than a century at that point. It was a more typical late eighteenth-century Barbadian sugar plantation in terms of its slave population (182) and its total plantation acreage (345). Although they were rockier, Seawell's lands, fields, and topsoil were "pretty much like that at Newton."[61] There was one significant agricultural difference. Some of the lands at Seawell were too close to the sea for quality cane. Longstaple cotton was sometimes cultivated on those fields. Newton had two wind-driven sugar mills, whereas Seawell had a single windmill. Despite its smaller size, contemporaries considered Seawell to be a plantation "of greater note" than Newton.[62] Indeed Seawell's profit rate in the 1790s (8.4 percent) was higher than the average Barbadian sugar plantation (6.1 percent), and Newton's (5.9 percent) was slightly lower.[63]

Standing in contrast in many ways to Newton and Seawell, Prospect was in Portland Parish in northeastern Jamaica. In was much younger than Newton and Seawell, and it focused almost exclusively on sugar production, along with a small amount of logging. Portland started as a sugar plantation at the beginning of the 1780s, when the Jamaican plantation system was still expanding. There is no evidence to indicate how financially successful the estate was. At its largest, in 1787, there were 162 slaves on the estate and it was close to 500 acres. In terms of its slave population and the size of its land, it was an average Jamaican sugar plantation. Unlike the low and mostly flat lands of Christ Church in Barbados, Portland was rugged and mountainous terrain, which made working conditions for slaves much more demanding. Whereas the planters at Newton and Seawell relied on oxen to transport canes to the mill, the Prospect planters were forced to use the more sure-footed and durable mule. Whereas the conditions for planting sugar in Christ Church tended toward too dry (especially on the southeastern coast around Seawell), Prospect was in an area of Jamaica where the average annual rainfall (about 5,000 mm per year) actually exceeded the ideal amount for sugar, forcing the slaves to work in chronically wet weather and in slippery, muddy, and rugged conditions.[64] Whereas African-born slaves were in a tiny minority at Newton and Seawell by the 1790s, the majority of Prospect slaves were

---

[61] "Report on the [Newton] Negroes," MS 523/288, Newton Family Papers, Senate House Library, University of London Archives.
[62] Bryan Edwards, "Map of the Island of Barbados for the History of the West Indies, 1794," in Tony Campbell, *The Printed Maps of Barbados: From the Earliest Times to 1873* (London: Map Collector's Circle, 1965), plate 19, no. 44.
[63] Ward, "Profitability of Sugar Planting," 204, 210.
[64] Edward Long, *History of Jamaica* vol. 2 (Montreal: McGill-Queen's University Press, 170).

African-born and recent imports. Whereas the Newton and Seawell population were close to being self-reproducing, there was only one year between 1784 and 1793 in which births exceeded deaths at Prospect.[65]

George Washington's Mount Vernon, in Fairfax County, in northern Virginia near Alexandria, was an enormous 8,000 acres by the time of his death in 1799 – sixteen times the size of Prospect or Newton and more than half the size of Portland Parish in Jamaica or of Christ Church Parish in Barbados. Washington was aggressively expansionist with the estate. When he acquired it, Mount Vernon was just 2,500 acres.[66] The slave population grew with the expanding farm. In the last quarter of the eighteenth century, the population more than doubled from 135 slaves to 317 slaves. The growth was almost entirely by natural reproduction.[67] After 1775, only a handful of the new slaves had been purchased by Washington, and almost all of the slaves Washington purchased in his life were creoles purchased from other planters. The number of slaves per acre at Mount Vernon was low – almost miniscule – compared to the same ratio on a sugar plantation. Nevertheless, Washington's estate had one of the highest slave-to-acre ratios among the top two dozen largest slave holders in the Chesapeake.[68] The top soils at Mount Vernon were poor, and Washington chose to stop growing tobacco in 1766, preferring to focus on corn, wheat, and other grains such as rye, oats, and barley.[69] The lands were relatively flat, making work conditions less demanding than they would have been on more rugged terrain and making the plowing necessary for grain cultivation easier. Mount Vernon became a collection of five working farm quarters rather than a single staple-crop plantation, and, Washington, to lower costs, became increasingly intent on using the abundant labor resources to make Mount Vernon entirely self-sufficient. Although slave labor was versatile and flexible, there were ultimately limits to the number of occupations or productive activities that Washington could envision at Mount Vernon for the slaves. By the summer of 1799, the

---

[65] S. D. Smith, "An Introduction to the Plantation Journals of the Prospect Sugar Estate," in *Records of the Jamaican Prospect Estate* [microform] (Wakefield, Eng.: Microform Academic Publishers, 2003), 1–25; "Report on the [Newton] Negroes," MS 523/288; and "Report on the Negroes of Seawell Plantation," MS 523/292, Newton Family Papers.

[66] Walsh, "Slavery and Agriculture at Mount Vernon," in Philip J. Schwarz, ed. *Slavery at the Home of George Washington* (Mount Vernon: Mount Vernon Ladies Association, 2002), 50.

[67] Jean B. Lee, "Mount Vernon: A Model for the Republic," in Schwarz, ed. *Slavery at the Home of George Washington*, 17, 36.

[68] Walsh, "Slavery and Agriculture," 48.

[69] Ibid., 56.

population had grown so large that Washington complained, "I have more working Negroes ... than can be employed to any advantage in the farming system."[70]

Mount Vernon was exceptionally large for a Chesapeake plantation, but its size and the land and labor resources available to Washington and his managers make the slaves' work routines and the managerial strategies more comparable to Jamaican and Barbadian estates. Combined, Mount Vernon was much larger than the average Chesapeake plantation but, separated into its constituent parts, the individual farm quarters begin to approximate what might be found on smaller holdings in the region. In this sense, the data from Mount Vernon could be seen as more representative of the region as a whole.

Slavery and Enlightenment in the British Atlantic is organized into two sections of three chapters each. The first three chapters address plantation management, labor organization, and agricultural practices and the ideas which shaped plantation management. The first chapter situates new and evolving systems of plantation management and accounting within broader Atlantic contexts. It demonstrates how plantation management strategies were transformed by the ideals of Enlightenment science, the accounting revolution of the Scottish Enlightenment, the rise of numeracy and political arithmetic, new ways of conceptualizing and tracking time, and the growth of an agricultural improvement movement. Scholars have long debated the impact of amelioration on the health of slaves in the Caribbean, focusing the debate on how widespread ameliorative ideas were and on the efficacy of ameliorative legislation. This chapter focuses instead on the shifting and evolving intellectual architecture of amelioration over time and on how amelioration related to other broader Enlightenment-inspired philanthropic projects.

The second chapter explores the seasonal rhythms of production in Barbados, Jamaica, and Virginia. It stresses the diversification of plantation production in all regions of the Americas, and explores the ways in which the quantity of labor expected from slaves rose throughout the late eighteenth century, particularly because of the elimination of downtime that came with the diversification of production. The seasonality of work and production has not been sufficiently emphasized in Atlantic historiography. Instead of making monolithic statements about the lived experience

---

[70] George Washington to Robert Lewis, August 17, 1799, in John Clement Fitzpatrick, ed. *The Writings of George Washington: From the Original Manuscript Sources, 1745–1799*, vol. 37 (Washington, DC: Government Printing Office, 1931), 338–339.

of slavery, this chapter underscores the impact of seasonal changes in work patterns on the enslaved.

The third chapter examines the key differences in gang labor organization among Barbados, Jamaica, and Virginia, stressing that Caribbean gangs were larger and much more regimented and severe in their labor discipline than were gangs in the Chesapeake. The gang system, this chapter shows, was one of the most significant sites of innovation and improvement in late eighteenth-century plantation management. Some planters saw the organization of labor as the key to extracting greater efforts from the enslaved while ameliorating the conditions of slavery.

The last three chapters of this book focus more directly on the lived experience of slavery within particular working environments. The fourth chapter explores the seasonal rhythms of health and work. Seasonality is, once again, a central theme in this chapter. I argue that illnesses and mortality rose among the enslaved in the Caribbean during the most demanding tasks, cane holing and manuring; yet, mortality and morbidity rates in the Chesapeake tended to be highest during the winter, when work was least demanding.

The fifth chapter explores the differences between skilled and unskilled work on plantations, suggesting that, in all regions, the boundaries between skilled and unskilled work were often porous and artificial. Tradesmen spent a significant amount of time in menial field labors. What constituted skilled work in the planter's mind was dependent in part on gendered and racialized ideas about who was capable of skilled work; the skill was in the worker and not the work.

The final chapter examines how the occupations held by the enslaved and their seasonal work routines shaped the formation of slave families and communities and their patterns of resistance to the institution. The key argument in this chapter is that a hierarchy existed within the slave community that drew on the occupations slaves held in the working world. Elite slave family groups emerged on plantations, and they tended to hold the most privileged work positions. Slaves who held the most privileged occupations had more opportunity to earn money, acquire wealth, and build and maintain stable families.

Slavery and Enlightenment in the British Atlantic contributes to the scholarly literature in several important ways. It offers more detailed evidence on eighteenth-century slave work routines than anything existing in the scholarly literature by closely examining and contextualizing a set of sources – plantation work logs – which have been almost entirely overlooked by scholars. It attempts to blend a business history of plantation management with a history of slave labor, and it forefronts the ways in which work was the most determinative factor in a slave's life. It broadens our perspective of slavery by bringing the historiography of mainland slavery and the historiography of Caribbean slavery into conversation. It examines a transitional phase that scholars often overlook between colonial and antebellum slavery – bridging the gap between those fields. It explores the ways in which plantation management and slave labor were shaped by Enlightenment-inspired improvement movements that strove to both ameliorate the conditions of slavery and improve profits from land and labor resources. It stresses that the amelioration movement usually gave ground to the planters' desire to extract more labor from the slaves, and some planters were able to intellectually reconcile the contradictions without being intentionally duplicitous. The key comparative point throughout this book is that triangulating Jamaica, Barbados, and Virginia permits the disaggregation of the regional category of Caribbean and yields a better understanding of the often significant differences between the sugar islands and the similarities between Virginia and Barbados or, to a much lesser extent, between Virginia and Jamaica. This kind of Atlantic history approach transcends the dictates of modern political boundaries and nationalist historiographies and questions the idea that the Caribbean was distinctly different from the U.S. mainland in the decades immediately after the American Revolution. In fact, managerial strategies and the working experiences of slaves in Virginia, Barbados, and Jamaica continued to be shaped by Anglo-American improvement movements from their rise in prominence in the mid-eighteenth century through the Revolution and into the early nineteenth century.

I

Clock Work

Time, Quantification, Amelioration, and the Enlightenment

In the 1760s, at Mount Vernon, in Virginia, George Washington used a pocket watch to conduct time-motion studies of his slaves at work, calculating his tradesmen's hourly rate of production, transforming the clock into a supervisory technology and making a science of slave management.[1] In 1789, he linked time and work again, identifying time as the key to compelling and measuring maximum labor efforts from his bondsmen without overtaxing them. He stressed that "lost labour can never be regained." Accordingly, "every labourer" should "do as much in the 24 hours as their strength, without endangering their health, or constitution, will allow."[2] In the 1790s, at Phillipsfield and Pleasant Hill, in Jamaica, the boiling house books noted the precise number of hours the mill was in operation and the hours at which groups of slaves began and ended their night shifts. In 1798, a relative and representative of the absentee owners of Newton and Seawell visited the estates during the cane harvest to see how their new manager, Sampson Wood, was conducting business. Wood was producing meticulous accounts and applying new kinds of supervisory tools such as daily work logs to better manage the estate's labor force, and he was achieving good profits.[3] Despite Wood's successes, the visitor was concerned that Wood was hamstrung in his

---

[1] George Washington Diary, February 5, 1760, http://memory.loc.gov/cgibin/ampage?collId=mgw1&fileName=mgw1b/gwpage602.db&recNum=24 (accessed on July 1, 2010); see also Lorena S. Walsh, *Motives of Honor* (Chapel Hill: University of North Carolina Press, 2010), 619–620.

[2] "George Washington to John Fairfax, January 1, 1789," in Dorothy Twohig, ed., *The Papers of George Washington*: Presidential series, vol. 1: September 1788–March 1789 (Charlottesville: University Press of Virginia, 1987), 223.

[3] Newton Abstract of Annual Accounts for 1798, MS 523/125, Newton Family Papers.

affairs because "He has no Clock, nothing but an Hour Glass to put the people to Work by."[4]

Late eighteenth-century planters conceptualized time as currency. Like money, it could be saved, exchanged, or spent. It had to be accounted for, and its successful calculation and manipulation could guarantee both a plantation's profits and the health of its slaves. Time was a tool of discipline and an aid to measuring performance. The manipulation and organization of work time and rest time, planters maintained, was the key to both improving an estate's productivity and ameliorating the conditions of slavery.

The clock and the precise divisions and systematic ordering of the work day that it enabled were integral parts of an Enlightenment-driven improvement project that transformed the plantation system of the British Americas from the early eighteenth century through the abolition of the slave trade in 1807. The rapidly expanding slave system in the British Americas created competition for resources, forcing adaptation and innovation. The Enlightenment pursuit of universal laws that would enable scientific, moral, and economic progress, and the time-work factory discipline that emerged with early industrialization spurred the development of new ways of conceptualizing and tracking the passage of time.[5] Statistical thinking and increasingly meticulous accounting techniques became more common in business management.[6] Plantation reforms in this era were focused on developing better and more integrated "systems" of management. Order, science, mathematical precision, and new ways of disciplining and compelling labor were at the heart of the

---

[4] Richard Lane to [Thomas Lane], Feb. 28, 1798, MS 523/332, Newton Family Papers.
[5] E. P. Thompson, "Time, Work Discipline and Industrial Capitalism," *Past and Present* 38 (December 1967), 56–97; Stuart Sherman, *Telling Time: Clocks, Diaries and the English Diurnal Form, 1660–1785* (Chicago: University of Chicago Press, 1996).
[6] B. S. Yamey, "Scientific Bookkeeping and the Rise of Capitalism," *Economic History Review* 1.2–3 (1949), 99–113; Patricia Cohen, *A Calculating People: The Spread of Numeracy in Early America* (Chicago: The University of Chicago Press, 1982); Peter A. Coclanis, "Bookkeeping in the Eighteenth-Century South: Evidence from Newspaper Advertisements," *South Carolina Historical Magazine* 91.1 (1990), 21–33; Richard K. Fleischman and Thomas N. Tyson, "Cost Accounting during the Industrial Revolution: The Present State of Historical Knowledge," *Economic History Review* 46.3 (August 1993), 503–517; M. J. Mepham, "The Scottish Enlightenment and the Development of Accounting," in R. H. Parker and B. S. Yamey, eds. *Accounting History: Some British Contributions* (Oxford: Clarendon Press, 1994), 268–93; Paolo Quattrone, "Is Time Spent, Passed or Counted? The Missing Link between Time and Accounting History," *Accounting Historians Journal* 32.1 (January 2005), 185–208.

plantation improvement movement. Land, time, and slave work were woven together in the minds of planters as elements of an intricate and interdependent plantation system – a machine.[7]

Planters normally linked increased economic efficiency with the amelioration of slavery, positioning them as part of the same project. The Enlightenment's unbridled faith in the practical and moral utility of progress and the mutually reinforcing nature of the two allowed planters to cast the plantation improvement project as both benevolent and profitable.[8] Reform-minded planters insisted that a more humanitarian management of slaves was in the economic interest of the planter; healthier and happier slaves would work harder. By inculcating better work habits in their slaves, planters sometimes suggested they could curb what they perceived as the moral depravity of the enslaved. Often, however, the efforts at improving the conditions of slavery clashed with the effort to improve agriculture by extracting more profit from plantation resources. Planters, for example, increased the supply of homegrown provisions by eliminating slack periods in the agricultural cycle to grow those crops, and they made their slaves work more each year to produce that food. When there was a conflict between improving the conditions of life among the slaves and increasing labor demands to extract more profits, it was usually

---

[7] Starkey, *Economic Geography of Barbados, A Study of the Relationships between Environmental Vairaions and Economic Development* (New York: Columbia University Press, 1939), 99–112; Drew Gilpin Faust, *James Henry Hammond and the Old South: A Design for Mastery* (Baton Rouge: Louisiana State University Press, 1982), 105–36; Mark Overton, *Agricultural Revolution in England: The Transformation of the Agrarian Economy* (New York: Cambridge University Press, 1996); Pamela Horn, "The Contribution of the Propagandist to Eighteenth-Century Agricultural Improvement," *Historical Journal* 25.2 (June 1982), 313–29; Watts, *West Indies: Patterns of Development, Culture, and Environmental Change since 1492* (Cambridge: Cambridge University Press, 1987), 384–392; Sarah Wilmot, "*The Business of Improvement*": *Agriculture and Scientific Culture in Britain, c. 1770–c. 1870* (Bristol: Historical Geography Research Group, 1990); Peter D. McClelland, *Sowing Modernity: America's First Agricultural Revolution* (Ithaca: Cornell University Press, 1992); Roy Porter, *Creation of the Modern World: The Untold Story of the British Enlightenment* (New York. W.W. Norton & Company, 2000); Sarah Tarlow, *The Archaeology of Improvement in Britain, 1750–1850* (Leiden: Cambridge University Press, 2007); Lynne Avery Hunt, *Inventing Human Rights: A History* (New York: Norton, 2007); Joel Mokyr, *The Enlightened Economy: An Economic History of Britain 1700–1850* (New Haven: Yale University Press, 2009).

[8] Roy Porter, *The Enlightenment* (New York: Palgrave Macmillan, 2001); Lorraine Daston, "Afterword: The Ethos of the Enlightenment," in Jan Golinski, William Clark, and Simon Schaffer, eds., *The Sciences in Enlightened Europe* (Chicago: University of Chicago Press, 1999), 495–504; Outram, *The Enlightenment*.

the former that gave way.⁹ Planters tried to reverse the constant decline of the slave population while increasing their slaves' work output. Plantation management schemes were geared toward total quantities of work production and mortality and fertility rates (quantity of life) among slaves rather than the slave's quality of life or their quality of work. Fertility rates improved and mortality rates declined slightly in the late eighteenth century but slaves were also forced to sacrifice leisure time for work time – coerced to exhibit work values and patterns that aligned with an industrious revolution transforming the British Atlantic.¹⁰

Historians have stressed that the modern ethos of industrial work and time discipline shaped labor patterns during the early stages of industrialization in Europe. New modes of labor discipline were central to the process of innovation during early industrialization.¹¹ Recent scholarship has clearly demonstrated that increases in the number of working hours and days were a critical factor in the productivity gains that accompanied early industrialization in Europe and, as this chapter will show, a remarkably similar process led to increased outputs per enslaved worker in the

---

⁹ Ward, *British West Indian Slavery, 1750–1834: The Process of Amelioration* (New York: Oxford University Press, 1988); Mary Turner, "Planter Profits and Slave Rewards: Amelioration Reconsidered," *West Indies Accounts: Essays on the History of the British Caribbean and the Atlantic Economy in Honour of Richard Sheridan* (Kingston, Jamaica: University of the West Indies Press, 1996), 232–252; Michael Craton, *Searching for the Invisible Man: Slaves and Plantation Life in Jamaica* (Cambridge, MA: Harvard University Press, 1978); Walsh, *Motives of Honor*, 623, 637.

¹⁰ Jan De Vries, "The Industrial Revolution and the Industrious Revolution," *The Journal of Economic History* 54.2 (June 1994), 249–270.

¹¹ Thompson, "Time, Work Discipline and Industrial Capitalism," 56–97; Leonard N. Rosenband, "Productivity and Labor Discipline in the Montgolfier Paper Mill, 1780–1805," *The Journal of Economic History* 45.2 (June 1985), 435–443; G.N. von Tunzelman, "Technological and Organizational Change in Industry During the Early Industrial Revolution," in Patrick O'Brien and Ronald Quinlet, eds. *The Industrial Revolution and British Society* (New York: Cambridge University Press, 1993), 258; Gary Hawke, "Reinterpretations of the Industrial Revolution," in O'Brien and Quinlet, eds. *Industrial Revolution and British Society* (New York: Cambridge University Press, 1993), 54–78; Gregory Clark, "Factory Discipline," *The Journal of Economic History* 54.1 (March 1994), 128–163; C. Evans "Work and Workloads During Industrialization: The Experience of Forgemen in the British Iron Industry 1750–1850," *International Review of Social History* 44.2 (August 1999), 197–215; Leonard Rosenband, Merritt Roe Smith, and Jeff Horn, "Introduction," in Rosenband, Smith, and Horn, eds. *Reconceptualizing the Industrial Revolution* (Cambridge, MA: MIT Press, 2010), 1–20; Mokyr, *Enlightened Economy*, 340–355; Leonard Rosenband, "Hiring and Firing at the Montgolfier Paper Mill," in L. N. Rosenband and M. Safley, eds., *The Workplace before the Factory: Artisans and Proletarians, 1500–1800* (Ithaca, NY: Cornell University Press, 1993), 225–240.

plantation Americas.[12] These new systems of labor and time discipline in Europe and in the slave Americas were shaped by the pursuit of useful knowledge and by the late Enlightenment's emphasis on the morally reforming capacity of work and time discipline.[13] The new systems of work and time discipline were applied in both urban and rural contexts, and they affected free and unfree laborers in the metropole and in the colonies. The increasingly rigorous and precise forms of labor and time discipline that drove productivity increases in early industrialization during the last third of the eighteenth century also transformed large slave plantations throughout the British Americas. In fact, clock-time discipline and the standardization and numerical precision that we associate with the labor management techniques of early industrialization were implemented on slave plantations decades before they transformed the early factory labor systems. It was this emphasis on industrial work and time discipline, as much as the sugar processing equipment itself, that made the sugar plantation a factory in the field.[14]

Records of crop yields on large plantations show that productivity levels per slave rose significantly in the late eighteenth century on Caribbean sugar plantations, as well as on large plantations in the Chesapeake. In the sugar islands, these productivity gains were particularly pronounced in the 1770s and 1780s. In the Chesapeake, the annual gains were more constant between 1740 and 1800.[15] The widespread increases in productivity per worker in both these slave societies can be explained in part by the many practices of the improvement project and by the diffusion of innovations in planting. Productivity increases in these slave societies were also the result of slave labor specialization and expertise with New World crops among an increasingly creolized slave population. However, for the most part, productivity was increasing because slaves, like workers in industrializing Europe, were working longer hours and more days throughout the year. Plantation accounts, such as work logs, and the new ways of tracking time apparent

---

[12] Joachim Voth, *Time and Work in England, 1750–1830* (New York: Oxford University Press, 2000).
[13] Porter, *Creation of the Modern World*, 377–384.
[14] Sidney W. Mintz, *Sweetness and Power: The Place of Sugar in Modern History* (New York: Penguin Books, 1986), 47.
[15] John McCusker, "The Economy of the British West Indies, 1763–1790: Growth, Stagnation or Decline," in McCusker, ed., *Essays in the Economic History of the Atlantic World*. (London: Routledge, 1997), 324; J. R. Ward, "The Amelioration of British West Indian Slavery, 1750–1834: Technical Change and the Plow," *New West-Indian Guide* 63.1–2 (1989), 43; Walsh, "Plantation Management in the Chesapeake, 1620–1820," *The Journal of Economic History* 49.2 (1989), 393–406.

in these accounts were among the technologies planters used to create a framework for defining and measuring productivity and extracting more work from their bondsmen.

Planters in the sugar islands participated in improvement discourses more readily than their counterparts in the Chesapeake but the central elements of this improvement project – amelioration and agricultural improvement – shaped plantation management strategies throughout the slave societies of the late eighteenth-century British Atlantic. After the American Revolution, the postcolonial world of Virginia was less subject to metropolitan standards than the Caribbean. Moreover, from the 1720s onward, and especially after the mid-eighteenth century, the Chesapeake slave population reproduced naturally with little effort on the part of planters, and the gradual switch to grain from the second quarter of the eighteenth century onward and the rapidly producing slave population created a surplus rather than a shortage of labor. Abolitionists, who became a significant force in the late 1780s, had more of an impact in the British Empire than in the new United States, and they focused their attention on pressuring large sugar planters to reform the conditions of slave life.[16]

Plantation work routines were transformed in the late eighteenth century by a variety of new improving practices in plantation management. This chapter will show how an Enlightenment faith in science and progress, the rise of numeracy and statistical thinking, and early humanitarian reform discourses shaped the day-to-day management of plantations. It will outline the ways in which planters conceptualized the interrelated elements of a plantation and strove to identify the universal rules of managing the plantation system. It will demonstrate that the amelioration of slavery was rooted in early eighteenth-century agricultural improvement schemes but was transformed by humanitarian discourses, rising slave prices, and abolitionist attacks on planters. Planters believed that amelioration and increases in work productivity were compatible but, as this chapter will show, the two goals were not always easy to reconcile. This chapter will situate new plantation accounting systems and the guiding principles of plantation management that undergirded these accounts within broader intellectual contexts and reconceptualize these

---

[16] There is a rich literature on abolition. For the best recent work, see Christopher L. Brown, *Moral Capital: Foundations of British Abolitionism* (Chapel Hill: University of North Carolina Press, 2006). See also David Brion Davis, *The Problem of Slavery in the Age of Revolution, 1770–1823* (New York: Oxford University Press, 1975) and Seymour Drescher, *Econocide: British Slavery in the Era of Abolition* (Pittsburgh: University of Pittsburgh Press, 1977).

new accounts as technological innovations in management systems and as core elements of the improvement project. Throughout, this chapter will contrast and compare the ways in which the improvement project was manifest in Chesapeake and Caribbean plantation management practices. Finally, it will demonstrate the extent to which new and more precise ways of conceptualizing and tracking time such as work logs – born of the broader Enlightenment context and the process of industrialization – drove productivity increases and led to more work for slaves.

SCIENCE, SYSTEMS, AND THE PLANTATION "MACHINE"

The rational pursuit of universal laws and principles generalized from cumulative experience linked Newtonian universalism and Baconian empiricism, which were the twin pillars of Enlightenment science.[17] These universal rules, once discovered, would enable the march of progress. Experimentation, empirical observation, and reason were lauded as the guiding principles of this spirit of investigation. Experiential and pragmatic applications were particularly common themes in British sugar plantation manuals. The author of a British Caribbean guide to the management of slaves, for example, described his book as "a series of rules deduced from experience."[18] A London review of Gordon Turnbull's *Letters to a Young Planter* praised it for its practical approach, contrasting it with a contemporary French plantation manual that was less useful because it was more "adapted to the study of the philosopher than the planter."[19]

Planters, especially in the sugar islands, strove to elevate plantership and acquire interpretive prestige by participating in genteel and metropolitan scientific discourses. Resident planters contributed their experiences in plantation management to the primary mouthpiece of agricultural improvement in Britain: Arthur Young's *Annals of Agriculture*.[20] Like

---

[17] Porter, *Creation of the Modern World*, 131–142; Mokyr, "European Enlightenment and the Origins of Economic Growth," in Jeff Horn et al., eds., *Reconceptulaizing the Industrial Revolution* (Cambridge, MA: MIT Press, 2010), 67–9.
[18] David Collins, *Practical Rules for the Management and Medical Treatment of Slaves in the Sugar Colonies* (London: Barfield, 1803).
[19] "Review of Gordon Turnbull's Letters to a Young Planter," in *The Monthly Review or Literary Journal* 74 (January to June, 1786), 65.
[20] See, for example, Patrick Blake, "Culture of Sugar in the West Indies," in Young, ed., *Annals of Agriculture* 31 (London, 1798), 360–370. For other important works in the eighteenth-century British agricultural improvement literature see Jethro Tull, *The Horse-Hoeing Husbandry* (Dublin: A. Rhames, 1733), and Arthur Young, *A Course of Experimental Agriculture*. (London: J. Dodsley, 1770).

Time, Quantification, Amelioration, and the Enlightenment 33

Britain's champions of agricultural improvement, improving planters in the islands and on the mainland trusted in the scientific pursuit of rules and principles to increase productivity and decrease mortality on their estates. In 1776, a Jamaican planter argued that "husbandry ought to be more generally understood as a science."[21] Through trial and error, agriculturalists would, he insisted, learn how to render the earth "more and more profitable."[22] In the first decade of the nineteenth century, the Barbadian Society for the Improvement of Plantership agreed that their members would need to study European developments in "chemistry, agriculture and mechanics" to devise the best systems of plantation management. To achieve this end, the "President ... laid before the Society a syllabus of a course of Lectures, prepared by their Secretary."[23] In 1775, a Jamaican writer insisted that planters should employ scientific principles in the boiling house rather than trusting enslaved sugar boilers. He recommended placing cane syrup on a small pane of clear glass and taking it outside the boiling house to examine it. Such methods were so commonly and successfully used by "Chemists" that he thought it "strange" that they not been universally "adopted in the Boiling House."[24] Improving planters insisted that a plantation manager needed to be educated in the sciences and, more specifically, needed to learn empirical methods of scientific observation and analysis, including the recording of evidence so that the manager could boil experience down to useful knowledge.

"Systems" were a central concept in the plantation improvement project. A system would be guided by predictable relationships between its component parts. The focus on systems was part of the effort to identify universal laws and principles in management. The key was to discover the systematic laws that undergirded the plantation. Washington directed his farm manager, James Anderson, to govern by specific sets of interrelated rules and guidelines because "in everything ... system is essential to carry on business well, and with ease."[25] According to a Barbadian plantation manual from 1786, "Men who manage without system, and form

---

[21] "Review of American Husbandry," *The Monthly Review* 65 [London, 1776], Art. VII. in Carmen, ed., *American Husbandry* (New York: Columbia University Press, 1939), xvii.
[22] Ibid.
[23] *Minutes of the Society for the Improvement of Plantership*, 27.
[24] I. P. Baker, *An Essay on the Art of Making Muscovado Sugar Wherein a New Process is Proposed* (Kingston, Jamaica: Joseph Weatherby, 1775), 37.
[25] George Washington to James Anderson, December 10, 1799, in John Clement Fitzpatrick, ed., *The Writings of George Washington from the Original Manuscript Sources*, vol. 37 (Washington, DC: Government Printing Office, 1931), 466.

expectations without *calculate*, must ever remain subject to the disappointment and failure which so many experience."[26] When a small group of elite Barbadian planters formed the Society for the Improvement of Plantership in 1804, they agreed that the society would only examine "certain topics and experiments ... tending to form a complete system of management."[27] The focus on systems in plantation life drew on the idea that all aspects of plantation production were interdependent and, ideally, mutually reinforcing. The Antiguan planter Samuel Martin, for example, articulated at mid-century what became a commonplace machine metaphor for plantation systems. According to Martin, "a plantation ought to be considered as a well-constructed machine, compounded of various wheels, turning different ways, and yet all contributing to the great end proposed."[28] Systems, as an organizing concept, made all aspects of production interrelated and drew together, conceptually, the health and productivity of the laborer, the land, and the stock. Planters could see technological innovation and the amelioration movement as part of the same project.

The machine metaphor that Martin and others used to describe plantations was grounded in mechanistic philosophies. The machine metaphor was commonly used in the late seventeenth and early eighteenth centuries to describe the natural world; the implication was that natural processes were part of a predictable and uniform system. Writers such as Francis Bacon helped extend the ways in which natural philosophy was conceptualized by attacking the distinction between things produced by human artifice and things produced by nature, and the machine metaphor became even more widely adopted as the distinctions between nature and human artifice began to break down. The metaphor could be used to understand both the natural world and human artifice. The clock, especially after the horological revolution of the 1660s and 1670s, when clocks became more accurate, was increasingly used as a referent in mechanistic philosophies.[29]

---

[26] Edwin Lascelles et al., *Instructions for the Management of a Plantation in Barbadoes and for the Treatment of Negroes* (London: [s.n.], 1786), 1 [emphasis added].

[27] *Minutes of the Society for the Improvement of Plantership*, 4.

[28] Samuel Martin, *Essay upon Plantership*, 2nd ed. (London: T. Smith 1750), 30; see also Kein, *An Essay upon Pen-Keeping and Plantership* (Kingston, Jamaica: His Majesty's Printing Office, 1796), 58. For more on Samuel Martin, see Richard Sheridan, "Samuel Martin, Innovating Planter of Antigua, 1750–1776," *Agricultural History* 34.3 (1960): 126–139.

[29] Steven Shapin, *The Scientific Revolution* (Chicago: The University of Chicago Press, 1996), 30–37; Margaret G. Cook, "Divine Artifice and Natural Mechanism: Robert Boyle's Mechanical Philosophy of Nature," *Osiris*, 2nd series, 16, "Science in Theistic Contexts: Cognitive Dimensions" (2001), 133–150; Sherman, *Telling Time*, 2–5; and

The clock was the master machine; it was an intricate device that relied on the coordination of interdependent parts.

The metaphor of the plantation as machine that planters adopted invoked the mechanistic natural philosophies and their focus on uniform rules. More specifically, it may have borrowed directly from seventeenth-century mechanistic philosophers' descriptions of a clockwork universe.[30] According to the mechanistic philosopher Robert Boyle, the universe was like a clock "put into such a motion, that though the numerous wheels, and other parts of it, move several ways ... yet each part performs its part to the various ends, for which it was contrived, as regularly and uniformly as if it knew and were concerned to do its duty."[31] By utilizing strikingly similar imagery in the description of an ideal plantation, Martin and his fellow planters were not only invoking the idea that the plantation had the same sort of predictable and uniform processes that natural philosophers sought but they were making the plantation analogous to a giant clock, stressing the rules of timing in plantation management and the cyclical nature of production. Martin, intent on timing, was especially careful to note that "if any one part [of the plantation machine] runs too fast or too slow in proportion to the rest, the main purpose is defeated."[32] For planters, the improvement and reform of their plantation machines would be grounded in the control of time.

TECHNOLOGY AND AGRICULTURE

Scholars used to depict the plantation Americas as slow to innovate or adapt and as resistant to change. They emphasized that plantations were sluggish and technologically retarded – a characterization that reiterated critiques first articulated by abolitionists and some English agricultural improvers.[33] In the eighteenth and early nineteenth centuries, the climate

Paul Glennie and Nigel Thrift, "Revolutions in the Times: Clocks and the Temporal Structures of Everyday Life," in David N. Livingstone and Charles W. J. Withers, eds., *Geography and Revolution* (Chicago: University of Chicago Press, 2005), 160–198; Mokyr, *Enlightened Economy*. 16.

[30] Porter, *Creation of the Modern World*, 56.
[31] Robert Boyle, "Essay Containing a Requisite Digression Concerning Those that Would Exclude the Deity From Intermeddling with Matter," in M. A. Stewart, ed., *Selected Philosophical Papers of Robert Boyle* (Indianapolis: Indiana University Press, 1991), 160; see also Shapin, *Scientific Revolution*, 34.
[32] Martin, *Essay upon Plantership*, 4th ed., 37.
[33] Arthur Young, *Political Essays Concerning the Present State of the British Empire* (London: Strahan and T. Cadell in the Strand, 1772), 278–279; Avery Craven, *Soil Exhaustion as a Factor in the Agricultural History of Virginia and Maryland,*

of the tropics was thought to retard ingenuity, making the slave societies of the Caribbean seem even less capable of innovation. Stage-based theories of development helped reinforce the argument by positing that slavery was fundamentally incompatible with technological advancement or with the higher levels of civilization.[34] The conflation of technological and moral progress, an Enlightenment legacy, helped buttress the idea that technological advancement was hindered by slavery. To say that slavery is efficient or that slave societies are capable of technological advancement is not to validate the morality of the institution.[35] However, more recent scholarly investigations are breaking down these base assumptions, demonstrating positive correlations between the extent of slavery in a society and the degree of technological innovation.[36]

Most large planters adapted to changing market conditions by striving for innovation and embracing enslaved labor as a component of that innovation. Innovative developments in labor management, such as the introduction of work patterns regulated by clocks, or in agricultural practices, such as increased manuring, were easier to introduce among enslaved workers than among free workers because the enslaved had far less negotiating power. Although there were some planters who were beginning to entertain the idea, which was growing rapidly in the late eighteenth century, that free labor was more productive than slave labor, the vast majority of planters never questioned whether an enslaved worker

1608–1840 (Gloucester: P. Smith, 1965[1926]); William A. Green "The Planter Class and British West Indian Sugar Production, before and after Emancipation," *Economic History Review* 26 (August 1973), 448–463; Lucille Mathurin Mair, "Women Field Workers in Jamaica during Slavery," in Brian L. Moore, ed., *Slavery, Freedom and Gender: The Dynamics of Caribbean Society* (Kingston, Jamaica: University of the West Indies Press, 2001), 189; Peter Boomard and Gert J. Oostindie, "Changing Sugar Technology and the Labour Nexus: The Caribbean, 1750–1900," *New West-Indian Guide* 63.1-2 (1989), 3–22; Russell Menard, "Colonial America's Mestizo Agriculture," in Cathy Matson, ed., *The Economy of Early America: Historical Perspectives and New Directions* (University Park: The Pennsylvania State University Press, 2006), 115–116; S. Max Edelson, *Plantation Enterprise in Colonial South Carolina* (Cambridge: Harvard University Press, 2006); Glenn A. Crothers, "Agricultural Improvement and Technological Innovation in a Slave Society: The Case of Early National Northern Virginia," *Agricultural History*, 75.2 (Spring 2001), 135–161; S. Drescher, *The Mighty Experiment: Free Labor Versus Slavery in British Emancipation* (New York: Oxford University Press, 2002), 19–33; R. W. Fogel, *The Slavery Debates: A Retrospective, 1952–1990* (Baton Rouge: Louisiana State University Press, 2003), 24–48.

[34] For more on the impact of these ideas, see Drescher, *Mighty Experiment*, 85–86.
[35] Fogel, *Slavery Debates*, 24–48.
[36] Rebecca J. Scott, *Slave Emancipation in Cuba: The Transition to Free Labour, 1860–1899* (Pittsburgh, PA: University of Pittsburgh Press, 2000), 3–44.

was better than a free worker.[37] By the twentieth century, this free labor ideology had become so pervasive that slavery scholars often took it for granted that slave labor was less efficient and less compatible with technological innovation. Yet, to a significant extent, a guaranteed, captive, and permanent labor force reduced the risks inherent in improvement schemes, thus encouraging experimentation and innovation. Permanent slave labor was always more constant and predictable than the hired labor market, whether free or enslaved.[38] Benjamin Franklin, one of the earliest colonial proponents of the superiority of free labor, was forced to concede that colonists probably continued to purchase slaves "because slaves may be kept as long as a man pleases, or has occasion for their labour; while hired men are continually leaving their master (often in the midst of his business) and setting up for themselves."[39]

It is easy to overlook technological innovation in agricultural societies. There appears, on a superficial level, to be little difference in how sugar was grown in the early modern era.[40] Planters in all settings used slave gangs equipped with nothing more than hand tools to grow cane and a large wind, water, or cattle mill to process it. It is somewhat easier to visualize agricultural transformation on large estates in the eighteenth-century Chesapeake than it is in the sugar islands because the dominant crops were changing. The planters in the Chesapeake began to grow more grains, which meant that they cleared and cultivated significantly more tracts of land for grain than they had for tobacco. A change in crops, however, is not necessarily sufficient evidence of extensive technological innovation. One way of assessing the degree of technological innovation is to focus on mechanization or tools. Although plows were adopted on some sugar plantations and throughout most of the large Chesapeake grain farms at

---

[37] David Barclay, *An Account of the Emancipation of the Slaves of Unity Valley Pen in Jamaica* (London: W. Phillips, 1801), 19; Drescher, *Mighty Experiment*; Eva Sheppard Wolf, "Early Free Labor Thought and the Contest over Slavery in the Early Republic," in John Craig Hammond and Matthew Mason, eds., *Contesting Slavery: The Politics of Bondage and Freedom in the New American Nation* (Charlottesville: University of Virginia Press, 2011), 32–48; R. J. Steinfeld, *The Invention of Free Labor: The Employment Relation in English and American Law and Culture, 1350–1870* (Chapel Hill: University of North Carolina Press, 1991).

[38] Roberts, "Uncertain Business: A Case Study of Barbadian Plantation Management, 1770–1793," *Slavery & Abolition*, 32.2 (June 2011), 254–255.

[39] Benjamin Franklin, *The Interest of Great Britain Considered with Regard to Her Colonies And the Acquisitions of Canada and Guadeloupe*, reprinted (London: B. Mecom, 1760), 54; Wolf, "Early Free Labor Thought."

[40] Russell R. Menard, *Sweet Negotiations: Sugar, Slavery and Plantation Agriculture in Early Babardos*. (Charlottesville: University of Virginia Press, 2006), 69–70.

the end of the eighteenth century, and threshing machines were used on some large grain plantations, there was little in the way of mechanical innovation in early modern agriculture. By this standard, slave plantations, or any early modern agricultural unit, could certainly be said to be slow to change or adapt.

A narrow definition of technology focused on innovations in machinery or processing equipment is not at all useful in understanding agricultural worlds with captive labor forces forming a major part of the plantation's capital stock.[41] In fact, if one focuses on new tools, the widespread adoption of plows for grain on large estates in the Chesapeake would make it seem that the mainland society had made greater strides in agricultural technology than the Caribbean – which would confirm the inverse relationship between the degree to which a society was committed to slavery and the degree to which it was capable of technological advancement. To appreciate innovations in early modern agriculture and to account for productivity increases in the late eighteenth century, one needs to focus on the minute details of production and the cumulative effect of small innovations in labor management, crop cultivation and combinations, accounting techniques, provision production, animal husbandry, or design details and building materials for the processing works that, collectively, had a significant impact on production and profits.[42] Human capital was usually the most significant portion of a planter's investment, and this is where scholars need to look most closely for innovation on slave plantations. Learning how to increase the longevity of this human stock or increase its productivity was central to technological improvement, particularly on plantations producing labor intensive crops such as sugar.

We have to use terms such as "productivity" and "efficiency" differently with slaves than with free laborers. Slaves were not paid by the hour. They were fixed capital. Planters owned their slaves and as long as a planter could get more out of his slaves each year without killing them, they increased the efficiency and productivity of their capital. This could mean simply reducing the number of days on which slaves missed work or increasing the daily hours expected of them. Labor management became central to innovation. It was possible for enslaved workers to actually become less efficient per hour and, in the planter's calculations, become

---

[41] Joel Mokyr, "Technological Change, 1700–1830," in Roderick Floud and Donald McCloskey, *The Economic History of Britain since 1700*, vol. 1: 1700–1860, 2nd ed. (New York: Cambridge University Press, 1994), 21.

[42] Menard, *Sweet Negotiations*, 69–70; Menard, "Colonial America's Mestizo Agriculture," 115–116; Joel Mokyr, "Technological Change," 21.

more productive overall because there was, cumulatively, more produced per slave each year. Planters were also motivated to diversify their economic production, especially in something as seasonal as agriculture, to avoid having their slaves be idle.[43]

When we think about innovation on slave plantations, it is important not only to consider new ways of using enslaved human capital but also to look beyond the total output of staple crops and productivity increases per hand. Plantations could improve profits in this era by lowering costs and becoming more self-sufficient – meaning that they could produce more of the goods internally that they had originally needed to purchase from outside the estate. Scholars have long debated the profitability of plantation enterprises – typically focusing on production levels – but because staple crop plantations have been thought of as monocropping businesses they have tended to overlook the improvements in self-sufficiency and the more efficient use of resources on individual plantations. Barbadian planters, with lower revenues than their counterparts in Jamaica, were particularly attentive to the importance of keeping costs low. A Barbadian plantation manual argued that "a proprietor of a plantation should put it under such a course of management that the net profits should more depend upon the smallness of the annual expense than upon the largeness of the crops."[44] By having slaves perform work previously done by free workers, by growing more provisions for cattle and slaves on site, and by improving the care and breeding of cattle or slaves to avoid having to purchase more, plantations could lower the costs involved in sugar production.[45] For Chesapeake planters, lowering the cost of production and crop diversification became critical to combating diminishing returns in tobacco cultivation. The American Revolution galvanized Chesapeake planters into focusing more fully on self-sufficiency rather than relying on goods imported from Britain, such as clothing for the enslaved.

In Barbados and Jamaica, residents and visitors often noted the innovations that were transforming agriculture, but they rarely focused on a specific development. In 1776, a Jamaican planter argued that "prodigious practical improvements [in sugar agriculture] have been made."[46] When a Barbadian overseer described conditions at his plantation in 1797, he drew attention to the "modern improvements" in sugar cultivation in Barbados,

---

[43] Robert E. Gallman and Ralph V. Anderson, "Slaves as Fixed Capital: Slave Labor and Southern Economic Development," *Journal of American History* 64.1 (June 1977), 24–46.
[44] Lascelles et al., *Management of a Plantation*, 2.
[45] Roberts, "Uncertain Business."
[46] "Review of American Husbandry," xvii.

and he assured the owner that "there have been many of late years."[47] It was the cumulative effect of the many small changes in practice that was transforming agriculture. The switch to Otaheite (Bourbon) cane in the 1790s; the improvements in livestock care that accompanied the adoption of Guinea or Scotch grass in the last half of the eighteenth century; the movement toward self-sufficiency in food production that helped planters cut costs; the increased use of manure; the development of better techniques for producing refined sugars or rum; the specialization of labor among slaves; and the increasing intercropping of provisions with cash crops to maintain soils, reduce weeding, and better utilize space all led to greater returns on sugar estates. The adoption of plantation hospitals after mid-century, more detailed accounting technologies, and more attention to the tracking and manipulation of time enabled planters to extract more labor from their slaves, making technological improvements in the manipulation of their human capital.

In Virginia, the switch to grains made it easier than it was in Jamaica or Barbados to incorporate the new strategies being used to improve agriculture in England because the climate of the Chesapeake was more comparable to England than was the tropical climate of a sugar plantation. Agriculture in England was transformed in the eighteenth century by the consolidation of lands and enclosures, by the more widespread use of the plow and manures, by improvements in animal husbandry, and by the Norfolk farming system – a new system of crop rotation using nitrogen-replacing crops, such as clover, that would allow planters to avoid fallowing.[48] Most of these improvements were readily transferable to the Chesapeake. Yet, until the eighteenth century, many large Virginian planters eschewed the English improvers' methods as unsuitable for the colonies.[49] After the middle of the eighteenth century, the largest planters in Virginia – men such as George Washington, Thomas Jefferson, and Landon Carter – turned more fully to the methods of English farmers, but they were also sensitive to adapting them to local conditions. They developed correspondence networks based on agricultural improvement and used their plantations as sites for scientific experiment, thus allowing them to participate in genteel discourses of Enlightenment science.[50] They also experimented

---

[47] Sampson Wood to Thomas Lane, October 15, 1797, MS 523/322, Newton Family Papers.
[48] Overton, *Agricultural Revolution*.
[49] Walsh, *Motives of Honor*, 224–225.
[50] Jean. B. Lee, "Mount Vernon: A Model for the Republic," in Philip J. Schwarz, ed., *Slavery at the Home of George Washington* (Mount Vernon: Mount Vernon Ladies Association, 2001), 18; "Landon Carter's Crop Book, Letters to Washington, October 27, 1796," *William and Mary Quarterly*, 1st ser., 21 (1912): 11–21.

continuously with the application of English techniques. In 1757, Landon Carter was pleased by how his crops were responding to "his method of introducing the English Husbandry with the tobacco planting." He meant that he was experimenting with different ways of manuring the soil, and he stressed the importance of empirical evidence and scientific method when he noted that he had "evidently discovered" that "tobacco will grow very unequal" even with the equal distribution of dung.[51] Likewise, a visitor to Mount Vernon in the 1790s described Washington as "always making experiments" with his lands.[52]

With declining soils, the Chesapeake tobacco economy slumped after 1680, and outputs per laborer fell from 1680 to 1740. But, from 1740 through 1790, the improvements in farming in the Chesapeake, greater levels of labor extraction, and the cultivation of more corn and wheat enabled plantations to gain returns per laborer that were once again equal to the returns from tobacco in the seventeenth century. The recovery of the Chesapeake plantation economy with these adaptations and improvements closely parallels the recovery of the Barbadian plantation economy in the late eighteenth century. The plow, the addition of grains, and the cultivation of more livestock fodder created significant changes on Virginian plantations.[53] Agricultural diversification and the training of slaves for a variety of skilled tasks led to greater self-sufficiency, which enabled large Chesapeake planters to achieve greater returns, especially after the 1760s.[54] By diversifying production, planters eliminated slack periods in annual agricultural cycles, coercing more labor from their slaves. On large plantations such as Mount Airy, Mount Vernon, or Monticello, more detailed accounting techniques allowed planters to extract even greater outputs from both their slaves and the land.

In the day-to-day operation of plantations, agricultural innovation was a contested process; it was never simply a matter of introducing a particular untested technique that had captured the planter's fancy or that would allow the overseer to carve out a reputation. Innovation had the potential to destabilize labor relations. The choice of agricultural techniques led to conflicts in labor negotiation, even between slaves and masters. Workers

---

[51] Jack P. Green, ed., *The Diary of Colonel Landon Carter of Sabine Hall, 1752–1778*, vol. 1 (Charlottesville: University Press of Virginia, 1965), 163.

[52] Journal of Samuel Vaughan, 1787, fol. 56, Mount Vernon Ladies' Association of the Union, as quoted in Lee, "Mount Vernon Plantation," 29.

[53] Walsh, "Plantation Management in the Chesapeake," 393–406; Walsh, *Motives of Honor*, 192–637.

[54] Walsh, *Motives of Honor*, 609.

were reluctant to adopt innovations that might require more work. Often owners and attorneys would argue with lower level managers about how to manage the estate and about whether a new method was appropriate. Enslaved workers, in particular, had developed strategies of survival and resistance that were dependent on the status quo in production. The improvements and experiments proposed by eager proprietors may not have always been so readily adopted by the people working on the estate, whether slave or free. Washington lamented the difficulties he had faced with slaves and overseers as he strove to introduce English agricultural practices. He had employed an English farmer who was well versed in that country's improved agricultural techniques but who would not persist in trying "to instruct the Negroes" in such techniques because it was too "troublesome." The slaves insisted on using their own techniques. Rather than compelling them "to the practice of his modes," the overseer, complained Washington, "slided into theirs" and "instead of proper flails for threshing the grain, I have found my people at work with hoop poles, and other things similar thereto."[55]

There were often significant tensions between tradition and innovations in planting, and traditional wisdom was sometimes used as a vehicle for spreading improvement schemes. A good example of such tensions between innovation and tradition comes in the Barbadian instructions of Henry Drax to his manager, and ways in which subsequent generations of planters used these instructions. Drax, a pioneer in sugar planting in Barbados, wrote these directives to his manager in the 1670s. A manuscript version of them survives in the Bodleian library in two separate hands. They were probably copied at some point from an original version, and they may have been revised during that process.[56] William Belgrove appended the instructions to his *A Treatise upon Husbandry or Planting*, published in 1755. He was a resident Barbadian planter who owned two plantations in the island. His version of Drax's instructions was a longer and heavily revised version of the Bodleian's copy. Belgrove quietly added sections on gang labor, on slave management, and on the kinds of accounts that should be kept on a plantation.[57] Drax's instructions were also included in a second manual published by a collection of planters in the

---

[55] George Washington to William Pearce, Jan. 25, 1795, Fitzpatrick, ed. *Writings of Washington*, Vol. 34, 103–104.

[56] Peter Thompson, "Henry Drax's Instructions on the Management of a Seventeenth-Century Barbadian Sugar Plantation, *William and Mary Quarterly* 3rd ser. 66.3 (July 2009), 566–604.

[57] Belgrove, *A Treatise upon Husbandry or Planting* (Boston: D. Fowle, 1755), 50–86.

1780s.[58] The instructions were an altogether new variant, but most of Belgrove's additions had been kept. In Barbados, Drax's instructions were a well-known and evolving document, and each new version became a testament to the growing body of community knowledge about sugar planting. At the same time, plantation reformers such as Belgrove continued to try gain legitimacy for their claims by grounding them in the authority of tradition and by attributing their plantation management strategies to one of Barbados' sugar pioneers. In Barbados, which had been an unqualified seventeenth-century economic success and which had a large population of resident sugar planters descended from the original families, new systems of management might have faced more resistance than in the newer sugar frontiers of Jamaica. Whereas Barbadian manuals cited the wisdom of men like Drax, manuals from elsewhere in the Caribbean often cited the skilled techniques of Barbadian planters, making Barbados the epicenter of a diaspora of sugar planting knowledge throughout the Caribbean.[59]

Self-sufficient provisioning, diversification, and, in the Chesapeake, the shift from tobacco to wheat, had economic benefits, but they also had significant moral dimensions. For large Chesapeake planters such as Washington and Jefferson, less tobacco and more grains – a less labor intensive crop – would keep them from being so dependent on slavery. They would cease to be planters and become farmers. Caribbean plantation manuals, beginning with Samuel Martin's in 1749, stressed the importance of self-sufficiency as both a cost cutting method and as a way to improve the health of slaves. A St. Vincent attorney, Michael Keane, in a 1790 letter to the plantation proprietor, most clearly articulated the links between self-sufficiency, improvement, and the amelioration project. He noted that the overseer on the estate was "very Considerably improving & meliorating the property by planting Plantaine Walks, which unquestionably are a Material Source for feeding slaves."[60] Such a perspective made the amelioration of a property synonymous with the planting of provisions on the estate and, as Keane's language makes clear, the property itself and not just the lives of the slaves could be ameliorated by planting provisions.

---

[58] Lascelles et al., *Management of a Plantation in Barbadoes*, 53–64.
[59] Martin, *Essay upon Plantership*, 4th ed., 7; Kein, *Pen-Keeping and Plantership*, 74.
[60] Michael Keane to John Crosbie, May 13, 1790, Letterbook of Michael Keane, 1787–1790, Mss1 K197 a 1, Section 1, Keane Family Papers, Virginia Historical Society.

AMELIORATING SLAVERY

Ameliorative practices were important elements of the plantation improvement project, and they were shaped by Enlightenment discourses of moral reform. Although "humanitarian" as a term was not used to connote a concern for human welfare until the nineteenth century, the origins of the humanitarian movement lie in the eighteenth century, when the interests of "humanity" were often invoked as a justification for moral reform and for philanthropic endeavors such as poor relief or hospitals.[61] The extent to which a society placed a value on human life was thought be a marker of civilization.[62] In the late Enlightenment, utilizing reason and knowledge to relieve human suffering and promote happiness became a core value.[63] These late Enlightenment values undergirded the institutionalization of care for the sick poor, the decline of torture and bodily punishments, the rise of penitentiaries, and, in the plantation Americas, the abolition and antislavery movements, the shifts from patriarchal to paternal understandings of the master–slave relationship, and the increasing importance placed on the amelioration of slavery.[64] Whiggish histories of the Enlightenment

---

[61] James Delbourgo, *A Most Amazing Science of Wonders: Electricity and Enlightenment in Early America* (Cambridge: Harvard University Press, 2006), 203, 220, 222. The rise of humanitarian sensibilities and their connection to abolition and antislavery projects have been hotly debated among scholars. See Roger Anstey, *The Atlantic Slave Trade and British Abolition* (Atlantic Highlands, NJ: Humanities Press, 1975); Thomas L. Haskell, "Capitalism and the Origins of the Humanitarian Sensibility, Part 1" *American Historical Review* 90.2 (April 1985), 331–362 and Thomas L. Haskell, "Capitalism and the Origins of the Humanitarian Sensibility, Part 2" *American Historical Review* 90.3 (June 1985), 547–566. For a response to Haskell, see John Ashworth, "The Relationship between Capitalism and Humanitariansim," *American Historical Review* 92.4 (October 1987), 813–828. See also Karen Halttunen, "Humanitarianism and the Pornography of Pain in Anglo-American Culture," *The American Historical Review* 100.2 (April 1995), 303–334; Hunt, *Inventing Human Rights*.

[62] Delbourgo, *Amazing Science of Wonders*, 222.

[63] Andrea A. Rusnock, "Biopolitics: Political Arithmetic in the Enlightenment," in Jan Golinski and Simon Schaffer, eds., *The Sciences in Enlightened Europe* (Chicago: University of Chicago Press, 1999), 49; Mokyr, *The Enlightened Economy*, 33; Porter, *Creation of the Modern World*, 418.

[64] Delbourgo, *Most Amazing Science of Wonders*, 222; Fiona A. Macdonald, "The Infirmary of the Glasgow Town's Hospital Patient Care, 1733–1800," in Paul Wood, ed., *The Scottish Enlightenment: Essays in Reinterpretation* (Rochester, NY: University of Rochester Press, 2000), 199; H. McMenemy, "The Hospital Movement of the Eighteenth Century and Its Development," in Frederick N.L. Poynter, ed., *The Evolution of Hospitals in Britain* (London: Pitman, 1964), 43–69; Michel Foucault, *Discipline and Punish: The Birth of the Prison* (New York: Vintage Books, 1995 [1977]); Robert Weiss, "Humanitarianism, Labour Exploitation, or Social Control? A Critical Survey of Theory and Research on the Origin and Development of Prisons," *Social History* 12.3 (October 1987), 331–350.

tend to trumpet the rise of natural rights, liberty, reason, and the emergence of humanitarian projects (such as abolition), but it is important to appreciate the extent to which discipline and the morally redemptive nature of work and industry were also influential strands of Enlightenment thought. This emphasis on work, discipline, and the restriction of autonomy as mechanisms of moral reform had as significant an effect on plantation management as other Enlightenment transformations such as the abolition and antislavery movements or the reduction in barbaric punishments.

Caribbean planters and overseers were the targets of abolitionist and antislavery advocates, but these same planters and overseers increasingly positioned themselves as part of the humanitarian reform projects. They were contesting the meaning and implication of the values of humanitarianism, civility, and the relief of suffering and the ways in which they might be achieved. The author of an 1803 Caribbean slave management manual maintained that the Caribbean planters' discussion of the "amelioration of the treatment of slaves long preceded the subject in Europe" and, he continued, "it is not unfair to suppose" that the desire to reform slavery "originated in the colonies, and was spontaneous, and that it resulted from the progress of the human mind."[65] Although the author's efforts to counteract the abolitionist stereotype of cruel and debased Caribbean planters are obvious and his explanation was simplistic, his identification of ameliorative sensibilities in the progress of the human mind highlights the cachet held by discourses of moral improvement.

The marked rise of humanitarianism discourses and the abolition and antislavery movements in the last quarter of the eighteenth century transformed the language of the amelioration project, but ameliorative management strategies were woven through the project of plantation improvement in the sugar islands in significant ways from the early eighteenth century onward. Elizabeth Alleyne, a widow, was managing Turner's Hall in Barbados in 1739. Her relatives in England worried about her being isolated in the rugged interior of Barbados, but she assured them that she was succeeding in managing the estate by adopting benevolent but disciplined management practices with the slaves. She never "let my overseer give any Chastisement without I give leave for you know that I can't Bear Cruelty," which meant that she had to closely supervise her slaves to ensure discipline. She was "engaged from five in ye Morning till Night," struggling to maintain discipline without brutality, "some times in peace & then War with my Black Family." The result, she explained, was that the cruelty on the

---

[65] Collins, *Management and Medical Treatment of Negro Slaves*, 24.

plantation before she took over had ended and the slaves were reproducing. She had "a very fine Young Family of Negroes Growing up and Many great Breeders."[66]

Alleyne's insistence on benevolent management was not uncommon at mid-century. The Antiguan Martin outlined proper agricultural techniques in his popular guide to plantation management in 1750, but he also insisted that "the good planter should be kind ... to his fellow creatures" by providing them with the best care, food, and housing.[67] In 1756, an overseer at Turner's Hall, after Elizabeth's death, assured the new owner that he would "take all the care in life of every thing that I am entrusted with, more especially the Negro's."[68] Jamaican planters, at mid-century, also attested to the importance of benevolent treatment. It is in "Ye Interest of every Master to treat his Slaves with Justice & Benevolence" insisted a Jamaican proprietor in his instructions to his overseer in 1754. To achieve this end, he maintained, the slaves had to be given sufficient time to grow their own provisions, and labor divisions had to be made carefully to ensure that "their work" was "proposition'd to their Strength."[69] This insistence on the kind and just management of slaves did precede the rise of abolitionist sentiment in the 1780s or the passage of amelioration laws in the last quarter of the century. Whether it was put into practice and how it was understood by planters is a different matter.

Ameliorationist sentiments of the pre-abolitionist era were most prominent in the older islands of the Eastern Caribbean (such as Barbados and Antigua) where planters, from the 1740s onward, were struggling to compete with the new sugar frontiers of the Western Caribbean (such as Jamaica and St. Domingue) for new African slaves. With the expansion of the sugar industry in the Caribbean came more competition for all plantation resources. The price of livestock, provisions, and slaves all rose. The acquisition of the Ceded Islands in 1763 led to even greater competition for labor. Between 1760 and 1807, as the slave system in the British Caribbean

---

[66] Elizabeth Alleyne to [Molly] Meynell, September 10, 1739, E20497; see also E20493: Mary Alleyne to [Molly] Meynell, May 14, 1738, Fitzherbert Papers, Barbados Department of Archives.

[67] Martin, *Essay upon Plantership*, 2nd ed.

[68] Samuel Rollstone to William Fitzherbert, July 12, 1756, E20511, Fitzherbert Papers.

[69] "Westmoreland, April 10, 1754. Mr. Richard Beckford's Instruction to Messrs. John Cope, Richard Lewingand Robert Mason," Monson 31.86, Thistlewood Papers, Lincoln County Record Office; see also John Dovaston, "Agricultura Americana or Improvements in West-India Husbandry Considered Wherein the Present System of Husbandry Used in England is Applied to the Cultiation or Growing of Sugar Canes to Advantage" [1774], Codex Eng 60, vol. 2. John Carter Brown Library.

expanded, the price of slaves doubled.[70] To a certain degree, the rise in prices after 1783 was a product of postwar inflation, but planters were also keenly aware of the rising price of slaves and the difficulties involved in securing a supply.[71] By improving the conditions of slaves or livestock and growing more provisions in the islands, planters were improving their plantations and finding ways to offset the increasing price of imported resources.

Ameliorative sensibilities had their origins in the agricultural improvement movement as much as in the rise of humanitarian sensibilities. To improve their plantations, planters needed to conserve, control, improve, and manipulate to their best advantage their land, labor, and livestock resources. The three were intricately linked in planters' minds as part of a complete system, and they could all be ameliorated. Planters argued that land could be "meliorated" by manuring it and rendering it more productive and by not overtaxing it.[72] Similarly, the condition of slaves and livestock could be ameliorated by feeding and not overtaxing them. A Jamaican proprietor insisted to his overseer in 1754 that "The Care of Mules & Cattle" was as "Essential for Carrying on ye operation of a Sugar Plantation as Negroes."[73] Virginian planters, such as Washington, were more likely to use the specific language of amelioration when they talked about their fields than when they talked about their slaves. For Washington, whose topsoils were very poor, the condition of the land was always more of an economic concern than replenishing the labor force, which was naturally reproducing. In the 1790s, as sugar planters began to focus their ameliorative strategies more specifically on the slave population, Washington worried about restoring his lands to "health and vigour," and he hoped that wheat would be "a great ameliorator of the soil."[74]

The approaches to improving animal husbandry and improving the management of slaves often mirrored each other. A "good planter" would, Martin insisted at mid-century, "be kind not only to his fellow

---

[70] Emma Christopher, *Slave Ship Sailors and Their Captive Cargoes, 1730–1807* (New York: Cambridge University Press, 2007), 34.
[71] David Beck Ryden, "Planters, Slaves and Decline," in Heather Cateau and S. H. H. Carrington, eds., *Capitalism and Slavery: Fifty Years Later* (New York: Peter Lang Publishing Inc., 2000), 155–170.
[72] Clement Caines, *Letters on the Cultivation of the Otaheite Cane* (London: Messers. Robinson,1801), 31.
[73] "Richard Beckford's Instruction," Monson 31.86.
[74] George Washington to William Pearce, December 18, 1793, in Fitzpatrick, ed., *Writings of Washington*, vol. 33, 188–189.

creatures, but merciful to his beasts."[75] Just as planters became more attentive to the work routines of slaves in this era, a Jamaican planter exhorted his estate manager to "see it [the mules and cattle] are not Work'd beyond their Strength."[76] Planters insisted that slaves had to be fed the most "wholesome food."[77] Likewise, planters pointed to the improvement of livestock fodder as integral to maintaining and improving their stock. Martin, for instance, maintained that stock, to improve their numbers, needed to be given "plenty and variety of wholesome food."[78] The Enlightenment critique of brutality and the decline of corporal punishment and torture throughout the British Atlantic also extended to the livestock.[79] Both slaves and cattle, Martin insisted, should be protected "from the flaying rope-lashes of a cruel driver."[80] The specifically humanitarian sensibilities of the amelioration project became more pronounced when the ameliorationist agenda came into dialogue with the abolition movement and the growing antislavery critiques of the 1780s.

Rooted in part in the agricultural improvement movement, amelioration did not need to be antislavery in its thrust. Although the amelioration and abolition or antislavery movements both articulated a concern with humanitarian reform and shared common intellectual and cultural origins, the planter-driven amelioration movement in Jamaica and Barbados was rarely a critique of the denial of freedom. In fact, efforts at amelioration in Barbados and Jamaica, such as the construction of plantation hospitals with barred windows and locked doors (see Chapter 4), sometimes involved greater restrictions on a slave's autonomy. Discipline and control were at the heart of moral improvement projects on sugar plantations. John Dovaston, the author of an unpublished 1774 Caribbean plantation manual, stressed that "good discipline is not inconsistent with humanity."[81] Planters in the plantation Americas were, in essence, offering alternative visions of modernity that did not see slavery and enlightened civilization or progress, moral or economic, as incompatible.

The humanitarian treatment of the slaves already within the Caribbean, many planters argued, could only be achieved within the framework of

---

[75] Martin, *Essay upon Plantership*, 2nd ed., 18.
[76] "Richard Beckford's Instruction," Monson 31.86; see also Martin, *Essay upon Plantership*, 2nd ed., 12.
[77] Kein, *Pen-Keeping and Plantership*, 20.
[78] Martin, *Essay upon Plantership*, 2nd ed., 12.
[79] Porter, *Creation of the Modern World*, 17.
[80] Ibid., 12.
[81] Dovaston, "Agricultura Americana," vol. 2.

slavery. Martin, in response to what he saw as a growing critique of slavery, published a proslavery pamphlet in 1775. In it he attacked the idea that slaves could "be happier under the slavery of *necessity*" that free workers experienced than "under masters bound by both the laws of humanity and *self-interest*, to protect, feed and cloath them."[82] Likewise, Russell Gill, overseer at Turner's Hall in Barbados, espoused humanitarian treatment of the slaves but thought that slavery was essential to the improvement of the laborers' conditions. "Twall be a very great misfortune for the poor Creatures," said Gill, "should a General Freedom ever take place."[83] Humanitarian reform movements that sought to reinforce rather than dismantle the institution of slavery heralded the growth of a paternalistic ethos and a proslavery defense that would come to be most fully articulated in the nineteenth-century U.S. South. This emphasis on the utility of slavery was consistent with elements of Enlightenment thought that stressed the need for self-discipline as part of the project of improvement. Those who lacked discipline – the unenlightened – would need, as historian Lorraine Daston explains, "the imposition of external discipline."[84]

During the Enlightenment and through the early stages of industrialization, a particular set of positive moral values about discipline, time thrift, and work habits became increasingly prevalent, shaping philanthropic endeavors in Britain for the underclasses, as well as for the early factory environment and plantation management schemes in the British Americas.[85] As early as 1697, John Locke had argued in his *Essay on the Poor Law* that poverty and unemployment were caused by a "relaxation of discipline and the corruption of manners," laying the blame squarely on the shoulders of the lower orders for their circumstances. For Locke, "virtue and industry" were "as constant companions on the one side as vice and idleness are on the other."[86] As the eighteenth century progressed, industry was tied ever more firmly to morality and sloth to vice, and work became a central tool in philanthropic projects. British Reformers in the metropole argued, echoing slaveholders' assessments of their slaves, that the poor naturally lacked the habits of industry, and they would have to be

---

[82] Samuel Martin, *A Short Treatise on the Slavery of Negroes in the British Colonies* (Antigua: Robert Mearns, 1775), 9.
[83] Russel Gill to Sarah Fitzherbert, June 3, 1793, E20565, Fitzherbert Collection.
[84] Daston, "Ethos of the Enlightenment," 502.
[85] Hawke, "Reinterpretations of the Industrial Revolution," 175.
[86] John Locke, "Essay on the Poor Law," in Mark Goldie, ed., *Locke: Political Essays*. Cambridge Texts in the History of Political Thought. (New York: Cambridge University Press, 1997), 184.

compelled to labor by either want or force. "The only way to make the poor industrious and therefore virtuous," William Temple, a clothier, argued in 1739, "is to lay them under the necessity of labouring all the time they can spare from rest and sleep."[87] Reform schemes for prisoners and the poor were often grounded on coerced labor. Reformers such as Jeremy Bentham and John Howard, who championed the development of imprisonment as a less barbaric and morally progressive form of punishment, stressed that convicts should be made to labor long hours, as many as fourteen hours a day, in order to discipline and instruct them but also to make them useful to society.[88] By the beginning of the nineteenth century, some reformers linked criminals and the underclasses by suggesting that they both failed to properly value work and time. Accordingly, time discipline was developed in factories, prisons, and workhouses as a means of instruction. Punctuality became a virtue. Enlightenment thinkers maintained that poor relief should be accompanied by a loss of liberty and forced labor, an assertion that helped to support the creation of workhouses for paupers. These workhouses were created in the late seventeenth century and, by 1776, there were approximately 2,000 of them spread across England.[89] Bentham associated sloth with vice and asserted the morally redemptive aspects of forced work when he argued that the workhouse would be "a mill to grind rogues honest, and idle men industrious."[90] Likewise, plantation hospitals in the Caribbean denied slaves' their liberty until they agreed to work again. Such measures were premised on the idea that slaves were naturally indolent.

Anglo-American reformers on both sides of the Atlantic insisted on the morally redemptive and socially useful potential of work and the need for

---

[87] William Temple, *The Case Between the Clothiers and the Weavers*, as quoted in Porter, *Creation of the Modern World*, 377, and in T.S. Ashton, *The Economic History of England: The Eighteenth Century* (New York: Routledge, 2006 [1955]), 20.

[88] Porter, *Creation of the Modern World*, 420–421; Hawke, "Reinterpretations of the Industrial Revolution," 175; Peter Spierenburg, "The Body and the State: Early Modern Europe," in Noval Morris and David J. Rothman, eds., *The Oxford History of the Prison: The Practice of Punishment in Western Society* (New York: Oxford University Press, 1998), 61–69; Randall McGowen, "The Well-Ordered Prison: England, 1780–1865," in Morris and Rothman, eds., *The Oxford History of the Prison* (New York: Oxford University Press, 1998), 78–80.

[89] Kirsten Olsen, *Daily Life in Eighteenth-Century England* (Westport, CT: Greenwood Press, 1999), 24–25.

[90] "Bentham to Brissot [1790]," in John Bowring, ed., *The Works of Jeremy Bentham*, vol. X (New York: Russell & Russell, 1962), 226. See also David Phillips, "Crime, Law and Punishment in the Industrial Revolution," in O'Brien and Quinault, eds., *The Industrial Revolution and British Society*, 172.

discipline and even coerced labor to inculcate habits of industry among the able-bodied poor, slaves, and criminals – the underclass. Planters directly associated slaves with criminals and the working poor. Martin, for example, compared slaves at the outset of his proslavery pamphlet to "the poor Labourers of Great Britain and Ireland."[91] Some plantation manuals directly modeled their advice for how to feed and manage slaves on European poor law policies.[92] The increasing emphasis on the morally redemptive aspects of work, the use of coerced labor as a tool in European social reform for criminals and the underclasses, and the associations between slaves and criminals or the working poor combined to give slaveholders' cultural and moral legitimacy for increasing working hours.[93]

Work became the Enlightened route to moral purification and the preferred mode of punishment, whereas punishments that encroached on bodily integrity, such as dismemberment or maiming, gradually declined throughout the British Atlantic. Whole bodies were able working bodies that would continue to be useful and that still had the capacity to be reformed and made useful. The introduction of the Penitentiary Act in Britain in 1779 was concurrent with calls for less physically barbaric punishments in plantation management and with the introduction of legislation against dismembering slaves on some of the sugar islands.[94] Caribbean managers began to insist that slaves should be confined rather than corporally punished. At Newton, in 1797, Wood wanted to assure the owner that "never has a Negro been destroyed never has a Negro been treated with unjust Severity since I have been here." He maintained that "good discipline" could be accomplished without severe physical punishments. Instead, there was a dungeon on the estate.[95] Chesapeake planters also insisted that their overseers curb their barbarity toward slaves. Planters focused on bodily punishments and tortures, particularly the

---

[91] Martin, *Short Treatise on the Slavery of Negroes*, 1; see also Dovaston, *Agricultura Americana*, Vol. 2.
[92] Simon David Smith, *Slavery, Family and Gentry Capitalism in the British Atlantic: The World of the Lascelles, 1648–1834* (New York: Cambridge University Press, 2006), 276–278.
[93] There were debates during the abolitionist era about the essential character of people of African descent and whether they were morally depraved; see "African Institution," *Edinburgh Review or the Critical Journal*, 2nd ed., vol. 15 (October 1809–January 1810), 490.
[94] Spierenburg, "Body and the State," McGowen, "Well-Ordered Prison," and Porter, *Creation of the Modern World*, 419–421.
[95] Sampson Wood to Thomas Lane, September 8, 1797 and Newton Work Log, 1796–1797, MS 523/110, 321, Newton Family Papers.

whip, as a measure of brutality. The Virginian planter William Cabell, in his agreement with the overseer Theoderick Suggs, insisted that Suggs was to do the "duty of an Overseer" but also that he was "not to Correct my slaves immoderately."[96] A month later, Suggs was dismissed. One of the principal problems was "his Cruelty to Slaves."[97] For Dovaston, the Jamaican author of an unpublished plantation manual in the 1770s, physical punishments would be less necessary "were Masters to Civilize their Slaves, and treat them as rational Creatures." He was certain that slaves could be reasoned with, without barbarity. If planters used "a fair and Soft Manner" with slaves, "we may expect & receive more profit from them."[98] The implication was that they would be content with slavery under the right conditions.

In the last two quarters of the eighteenth century, the growth of humanitarian reform discourses throughout the Atlantic and the sharp rise of abolitionist and antislavery sentiments increasingly helped to draw distinctions between the ameliorative project and the agricultural improvement project. By destabilizing the idea that slavery was natural and focusing on the treatment of slaves rather than on the plantation machine as a unit in need of improvement, antislavery and abolition activists helped to transform the ameliorative discussion into one concerned far more with people than with land and cattle. Humanitarian sensibilities were increasingly privileged after the 1780s as the principal justifications for amelioration, signaling the transformation of the ameliorative project. The estate manager on the Codrington plantations in 1796 assured the owner that it was "a principal part of my Business ... to take care of the Negroes & preserve their health; not for their services alone but through the principles of Humanity & Religion."[99] Jamaicans, likewise, began to focus on a humanitarian creed as the key reason for amelioration after the 1780s. Patrick Kein, for example, argued that "the right or rational method, of treating negroes ... is with humanity and benevolence, as our fellow-creatures, created by the same Almighty hand."[100]

---

[96] July 20, 1773, William Cabell commonplace book, vol. 4, Mss5:5C1117:4. Virginia Historical Society.
[97] August 23, 1773, William Cabell commonplace book, vol. 4.
[98] Dovaston, *Agricultura Americana*, vol. 1.
[99] Edward Clarke to John Brathwaite June 1, 1796, Correspondence of Edward Clarke, Estate Manager, 1795–1800, C/COD/46, Codrington Papers, C series, United Society for the Propagation of the Gospel Archives; see also Sir John Gay Alleyne to Sarah Fitzherbert, [1792?], E20563, Fitzherbert Papers.
[100] Kein, *Pen-Keeping and Plantership*, 18–19.

Caribbean to make a master's first intentional murder of a slave illegal. It built on an earlier Jamaican law, passed in 1696, which had made the second offense a punishable crime. The ameliorative legislation of the late eighteenth and early nineteenth century showed a different understanding of the role of corporeal punishment in slavery and an emerging value being placed on bodily integrity. There were laws in some of the islands against dismembering slaves as punishment from 1775 onward, reflecting the gradual growth of a humanitarian sensibility and a desire to civilize the appearance of slavery, but planters were not adamant about maintaining these laws. In Jamaica, laws against dismemberment were passed in 1775, but they were allowed to lapse in 1784, even though stricter laws were enacted that same year to prevent slaves from stealing or injuring livestock. There was no significant legislation within the islands against whipping until the nineteenthcentury.[108] Overall, ameliorative legislation served chiefly to support the planters' goals of greater labor extraction and risk and cost reduction.

There was never a direct correlation between mortality rates among slaves or the severity of labor and the degree to which ameliorationist sentiments were articulated. Planters in Barbados were more vocal than their Jamaican counterparts about amelioration and Barbados, by the turn of the nineteenth century, had the only naturally reproducing slave population in the sugar islands. Whereas the health of the Chesapeake slave population was the product of the crops being worked rather than of humanitarian sensibilities or ameliorative policies, the reproduction rates among the slaves in Barbados seem to have been improved by the rise of ameliorationist and pro-natalist management practices.

Overall, the scholarship suggests that, during the era of amelioration, there were some improvements in the living conditions for slaves in the Caribbean and in the Chesapeake that extended their life expectancy or the *quantity* of their lives.[109] At the same time, most planters were also focused on employing new technologies and agricultural innovations to extract increasingly higher levels of labor from their bondsmen.[110] Planters

---

[108] Ward, *British West Indian Slavery*, 110–15, 202–5; E. V. Goveia, *The West Indian Slave Laws of the Eighteenth Century* (Bridgetown: Caribbean Universities Press, 1970): 9–56.

[109] Ward, *British West Indian Slavery*; Turner, "Planter Profits and Slave Rewards," 232–252; Craton, *Searching for the Invisible Man*. For a recent article that suggests that slave diets may not have improved significantly during amelioration, see James E. Candow, "A Reassessment of the Provision of Food to Enslaved Persons, with Special Reference to Salted Cod in Barbados," *Journal of Caribbean History* 43.2 (December 2009), 265–281.

[110] Walsh, *Motives of Honor*, 621, 623.

equated the quantity of their slaves' lives with quality of life, relying on birth and death rates as crude measurements of how well their slaves were treated. From a historical perspective, however, one must be careful not to assume that mortality and fertility rates necessarily reflect improvements in the lives of slaves. Whether the slaves agreed with planters that the improvement projects of the late eighteenth century led to a better *quality* of life is questionable.

TABULATING IMPROVEMENT

To assess their plantation systems, achieve balance within them, and establish rules of cultivation and governance that would improve their estates and preserve the bodies of the enslaved, planters believed they had to strive for regularity and precision in both their methods and their documentation. Belgrove's mid-century Barbadian plantation manual strongly encouraged its readers to lay out their plantations "in Chequer Order" (essentially a grid) with each field being exactly ten acres to allow for precision in management.[111] Compared to other sugar islands, the Barbadian terrain was flat and uniform, making Belgrove's scheme easier to adopt. Regularity in field design was unsuited to the terrain in many islands, yet there were planters who sought regularity and order in their field design at the cost of production. According to a planter who had experience with estates in the steep and mountainous terrain of St. Kitts, some planters "always sacrifice the growth of a part of their canes, to the appearance of their holed land" by making certain that the rows terminate with the end of a piece which "makes them run even and look neat."[112] This practice of standardizing the plantation's lands was supported by the development of meticulous and detailed plantation accounts, which defined slaves and land – as much as it was possible to do – as interchangeable units of production.

The numeracy and precision that Belgrove advocated was central to the project of improved plantership. It reflected the "quantifying spirit" of the eighteenth century and the growth of numeracy in the colonies.[113] Those principles undergirded his 1755 guide to improving plantations. He encouraged planters, for example, to calculate "to a Certainty the

[111] Belgrove, *Treatise upon Husbandry or Planting*, 31.
[112] Caines, *Cultivation of the Otaheite Cane*, 41.
[113] Tore Frängsmyr, John L. Heilbron, Robin E. Rider, *The Quantifying Spirit in the Eighteenth Century* (Berkeley: University of California Press, 1990); Cohen, *Calculating People*.

Quantity of Dung you'll require ... for the whole Crop you propose to plant; without which Adjustment you cannot be regular in your Dung."[114] Bookkeeping and statistical precision became so essential to late eighteenth-century planting that the author of a Jamaican plantation manual derided overseers and planters who thought of themselves as skilled even "though they could not make out a list of the negroes or stock on an estate, with any regularity." A skilful planter, he insisted, had to be "adept in figures."[115]

The business records of large plantations, particularly sugar plantations, grew more detailed and methodical from the first quarter of the eighteenth century onward to accommodate growing absenteeism but also to engender improved management. The new accounting systems showed increasing concern with the internal day-to-day processes of the estate.[116] New kinds of accounts – such as work logs and increase and decrease of stock accounts and more elaborate versions of inventories, boiling house books, and yearly financial reports – emerged as part of the apparatus of plantation management in the 1740s and 1750s. So much of agricultural production, planters and overseers protested, was difficult to control, which made the application and identification of natural laws governing production difficult to achieve.[117] The amount of capital invested in sugar processing equipment and the threat of hurricanes, warfare, and large-scale slave revolts in Caribbean agriculture made production riskier than it was in the Chesapeake. Detailed accounts helped improving planters assess their experiences, form precise rules of management, and predict the outcomes of production schemes.

Throughout the eighteenth century in the British Atlantic, business records, especially in double-entry bookkeeping, became more precise and methodical.[118] These changes were driven in part by an accounting revolution, with its locus in Scotland, articulated by books such as John

---

[114] Belgrove, *Treatise upon Husbandry or Planting*, 3.
[115] Kein, *Pen-Keeping and Plantership*, 11, 15.
[116] Walsh, *Motives of Honor*, 228–237.
[117] Roberts, "Uncertain Business," 247–268.
[118] See John Mair, *Book-Keeping Methodiz'd: or, a Methodical Treatise of Merchant-Accompts, According to the Italian form*. ...7th ed. (Edinburgh: Sands, Donaldson, Murray, and Cochran, 1763), 235–368; Mepham "The Scottish Enlightenment and the Development of Accounting," 268–293. See also Coclanis, "Bookkeeping in the Eighteenth-Century South," 21–33; Fleischman and Tyson, "Cost Accounting during the Industrial Revolution," 503–517; Quattrone, "Is Time Spent, Passed or Counted?," 185–208. For older work on this subject, see B. S. Yamey, "Scientific Bookkeeping," 99–113.

Mair's *Book-keeping Methodiz'd*. First published in 1736, Mair's work was the most popular British accounting book of the eighteenth century; it went through several editions. The 1741 edition included, for the first time, a discussion of the basic accounts that should be kept in tobacco production and trade, and the 1757 edition did the same for sugar.[119] Mair's sections on accounting in the sugar colonies actually drew on Weston William's 1754 treatise on accounting. Whereas Mair focused for the most part on bookkeeping in merchant's houses, Weston stressed the need for accuracy in both plantation and merchant accounting.[120]

According to Weston, the internal account most universally kept at mid-century on sugar plantations was the boiling house book, which he described as being kept by the "by the *White-Man* on Duty, and weekly delivered to the Overseer, who examines it."[121] The boiling house book recorded when the works were operating and how much sugar was produced. Sometimes, separate but similar books were kept for the still house, accounting for rum production. To keep a boiling house book and supervise the slaves, the observer, according to a Jamaican chronicler, had "to sit up the whole night." It was "a most severe and distressing duty" that "tends to destroy his health throw a damp upon his spirits, and finally shorten his days."[122] Collecting statistics to track the management of a plantation was such an essential part of an overseer's apprenticeship that the overseer's assistants on large sugar estates were entrusted with this boiling house accounting, and they were referred to as "bookkeepers." Overseers increasingly served "a certain number of years as a bookkeeper" before rising to their station.[123] Wood, in a letter to the owners, outlined the kinds of accounts he would send, but he acknowledged that it was the bookkeepers who kept the accounts, and he apologized for the "badness of their spelling."[124] These accounts became a scientific record of experiments and observations, and they took the place of direct observation, extending the sphere of control for higher level managers such as

---

[119] M. J. Mepham "Scottish Enlightenment and the Development of Accounting," 272–273.
[120] John Mair, *Book-Keeping Methodiz'd: or, a Methodical Treatise of Merchant-Accompts, According to the Italian form*. ...2nd ed. (Edinburgh: Sands, Brymer, Murray and Cochran, 1741); Ibid., 5th ed. (Edinburgh: Sands, Brymer, Murray and Cochran, 1757).
[121] William Weston, *The Complete Merchant's clerk: or, British and American Compting-House* (London: Charles Rivington, 1754), 24.
[122] Stewart, *An Account of Jamaica and Its Inhabitants* (London: Hurst, Rees and Orme, 1808), 112.
[123] Ibid., 129. See also Charles Ruddach to Charles Stewart, July 25, 1779, Jamaica Manuscripts Collection, Special Collections, University of Miami Libraries.
[124] "Report on the [Newton] Negroes." MS 523/288, Newton Family Papers.

owners and attorneys and thus allowing for multilayered systems of management.

In the middle of the eighteenth century, more detailed and numerical sets of increase and decrease of stock accounts joined boiling books and basic inventories and expenditure accounts as a regular part of the sugar plantation's managerial apparatus. Increase and decrease accounts were developed in conjunction with the efforts at ameliorating the conditions of both slaves and livestock. Increase and decrease accounts showed a careful inventory at the beginning and end of the year of slaves and livestock, and they recorded births and deaths in those populations sequentially. They resembled an early modern business waste book in their design, recording the loss of life or the addition of birth as transactions in the order in which they occurred.[125] Because these accounts included the dates of births and deaths in order, observable at a glance, they made the seasonal timing of deaths and births significant. The increasing use of these accounts on sugar plantations parallels a growing Enlightenment interest in quantifying populations. The term "population" was not used in the seventeenth century, and the idea that one should study total populations had not yet become popular. The tracking of total populations became more common at the end of the seventeenth century as demography and political arithmetic emerged as legitimate fields of inquiry.[126] Although few records of plantation management survive from the late seventeenth century, the surviving evidence suggests that increase and decrease accounts were not an entirely new invention in the eighteenth century. In the 1690s, a Jamaican planter, in a letter to his relative and financial partner, set apart his descriptions of the loss and addition of enslaved workers by writing "Now follows the accot. of the Increase & Decrease of Negroes since ye Departed." The list that followed, however, was simply a descriptive narration of individual deaths and their causes and new slave births and purchases, with no effort at quantification. The increase and decrease accounts that appeared in the middle of the eighteenth century were statistically precise, and they were drawn as a separate account, normally in tables.[127] The rise of these more

---

[125] Mair, *Book-Keeping Methodiz'd*, 7th ed., 3–7.
[126] Andrea A. Rusnock, "Biopolitics and the Mathematics of Population," 49–68; see also Andrea Rusnock, *Vital Accounts: Quantifying Health and Population in Eighteenth-Century England and France* (New York, 2002).
[127] Cary Heylar to William Heylar, March 18, 1689/1690, Heylar Manuscripts, Somerset Record Office; see also J. Harry Bennett, "Cary Heylar, Merchant and Planter of Seventeenth Century Jamaica," *The William and Mary Quarterly*, 3rd ser. 21.1 (January 1964), 53–76.

detailed tabular accounts on plantations parallels the publication of monthly tables of mortality in periodicals such as the *Gentleman's Magazine* in London and Benjamin Franklin's first musings on population in his "Observations Concerning the Increase of Mankind," originally published in 1751.[128] Chesapeake planters rarely kept statistics on the mortality and fertility of their workers because their slaves were naturally reproducing.

Increase and decrease accounts verified that efforts were being made to maintain slaves and livestock. In 1786, a Barbadian plantation manual maintained that "the increase is the only test of care with which they are treated."[129] When the Jamaican attorney Simon Taylor wanted to convince the owner, in 1782, that the overseer was not taking sufficient care of the slaves, he insisted that the owner look to "The Increase & Decrease of your Negroes," because those accounts "will show whether they have been properly attended to."[130] In 1790, Thomas Barritt assured the owner of Pleasant Hill in Jamaica that he was sending the customary plantation accounts, including "The Diary of the Estates work, with Increase & Decrease Accot."[131] By the end of the first decade of the nineteenth century, particularly after abolition, these accounts had become so ubiquitous and essential to plantation management that, according to a Jamaican observer, the "care of Negroes" and, specifically, "the causes of increase and decrease" had become "the subjects of common conversation."[132]

For many planters, the increase and decrease of slaves became a way of quantifying the success of ameliorative practices, a way of calculating happiness, especially by the end of the eighteenth century. When Sampson Wood wanted to assure the owner of Newton in 1798 that "everything is as it should be," he pointed out the slave population was "but happy & upwardly increasing, a certain sign of Happiness & good treatment."[133] This focus in increase and decrease accounts was on the

---

[128] Porter, *Creation of the Modern World*, 149; Eva Sheppard Wolf, "Early Free Labor Thought," 32–48.
[129] Lascelles et al., *Management of a Plantation*, 2.
[130] Simon Taylor to Chalenor Arcedeckne Esq., January 30, 1782, Vanneck-Arc/ 3A/ 1782/ 2, Cambridge University Library.
[131] Thomas Barritt, Pleasant Hill, Jamaica, to Nathaniel Phillips, December 25, 1790, #8351, Slebech Papers.
[132] Gilbert. F. Mathison, *Notices Respecting Jamaica in 1808, 1809, 1810* (London: J. Stockdale, 1811), 12.
[133] Sampson Wood to Thomas Lane, March 31, 1798, MS 523/334, Newton Family Papers; see also Collins, *Management and Treatment of Slaves*, 20.

Time, Quantification, Amelioration, and the Enlightenment 61

quantity of slave life, and the slaves' health and happiness was being measured as a uniform collective, as a total population. Such evaluations of slaves' happiness were strikingly similar to the moral principles of utilitarians such as Bentham. who argued that the only true measure of right or wrong was the greatest happiness of the greatest number. As the century closed, "happiness" itself was becoming a measureable quality and a key Enlightenment value.[134]

Detailed work logs joined increase and decrease accounts as major innovations in plantation accounting in the middle of the eighteenth century, and they were used on both the mainland and in the islands (see Figures 1.1 through 1.5). In 1801, a St. Kitts planter, Clement Caines, called the work log, "the most minute, exact, and perfect invention that ever was devised for ... giving information of whatever is necessary on a Caribbean estate."[135] Drax's original instructions to his plantation manager in the 1670s included descriptions of all the records that should be kept, and he did not mention work logs or increase and decrease accounts.[136] In 1745, however, Walter Tulldeph, an attorney in Antigua, noted that the overseer of the plantation was keeping an "exact Journall of the Plantation worke" which "he will transmitt you soon." This work log was novel enough in 1745 to merit comment.[137] No copies of the log survive. The oldest surviving detailed work log is from 1759, for a sugar plantation in St. Croix in the Danish Caribbean.[138] In 1755, when Belgrove republished Drax's instructions, he added the request that "commonly every Fortnight, and sometimes oftner, a List" would be made "where every Negro in the Plantation was employed."[139] By claiming these were seventeenth-century instructions, he grounded the new work accounts in tradition, strengthening their legitimacy. The minimum two-week intervals of work reports that Belgrove was calling for at mid-century became far more detailed over the last fifty years of the eighteenth century. By the 1780s, some planters were using preprinted proforma log sheets for daily reports (see Figure 1.5). Washington began using logs at Mount

---

[134] Porter, *Creation of the Modern World*, 418; Mokyr, "The Enlightened Economy," 33 in O'Brien and Quinlet, *Industrial Revolution and British Society*.
[135] Caines, *Cultivation of the Otaheite Cane*, 248.
[136] Thompson, "Henry Drax's Instructions," 582–604.
[137] "Dr. Walter Tulldeph to Governor George Thomas, August 8, 1745," in Richard Sheridan, ed., "Letters from a Sugar Plantation in Antigua, 1739–1758," *Agricultural History*, 31 (July, 1957), 11.
[138] Jens Vibæk, "Dansk Vestindien 1755–1848," in Johannes Brøndsted, ed., *Vore Gamle Tropekolonier*, 2nd ed., vol. 2. (Copenhagen: Fremad, 1966–1968 [1952–1953]), 110–111.
[139] Belgrove, *Treatise upon Husbandry or Planting*, 65–66.

FIGURE 1.1. Work log entry, Somerset Vale, October 13 to November 9, 1776. *Source*: Somerset Vale Work Logs, 1776–1780, Codex Eng 180. Courtesy of the John Carter Brown Library at Brown University.

FIGURE 1.2. Work log entry, Seawell, May 3, 1796.
Source: Seawell Work Log, 1796–1797, MS 523/111, Newton Family Papers. Courtesy of the Senate House Library, University of London Archives.

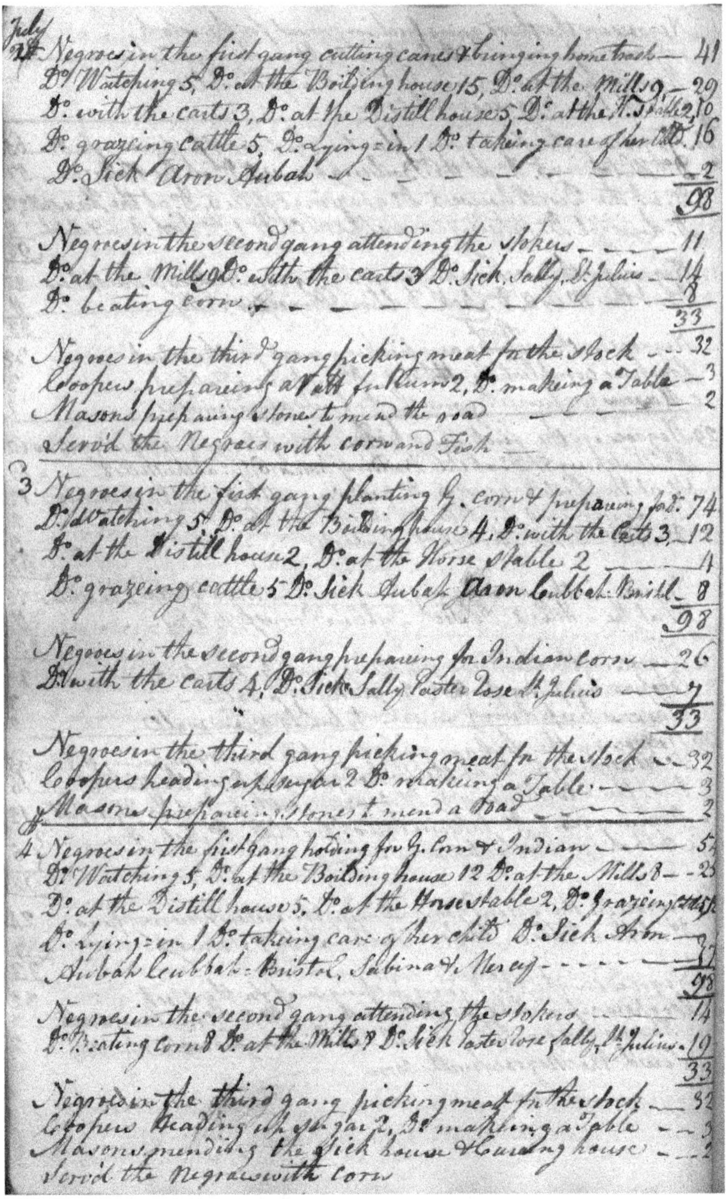

FIGURE 1.3. Work log entry, Newton, July 4, 1798.
Source: Newton Work Log, 1797–1798, MS 523/123, Newton Family Papers. Courtesy of the Senate House Library, University of London Archives.

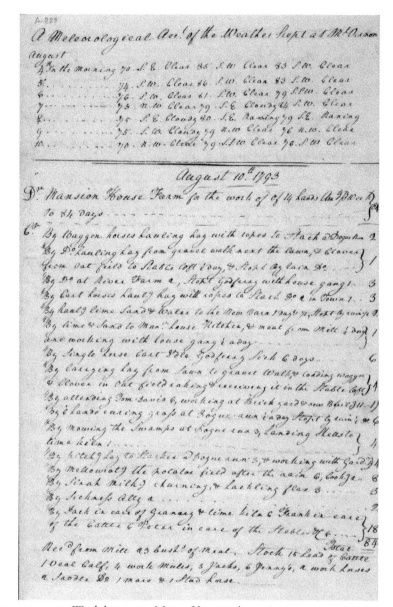

FIGURE 1.4. Work log entry, Mount Vernon, August 4–10, 1793.
Source: CT 6714-1. Courtesy of Mount Vernon Ladies' Association.

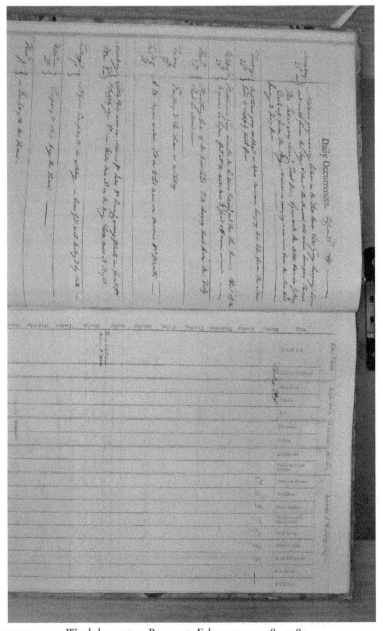

FIGURE 1.5. Work log entry, Prospect, February 23–28, 1789.
Source: Prospect Plantation Journals 1787–1793, 0627-0019. Courtesy of Barclays Group Archive.

Vernon in 1785, the earliest surviving logs from the Chesapeake.[140] They became increasingly common with the spread of scientific agriculture on the North American mainland in the nineteenth century, particularly on large cotton estates in the Deep South.[141] Although the emphasis in work logs was on utilizing rather than maintaining the slave population, planters sometimes described the better organization of labor as one of the keys to ameliorating slavery. Work logs were seen as evidence of the kind of "forward" and civil management that would contribute to both higher profits and lower mortality among the slaves. When Tulldeph mentioned the early Antiguan work log in 1745, he used the work accounts as evidence of the overseer's "industrious" nature and managerial skills. Tulldeph described the overseer as a man who could "effectually" work an estate but still be "carefull & humane," the implication seeming to be that the records themselves and the "industrious" management that they exemplified would enable the overseer to be both humane and productive.[142] Planters believed that by recording labor they could monitor and control its impact on enslaved workers. "To prevent all waste and misapplication of labour," Caines argued in 1801, "is a consideration that should be unremittingly attended to." Otherwise, he explained, a planter's "slaves will become the victims of fatigue, or the cultivation of his estate must cease to be prosecuted with spirit and to advantage."[143]

With a work log, a planter could track labor patterns over longer periods at a single glance. It was a way of encapsulating and organizing time. Caines stressed that the work log exhibited "*at one view* every application and misapplication of labour on a West Indian estate."[144] Being able to take in a large amount of evidence and a broad expanse of time all in one glance was an important part of the account's design, originating in Francis Bacon's theory that such a design was necessary

---

[140] The only other log I have found for the Chesapeake in this period was from Mount Airy. See Mount Airy Work Log, Mss1 T2118 a8, Virginia Historical Society. For a discusson of this log, see Richard Dunn, "After Tobacco: The Slave Labour Pattern on a Large Chesapeake Grain-and-Livestock Plantation in the Early Nineteenth Century," in Kenneth Morgan and John J. McCusker, eds., *The Early Modern Atlantic Economy* (New York: Cambridge University Press, 2000), 344–363.

[141] Jacob Metzer, "Rational Management: Modern Business Practices and Economies of Scale in the Ante-Bellum Southern Plantations," *Explorations in Economic History* 12.1 (1975), 123–150.

[142] "Tulldeph to Thomas, August 8, 1745," in Sheridan, ed., "Letters from a Sugar Plantation," 11.

[143] Caines, *Cultivation of the Otaheite Cane*, 50.

[144] Ibid., 247.

for a process of inductive reasoning. Seventeenth- and eighteenth-century weather records, which were also becoming meticulously detailed during the Enlightenment, similarly stressed the need for such an organization of the data onto a page that could be taken in at a glance.[145] Many work logs had a dual function, tracking both labor and weather patterns on that single page.

At Mount Vernon, Washington required meticulous weekly statistics from his managers, particularly when it came to tracking slaves' sick days. He employed a double-entry bookkeeping system in the design of his work logs, making it clear that work logs were about the maximum utilization of resources and that they drew heavily on contemporary accounting theory. Washington required that his managers use a system of debiting and crediting his labor account in the farm reports. The total labor pool appeared as a credit above each farm or group of skilled slaves (such as the gardeners), and the tasks done by slaves, as well as their sicknesses, pregnancies, or absences, were recorded as debits to that account. Washington's letters to his farm managers offer insight into how carefully he reviewed these accounts. On December 18, 1796, he asked, "What has Frank, Hercules and Cyrus been employed in?" because "no mention is made of any work performed by them in the Gardeners or other Reports."[146] From timing his slaves to tracking missing individuals in meticulously detailed work logs, Washington was improving his estate by ensuring that no time was lost.

CLOCK WORK

Clock time and standardized industrial time were central to the accounting systems of the improvement movement, challenging traditional agricultural ways of understanding time. In preindustrial agricultural societies, day-to-day work schedules were generally dominated by methods of measuring the passage of time that were based on seasonal cycles, agricultural tasks, and diurnal rhythms.[147] Sugar plantations were unique and revolutionary among early modern agricultural enterprises precisely because they did not strictly follow the dictates of diurnal cultivation. They were "factories in the field," proto-industrial enterprises, relying on processing

---

[145] Jan Golinski, *British Weather and the Climate of Enlightenment* (Chicago: University of Chicago Press, 2007) 83.
[146] Washington to William Pearce, December 18, 1796 in Fitzpatrick, ed., *Writings of Washington*, vol. 35, 338.
[147] Thompson, "Time, Work-Discipline and Industrial Capitalism," 58–60.

Time, Quantification, Amelioration, and the Enlightenment 69

equipment and indoor labor to an unparalleled degree in agriculture. Precise timing was always paramount in early modern sugar production. Once cut, canes had to be harvested immediately or they would become dry and sour. During the harvest, mills and boiling houses ran late into the night and sometimes around the clock to accomplish the demands of the harvest. Slaves would toil in the field from sunup to sundown and continue their labors through the night, working in squads, in shifts or "spells," before snatching a few hours of sleep and working again. Although sugar could be planted or harvested at any time of the year in the early modern Caribbean, the rainy season made the crop difficult to harvest, and the onset of the hurricane season always threatened to impede shipping so work had to be completed quickly. Until the introduction of a new variety of cane in the 1790s, sugar took more than a year to mature, so planters had to carefully time the sequence of harvesting or planting their fields, often performing both tasks simultaneously. They also had to impose more standard annual definitions of time in order to record and narrate that extended cane cultivation cycle in one-year accounting formats. They redefined the natural growth cycles to create standardized one-year accounts that would be in accordance with one-year accounting and credit and debt collection systems elsewhere in the Atlantic. Because of the unique demands of sugar, planters were always anxious about timing and, by the middle of the eighteenth century, they were striving to organize and discipline their labor force and their production schedule by the clock. They became attentive to using standardized, interchangeable, and clock-based units of time in their management, especially within the boiling house.

References to mechanical or clock time increasingly peppered the language of plantation improvement. Historian Mark Smith has argued that this attention to clock-based and industrial modes of defining and tracking time did not emerge fully in the U.S. South until the 1830s. The evidence, however, suggests that planters, particularly in the Caribbean, were using clock-based time and conceptualizing time itself as a currency at least a century before then.[148] Given the agricultural setting, reform-minded planters throughout the plantation Americas relied to a remarkable degree on mechanical time in establishing rules of management. Washington, for example, stressed the need to extract as much as possible from slaves in

---

[148] Mark Smith, *Mastered by the Clock: Time, Slavery and Freedom in the American South* (University of North Carolina Press, 1997).

"24 hours."[149] The discipline of the clock, which rose to the fore during the harvest on sugar plantations, became central to extracting more slave labor but also, significantly, to the amelioration project. William Belgrove, in the mid-eighteenth century, warned the readers of his manual that "you should never boil after 11 o'Clock at Night at the latest" because it was too draining for slaves.[150] Likewise, Wood complained that he had seen slaves' health destroyed by being put to work in the Boiling House "at six or seven o'clock one morning" and being made to work until "the same hour the next Morning." He assured the owners of the plantation "that our Negroes shall never work after nine or ten o'clock at night."[151] The slaves were not the only plantation workers who were subject to the discipline of the clock. In 1766, Martin, who made the operations of his plantation analogous to a clockwork universe, dismissed an overseer because he "lay in Bed every Morning till 9 a Clock with a negro whore."[152] Martin closely associated the overseer's refusal to regulate his life by the clock with sexual debauchery; tardiness was not only inefficient, but it was also interwoven with immorality.[153] Clocks offered the opportunity for precise measurement, they facilitated the application of universal rules based on standardized measurements of time, and they enabled an exact coordination of work schedules.

The diary of Thomas Thistlewood, a Jamaican overseer who came to the island from Britain in 1750, offers strong evidence of how prevalent time consciousness was becoming in the 1750s.[154] It also offers more insight into how an overseer conceptualized and used time in the management of the plantation. From September 15, 1748 to September 15, 1749, before he traveled to Jamaica, Thistlewood made 350 references to a unit of time when he recorded his daily activities or events he had witnessed. He most commonly used less precise divisions of time such "forenoon" and "afternoon" or "night" to denote the timing of daily activities and events. For a couple of months, he used "AM" and "PM" to note activities.

---

[149] "George Washington to John Fairfax, January 1, 1789," in Abbot et al., eds., *The Papers of George Washington*: Presidential series, vol. 1, 223.

[150] Belgrove, *Treatise upon Husbandry or Planting*, 12.

[151] "Report on the Buildings at Newton," MS 523/290, Newton Family Papers.

[152] Samuel Martin to "Mr. Pooley," March 6, 1766, MS 41350, Martin Papers, British Library.

[153] Hawke, "Reinterpretations of the Industrial Revolution," 175.

[154] For more on Thomas Thistlewood, see Trevor Burnard, *Mastery, Tyranny and Desire: Thomas Thistlewood and his Slaves in the Anglo-Jamaican World* (Chapel Hill: University of North Carolina Press, 2004).

Time, Quantification, Amelioration, and the Enlightenment 71

Approximately one-quarter of his time references were to clock time. His use of clock time rose sharply when he traveled onboard a ship. He was very careful then to note arrivals and departures, and he made as many as five references to the clock each day on board a ship. Otherwise, when he was in Europe, he rarely noted clock time.[155]

In 1752, during his first full year on a sugar plantation called Egypt, Thistlewood struggled to coordinate and control the enslaved workers.[156] He noted the time at which events took place in his diary nearly twice as often in 1752 on a sugar plantation as he had in 1748–1749, when he was in Britain and traveling in Europe. Despite never traveling aboard a ship during his first year as a Jamaican overseer, he made slightly more references to specific clock time while at Egypt than he had in Europe. He also made more references to meal time (such as "at dinner" or "before breakfast") in Jamaica than he had in Europe, suggesting the extent to which the feeding of enslaved workers might have shaped his perception of time on the plantation. In Jamaica, he began to much more carefully divide almost every day into three sections instead of two: "morning, evening and night." There were two months in which he was especially careful to note clock time at Egypt: March and October. March was in the middle of their sugar harvest that year, and Thistlewood regularly noted in his diary the specific time the mill was starting and stopping. His experience with the mill itself was influencing his perception of time. In October, Thistlewood's increasing use of clock time corresponds with his increased sexual activity. In 71 percent of all his sexual encounters in 1752, Thistlewood recorded the time. Sex was the one activity that most consistently led him to record specific clock time. Throughout the year, he often noted clock time when certain field tasks stopped, especially when slaves were performing more than two tasks in a day. The adoption of clock time clearly facilitated the organization of labor. He also noted specific clock times when he was hunting or when there were visitors or when he traveled to places near Egypt, such as Salt River.[157] He continued to use clock time in relation to labor during his years at Egypt. For example, on January 5, 1760, he observed "negroes working on the road, return home 3 p.m" and,

---

[155] Thomas Thistlewood Diary, September 15, 1748 to September 14, 1749, Monson, 31/1, Thistlewood Papers.
[156] For example, see Thomas Thistlewood Diary, December 27, 1752, Monson, 31/3, Thistlewood Papers.
[157] Thomas Thistlewood Diary, January 1, 1752 to December 31, 1752, Monson 31/3, Thistlewood Papers.

on November 17, 1760, he noted that "Sambo, slave comes with McDonald's negroes to work here, 9:30 a.m."[158]

The sugar mill and boiling house were the epicenter of clock time consciousness on a sugar plantation, and the plantation was oriented in space around those works. The works, which required significant capital investment, anchored a plantation in space; they could not be easily moved or inexpensively rebuilt, and the distance of the sugar fields from the mill was limited by the amount of time it would take to traverse that ground and transport cane to the works. Essentially, there was an outer limit to the distance that the plantation could grow away from the works, and the cost of the mill inhibited any relocation of the plantation. The works were set in the plantation yard, near store houses and often near the slave village and the manager's house. This area was the place on the plantation in which slaves were most closely supervised. The works were also the one place on a plantation in which the hours of labor regularly exceeded the hours of daylight. It was the place in which planters and overseers most commonly utilized clock time. Boiling house books commonly recorded the exact hours at which the mill stopped and started, and planters timed the length of the slaves' night shifts or "spells" at the works. As early as the seventeenth century, sugar planters were using clock time when they discussed events at the mill. In 1690, at Bybrooke plantation in Jamaica, for example, a sugar planter described a slave who "accidentally about Eight of the Clock in ye Morning fell to his armes between the Cases of ye Mill & soo dyed."[159] That the accident occurred at the mill appears to have been the most important factor in his decision to note time. At several other points in this series of letters about the management of the young plantation, the planter mentioned the deaths of enslaved workers without noting time. Thistlewood was more likely to record clock time for work at the mill than for any other type of labor activity.

On large Virginian plantations, in contrast, the demands of processing were not nocturnal and there were no central works driving the adoption of clock time. The use of clock time on Virginian plantations, despite these differences from sugar plantations, is a testament to the strength of the growing interest in the clock as a way of compelling time discipline. The diary of Landon Carter, a Virginian planter, offers a useful point of

---

[158] Thomas Thistlewood Diary, January 5, 1760 and November 17, 1760, Monson 31/11, Thistlewood Papers.

[159] Cary Heylar to William Heylar, March 18, 1689/1690, Heylar Manuscripts, Somerset Record Office.

comparison to Thomas Thsitlewood's diary. Not surprisingly, without a mill, Carter was less attentive to clock time than Thistlewood. Whereas Thistlewood made ninety-nine references to clock time in 1752, Carter made only twenty references to clock time in 1757.[160] Most of his references were connected to monitoring the signs of sickness in slaves or administering treatments. The difference between Thistlewood and Carter is certainly suggestive of a keener attention to clock time in Jamaica than in Virginia, but the evidence must be handled with care; it could simply be a difference in the conventions Carter and Thistlewood were adopting in drafting these diaries. Carter was clearly invested in instilling time discipline in his slaves and maximizing their production. On January 21, 1757, he complained about his enslaved threshers because they wanted "to thresh no more per day than they did when the days were 20 minutes shorter." Carter quickly punished them for their "evident lazyness" and "ordered them Correction" for "three days running."[161]

As much as clock time was transforming plantation management over the course of the eighteenth century, diurnal rhythms still controlled most field labors. The sun lit the slaves' labors, and slaves were sent to the field by its rise and fall. Slaves "usually work from Sun to Sun," a Barbadian planter explained in 1789. Planters allowed the slaves a break for breakfast and then "two Hours" at "Noon" during the hottest part of the day when the sun had reached its highest point in the sky.[162] The standardization of time and the rise of clock-based time began to discipline and standardize the rhythms of plantation life in the late eighteenth century, but older ways of defining time and its relationship to work and life persisted and coexisted on plantations and there were always competing and contested definitions of time. Both planters and slaves, for example, consistently referred to the harvest as "Crop Time," which could last as little two months or as many as six months. In fact, on some Jamaican estates it occurred twice a year. Slaves had their own ways of understanding the passage of time; they were often focused on the cyclical rise and fall of food supplies. In Barbados, for example, slaves tended to refer to July and August, before the corn harvest, as the "hungry-time" or the "hard-time."[163]

---

[160] Jack P. Greene, ed., *The Diary of Colonel Landon Carter of Sabine Hall, 1752–1778*, vol. 1 (Charlottesville, 1965), 137–198.
[161] Greene, ed., *Diary of Colonel Landon Carter*, vol. 1, 138.
[162] "British Sessional Papers, Commons, Accounts and Papers," 1789, Pt. III, 90.
[163] Gad Heuman, "Runaway Slaves in Nineteenth-Century Barbados," in Gad Heuman, ed., *Out of the House of Bondage: Runaways, Resistance and Maroonage in Africa and the New World* (London: Frank Cass, 1986), 102.

Time, in the hands of planters, was currency to be saved or spent, and work was defined by its relationship to time. The amount of slave energy that could be expended within a certain period of time was not a significant concern on sugar plantations or on large grain plantations in the Chesapeake. Whereas rice planters in the Lowcountry, who relied on task labor, developed labor quotas and used free time as an incentive for slaves to work harder, planters in Barbados, Virginia, and Jamaica focused on increasing the amount of time slaves spent working. Labor efforts on these gang labor plantations tended to be depicted as constant within a given unit of time. Time and slave work were blended together, becoming nearly synonymous. By equating the amount of available work with time itself, planters were effacing and naturalizing both the work efforts of the slaves and the force that was necessary to coerce these efforts. A mid-eighteenth century Barbadian plantation manual, for example, encouraged planters to "finish your Holeing," in October, and then "entirely *employ your Time* in planting Canes."[164] Note that it was time and not the slaves being put to work. Work logs were the tools that improving planters used to assess the precise number of days necessary to accomplish the labors of an estate. The Barbadian Society for Plantership discussed and debated exactly how many "labour days" an estate had. They conceptualized a total pool of "labour days" (counting work by the first gang as a full day's labor and by the second gang as two-thirds of a day) and noted, with resignation, that from this pool of days "a due proportion of labour must be deducted for sickness, absence and weather."[165] The planters met to determine how many "labour days" it took to cultivate ten acres of canes. "Labour days" like the man-days that came to be used later in industrial settings, was a term that merged work with time, regularizing and naturalizing the amount of labor that a worker should produce in a day.

Productivity rates per slave within a given period of time were not commonly recorded in work logs. The planters' underlying assumption seems to have been that the efforts of the field slaves, which were the majority of the slaves being tracked in work logs, would be constant and maximal each day because of the presence of a driver. Indeed, the anthropometric evidence suggests that slaves in the Caribbean and in the Chesapeake were working at near maximal levels of physical intensity. Recent studies of slave skeletons have demonstrated that field slaves had

---

[164] Belgrove, *Treatise upon Husbandry or Planting*, 18 [emphasis added].
[165] *Society for the Improvement of Plantership*, 13.

thicker bone structure and muscle density in load bearing areas and higher rates of degenerative joint disease than did free laborers, suggesting that they often labored at greater intensity than did free workers.[166] The improvement project of the last half of the eighteenth century was probably focused on making slaves work longer while maintaining this already maximal speed and intensity per hour. New plantation accounting systems were designed to encourage a greater quantity of maximal labor days. Accordingly, instead of tracking the intensity or output of labor each day, work logs normally counted the total volume of labor days. The boiling house was the one work site on a sugar plantation at which productivity rates per day or hour or acre were carefully recorded; yet, there was almost never any notation of how many slaves worked in the boiling house and thus little thought was given to productivity rates per person. Carter and Washington did perform time and motion studies of slaves at work to compel greater labor intensity, but they focused on skilled slaves or on slaves who were not already being supervised throughout the day by a driver. Work quotas were often used with these unsupervised slaves. The Mount Vernon farm reports, for example, list the precise amount of work produced by the spinners and knitters each week.[167] The work quotas imposed in these specialized work sites were designed as standards that slaves would need to meet in order to avoid the field. Without a driver, there was no guarantee that their labor would be maximal. Washington threatened to send spinners to the field, where they would face "the overseer's thereat [sic]" if they fell below their quotas.[168] In field labors, the productivity gains of the late eighteenth century were more closely related

---

[166] Kristrina A. Shuler, "Health, History, and Sugar: A Bioarchaeological Study of Enslaved Africans from Newton Plantation, Barbados, West Indies" (Ph.D. Dissertation, Department of Anthropology, Southern Illinois University Carbondale, 2005); Lorena Walsh, "Work and the Slave Economy," in Gad Heuman and Trevor Burnard, eds., *The Routledge History of Slavery* (New York: Routledge, 2011), 112.

[167] Mount Vernon Farm Reports, 1797-1798 in Theodore J. Crackel, ed., *The Papers of George Washington Digital Edition* (Charlottesville: The University of Virginia Press, 2009). For an individual example of these reports, see "Farm Repors, 2-8 April, 1797," in W.W. Abbot, ed., *The Papers of George Washington: Retirement Series*, vol. 1 (Charlottesville: University Press of Virginia, 1998), 60-69. The collection of 1797 weekly farm reports used throughout this book has been gathered from original manuscripts and photostats at the Mount Vernon Ladies Association Archives and the Library of Congress. This collection will be hereafter cited as Mount Vernon Farm Reports with the appropriate year.

[168] George Washington to Anthony Whiting, December 23, 1792 in Fitzpatrick, ed., *Writings of Washington*, vol. 32, 277.

to an increased amount of absolute work time being extracted from slaves rather than increases in work intensity, and the lack of productive totals in work logs are a testament to this focus.

Specific clock times were uncommon in work logs, but the unit of work time being analyzed (the "day") was, to some extent, an artificial construct. Although days were never exactly the same length because the sun rose and set at different times during the year, the day was made the critical unit of analysis in the work log. In Virginia, the slaves worked in the field from sunup to sundown but their daily hours varied significantly. There are approximately nine and a half hours of sunlight in Virginia in December and nearly fifteen hours during the longest days in June. Not only was there less field cultivation and generally lighter labors in the winter than in the summer, there were also nearly six fewer hours in the working day. Although slaves' efforts during the short summer grain harvest were faster paced and more demanding, the work logs do not account for any difference in a day's work. In the Caribbean, closer to the equator, the amount of sunlight in a day is more constant, but what makes the unit of time (a day) even more arbitrary in sugar plantation work logs is that they did not record night labors during the harvest, which could last as long as six months each year in Jamaica. A working day during the harvest was significantly longer than a working day outside the harvest. Without the rhythms of sunup and sundown to mark the passage of time, Caribbean planters began to rely on the clock to divide work shifts and record productive activities during the harvest. Boiling house books were attentive to the precise number of clock hours during which the mill was running.

The work log was part of a project of delineating between work time – during which slaves should be laboring maximally – and nonwork time. Work logs were supposed to allow planters the opportunity to maximize time and labor resources. They achieved this in part by constructing and imposing definitions of work time and rest time – a way of coercing full labor efforts during the work day. Weekly recordings of labor were anchored around the Sunday day off. Regardless of how demanding the agricultural tasks were at any given point in the year, these rest days came at regular seven-day intervals. Although logs demarcated between work time and rest time, this was largely an artificial distinction for slaves, who were expected to sustain themselves, at least in part, from working their own grounds on Sundays. "To expect the slaves, in general, worn down as many of them are, by daily, and in crop time, by nightly labour, to support themselves, by working on Sundays, in their own grounds," noted one

Time, Quantification, Amelioration, and the Enlightenment 77

Barbadian observer, "is, to say the least of it, extremely impolitic."[169] Provision work done during regular plantation work hours was carefully recorded in the logs but a slave's Sunday labors on provision grounds went unsupervised so they were simply not counted. Planters were attentive to the number of days slaves missed and to the size of work gangs during the work week, but these details on Sundays went overlooked. In some logs, Sunday never appeared and the date skipped. In others, the only notation was "Negroes in their Grounds."[170] Although sugar mills often operated until the early hours of Sunday and began again late on Sunday afternoon, work logs failed to acknowledge this as work being done on Sunday, defining this time instead as part of Saturday or Monday labor, thus effectively increasing the amount of time demanded from slaves by reshaping the definition of a day's labor. Account books elided the productive activities of slaves, and planters described Sundays, despite the operation of the mill, as rest days for slaves. Wood, for example, defied "any Negro Man to say He labours harder in his vocation, or more constantly than I do" because "they have their days of rest." In contrast, Wood lamented, on Sundays, he was in his office in the boiling house revising "the Books & the works of the antecedent week."[171]

By the last quarter of the eighteenth century, as part of the determined effort to extract more work from slaves and systematically control every moment of plantation time, a few sugar planters began to argue in favor of using drivers to compel the slaves to toil on Sunday. In 1773, a physician and pen-keeper in Jamaica visited his slaves' provision fields and "found that the negroes had entirely and absolutely neglected their grounds." His solution was "to work them in a gang in their own grounds every Sunday."[172] John Dovaston explained to the projected reader of his unpublished plantation manual in 1774 that "As Sundays are assigned to Negroes to labour and cultivate their own lands ... the Driver of them should See that they did their duty to you."[173] In 1786, the Dominican planter Gordon Turnbull recommended that managers inspect their slaves' grounds weekly "to see that they are properly cultivated; and the negroes who neglect this must be punished."[174] In 1793, the Jamaican Bryan

---

[169] William Dickson, *Mitigation of Slavery in Two Parts* (Miami, [1814], 1969), 316.
[170] Somerset Vale Work Logs, 1776–1780, Codex Eng 180, John Carter Brown Library.
[171] Sampson Wood to Thomas Lane, April 24, 1798, MS 523/335/1, Newton Papers.
[172] Alexander Johnston Daybook, August 21, 1773, ser. XII, vol. 334, box #1582, Powell Collection, Historical Society of Pennsylvania.
[173] Dovaston, "Agricultura Americana," vol. 2.
[174] Gordon Turnbull, *Letters to a Young Planter* (London: Stuart and Stevenson, 1785), 41.

Edwards suggested that planters should, in order to continue "meliorating the condition of the slaves," abolish the slave market on Sundays, make it a day of religious devotion, and "compel them to work in their own gardens four or five hours every Sunday morning."[175] In 1808, a Jamaican attorney assured the plantation owner at Running Gutt that the "Negroe Grounds" were inspected at least "once per week" and "I have been obliged to form a Gang of the lazy ones and work them together with a driver after them."[176] Slaves would not be expected to tend to canes on Sundays but they would be made – sometimes under the watch of a driver – to cultivate more provisions, which, despite taking away slaves' free time, was fully consistent with the amelioration project.

CONCLUSION

Planters participated in discourses of improvement that spread throughout the late eighteenth-century Atlantic. They believed that moral and economic progress and slavery were compatible and, in the late eighteenth century, as slavery and the slave trade came under increasing scrutiny and as some theorists began to celebrate the superior efficiency of free labor, planters offered competing notions of progress and modernity – notions that embraced restrictions on freedom. For planters, the control and discipline of slaves' time was central to progress. The plantation was a machine with interrelated parts that could be predicted and controlled if planters could identify sets of universal rules that governed that system. Slaves were an integral and inseparable part of that system. They were the chief capital stock of a plantation. Improving their condition by growing more provisions and by raising their fertility and lowering their mortality was a principal part of the agricultural improvement movement. Amelioration was just one component of that project. By the end of the eighteenth century, with the rise of humanitarian sensibilities, antislavery, and abolition, the language of amelioration and the justifications for it shifted; amelioration was increasingly moralized.

Torture and corporal punishment declined over the course of the eighteenth century and the provisions available for slaves tended to increase, but planters also demanded more work time. Plantation accounting

---

[175] Bryan Edwards, *The History, Civil and Commercial of the British Colonies in the West Indies*, 2 vols. (Dublin: Luke White, 1793), 146–148.
[176] "Doctor M. Campbell to John Taylor, December 13th 1808," series XIII, box 60, folder 6, Powell Collection.

systems were transformed in the late eighteenth century and new accounts such as work logs, boiling house books, and increase and decrease of stock accounts became important technological innovations, particularly in the sugar islands. These accounts enabled planters to extract more labor. By the end of the eighteenth century, some planters in the Caribbean were so intent on maximizing labor that they were beginning to encroach on the slaves' Sundays. Likewise, on some sugar plantations in Barbados and Jamaica, and throughout the largest plantations in the Chesapeake, planters began to diversify their crops enough to eliminate all slack periods in the agricultural cycle. Work logs enabled the coordination of the many productive activities on these estates.

The improvement movement shaped plantation management both in the Caribbean and the Chesapeake. In Virginia, amelioration was less pronounced. Perpetuating life was less of an issue where slaves naturally reproduced. Amelioration was most pronounced in Barbados, where planters working older lands were forced to contend with the rising costs of slaves and competition from the new sugar frontiers. Nevertheless, planters on the mainland and throughout the sugar islands were committed to experimentation and the application of reason in plantation management. Not all planters were equally committed to improvement, but there were enough that there were significant increases in productivity, and the best-practice standard in plantation management enabled planters to achieve very high profits. There were a variety of improving practices in the late eighteenth century. Not all of them were adopted on every plantation, and not all of them were profitable. Planters found a greater variety of crops to grow, increased their use of manure, grew better grasses for their cattle, became more self-sufficient, grew more provisions, and turned their fields into grids. They tracked the mortality and fertility of their slaves and livestock, and they noted the working days and sometimes the hours of cultivation. They meticulously accounted for all of their resources and took more time from their bondsmen. As they counted, coerced, and watched their clocks, they tightened the screws on their plantation machines.

2

Sunup to Sundown

Agricultural Diversity and Seasonal Patterns of Work

"It will be in the Power of the Husband-man to do every Thing in its most proper Season," insisted William Belgrove, the author of one of the earliest published plantation manuals in 1755, "I mean not to be a Planting when he ought to be Reaping, or a Reaping when he ought to be Planting."[1] Belgrove laid out a month-by-month plan of when to undertake tasks on a sugar plantation. He stressed proper timing as the key to the most efficient use of resources. His monthly system of planting was not unique. It was probably adapted from the English agricultural improvement literature. William Ellis' popular manual *Modern Husbandmen or Practice of Farming* (1731) was laid out as a set of monthly instructions. Likewise, the English improver Arthur Young adopted a month-by-month set of instructions in his book *The Farmer's Kalendar* (1770).[2] Belgrove's insistence on knowing the "proper Season" of cultivation was driven by an Enlightenment interest in systematizing plantation agriculture and in identifying the universal rules of cultivation that would allow nature to be disciplined. At the same time, Belgrove's monthly schedule highlights the importance of seasonality in early modern plantation agriculture. Just as the rhythms of labor changed with the season in British farming, there was never a typical day of labor on a Chesapeake grain plantation or a Caribbean sugar plantation. The season of production and the weather on any given day dictated the daily labors of slaves. There were distinct rhythms to plantation life, particularly in the Chesapeake. Although

---

[1] William Belgrove, *A Treatise Upon Husbandry or Planting* (Boston: D. Fowle, 1755), 34.
[2] Joel Mokyr, *The Enlightened Economy: An Economic History of Britain, 1700–1850* (New Haven: Yale University Press), 185.

historians are becoming attentive to how particular crops shaped the experience of slavery, they still tend to gloss over the seasonality of plantation life and work (see Appendix B, Tables A1 to A5).

In the improving era, planters sought uniformity and predictability in the management of their plantations, and they hoped to extract more labor from slaves by having them work maximally throughout the year. However, indoor work with nonorganic products led more easily than agricultural field work to constant and uniform working conditions. Even though sugar plantations are sometimes described as agroindustrial operations or "factories in the field," and even though planters throughout the Americas strove to dictate the pace and the motions of slave laborers in ways that foreshadow later developments in factory labor, the rhythms of work on plantations changed with the season.[3]

The demands of tending to the staple crops dictated the pace of work throughout the year and shaped how planters allocated labor. Every crop had periods of higher and lower intensity in its labor demands. Wheat was among the most markedly seasonal crop grown in the plantation Americas because it required little labor outside of the harvest. Tobacco, in contrast, required a more constant labor effort.[4] Cane can be planted and harvested at almost any point of the year, but it could also be a seasonal crop because of the pace of work required during the sugar harvest and because it needed to be cut and shipped during the dry part of the year, before the hurricane season. To increase the slaves' total hours of annual labor, planters found ways to offset the highs and lows in the cycle of a staple crop. By diversifying their crops and including work activities that required more constant efforts, such as craft production or animal husbandry, planters ensured a full daily employment of the available labor pool. Planters also sought to diversify because it would offset the market risks and the threat of pests and crop failures that came with the cultivation of a single staple crop. Overspecialization in a single crop leads to cycles of boom and bust. Diversification makes profits more certain. This risk-reducing function of diversification, coupled with the reduction of dependence on physically taxing staple crops, such as sugar or tobacco, made diversification central to the amelioration project. To balance an increasingly wide array of crops and productive activities, the timing of tasks and

---

[3] Sidney Mintz, *Sweetness and Power: The Place of Sugar in Modern History* (New York: Penguin Books, 1985), 48–52.
[4] Philip. D. Morgan, *Slave Counterpoint: Black Culture in the Eighteenth-Century Chesapeake and Lowcountry* (Chapel Hill: University of North Carolina Press), 175–178.

attention to the seasons of production was essential. Given that slaves were fixed capital, any time they spent idle was an expense to the planter. Planters were highly motivated to pursue economic activities that would allow them to keep their slaves fully employed throughout the year.[5]

Eighteenth-century planters were increasingly aware that lost time, like a relaxed pace, meant a lower return on fixed capital (such as the land and the mill) but also on the flexible stock (slaves and livestock) of an estate. Every task performed on a plantation had an opportunity cost, and planters made careful economic decisions about these opportunity costs; they dwelled on how to maximize land space and spend, save, or increase the amount of labor time available on an estate. Their decisions were rational, given their most basic assumptions about the nature of their land and labor resources. On plantations that relied on gang labor organization among a fixed and guaranteed supply of slave laborers, the units of available time and the units of available work became essentially synonymous, and planters struggled to control, manipulate, and maximize these units of work and time.

Slaves worked for the vast majority of their waking hours, and that time was shaped by managerial strategies and by the cultivation demands of particular crops. There were many possible management schemes in the production of any staple crop, and the degree to which planters diversified production or produced primary and secondary staple crops varied considerably. This chapter compares the total annual amount of labor and seasonal changes in working hours on large plantations in the Chesapeake and the Caribbean. It examines the amount of time devoted to primary and secondary cash crops and provisions on plantations in each region. It contrasts and compares two systems of production: multicropping and monocropping. It explores the relationship between seasonal crop demands and labor patterns by examining specific aspects of cultivation: holing and plowing, cleaning and weeding, manuring and the care of livestock, and, finally, the harvest. Overall, the chapter seeks to determine how the daily routines of plantation workers were shaped by Enlightenment-inspired improvement movements in this era.

TOTAL ANNUAL LABOR

The exact number of days slaves spent working each year was a common subject of discussion for plantation improvers in the late eighteenth

[5] Robert. E. Gallman and Ralph. V. Anderson, "Slaves as Fixed Capital: Slave Labor and Southern Economic Development," *Journal of American History* 64.1 (June 1977): 24–46.

century, especially in Barbados. It was part of the increasing numeracy in plantation management. Improving planters debated the precise number of work days they could expect from their slaves, and they recorded the exact number of days they managed to attain. Work logs were central to this increasing emphasis on tracking, regulating, and compelling maximum labor participation. Total annual work days became a finite and calculable resource that a plantation manager could spend on a variety of tasks. Planters never questioned their ownership of that time. The Barbadian Society for the Improvement of Plantership met in 1805 to calculate the exact number of days planters could expect from their slave gangs and determine how that number of days should be spent. One member of the Society insisted that it was "essential to ascertain the quantum of labour" that a planter would spend on each task.[6] In 1804 and 1805, a Jamaican pen keeper designed a work account in which he recorded not only the tasks his slaves were performing each day but also the value of his slaves' working days as a deduction in his accounting book when they were spent. Quite tellingly, he also differentiated between tasks when he was determining the value of a day's labor. Presumably, this was based on the standard island rate at which slaves would have been hired for such tasks. The most demanding chores, such as road building, were more costly than provision work. In this case, the planter appears to have been factoring in a kind of depreciation cost, determining how draining each chore would be on the health of his own slaves.[7] To grant his slaves a day off or a sick day was literally a calculated expense. In the early nineteenth century, Barbadian William Dickson, relying on information gleaned from the Barbadian planter Joshua Steele, used precise estimates of the number of annual work days to support his ameliorationist stance. He maintained that individual Caribbean field workers, because of high sickness rates and because of frequent long- and short-term runaways, worked, on average, no more than 266 days each year (see Figure 2.1). Slaves, for Dickson, were simply too overworked and underfed to work more than that, but amelioration would, he implied, give planters not only a larger number of days but also a more predictable and consistent amount.[8]

---

[6] *Minutes of the Society for the Improvement of Plantership in the Island of Barbados* (Liverpool: Thomas Kaye, 1811), 13.
[7] "Occurrences & Amount of Negro Labour Weekly," Retirement and Harmony Hill Plantation Book, 1804–1805, Folder 5, Box 59, Case/Box #1582, Powel Family Papers.
[8] William Dickson, *Mitigation of Slavery, In Two Parts* (Miami, FL: Mnemosyne Pub. Inc., [1814] 1969), 435.

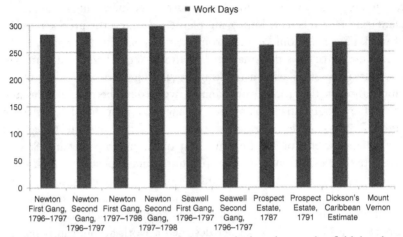

FIGURE 2.1. Average number of days worked each year by field hands at Prospect (1787 and 1791), Mount Vernon (1797), Newton (1796–1797), and Seawell (1796–1797).
Sources: Prospect Plantation Journals 1787–1793, 0627-0019; Newton Work Logs, 1796–1798 and Seawell Work Log, 1796–1797, MS 523/110, 111, 123, Newton Family Papers; Mount Vernon Farm Reports, 1797; Dickson, Mitigation of Slavery, 435.

Surviving plantation work logs show that Dickson was actually vastly underestimating the average number of days the average slave was working each year, probably exaggerating to support his argument. Through a mixture of coercive tactics, greater labor discipline, and new forms of plantation accounting, the managers in the 1790s at Newton and Seawell in Barbados and at Prospect in Jamaica forcefully extracted more from their slaves each year than Dickson's estimate. The adults who worked in the fields on these estates averaged between 279 and 297 days per year (see Figure 2.1 and Appendix B, Tables A6 to A8). By comparison, slaves on cotton and rice plantations in the nineteenth-century U.S. South worked an average of 280 to 290 days per year.[9] The number of days slaves worked each year were strikingly consistent throughout the plantation Americas because almost all planters granted their slaves Sundays and three or four other days off each year. Likewise, the average number of days lost to sickness, bad weather, or other occurrences was remarkably uniform across the plantations of the Anglo-American world. Jamaican

---

[9] Robert. W. Fogel, Without Consent or Contract: The Rise and Fall of American Slavery (New York: Norton, 1989), 77; Gallman and Anderson, "Slaves as Fixed Capital," 30.

plantations were more likely than Barbadian or Virginian plantations to fall below that standard. There were specific circumstances, such as severe epidemics or famines, large numbers of runaways, and long bouts of bad weather, in which the average number of days slaves worked could fall well below 280. Jamaican plantations were most subject to all of these circumstances. Jamaican planters also set aside more "days off" for their slaves to cultivate their own provision grounds, which tended to keep the number of supervised work days lower than elsewhere. The days slaves spent working on provision grounds were not leisure time, but planters refused to acknowledge them as work days even if, by the end of the eighteenth century, many planters, especially Jamaicans, began to use drivers to compel slaves on Sundays.

Plantations high in the mountains of Jamaica or in the island's frontier areas, such as Prospect, were particularly subject to lost working days. The labor on these steep, heavily forested grounds was more severe, taxing the slaves and increasing the amount of time they spent sick. The heavy forest cover and more isolated location of these plantations also created conditions that were more conducive to running away, if only for a few days at a time. In Barbados, by contrast, the consistent and mostly clear-cut terrain and the established plantations probably allowed for greater uniformity in labor conditions and more working days. It took time for planters to standardize their work routines and achieve a more predictable number of annual work days. In 1787, for example, Prospect was a new estate with a large number of recently imported African workers still undergoing seasoning in a mountainous sugar frontier in northeastern Jamaica. The hard work of clearing the plantation was not finished, and the slaves were harvesting both sugar and logwood. The backbreaking work of logging offered no relief from the brutal chore of digging cane holes. There was so much sickness and disease that year that the average slave worked only 261 days, less than Dickson's estimate. Four years later, with far less logging, the Prospect slaves worked an average of 281 days each.

Given that the natural decline of the enslaved workers was greatest in Jamaica, that that the Virginian slaves were reproducing naturally at a significant rate, and that the Barbadian slaves were almost naturally reproducing, it is striking that Virginian and Barbadian slaves worked more days on average than their counterparts on Jamaican estates. If anything, there was an inverse relationship between the total number of days worked and the reproductive rates in these three locales. One of the central strategies in the plantation improvement project was to increase labor discipline and employ supervisory tools, such as work logs and

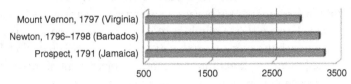

FIGURE 2.2. Annual number of hours worked per field hand at Newton, Prospect, and Mount Vernon.

Note: Estimates are based on the average number of days worked each month per slave (excluding all individual and group days off), the number of days in which sugar mills were in operation, an estimate of four hours of night work for each day a sugar mill was running, and the hours of daylight in each location. Two hours of break time during daylight have been included in the estimates. Two years of full work logs were used to calculate the average at Newton.

Sources: Prospect Plantation Journals, 1787–1793, 0627-0019; Newton Work Logs, 1796–1798, MS 523/110, 123, Newton Family Papers; Mount Vernon Farm Reports, 1797.

coercive medical measures, to increase the number of days slaves spent working each year, but the rising number of working days per slave did not necessarily have a negative impact on the mortality and fertility rates of the bondsmen.

Although the number of days slaves worked was somewhat consistent throughout the plantation Americas, the number of hours could vary significantly, particularly between the sugar islands and the mainland. Sugar slaves had the additional burden of harvest night work. The average number of hours worked each year by field workers was higher at Prospect (3,288) than it was at Newton (3,209) or at Mount Vernon (2,919) (see Figure 2.2). Slaves at Mount Vernon would have had to work another month and a half each year of regular labors to meet the labor demands placed on slaves at Prospect. There was little difference between the average number of hours each Barbadian slave worked and the average each Jamaican slave worked, but this could vary quite a bit each year, depending on the size of the sugar crop. In 1796–1797, the cane yield at Newton was low, there was less harvest work to be done, and slaves worked less than 3,000 hours each. However, in 1797–1798 the cane yield was above average and slaves worked more than 3,400 hours each.[10] Slaves in Jamaica received more time off to tend their own grounds, but the length of the harvest was longer, which meant more hours of night labor. By comparison, slaves on antebellum U.S. cotton plantations, where slaves were naturally reproducing at a remarkable rate, worked far less (2,800 hours per year) than eighteenth-century slaves in Barbados, Jamaica, and Virginia.

Did long hours play a significant role in the health of the enslaved on sugar plantations? Despite the similar number of hours worked, the Barbadian slave population did not decline in the way that the Jamaican population did. It is important not to reduce the demands of a particular labor regime and their impacts on workers' health to the hours alone. Free farmers in the U.S. north in the nineteenth century worked almost as much as eighteenth-century Jamaican and Barbadian slaves, an average of 3,200 hours per year.[11] Workers in early nineteenth-century English textile mills probably worked more hours for their employers than did sugar slaves, averaging as many as 4,000 hours per year.[12] Yet, if one includes the slaves' work on their own provision grounds as labor, then slaves in a good harvest year on a sugar plantation were working nearly as many hours as early nineteenth-century industrial workers. Given the similar efforts of factory and plantation owners to increase labor discipline and compel more hours of work through close supervision and better accounting technologies, it is not surprising that the time spent working by slaves and factory workers were comparable.

The hours of labor varied considerably with the season on plantations. In the Chesapeake, sunlight dictated the working hours. Mount Vernon field hands worked many more hours during the long days of June than during the short days of December (see Figure 2.3). In the Caribbean, by contrast, the length of the day was more constant throughout the year, but the work day grew longer during the harvest. During the cane harvest, field hands, after a full day of labor, served a shift or "spell" in the mill for three to six hours each night. Larger plantations were able to use three rotating shifts, whereas smaller estates used two, suggesting that slaves on the largest plantations probably worked slightly fewer

---

[10] Sampson Wood to Thomas Lane, 31 March 1798 and Sampson Wood to Thomas Land, 24 April 1798, MS 523/334, 334/1, Newton Family Papers.
[11] Fogel, *Without Consent or Contract*, 78.
[12] Ibid., 28; Herman Freudenberger and Gaylord Cummins, "Health, Work, and Leisure before the Industrial Revolution," *Explorations in Economic History* 13.1 (1976), 6.

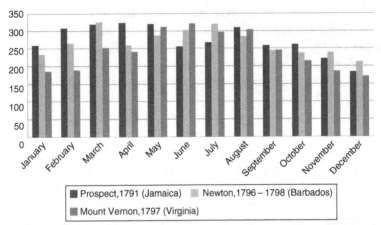

FIGURE 2.3. Average number of hours worked each month by field hands at Prospect, Mount Vernon, and Newton.
Note: The hours have been calculated in the same way as in Figure 2.2. The data for Newton represent the average derived from two full years of work logs.
Sources: Prospect Plantation Journals, 1787–1793, 0627-0019; Newton Work Logs, 1796–1798, MS 523/110, 123, Newton Family Papers; Mount Vernon Farm Reports, 1797.

hours each year.[13] The peak season of labor in Virginia was May through July. With nearly fifteen hours of sunlight, these were the longest days of the year – nearly six hours longer than the winter days of December. In the Caribbean, by contrast, the sunlight is more constant. It ranges from eleven hours to thirteen hours in Jamaica and from eleven and a half to thirteen hours in Barbados, closer to the equator. The longest work days on sugar plantations were at the height of the harvest. At Prospect, the hours of work increased significantly from February through May. At Newton, the longest hours came from March through July. In both the Caribbean and Virginia, the hours of work per month fell sharply in November and December, with shorter days in Virginia and less harvest work to be done in the Caribbean. In January and February, the hours of work per month tended to remain low in the Chesapeake, but they rose in the Caribbean because the harvest traditionally began after the Christmas holiday with the onset of the dry season. The difference

[13] John Weddenbrun to Roger Hope Elleton, February 24, 1760, West Indies Box 1, Letters & Accounts Regarding the Blue Castle Estate, Stowe Papers, Huntington Library; see also B. W. Higman, *Slave Populations of the British Caribbean, 1807–1834* (Baltimore: Johns Hopkins University, 1984), 182–183.

between a harvest month and a nonharvest month on a sugar plantation was often remarkable. For example, in July 1798, the Newton slaves rushed to finish harvesting a bumper crop before the onset of the hurricane season. They worked more than 370 hours that month. The mill ran almost continually. In sharp contrast, just a few months earlier, in December 1797, before the harvest began, the average slave spent approximately 210 hours in the field. That difference of nearly 160 hours in a single month had a significant impact on the lives these workers were able to shape away from their chores.

The amount of time spent working was rising in both the Chesapeake and the Caribbean in the late eighteenth century. The increasing diversification of production in the Chesapeake meant less "down time" during the year. Chesapeake planters extracted a greater amount of labor from their slaves than ever before, including more hours and days per year.[14] The creolization of the enslaved population in Jamaica, and especially in Barbados, meant a healthier slave population, acclimatized to the Caribbean disease environment. Accordingly, both the average number of days and hours worked each year appear to have risen in the late eighteenth and early nineteenth centuries. Just as the increase in productivity in Britain during the Industrial Revolution may have been due more to longer hours than to increasing levels of worker productivity, the rising number of days and hours on slave plantations in this era was one of the most significant factors in increased productivity.[15] Labor discipline rather than mechanization was the key to productivity gains throughout the British Atlantic in this era.

CASH CROPS AND PROVISIONS

Slaves were flexible capital assets, and planters could assign them a wide array of chores, including working on multiple cash crops or a combination of cash and provision crops. Assuming a sufficient labor force, the

---

[14] Lorena S. Walsh, "Slave Life, Slave Society, and Tobacco Production in the Tidewater Chesapeake, 1620–1820," in Ira Berlin and Philip D. Morgan, ed., *Cultivation and Culture: Labor and the Shaping of Slave Life in the Americas* (Charlottesville: University Press of Virginia, 1993), 170–202.

[15] Joachim Voth, *Time and Work in England, 1750–1830* (New York: Oxford University Press, 2000); John McCusker, "The Economy of the British West Indies, 1763–1790: Growth, Stagnation or Decline," in McCusker, ed. *Essays in the Economic History of the Atlantic World* (London: Routledge, 1997), 324; J. R. Ward, "The Amelioration of British West Indian Slavery, 1750–1834: Technical Change and the Plow," *New West-Indian Guide* 63.1–2 (1989), 43.

limiting factor in production schemes was not what the slaves were capable of doing but what the land would support. Slaves were often more skilled at cultivating a particular cash crop, and there was a learning curve with the introduction of new crops, but the benefits that came with growing multiple crops encouraged many planters to diversify. Cash crops were revenue generators, but keeping expenses down was often the best way to make profits more consistent and predictable on a plantation, and this meant relying more heavily on internally grown provisions. The reduction of plantation expenditures and risks was a central goal in the improvement movement. The risk of obtaining provisions at reasonable prices, for example, could be offset by growing more provisions, essentially ameliorating the estate.

Diversification allowed planters to maximize the available land and labor resources and offset the erratic highs and lows in income that came with the reliance on the market price of a single crop, as well as the risks of crop failure that attended cash crop monoculture. Many planters eliminated slack periods in labor demands by combining multiple, ideally complementary, crops for sale and for use on the plantation and by devoting labor to raising more livestock or improving the lands and structures of the estate. Economic historians have found that diversification tended to be the rule rather than the norm on staple crop slave plantations in the antebellum U.S. South. On cotton plantations, for example, slaves spent only a third of their time growing the staple crop.[16] In the Chesapeake, wheat, as a cash crop, required only short bursts of effort each year, and it could be combined easily with other crops. The seasonal requirements of tobacco meshed particularly well with corn and wheat cultivation.[17] The seasonal requirements of cane were such that sugar planters could also cultivate other less labor intensive provision crops, such as corn, potatoes, or yams, fairly easy, but secondary cash crops were harder to incorporate on sugar plantations than on large Chesapeake plantations.

Few plantations were ever solely devoted to the production of a single crop, but Barbadian and Jamaican planters were more likely than their Virginian counterparts to favor a near monoculture over a multicropping system. Planters cultivated different crops and different ratios of crops

---

[16] Robert William Fogel and Stanley L. Engerman, *Time on the Cross: The Economics of American Negro Slavery* (Boston: Little & Brown, 1974), 41–42.

[17] James R. Irwin, "Slave Agriculture and Staple Crops in the Virginia Piedmont" (PhD. Dissertation, University of Rochester, 1986), v.

every year. If sugar prices were high, a sugar planter could devote more acreage and labor to that staple crop. If sugar prices were falling relative to the price of other cash crops, a planter might turn to the cultivation of other staples. Barbadians turned to cotton, particularly along the south coast of Barbados in the 1780s and 1790s, and Jamaicans began turning to coffee in the mountains of the island, especially in the 1790s and during the first decade of the 1800s. On some Jamaican plantations, such as Somerset Vale, slaves worked annually on both coffee and cane.[18] As the cost of imported provisions rose, particularly during the American Revolution, sugar planters could plant less staple crops and have slaves grow more provisions internally. To be successful, planters had to predict future changes in markets and prices and adapt. They had to consider the opportunity costs of any system of cultivation.

In Virginia, planters began to add more corn and wheat to their tobacco staple from the 1730s onward and especially in the last quarter of the eighteenth century.[19] The largest planters even began to diversify into other productive activities, such as fishing, planting orchards, or distilling.[20] By the 1790s, Washington's Mount Vernon in northern Virginia was what contemporaries would have thought of as a farm rather than a plantation because of the enormous range of productive activities and because such a minor share of the annual labor was devoted to the production of a single staple crop.[21] There were a wide variety of grains, fodder, and other crops being grown at Mount Vernon. Wheat was the primary cash crop at Mount Vernon, but corn was also grown in large quantities. Whereas on a sugar plantation corn was almost exclusively cultivated to feed the slaves and livestock, large Chesapeake planters grew corn as both a cash crop and as a provision crop for the livestock and slaves. Approximately 90 percent of the wheat and 50 percent of the corn produced was grown for sale.[22]

---

[18] Somerset Vale Work Logs, 1776–1780, Codex Eng. 180.
[19] Richard B. Sheridan, "Strategies of Slave Subsistence: The Jamaican Case Reconsidered," in Mary Turner, ed., *From Chattel Slaves to Wage Slaves; The Dynamics of Labour Bargaining in the Americas* (Bloomington: Indiana University Press, 1995), 48; Otis P. Starkey, *The Economic Geography of Barbados: A Study of the Relationships between Environmental Variations and Economic Development* (New York: Columbia University Press, 1939), 106; Lorena S. Walsh, "Plantation Management in the Chesapeake, 1620–1820," *The Journal of Economic History* 49.2 (June 1989), 397.
[20] Walsh, "Plantation Management."
[21] Morgan, *Slave Counterpoint*, 174.
[22] Ibid., 397.

Tobacco production at Mount Vernon, on a large scale, had ended in the 1760s because of poor-quality top soils and declining tobacco prices. Washington was growing wheat, corn, and fodder crops. Wheat required less labor than sugar, rice, cotton, or tobacco, the other major crops in the plantation Americas. To obtain as much revenue, it also required far more cultivated acreage than tobacco. This search for new and larger grain fields led Washington to expand Mount Vernon from 2,000 to 8,000 acres before his death in 1799. Mount Vernon's outlying farms were the primary producers, and Washington planned to distance himself from the production cycles of cash crops and end all cultivation at his seat, the Mansion House farm, in 1798.[23]

Unlike their counterparts in the sugar islands, Washington's slaves spent little time each year cultivating the primary cash crop: wheat. Mount Vernon was the quintessential multicropping estate. In 1797, slaves spent less than a fifth (19 percent) of their time raising wheat (see Appendix B, Tables A9 and A10). The demands of wheat peaked in the summer during the harvest, but an even greater spike came in September when the slaves spent nearly half of their work days plowing and harrowing a new crop of wheat.[24] From January through May, in August after the harvest, and in October and November, the production of wheat required very minimal effort from field hands, allowing the Mount Vernon managers to assign the workers to the production of secondary or provision crops or to other nonfield activities such as fishing or the improvement of plantation structures. Washington, for example, had designed a sixteen-sided barn on his Dogue Run farm, which he hoped would increase efficiency.

Washington's goal was to make Mount Vernon almost entirely self-sufficient, and raising large volumes of corn helped him achieve it. Corn, grown both as a cash crop and to feed the estate's slaves and livestock, required more annual labor than wheat on all of the Mount Vernon farm quarters. At least 26 percent of all work days were spent cultivating corn and, including some of the plowing or harrowing done on unspecified crops, the amount of time spent cultivating corn was probably closer to 31 percent of all work days (see Appendix B, Tables A9 and A10). In other words, the field hands at Mount Vernon were as much corn slaves as they were wheat slaves. There were only two months of the year in which wheat

---

[23] George Washington to James Anderson, June 18, 1797, W.W. Abbot, ed., *The Papers of George Washington: Retirement Series*, vol. 1: March–December 1797 (Charlottesville: University Press of Virginia, 1998), 191–195.

[24] Irwin, "Slave Agriculture and Staple Crops," 50–51.

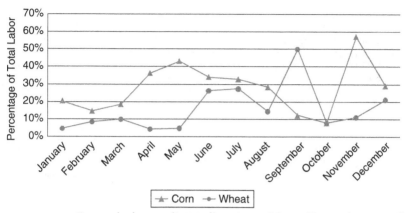

FIGURE 2.4. Seasonal wheat and corn allocation at Mount Vernon in 1797 (all outlying farms).
Note: The calculations for this figure include not only all days described as wheat or corn cultivation but also a portion of all days spent doing unspecified harrowing, plowing, and grubbing tasks. One-third of these days were counted as wheat and one-third as corn.
Source: Mount Vernon Farm Reports, 1797.

required more working days than corn: September and October. In November, the corn harvest required nearly 60 percent of the slaves' total working days (see Figure 2.4).

The greatest share of work on any sugar plantation was always invested directly in cultivating the staple, but the degree to which the estates focused on sugar varied from almost a sole focus on sugar to a multicropping system. The production strategy at Prospect, in Jamaica, was an extreme example of sugar monoculture. In 1785, 1787, and 1791, the field hands on that plantation spent no less than 70 percent and as much as 90 percent of their work days toiling in the cane fields and at the mill to obtain high yields (see Appendix B, Tables A11–A13). There was some division of labor on tasks at Prospect, but all field workers could expect to spend the vast majority of almost every month of the year toiling in the canes. January, February, November, and August were the months in which Prospect slaves spent the least days cultivating canes (see Figure 2.5).

The amount of time slaves spent tending to sugar on the Barbadian plantations of Newton and Seawell stands in sharp contrast to the time spent at Prospect, demonstrating the range of possibilities in sugar production. What is most remarkable about the daily work routines at Newton and Seawell is that the slaves, on an island that had gained a reputation as a foreign-fed colony geared toward sugar production alone,

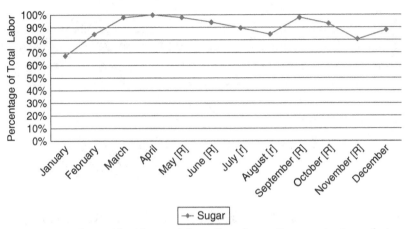

FIGURE 2.5. Seasonal cash crop labor allocation at Prospect (1787 and 1791 combined).
Note: [R] = Peak Rain Season, [r] = Rain Season.
Source: Prospect Plantation Journals, 1787–1793, 0627-0019.

were working directly on cash crops for as little as a third of their working days. At the start of the 1797 crop, the manager at Newton and Seawell predicted that the crop was going to be "very short" because "the weather throughout the whole year has been uncommonly dry & severe."[25] Newton slaves spent only 35 percent of their time cultivating canes and working at the mill in 1796–1797. Questions could obviously be raised about the typicality of the low cash crop production at Newton that year. Drought did significantly hamper the size of the 1797 sugar crop.[26] However, the amount of time Newton slaves spent on cane cultivation did not rise significantly with better crops. The crop of 1798 was among the best that Newton had seen in the late eighteenth century. The 1798 revenues were more than three times higher than they had been in 1797.[27] Yet, even though the plantation went from an extreme drought year with a poor yield to ideal conditions for sugar, the amount of time slaves spent

[25] Sampson Wood to Thomas Lane, March 26, 1797, MS 523/295, Newton Family Papers. Others agreed that excessively dry weather had hurt the crop of 1797; see Edward Clarke to John Brathwaite, May 1, 1797, Correspondence of Edward Clarke, Estate Manager, 1795–1800, C/COD/46, Codrington Papers C Series.
[26] Sampson Wood to Thomas Lane, March 26, 1797, MS 523/295, Newton Family Papers.
[27] Sampson Wood to Thomas Lane, March 31, 1798, Sampson Wood to Thomas Lane, April 24, 1798, Newton Annual Abstracts of Accounts for 1797 and 1798, MS 523/45, 46, 334, 334/1, Newton Family Papers.

tending and harvesting canes at Newton only rose from 35 to 39 percent over these two years. Clearly, weather and the crop yield did not significantly alter the number of days slaves spent producing sugar each year. At Seawell, in 1796–1797, slaves spent 42 percent of their work days cultivating a combination of cotton and canes. In other words, even with two cash crops to juggle, the Seawell slaves spent the majority of the year working on tasks not directly connected to either of those staple crops. The first gang at each plantation spent an even smaller share of time than the second gang tending to cash crops (see Appendix B, Tables A14–A17). Even if one includes the closely connected and labor intensive tasks of making and distributing dung – which was not used exclusively on cotton or canes – Newton and Seawell hands spent less than half of their time on cash crops during any year. Instead, these estates grew a diverse array of cash and provision crops with regular gang labors.

The biggest difference between a drought year and a boom year in sugar cultivation was in the amount of time the slaves spent harvesting canes. In years when drought or pests hindered the growth of canes, the enslaved workers spent less time harvesting canes but, instead of turning away from the canes altogether, they spent an almost equal number of days weeding and otherwise tending to the poor-quality canes to maximize their limited potential. A poor harvest meant they could avoid night work in the boiling house, but it also meant that they would lose a food source because slaves often sucked on cane stalks during the harvest.

Most of the more demanding tasks in the cane cultivation cycle were strictly seasonal, which meant that the demands of sugar were staggered, especially in Barbados. At Newton, over the course of two years of work, field hands spent much as 63 percent of their days on canes during months when slaves were digging cane holes or harvesting and milling canes (see Figure 2.6). These activities often overlapped between January and May. During the peak periods of cane cultivation in Barbados, Newton came much closer to resembling the stereotypical monoculture sugar plantation. Yet even during the sugar harvest, with canes threatening to rot, at least a third of the first gang's labor was normally invested in a variety of other activities such as tending to corn and livestock pens. When the harvest was over and provision work became the focus, Newton field hands spent as little as 21 percent (in July) of their labors on sugar production.

Likewise at Seawell, in 1796–1797, the months spent harvesting canes (February to April), holing canes (July and December), or picking cotton (January to March) led to considerable increases in the amount of time slaves tended to cash crops. In March, 82 percent of the Seawell slaves'

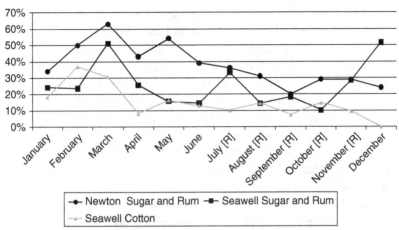

FIGURE 2.6. Percentage of first-gang labors spent on cash crops each month at Newton and Seawell, 1796–1798.
Note: [R] = Rain Season.
Sources: Newton Work Logs, 1796–1798 and Seawell Work Log, 1796–1797, MS 523/110, 111, 123, Newton Family Papers.

work days were spent harvesting sugar and cotton, as slaves alternated between the two. During other months, the Seawell cash crops received much less attention. In October, only 25 percent of the slaves' labors were allocated to the two cash crops. Overall, the percentage of total work days devoted to cash crop cultivation on Barbadian estates tended to be much higher during the dry harvest season than during the rainy season (Figure 2.6).

The proportion of time that Newton and Seawell slaves spent on cash crops was close to standard practice for large Barbadian sugar estates at the end of the eighteenth century. If anything, field workers at Newton and Seawell spent a greater than ideal amount of time on cash crops. In 1805, prominent local planters in the Barbadian Society for the Improvement of Plantership estimated that slaves on a hypothetical sugar plantation would need to spend from 33 to 38 percent of their work days on canes and on making and distributing dung. The remaining work days could be allocated to "the raising of food for the slaves and the stock."[28] The managers at Newton and even at Seawell, where some fields were devoted to cotton, cultivated more cane acreage per field hand and a higher ratio of plant canes to ratoon canes (canes that are harvested without replanting) than the society's ideal model, which required the Newton slaves to spend more of their time on cash

[28] *Society for the Improvement of Plantership*, 11–13.

crops than the society's improving members thought best. Barbadian plantations countered the competition that came with the rapid expansion of the sugar industry in the Caribbean by growing more food internally and by ensuring that slaves worked those provisions to their fullest potential by forcing them to cultivate provisions as part of their regular gang labors.

Planters in the Chesapeake were, like their Caribbean counterparts, quick to exploit whatever economic opportunities were available. By the last half of the eighteenth century, many Chesapeake planters were combining wheat, corn, and livestock farming with the traditional tobacco staple while also adding fodder crops, tending to fruit orchards, or even operating fisheries along the major rivers. Slaves worked intensely year round. With an abundant labor supply and crops that required little annual labor, Washington experimented with several economic activities to supplement his income from grains. He operated a brick kiln at Mount Vernon and a fishery along the Potomac. Field hands from all of the quarters assisted with the labor at these sites. The haddock and shad hauled in by nets at the fishery brought more income in some years than the income from all the cultivated crops at Mount Vernon, but it required an investment of less than 1 percent of all work days in 1797 (see Appendix B, Tables A9 and A10).[29] The most financially lucrative tasks were not always the most labor intensive.

There has been a tendency to overlook the degree of economic diversification that was possible on a large sugar estate.[30] Although sugar reigned in the Caribbean, its planters often tried to increase profits by developing secondary and tertiary economic activities on their estates. Depending on where their estate was located, planters in Jamaica could grow coffee, cut logwood, and sell livestock for additional profits. In Barbados, planters had less arable land, less woodland, and less economic opportunities available to them, but many of them raised and sold cattle, grew cotton, or raised other small crops. The managers of Newton and Seawell, for example, raised livestock for sale and cultivated arrowroot commercially in addition to growing large amounts of cotton.[31] Long-established estates with a large population of creole slaves often had many enslaved

---

[29] Lorena. S. Walsh, "Slavery and Agriculture at Mount Vernon," in Philip J. Schwarz, ed. *Slavery at the Home of George Washington* (Mount Vernon: Mount Vernon Ladies Association, 2002), 52.

[30] David Eltis, *The Rise of African Slavery in the Americas* (New York: Cambridge University Press, 2000), 202.

[31] Jerome S. Handler, "The History of Arrowroot and the Origin of Peasantries in the British West Indies," *Journal of Caribbean History* 2 (May 1971): 46–93.

craftsmen, and they could make substantial sums from hiring out these craftsmen to surrounding plantations.[32] Planters would turn to these secondary opportunities when there was a depression in the sugar market.

The ways in which planters combined cotton and canes in Barbados in the last quarter of the eighteenth century offers an opportunity to think about how and why planters chose which staple crops to pursue and in what combinations. In Barbados, cotton production was greatest in the 1780s, immediately after the 1780 hurricane.[33] Although cotton exports from Barbados peaked in the 1780s, production seems to have continued on a smaller scale into at least the early nineteenth century. John Forster Alleyne, once a resident planter but living in England at the turn of the nineteenth century, owned three Barbadian estates, and he had grown cotton with the canes on these estates, depending, he said, on shifting "circumstances." Alleyne intended to sell most of his cotton on the internal Barbadian market. In 1802, Alleyne worried that cotton was being produced in "the American States Georgia and Carolina ... upon a large and increasing Scale" and that it was much "better" than Barbadian cotton. He predicted that Barbados would be unable to compete with the United States in cotton production.[34] Although the rise of U.S. cotton probably destroyed large-scale cotton production in Barbados, cotton production continued in the island on a small scale. Most of it was marketed internally. In 1827, at Lowther, a sugar plantation in Christ Church, 6 percent of total revenues came from cotton, all of which was sold in the island. Presumably, the only way for Barbadian cotton growers to compete with the rapidly expanding U.S. market was to avoid shipping costs.[35]

Why did so many Barbadian planters turn to cotton on lands previously used for canes? The potential returns from cotton on good cane lands with an adequate labor force were never as high as the potential returns from sugar. Managers and overseers based decisions about whether to include cotton in their plantation production strategies on a range of variables, including sugar and cotton prices, droughts, pests, the available labor

---

[32] Lowthers Plantation Annual Financial Abstract, 1756, MSS 43507, Papers of the Duke of Cleveland, British Library.
[33] Starkey, *Economic Geography*, 106.
[34] John Forster Alleyne to George Marsh, October 8, 1801, Alleyne to Richard Henry Smith, October 21, 1801, November 19, 1801, March 17, 1802, Alleyne to Benjamin Storey, March 16, 1802, J. F. Alleyne Letterbook, 1799–1804, WIC/3/ALL, Institute for Commonwealth Studies.
[35] Lowthers Plantation Financial Abstract, 1827, Lowthers Family Papers, MSS 43507, British Library.

supply, recent yields, and whether the sugar works needed to be repaired. Cotton grew well on lands along the sea coast.[36] It was a crop that could be resorted to in case canes were suffering from poor prices or pests, even after the canes had already been planted. Alleyne, for example, told his manager in 1801 that "if the Canes are destroyed in the manner you represent those at Porters [Plantation] to be. We must have Recourse to Cotton from which something may probably be made."[37] Cotton matured more quickly and yielded faster returns than sugar, so a cane field infested with borers could be dug up and replanted with cotton to avoid a complete loss. Rats were also less likely to infest cotton fields. Cotton could be grown on soils where sugar had ceased to generate good returns, and it did not require the expensive processing equipment that sugar did. Corn was more commonly intercropped between the rows of cotton than between the rows of canes, making more use of limited land space, and, although there were concerns about growing sugar and cotton together, no planters complained about growing corn and cotton together in the same field. When sugar works were badly damaged by hurricanes or in need of a major overhaul, cotton was a blessing. The price of slaves and the cost of hiring jobbing gangs for cane holing (common practice on Barbadian sugar plantations) were rising in the last quarter of the eighteenth century, and cotton was a less labor intensive crop.

The combination of cotton and canes on Barbadian plantations became so common by the end of the eighteenth century that in the fall of 1806, the Barbadian Society for the Improvement of Plantership debated at length "the comparative advantages and disadvantages of the combined culture of Canes and Cotton." The key advantage, they argued, was that cotton cultivation could take place on lands distant from the mill, whereas the more distant a cane field was the more labor, time, and livestock would be required to cart canes to the mill. Overall, however, the planters decided that such a juggling act between two cash crops was difficult to maintain and, in most cases, "it was better to pursue that crop solely which appeared to be the most certain."[38]

In the thirteen years from 1788, when cotton was first grown at Seawell, to 1801, when complete financial records for the estate cease, the managers experimented often with cotton. Rather than planting a consistent amount

---

[36] Alleyne to Smith, November 19, 1801, J. F. Alleyne Letterbook, 1799–1804, WIC/3/ALL, Institute for Commonwealth Studies.
[37] Alleyne to Smith, October 21, 1801, J. F. Alleyne Letterbook, 1799–1804, WIC/3/ALL (underlining in original).
[38] *Society for the Improvement of Plantership*, 44.

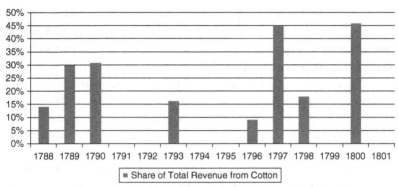

FIGURE 2.7. Share of total revenue from cotton at Seawell, 1788–1801.
Sources: Annual Abstracts from Seawell Plantation, 1788–1801, MS 523/34, 36, 38, 40, 43, 45–46, 49, 51, 54, 58, 62, 66, 74, 78, 83, 87, 91, 95, 99, 101, 103, 109, 115, 127, 137, 141, 145, Newton Family Papers.

every year, they based their land allocation strategies on speculations and rumors about market prices and on soil and labor conditions, on what Alleyne would have called "circumstances." In some years, Seawell produced nothing but sugar. In others, it produced both cotton and canes. The managers never settled on a consistent production strategy, demonstrating how dynamic agricultural production choices could be in the sugar islands. Even during the boom market years for sugar planters, which extended from 1792 to 1799, when the Haitian Revolution and the collapse of St. Domingue drove up sugar prices, Seawell workers continued to tend to large cotton crops (see Figure 2.7).

Cotton production at Seawell was always a secondary activity, but it was not an insignificant one. The Seawell manager even entertained the idea in 1796 that Seawell might profit more if it was turned permanently into a "cotton plantation rather than a Sugar one."[39] Two years later, the manager gave up on the idea, then he tried it once more for the harvest of 1800. During 1796–1797, when there was an unusually large crop of cotton planted and harvested at Seawell, field workers spent 15 percent of their work days on cotton cultivation. It was not necessarily a crop grown to fill the slack periods in the cane cultivation cycle (a role that provision crops or livestock farming could play). There was not a significant degree of complementarity in cane and cotton production. They were harvested at the same time, requiring Seawell overseers to juggle daily

---

[39] "Report on the Lands of Seawell Plantation," MS 523/291, Newton Family Papers.

work assignments, which explains why the Barbadian Society for the Improvement of Plantership expressed concerns about the combination of these crops. Indeed, Sampson Wood, the Newton and Seawell manager, beginning in 1795, found the balancing act exasperating at times. "The worst of planting the two articles Sugar & Cotton on the same Estates," he complained to the owner, "is that the one interferes so much with the other. You cannot employ yourself in both, & each requires attention at the same period."[40] Yet, he continued to plant both crops to get the largest revenues possible from soils that were less than ideal for sugar.

In Jamaica, both Prospect and Somerset Vale slaves juggled primary and secondary cash crops, but at Prospect the plantation managers did little more than dabble with secondary cash crops, spending almost no time on their cultivation. The Somerset Vale slaves, in contrast, spent time cultivating both coffee and canes during 1776–1777, with sugar being the primary crop and coffee the secondary. Just as the second gang specialized in cotton at Seawell, the weaker slaves at Somerset Vale usually cultivated coffee, while the stronger workers toiled in the canes. At Prospect, in 1785, the slaves planted and harvested dyewoods during those months when canes required less attention. Although dyewoods were produced for the market, they were was a distant second in importance to canes, demanding less than 2 percent of the field hand's annual work days. Likewise, in 1787, the managers at Prospect experimented with growing some coffee, a suitable crop for a mountain estate, but they spent only twenty total work days, less than 1 percent, on the slaves' annual labor time on the crop.

Some sugar planters juggled more than just cash crops. The work routines of field workers at Newton and Seawell demonstrated the management's thorough commitment to self-sufficiency. These slaves grew a wide array of provisions and, in total, the cultivation of provisions required 29 to 30 percent of the slaves' work days in 1796–1797, almost as much time as they spent toiling in the canes and only slightly less time than the Mount Vernon hands spent growing corn (see Appendix B, Tables A14–A17). Even during the boom year at Newton, the amount of time slaves spent on provisions remained as high as one-fifth of all work days.

As the evidence from Newton and Seawell shows, Barbadian slaves cultivated provisions as part of their regular work routines, with the controlled pace and close supervision of gang labor. With little spare land, Barbadian planters who tried to raise food for the plantation grew Indian corn, Guinea corn, potatoes, yams, and peas between the rows of

---

[40] Sampson Wood to Thomas Lane, May 3, 1797, MS 523/303, Newton Family Papers.

their canes (on the banks of soil alongside the cane holes), and they cultivated Guinea corn, a hardy crop that required little tending, on whatever land was unsuitable for canes. Intercropping in a cane field helped reduce the need for weeding and reduced soil erosion by providing more roots and ground coverage. Proper crop combinations also helped maintain soil fertility.[41] Moreover, large numbers of slaves could work on different crops in the same field. The managers, overseers, rangers, drivers, and watchmen could see more slaves at once, thereby reducing the need to employ additional supervision or coercive controls. These intercropping strategies were not new innovations. Late seventeenth-century planters in both Barbados and Jamaica grew corn between the rows of their canes, and they thought the intercropped corn offered "great helps" for feeding the slaves.[42] Even on the land-poor island of Barbados, sugar planters sometimes used sugar fields to cultivate provisions on their own. In the late seventeenth century, the Barbadian sugar pioneer Henry Drax, probably borrowing from English crop rotation schemes, argued that rotating sugar and potatoes in poor-quality cane fields would improve the soils.[43]

On the large island of Jamaica, planters adopted a greater variety of provisioning systems than in Barbados, from having slaves grow food on land and during time allotted to them, to relying on gang labor and growing provisions in the cane fields, to purchasing imported provisions, to some mixture of the three. In terms of the amount of time spent on provisions, Somerset Vale in Jamaica in 1776–1777 was strikingly similar to Newton and Seawell. Slaves at Somerset Vale worked regularly as a gang under the overseer's supervision on provisions that were both intercropped with cane and cultivated separately.[44] On some days, "all hands" at Somerset Vale, "planted corn & french Beans in ye young Canes," and, on other days, the field hands were sent to clean or harvest the Plantain

---

[41] Donald Q. Innis, *Intercropping and the Scientific Basis of Traditional Agriculture* (London: Intermediate Technology Publishing, 1997); Matt Liebman and Elizabeth Dyck, "Crop Rotation and Intercropping Strategies for Weed Management," *Ecological Applications* 3, no. 1 (February, 1993), 92–122; John Vandermeer, *The Ecology of Intercropping* (Cambridge, 1992); Laura S. Meitzner and Martin L. Price, *Amaranth to Zai Holes: Ideas for Growing Food under Difficult Conditions* (North Fort Myers, FL: ECHO, 1996), 141–145; Thomas A. Lyson and Rick Welsh, "The Production Function, Crop Diversity, and the Debate between Conventional and Sustainable Agriculture," *Rural Sociology* 58.3 (Fall 1993), 424–439.

[42] Peter Thompson, "Henry Drax's Instructions on the Management of a Seventeenth-Century Barbadian Plantation," *William and Mary Quarterly* 3rd ser. 86.3 (2009), 586; Cary Heylar to William Heylar, March 18, 1689/1690, Heylar Manuscripts.

[43] Thompson, "Henry Drax's Instructions," 585.

[44] Somerset Vale Work Logs, 1776–1780, Codex Eng 180.

walk or fields full of yams. On approximately 70 of the 311 working days in 1776–1777, the Somerset Vale workers tended to provisions as part of their regular plantation work routine. In addition, every Sunday, the overseer noted that the slaves were "in their Grounds," tending to their own crops.[45] At Prospect, by contrast, the managers invested almost none of the gang's regular work routine in provisions – between 1 and 2 percent of their time in 1785, 1787, and 1791. Instead, the managers purchased provisions or made the workers grow their own and focused on sugar production. They cultivated enough to account for emergencies in supply.

Early modern sugar plantations were highly flexible business entities. There was a continuum in sugar production from monocultural estates that grew nothing but canes and focused their labor on that crop (while importing anything that was needed) to estates that practiced multicropping, growing a wide array of provisions with gang regular labor and adopting secondary cash crops. These production schemes, as the production of cotton at Seawell suggests, were constantly changing, depending on circumstances. Management decisions about secondary crops, about provision crops, or about the degree to which the final sugar product was refined or made into rum depended on both external market and internal production factors, indicating the adaptability of plantation production schemes and the responsiveness of planters. At Turner's Hall, in the interior of Barbados, for example, the planters reduced the acreage under sugar cultivation during the American Revolution and reallocated that land and labor to growing provisions. In 1770, they had spent £285 on corn imports, but by 1777, despite inflation and the skyrocketing price of provisions, they spent only £10 on corn, growing the rest within the estate. After the Revolution, the Turner's Hall managers reallocated some of the corn land and labor to sugar, but they did not return entirely to prewar productions schemes, preferring the safety that came with continuing to grow some provisions on the estate.[46] Likewise, after the Revolution, Barbadian planter George Brathwaite explained, "Upon my estates in the year 1774, upon an Apprehension of Distress, I reduced the Quantity of Acres in Sugar by Sixty Acres to sow it with Corn; and I had the satisfaction to find that my Negroes experienced no distress."[47] Planters grew more provisions when it seemed likely that the supply would be hindered.[48]

---

[45] Ibid.
[46] Abstract of Accounts, 1770–1793, E20680-E20700, Fitzherbert Papers.
[47] British Sessional Papers, Commons, Accounts and Papers, 1789, Part III, 94.
[48] Justin Roberts, "Uncertain Business: A Case Study of Barbadian Plantation Management, 1770–1793," *Slavery & Abolition* 32.2 (June 2011), 247–248.

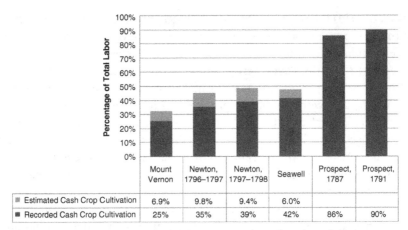

FIGURE 2.8. Cash crop production as a percentage of total work days.
Note: This chart shows calculations for cultivation tasks that were clearly cash crop, as well as calculations for unspecified tasks that were probably cash crop.
Sources: See Appendix B, Tables A4–A12.

As the work routines on these estates show, the amount of time devoted to cash crop production could vary considerably. At Mount Vernon, in total, the slaves spent less than a third and, perhaps, as little as a quarter of their total work days producing cash crops. Sugar slaves at Newton and Seawell spent only slightly more of their time working on cash crops. At Newton, field hands devoted as little as one-third and no more than one-half of their time to cash crops (see Figure 2.8). At Seawell, the juggling of canes and cotton led to slightly more time being devoted to cash crops, but it was still less than half of all work days. By comparison, the amount of time spent on cash crop cultivation at Prospect is remarkable (see Figure 2.8). The Prospect field workers spent approximately 90 percent of their time on cash crops. Multicropping systems of sugar production were not necessarily less profitable. Newton, for example, had an enormous profit of £4,655 in 1798.[49] The difference between Newton or Seawell and Prospect was not necessarily a Barbadian versus Jamaican scheme of production either. The evidence from Somerset Vale in Jamaica is not as detailed as it is from Newton and Seawell, but it does show slaves

---

[49] Newton Plantation Financial Abstract, 1797, and Newton Plantation Financial Abstract, 1797, MS 523/113,125, Newton Family Papers.

cultivating sugar as a primary crop, coffee as a secondary crop, and a variety of provision crops as part of their regular gang labors.

BREAKING GROUND

Breaking the soil to get the crop into the ground demanded significant force and exertion from slaves in both the Chesapeake and the Caribbean. Of all the specific jobs done during an annual sugar cycle, the most arduous was cane holing, followed closely by the various tasks associated with making and distributing manure. Harvest work, despite its long days, was a distant third in sheer work intensity. Cane holing demanded an enormous share of the field hands daily labor on Caribbean sugar plantations. It was among the most backbreaking of all tasks performed by slaves in the Americas. Most contemporaries agreed that it contributed to the high mortality and morbidity rates on sugar plantations.[50] Planters with sufficient revenue tried to reduce the demands of holing on their slaves by hiring jobbing gangs of slaves from outside the estate to do a share of the task. In Chesapeake grain cultivation, plows, guided by slaves with sufficient upper-body strength and drawn by livestock, helped to reduce the physical exertion required of slaves in breaking the soil.

Holing the ground for cane was normally a task performed by only the strongest and most able on an estate, and these people were sometimes referred to as "the holing gang" or "the holers."[51] Plantation manuals warned mangers to be careful not to overtax slaves while digging cane holes.[52] Dry soils could make the job seem nearly impossible. After a long stint without rain, a Jamaican planter and attorney found the ground "so hard a Hoe would not enter it."[53] In dry weather, another Jamaican insisted, the best soils often acquired "the hardness of a brick."[54]

In Barbados, the Newton manager complained one year that the regular period of holing and planting had been "so void of moisture that People could not get a third of the crop in the ground" during these months, which had upset the delicate timing of the sugar cycle.[55] Some soils were naturally

---

[50] Dickson, *Mitigation of Slavery*, 164.
[51] David Collins, *Practical Rules for the Management and Medical Treatment of Negro Slaves in the Sugar Colonies* (London: J. Barfield, 1803), 178.
[52] Samuel Martin, *An Essay Upon Plantership*, 4th ed. (London: Samuel Chapman, 1765), 3.
[53] Simon Taylor to Sir Chalenor Arcedeckne, September 9, 1782, Vanneck-Arc/3A/1782/ 36.
[54] Mathison, *Notices Respecting Jamaica*, 37.
[55] Sampson Wood to Thomas Lane, May 3, 1797, MS 523/303, Newton Family Papers.

hard and stiff, and plantation manuals warned that, on these soils, the planters needed to avoid long spells of holing by alternating the task with "easier work" or the slaves would wear out.[56] The years slaves spent digging cane holes left their toll. The majority of slave skeletons from Newton Plantation show widespread levels of arthritic joint degeneration of the thoracic vertebrae and knees, suggesting the kinds of wear and tear that would come from the heavy stooped labor of digging holes.[57]

Several stages of labor went into digging cane holes. Most holes were dug between September and November, during the wetter months of the year, but it was a task that could be done at any time of year. The ground would have been easier to break in the wet months. Planters began by having two slaves carefully measure and lay out a grid pattern on a field. After a grid had been lined on the field, prime field hands started digging holes – four feet by five feet was a common measurement – in the center of each square. The lining and the gang system went hand in hand, allowing planters to more efficiently extract labor from the gangs by controlling and dictating the slaves' pace and workload. According to one planter, "by lining the land before it is hoe-ploughed, each negro may have an equal share to dig."[58] Stragglers faced the whip. This planter's emphasis on a standardized task was common during the improvement era. It was part of the project of making the labor process more predictable and uniform and making the workers into interchangeable elements of production. While the holes were being dug, the dirt was carefully molded into banks on either side of the squares. Then the holes were made a little deeper through a process called "cross-holeing," and this extra dirt was piled on the top and bottom of the squares.[59] Planters debated, almost endlessly, the best size and depth of these holes and the distance between them. The number of holes a slave was expected to dig in a day varied with the size of the holes. A Jamaican suggested that the standard was approximately 100 holes per slave per day.[60] Using nothing more than hand tools, an

---

[56] Patrick Kein, *An Essay upon Pen-Keeping and Plantership* (Kingston, Jamaica: His Majesty's Printing Office, 1796), 20f.

[57] Kristrina A Shuler, "Health, History, and Sugar: A Bioarchaeological Study of Enslaved Africans from Newton Plantation, Barbados, West Indies" (Ph.D. Dissertation, Southern Illinois University, Carbondale, 2005), 302.

[58] Kein, *Pen-Keeping and Plantership*, 46.

[59] Joseph Galloway, *Sugar Cane Industry: An Historical Geography from its Origins to 1914* (New York: Cambridge University Press, 1989), 100–102, and Thomas Kerr, *A Practical Treatise on the Cultivation of the Sugar Cane and the Manufacture of Sugar* (London: J.J. Griffin & Company, 1851), 17–19.

[60] H. T. De La Beche, *Notes on the Present Condition of the Negroes in Jamaica* (London: T Cadell in the Strand, 1825), 6.

individual slave would dig and move between 640 and 1,500 cubic feet of earth in a day of holing.[61]

Digging cane holes required more days from the slaves than any other single task in the sugar cycle, especially in the older islands of Antigua and Barbados, where planters relied less heavily on ratooning than in Jamaica and where planters paid more attention to careful holing to avoid soil erosion. According to the Barbadian Society for the Improvement of Plantership, if first-gang hands on a large sugar estate dug cane holes without the assistance of other gangs, it would require 9–10 percent of their annual work days.[62] Because they advocated a greater reliance on ratoon canes and a lower ratio of cane acreage per hand, the amount of time slaves spent holing at Newton and Seawell was sometimes higher than the Society suggested. Digging and clearing cane holes and cross-holing required 10–18 percent of the first gang's annual labors at Newton and Seawell. No other specific agricultural task required more work on these plantations.[63]

In Jamaica, instead of relying on a Barbadian cane holing grid with square holes, slaves often dug longer and broader trenches in rows into which the canes were put.[64] Trenches required less labor to dig, clear, and keep tidy but made less-efficient use of the land because soil erosion was more likely and because there was less room for food crops to be grown around the cane plants. It was easier to apply the plow to trenching. Indeed, although the plow never gained much popularity in Barbados, it appears to have been adopted by many planters in Jamaica in the 1770s and 1780s as a potential labor-saving device and an ameliorative strategy to lessen the slaves' workload in their most onerous task. The plow fell into disuse in Jamaica after the 1780s. Planters decided it was not appropriate for Caribbean planting conditions.[65]

Jamaicans spent slightly less time than Barbadians digging cane holes because they tended to allow canes to regrow from their stump rather than

---

[61] Higman, *Slave Populations of the British Caribbean*, 162.
[62] *Society for the Improvement of Plantership*, 11–13.
[63] Newton Work Log, 1796–1798 and Seawell Work Log, 1796–1797, MS 523/110, 111, 123, Newton Family Papers.
[64] "The Cultivation and Manufacture of Sugar in America," *The London Magazine: The Gentleman's Monthly Intelligencer* 38 (June 1769), 319; J.B. Moreton, *West India Customs and Manners: Strictures on the Soil, Cultivation, Produce, Trade, Officers and Inhabitants with the Method of Establishing and Conducting a Sugar Plantation to which is Added the Practice of Training New Slaves*, rev. ed. (London: J. Parsons; W. Richardson; H. Gardner; and J. Walter, 1793), 43–44.
[65] Ward, "Amelioration of British West Indian Slavery."

replant them. At Prospect, slaves were "holing" on some days and "trenching" on others. Occasionally, the task was recorded as "trenching and holing." The two terms were sometimes used synonymously in Jamaica but, given the attempt to differentiate between the two on days in which they were both performed, planters at Prospect probably used both systems of digging cane holes. The type of hole being dug depended on, among many factors, the gradient of the fields, the degree of exposure to the elements, the amount of labor available, and the quality of the soil.[66] Barbadian-style cane holes were particularly useful for preventing soil erosion on steep ground. In total, field hands at Prospect spent between 5 and 11 percent of their annual labor holing and trenching for canes. Although the logs do not allow for more detailed analysis, the first-gang Prospect slaves almost certainly specialized in cane hole digging and spent slightly more time on the task. Like Prospect, Somerset Vale relied heavily on ratoon cane. Somerset Vale field workers spent approximately 11 percent of their total work time digging cane holes, approximately the same amount of time the task took at Prospect.

The optimum size of a holing gang during the holing season appears to have been between thirty and fifty workers.[67] If the great gang was larger than fifty slaves, planters tended to divide the great gang and assign the weaker laborers beyond the first fifty slaves to other tasks. The optimum size of a holing gang may have been determined by how many slaves could be effectively supervised by a single driver and how many slaves could be made to work efficiently as a unit. The size may have also been determined by the amount of labor required to hole an acre, giving the gang a task that could be completed in a day. Contemporary estimates of how many slaves it took to hole an acre of cane in a day were reasonably consistent, ranging from twenty-five to thirty-six depending on the land, the number of holes per acre, the location, and the number of newly imported and untrained African workers in the gang.[68] These estimates accord with the average

---

[66] Clement Caines, *Letters on the Cultivation of the Otaheite cane: the manufacture of sugar and rum; the saving of melasses; the care and preservation of stock; with the attention and anxiety which is due to Negroes: To these topics are added, a few other particulars analogous to the subject of the letters; and also a speech on the slave trade, the most important feature in West Indian cultivation* (London: Messrs. Robinson, 1801), 45–46.

[67] Newton Work Logs, 1796–1798 and Seawell Work Log, 1796–1797 and 1798, MS 523/110, 111, 122, 123, Newton Family Papers; Prospect Plantation Journals 1785 and 1787–1793, 0627-0017 and 0627-0019.

[68] De La Beche, *Present Condition of the Negroes in Jamaica*, 6; Belgrove, *A Treatise upon Husbandry or Planting*, 4; Dickson, *Mitigation of Slavery*, 263; James Ramsay, *An Essay on the Treatment and Conversion of African Slaves in the British Sugar Colonies* (London:

amount of time it took to accomplish these tasks at Prospect, Newton, and Seawell. At Prospect, it took an average of thirty-two work days per acre to dig cane holes for plant canes. At Newton, first-gang hands spent thirty-seven work days per acre of young cane holing the ground. At Seawell, it took twenty-five first-gang work days per acre of young cane, about five to ten days less than most contemporary estimates. The annual accounts show that no slaves were hired from off the estate to dig holes in 1796 or 1797 to do holing work, but it is possible that some of the holing work for the 1797 crop was done before or after the one-year log was recorded. It is also possible that the Seawell gang was particularly adept at holing, that they were being driven faster, or that the ground was easier to penetrate.[69]

The amount of time required to dig cane holes was remarkably consistent across Caribbean sugar plantations, indicating that slaves were working at a similar pace and consistency throughout the sugar islands. Some planters would reduce the speed at which holing was done when slaves were short on provisions or when epidemics threatened the plantation. A reduced pace in cane holing was also one of the many ameliorative strategies with which planters experimented. Thomas Barritt, the attorney at Pleasant Hill and at Phillipsfield in St. Thomas in the East in Jamaica, assured the owner that the slaves had "not been pressed too much in holing last year, for we took great time in doing what was done in that way." Significantly, Barritt allayed the concerns of the owner for only this one task – the most onerous on a sugar plantation.[70]

Holing the ground was so destructive to the health of field workers and required so much labor for brief periods of time that planters with adequate revenues or planters who were shorthanded in labor would often hire specialized groups of slaves or "jobbing gangs" from off the estate to hole at least some of their acreage. One Barbadian plantation manual recommended that an average-sized estate with sixty field hands should try to cultivate 160 acres of cane and that the planter should, in order to grow that much cane, factor in the expense of getting "twenty acres of land holed for canes by hired labor."[71] Whereas jobbing gangs were regularly relied on to make up deficiencies in the labor supply, they were not hired as often during the cane harvest, another period of intensive

T. Walker, C. Jenkin, R. Marchbank, L. White, R. Burton, P. Byrne, 1784), 119; *Society for the Improvement of Plantership*, 12.

[69] Seawell Annual Abstracts for 1796 and 1797, MS 523/ 109, 115, Newton Family Papers.
[70] Thomas Barritt to Nathaniel Phillips, February 8, 1792, MS8388, Slebech Papers.
[71] Edwin Lascelles et al., *Instructions for the Management of a Plantation in Barbadoes. And for the Treatment of Negroes, etc., etc., etc.* (London: [s.n.], 1786), 6.

labor in the cane cultivation cycle. The primary work of holing could be done only by strong and mature hands, and these slaves were in limited supply. In contrast, planters could rely on a larger proportion of the population to cut and mill sugar. Without the assistance of jobbing gangs, holing would be slowed considerably, the work might be poorly done, and mortality and morbidity rates would be higher. In contrast, during the harvest, it was more common for planters to purchase new slaves than to hire them.[72] Even in their weakened state, suffering from the effects of the middle passage and trying to acclimatize to the plantations, new slaves could be put to work in the harvest.

With the shift to grain and the adoption of the plow in the Chesapeake, field hands were increasingly able to avoid the strenuous work of holing fields with hand held hoes. Much of the labor involved in breaking the soil for planting was transferred to draft animals. At Mount Vernon, almost one in five of the slaves' work days were spent plowing the soil to prepare it for cultivating, suggesting that, although the work may have been easier with a plow, the task of plowing still required – because of the increasing amount of acreage being cultivated with the switch to grain – a large share of the slaves' annual labor. On tobacco fields, slaves were able to work around tree stumps or extensive roots as they planted by hand. In some ways, the switch to plowing alleviated the slaves' burden, but it also increased it. With plowing and the switch to grains, slaves needed to spend more time clearing trees, bushes, and roots for large and level grain fields that could accommodate a plow. Deep plowing, adopted by many planters in the region, penetrated the soil to a greater depth than ever before. The combination of more extensive clearing and greater soil penetration that came with the new system of plowing and grain agriculture caused extensive soil depletion; in turn, the soil depletion forced planters to manure more extensively to maintain crop yields.[73]

---

[72] See, for example, Lauchr. McLaine to John Taylor, January 28, 1801 and February 13, 1801; John Beaufin Irving to John Taylor, February 10, 1801, series XIII, box 59, folder 10, Powell Collection, Historical Society of Pennsylvania.

[73] Lorena S. Walsh, "Land Use, Settlement Patterns and the Impact of European Agriculture, 1620–1820," in Philip D. Curtin et al., eds., *Discovering the Chesapeake: The History of an Ecosystem* (Baltimore: Johns Hopkins University Press, 2001), 242; Earle Carville, and Ronald Hoffman, "The Ecological Consequences of Agrarian Reform in the Chesapeake, 1730–1840," in Curtin et al., *Discovering the Chesapeake: The History of an Ecosystem* (Baltimore: Johns Hopkins University Press, 2001).

TENDING THE CROP

Although holing or plowing, planting or seeding, and harvesting the crops were the key phases in the agricultural cycle, the crops required nurturing between these phases to ensure a strong yield. The Caribbean climate was particularly conducive to the growth of grasses such as sugar cane. Weeds, however, found those same conditions ideal. Cleaning the bushes and unwanted vegetation or weeds that sprang up in and around crop fields was a major concern for all planters. Unwanted vegetation choked the cash crops, threatening profits. Weeding and cleaning fields made the labor demands of annual crop cycles more constant. Weeding was not an essential task, like holing or harvesting, but planters believed that "timely" and thorough weeding could make the difference between a mediocre crop and a great one. Without weeding, crops could still grow but if this tedious and time-consuming task was neglected, one plantation manual warned, "the grand and very arduous labour of ploughing, holing, and planting, is in a great measure defeated."[74] One agricultural writer argued that Jamaican planters, trying to maximize profit, would often grow more cane than their laborers could properly weed, which robbed the planter of his returns. The opportunity costs of the labor lost in trying to combat so many weeds were severe. Routine plantation maintenance or provision cultivation would have to be sacrificed in favor of weeding. With "overplanting," the weeds would choke the fields and everything on the plantation would suffer as the slaves struggled to keep the crops clean.[75] Weeds had been the bane of British Caribbean sugar planters since the rise of sugar plantations in Barbados. A seventeenth-century Barbadian planter insisted to his manager that when weeds appeared he must "leave all worke what ever & goe to weeding."[76]

The amount of time devoted to weeding on sugar plantations varied considerably. At Prospect, slaves waged a constant war on weeds through most of 1785. The estate was young, and slaves were still struggling to carve cane fields out of the mountainside, battling local vegetation as they transformed the ecosystem. Weeding the cane fields at Prospect required one-fifth of all the slaves' work days, twice as much annual labor as holing and trenching canes that year. The amount of time they spent weeding that

---

[74] Kein, *Pen-Keeping and Plantership*, 85.
[75] Nicholas Robson, *Hints for a General View of the Agricultural State of St. James in the Island of Jamaica* (London, 1796), 26.
[76] Thompson, "Henry Drax's Instructions," 591.

year probably represents the upper limit for a sugar plantation. Over time, the weeds required less cleaning and clearing. In 1787, the Prospect slaves spent just 15 percent of their time weeding, and by 1791 this task required only 3 percent of work days. When planters relied on intercropping of provisions and canes in multicropping estates, they could better restrict the growth of weeds but the task still required a significant share of annual labor.[77] At Somerset Vale, a multicropping plantation, slaves were often listed as "Cleaning Corn & Cane" on a given field because the crops were mixed together on the same ground. The records do not allow for a more precise estimate of how much weeding was done at Somerset Vale. At Newton and Seawell, in 1796–1797, where multicropping and intercropping were practiced extensively, the slaves weeded both the canes and the provisions as part of their regular gang labors. In total, on these two plantations, enslaved workers spent approximately 15 percent of their work year weeding the various crops.

Because of its size, there was far less time invested in weeding per acre at Mount Vernon, but the slaves spent only slightly less time each year cleaning the fields than their Caribbean counterparts. According to the farm reports, the Mount Vernon field hands were actually "weeding" crops for less than 1 percent of their days, but they were often hard at work on related tasks such as "grubbing" or clearing and burning bushes, brush, and briars. It was bushes rather than grasses that plagued the Virginian planter. Approximately one in ten work days performed by Mount Vernon field hands involved some form of field cleaning and clearing. Much of this time was spent grubbing in roads or to expand the estate's cultivated fields into "new grounds." On one particular outlying farm, Muddy Hole, the field hands spent a vast share of their time, almost a fifth of work days, clearing fields. Most of their work was done in new ground.

Weeding was tedious but manuring could be deadly. Field hands on Caribbean and Chesapeake plantations of the late eighteenth century spent a larger share of their time than they ever had before working with livestock and with the essential dung that the stock provided. Dung was a key tool in the agricultural improvement movement, particularly in Virginia and Barbados. Manure maintained the soil quality in two of the oldest colonies in the British Americas. In Jamaica, field hands on sugar plantations spent much less time caring for livestock and less time making and distributing manure. Although many Jamaican planters championed the value of dung in maintaining the island's soils, the lands had not been as intensively cultivated

---

[77] Seawell Work Log, 1796–1797, MS 523/111, Newton Family Papers.

for as many years as they had in the Chesapeake and Barbados. Jamaican planters could rely more on the quality of the soil alone to yield a good crop.[78] There was, however, more livestock in Jamaica than in Barbados or Virginia. Livestock husbandry tended to be separate from the sugar plantation. By the 1770s, almost every large Jamaican sugar plantation had a satellite operation, known as a "pen," for raising stock.[79]

Historians have a tendency to skirt "timidly around the dung pile," ignoring its importance in early modern agriculture.[80] Plantation managers could not afford to make that mistake. In *Sugar Cane* (1764), the poet James Grainger advised prospective planters to learn to enjoy the thought and sight of "old fat dung."[81] Fallowing, one of the most common forms of soil management in England, and in the Chesapeake in tobacco cultivation, never gained much popularity in the Caribbean. Planters feared that fallow land was too liable to be "baked by the sun."[82] They relied on crop combinations or rotations to manage the soil, and dunging became a crucial part of sustainable plantation agriculture. Dung from the pens and a mixture of other soil improvement agents like marl, lime, sand, seaweed, rags, animal bones, cane tops, and crop "trash" or debris brought new life to cane fields and maintained or improved crop yields.[83]

Dunging was particularly important to the sugar industry in the Lesser Antilles, where, by the late eighteenth century, most of the cane fields had

---

[78] Kein, *Pen-Keeping and Plantership*, 26.
[79] Philip D. Morgan, "Slaves and Livestock in Eighteenth-Century Jamaica, Vineyard Pen, 1750–1751," *William and Mary Quarterly* 52.1 (1995), 47–76; Verene A. Shepherd, "Livestock and Sugar: Aspects of Jamaica's Agricultural Development from the Late Seventeenth to the Early Nineteenth Century," *The Historical Journal* 34.3 (September 1991), 634.
[80] Donald Woodward, "An Essay on Manures: Changing Attitudes to Fertilization in England, 1500–1800" in John Chartes and David Hays, eds., *English Rural Society, 1500–1800: Essays in Honour of Joan Thirsk* (New York: Cambridge University Press, 1990), 252.
[81] James Grainger, "Sugar Cane: A Poem in Four Books," in Thomas Krise, ed., *Caribbeana: An Anthology of English Literature of the West Indies, 1657–1777* (Chicago: University of Chicago Press, 1999), 180.
[82] Martin, *Essay Upon Plantership*, 4th ed., 62.
[83] David Watts, *The West Indies: Patterns of Development, Culture, and Environmental Change since 1492* (Cambridge: Cambridge University Press, 1987), 396–404; Richard Grove, *Green Imperialism: Colonial Expansion, Tropical Island Edens, and the Origins of Environmentalism, 1600–1860* (New York: Cambridge University Press, 1995), 5, 116–120; Martin, *Essay Upon Plantership*, 4th ed., 15; Eltis, *Rise of African Slavery*, 202; Harry J. Carman, *American Husbandry* (New York: Columbia University Press [1775] 1939), 417; Grainger, *Sugar Cane*, 180; J.R. Ward, *British West Indian Slavery, 1750–1834: The Process of Amelioration* (New York: Oxford University Press, 1988), 75.

been regularly tilled for well over a century. Dunging was used on Barbadian sugar plantations as early as the 1650s, but their reliance on the fertilizing agent grew over time. In the early eighteenth century, some proprietors in Barbados went so far as to manage dung farms, raising stock solely for their dung and selling the produce to surrounding planters.[84] By the mid-eighteenth century, Barbadian planters were insisting that "Dung" was "the article upon which the success of Crop almost intirely depends."[85] In 1801, John Forster Alleyne, a member of the most prominent family of planters in Barbados and the owner of three sugar plantations, continued to call "Dung ... the most essential Point in the Management of an Estate." He warned his manager to be sure to manure all crops.[86] Planting had been reduced, in large part, to how much dung the slaves could get to the crops.

Hauling manure was a brutal task and slaves were expected to haul increasingly larger loads of manure in the improvement era. Dung baskets could weigh as much as eighty pounds each.[87] According to Dickson, the "most laborious tasks of the negroes" were "*holing* land and *turning* or carrying out dung."[88] David Collins, a Caribbean physician and the author of a slave management guide, thought that carrying dung over long distances or steep terrain was "The source of more racking and incurable pains in the stomach, than every other species of plantation labour united."[89] Another Barbadian manager agreed that carrying dung "is almost the hardest work they have."[90] The dung basket was the source of some of the greatest tensions in Caribbean plantation management. Planters had to strike a balance between asking too much of their labor force or giving too little to the soil. Planters and overseers recommended an array of solutions to lighten the slaves' labor loads, from fly-penning to wheelbarrows, without reducing the amount of dung. "I am ever studying the case," Sampson Wood promised the owner of Newton.[91]

---

[84] Starkey, *Economic Geography of Barbados*, 8–9.
[85] Belgrove, *Treatise upon Husbandry or Planting*, 6.
[86] John Forster Alleyne to Richard Henry Smith, September 20, 1801, J. F. Alleyne Letterbook, 1799–1804, WIC/3/All.
[87] Ibid., 164.
[88] William Dickson, *Letters on Slavery: To which are added, addresses to the whites, and to the free Negroes of Barbadoes; and accounts of some Negroes eminent for their virtues and abilities* (Westport: Negro Universities Press, [1789] 1970), 22.
[89] Caines, *Cultivation of the Otaheite Cane*, 27; Kein, *Pen-Keeping and Plantership*, 59.
[90] Sampson Wood to Thomas Lane, October 15, 1797, MS 523/322, Newton Family Papers.
[91] Kein, *Pen-Keeping and Plantership*, 59; Sampson Wood to Thomas Lane, October 15, 1797; MS 523/322, Newton Family Papers.

Agricultural Diversity and Seasonal Patterns of Work 115

To throw out dung, slaves marched back and forth from dung piles to the canes in long lines, carrying dung in baskets on their heads. The number, size, and location of dung piles or stock pens varied. The distance of the dung from the cane field made a difference in how many work days it took to carry and in how hard the task was for slaves. The gang's movement patterns and work pace during dunging were controlled by the driver just as they were in other field tasks. Slaves moved, ideally, at the same speed in the line and each slave carried the same amount of dung in his or her basket. It was part of the project of standardizing work to improve labor discipline and make the labor output more constant and predictable. Some planters had two gangs work interdependently on this task when they reached the field "so that the [second gang] may follow and cover up the dung as fast as the [first gang] throw it out."[92] Some plantation manuals advised their readers to lessen the load by never asking slaves to carry rain-soaked dung.[93] Others insisted that the dung worked best when it was wet, with little thought to the heavier loads. Dunging, one author insisted, should always be done "in rainy weather."[94]

Dung piles were regularly turned to help them rot, adding to the slaves' workload. In Barbados, turning dung and carrying it to the fields, like cane holing, was a task normally reserved exclusively for the strongest workers. In total, first-gang workers at Newton and Seawell spent 2 percent of their days turning dung. Slaves also gathered dung in baskets and "bedded" the growing crops as part of the regular cultivation cycle, and they transported and cast manure more generally over the lands. This process of throwing dung onto the fields was the hardest for slaves. The first-gang workers at Newton and Seawell spent a total of 12 percent of their days throwing dung onto the fields. Far from being a minor task, this distribution of dung occupied more work days at Seawell (917) in 1796–1797 than cutting canes (908).

Just as Barbadian planters hired gangs to assist in holing the land, they also hired gangs, although far less often, for "Throwing out Dung" onto the fields.[95] The task, like holing, was demanding enough that planters were either unable to find enough prime hands on their estates to distribute as much dung as they wanted or they recognized the negative effects of

---

[92] Lascelles et al., *Management of a Plantation*, 9.
[93] Dickson, *Mitigation of Slavery*, 164.
[94] Gordon Turnbull, *Letters to a Young Planter; Or Observations on the Management of a Sugar Plantation* (London: Stuart and Stevenson, 1785), 7.
[95] Turners Hall Financial Abstracts for 1785, 1787, and 1789, E20699, E20698, E20696, Fitzherbert Collection.

distributing dung on the health of their laborers. Jobbing gangs were also used for throwing out dung because it was the kind of work that could be done piece rate. A set amount of dung could be distributed over a specific number of acres. Some planters, for example, advocated one basket per cane hole immediately after holing.

Unlike their Barbadian counterparts, the Prospect slaves spent very little time manuring. In 1785, 1787, and 1791, the slaves carried dung to the fields for less than 1 percent of their work days. Prospect, as a young estate, may have been atypical in this respect. Jamaican authors of plantation management guides did emphasize the importance of regular manuring, if not as emphatically as Barbadians. The difference between the amount of manuring at Seawell or Newton and the amount at Prospect demonstrates the wide range of possibilities in sugar cultivation. On the older estates, spread across the long and intensively cultivated Barbadian landscape, dunging was among the most important tasks in the annual cultivation cycle. On younger estates in new sugar frontiers, such as Prospect in the northeastern mountains of Jamaica, weeding and clearing the lands required massive work commitments but dunging was almost unnecessary.

Manuring was important to the agricultural cycle at Mount Vernon, where much of the soil was thin or exhausted, but it still did not require nearly as much time as it did in Barbados. Including time spent generally carting and hauling manure and the time spent delivering the fertilizer to a specific crop, meadow, or new ground, slaves at Mount Vernon were working with manure for only 3 percent of their work days. The stock-drawn plows in the Chesapeake made the delivery of dung to the fields a little easier, lessening the work load for slaves. Over the course of the day, draft animals would also leave at least some of their dung in the field. Chesapeake planters relied more heavily than their Caribbean counterparts on carts drawn by the stock to deliver dung, which saved even more human labor. Washington witnessed how much manure Barbadian planters were using during a visit to the island in 1751 and he would, ideally, have preferred that his slaves spend more time manuring, but he complained to his manager that "Manure can not be had in the abundance the fields require." Mount Vernon, which was more than twenty times the size of even a large sugar plantation, was simply too vast for concentrated manuring.[96]

---

[96] George Washington to William Pearce, December 18, 1793, in Fitzpatrick, ed., *Writings of Washington*, 33, 188; Richard B. Goddard, ed. *George Washington's Visit to Barbados, 1751*. (Wildey, St. Michael, Barbados: Cole's Printery Ltd, 1997).

Agricultural Diversity and Seasonal Patterns of Work 117

To revive the fields with manure, planters in the Chesapeake and on older islands in the Caribbean had to become more involved in animal husbandry on the plantations themselves. In 1765, an Antiguan planter noted that Barbadians, "in particular," kept large quantities of livestock because the fields needed "plenty of dung."[97] In 1775, the author of *American Husbandry* argued that "the [Chesapeake] planters are obliged, on account of manure, to keep great stock."[98] Livestock had their drawbacks. They trampled the soil, which could not then absorb as much moisture, which in turn led to increased soil erosion. Unless contained or kept under close supervision, large stock could also damage growing crops.[99] Livestock also brought many benefits. Cattle, mules, or horses provided locomotive power to help slaves transport harvested crops, and they provided much-needed fertilizer.

At Prospect, where manure was less essential, the regular field hands did little work with the stock. Normally, seven or eight of the field hands served as mulemen during the harvest but, rather than being keepers of the stock, these mulemen were, essentially, cart drivers, bringing canes to the mill. As the plantation expanded and more canes were cultivated in 1787 and 1791, the number of slaves serving as mulemen and carrying canes to the mill increased to twelve. Such a task was not necessarily part of animal husbandry as much as it was transport work. Prospect slaves also tended and gathered grass to feed livestock and built pens but, at most, the field workers spent only 6 percent of their days tending to livestock. Newton and Seawell used field hands for the same purpose, but the work of carting canes to the mill took only 1–2 percent of work days on those plantations because they cultivated less canes and the terrain was easier to navigate.

Because of the increasing numbers of livestock necessary for plowing, Chesapeake planters were applying more of their labor resources to clearing and cleaning pasture, growing fodder, and building fences. On large estates, the care of livestock could become an enormous undertaking, and overseers often found it difficult to take the slaves away from crops to accomplish work for the livestock, such as clearing adequate pasture lands. In 1778, William Lee, an absentee owner of a property near Richmond, Virginia, had few directions for his overseer about how to manage the plantation other than "in general I wish to have as much of the swampy

---

[97] Martin, *Essay upon Plantership*, 4th ed., 7.
[98] Carman, *American Husbandry*, 190.
[99] Watts, *West Indies*, 117, 119, and 126.

lands as possible made into Timothy Meadow" and "instead of sellg. any Hay or Fodder, I think they will be more beneficially imployed in increasing & supporting well a Large Stock of Cattle & Sheep." Four years later, after repeating his suggestions a few times, the meadow was still a swamp and Lee had grown frustrated. "This shd. be the grand object at present," he told his brother, "even to ye. Partial neglect of Crops of Tobacco." Still waiting three months later, he tried a more direct order: "3 or 4 proper Fellows, or more of necessary, shd. be kept Constantly employ'd in Ditching, Draining & Clearing ye. Swamp."[100] The increasingly diversified production on large Virginian estates was not without its drawbacks. It could become a juggling act, as exasperating as it was beneficial.

Once ground was cleared, Chesapeake planters had to fence the land to keep wild or feral animals out and livestock in or to concentrate manure on a particular spot.[101] With the ever-expanding acreage needed for growing grains, planters found it difficult to find sufficient labor to spend as much time on fencing as was ideal. In 1775, the author of *American Husbandry* criticized Chesapeake planters because, compared to farms in England, Chesapeake "fences are extremely incomplete and kept in very bad order."[102] Fencing was among the most labor intensive tasks at Mount Vernon. Field hands at Mount Vernon spent almost one in every ten work days making and repairing fences. The cultivation of fodder, grasses, and meadow ground increased the labor demands of livestock care even further, requiring another 2 percent of annual labor. Finally, the direct work of animal husbandry (including tasks such as hauling feed to the mules, horses, and cattle; castrating or slaughtering stock; capturing wayward animals; or repairing and building barns, pens, and shelters) required an additional 4 percent of annual labor at Mount Vernon. In total, the work of fencing, cultivating fodder crops or pasturage, feeding and minding the stock, and maintaining shelters took nearly a quarter (22 percent) of the field hand's work days, demonstrating the commitment to animal husbandry as a central part of Mount Vernon's mixed farming operation.

Barbadian planters were not normally as deeply invested in animal husbandry as large Chesapeake planters, but they were certainly more

---

[100] William Lee to Mr. Ellis, June 24, 1778, Mss1 L51f 416, section 115, William Lee's Letterbook, August 1777 to June 1778; William Lee to [Richard Henry Lee], July 12, 1782 and William Lee to Richard Henry Lee, October 1, 1782, William Lee's Letterbook, December 1780–June 1783, Mss1 L51f 420, section 119 Virginia Historical Society.
[101] Virginia DeJohn Anderson, *Creatures of Empire: How Domestic Animals Transformed Early America* (New York: Oxford University Press, 2004).
[102] Carman, *American Husbandry*, 190.

Agricultural Diversity and Seasonal Patterns of Work 119

committed to livestock care than many of their fellow Caribbean planters. At Newton and Seawell, between 1796 and 1798, first-gang field workers spent between 10 and 11 percent of work days on tasks related to livestock care. In 1797, Newton was "full stocked" with 103 cattle and 12 horses. Seawell had slightly less livestock to tend: 59 cattle and 8 horses.[103] There was roughly one large grazing animal producing dung for every 2.1 acres of regularly cultivated soil at Newton and one for every 3.9 at Seawell. The extra livestock per acre at Newton allowed for more manuring and for a more focused soil improvement strategy. Indeed, Wood claimed that the "increased quantity of manure" that they were getting "from an increase of stock" would "improve our lands considerably."[104]

Both Newton and Seawell used an innovative system of fertilizing that was sometimes called "fly-penning" or "fold-coursing" to distribute dung. Fly-penning was used extensively with sheep in medieval Europe.[105] This task reveals careful attention to soil management and sustainable agriculture on these two sugar plantations. It also shows the manager's commitment to alleviating the slaves of some of their backbreaking dunging work. Under this system, the stock were kept in temporary enclosures ("pens") that were rotated around the plantation to concentrate their fertilizer on a chosen spot. In Europe, the system was used to revitalize fallow lands. In the Caribbean, lands were rarely left fallow. Rather than being placed on the field, Caribbean fly-pens were usually placed near the field so that "the manure," the Newton manager explained, "may be at hand for the Negroes to throw it into the cane holes."[106] Placing the pens close to but not on the field kept the soil or fresh holes or young plants from being trampled while still saving some of the labor involved in carrying dung from distant dung heaps.[107] Most of the stock were left in these pens during the day. Occasionally, some of the "poor cattle" were taken out of the pen during the day to better pastures or shadier areas to graze under the supervision of one or two field hands. From 1796 to 1798, the greatest share of first-gang livestock labors at Newton and Seawell was spent building or maintaining pens (between 8

---

[103] "Seawell's Land and Stock Account," and "Newton Stock and Land Account," MS 523/116, 119, Newton Family Papers.
[104] "Report on the [Newton] Lands," MS 523/289, Newton Family Papers.
[105] Richard K. Ormrod, "The Evolution of Soil Management Practices in Early Jamaican Sugar Planting," *Journal of Historical Geography* 5.2 (1979), 16; Sampson Wood to Thomas Lane, October 15, 1797, MS 523/322, Newton Family Papers; see also Turnbull, *Letters to a Young Planter*, 7.
[106] Sampson Wood to Thomas Lane, October 15, 1797, MS 523/322, Newton Family Papers.
[107] Ibid.

and 12 percent).[108] For at least a day of almost every month of the year, the majority of the first gang would be assigned to this task. Second-gang slaves almost never assisted with the task.

THE HARVEST

On plantations throughout the Americas, slaves (and sometimes masters) celebrated the end of the harvest with festivals. A Jamaican overseer, for example, referred to the festivities as "Merry New Crop Over."[109] The pace of work was at its highest during the harvest but, depending on the crops being grown on a plantation, the intensity of labor required and the length of the harvest varied. In the last half of the eighteenth century, Chesapeake, Barbadian, and Jamaican plantations became more diversified in their production and, with more than one crop, there could be more than just one harvest per year. Juggling the harvest demands of multiple crops could, depending on the crops, make timing and speed during the harvest even more essential.

Harvest was a leveling experience for enslaved workers on a sugar plantation. Tradesmen and domestics would often join the line alongside a cutting gang. Meanwhile, field slaves with specialized skills would move into the works to assume positions as boilers, clarifiers, and distillers. Harvest work also demanded a broader range of tasks than, for example, cane holing or weeding, and many of these were done by individual slaves or gangs working interdependently. From among the field workers, weaker slaves could be drawn to carry canes back to the mill or guide mules laden with the crop or oxen pulling carts with canes to the mills. Weaker slaves were also chosen to gather field trash as fuel for the mill or as cattle fodder, and they were assigned to feed canes into the mill. After the canes were cut, the mill continued to run into the night – ideally until the last of the canes were milled – to avoid having the cane rot or dry, which it did quickly once cut. After cutting canes, field hands would divide into smaller groups and work through the night in rotating shifts at the mill and at the boiling house.[110]

---

[108] Martin, *Essay upon Plantership*, 4th ed., 9–10.
[109] Thomas Thistlewood Diary, April 11, 1752, Monson 31/3; Hilary Beckles, "Crop Fetes and Festivals in Caribbean Slavery," in Alvin O. Thompson, ed., *In The Shadow of the Plantation: Caribbean, History and Legacy* (Kingston, Jamaica: Ian Randle Publishers, 2002), 246–265.
[110] De la Beche, *Present Condition of the Negroes*, 7.

Cane took more than a year to mature, and it could be harvested during any month of the year. Caribbean planters tried to plan the harvest for the first five to seven months of the year, from January through July, before the hurricane season arrived. Planters also competed with each other to get their harvests shipped. The price that sugar could fetch in Britain tended to be higher earlier in the harvest (before May) and decline as it continued.[111] This strategy of beginning the harvest in January at the start of the dry season and ending before the rains began also enabled them to harvest more easily. In wet weather, canes often sprung from the blades during cutting, and the wet canes and poor visibility made accidents more likely.[112] On days in which the rains were too heavy, the mills were often halted and all cutting was stopped until the rain subsided. In Jamaica, when rains prevented planters from harvesting canes, they sometimes used the opportunity and stopped the harvest for long enough to plant corn.[113] At Newton and Seawell, the cane harvest was distinct from the rest of the year. In 1797, it lasted only two months. In 1798 at Newton, with a bumper crop, it was more than twice as long (see Figure 2.9). At Somerset Vale, in 1776–1777, it was quite short, lasting for only the two months of April and May (see Figure 2.10). At the other end of the

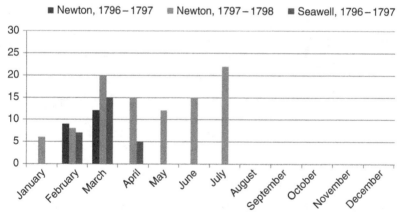

FIGURE 2.9. Number of days each month the primary mill was operating at Newton and Seawell (Barbados) in 1796–1798.
Source: Newton Work Log, 1796–1798; Seawell Work Log, 1796–1797, MS 523/110, 111, 123, Newton Family Papers.

[111] David Beck Ryden, *West Indian Slavery and British Abolition, 1783–1907* (Cambridge: New York University Press, 2009), 94.
[112] Simon Taylor to Chalenor Arcedeckne, October 10, 1783, Vanneck-Arc/ 3A/ 1783/39.
[113] Peter Marsden, *An Account of the Island of Jamaica* (Newcastle: S. Hodgson, 1788), 36.

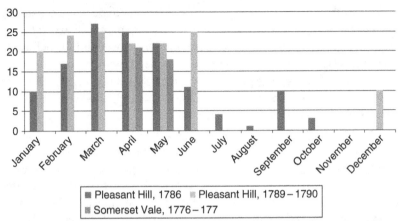

FIGURE 2.10. Number of days each month the primary mill was operating at Pleasant Hill (Jamaica) in 1786 and 1789–1790 and at Somerset Vale in 1776–1777. The crop of 1790 at Pleasant hill began in December, 1789. The Somerset Vale logs cover the period from October 1776 through October 1777.
Source: Pleasant Hill Boiling House and Crop Books, MS 8441, MS 11496, Slebech Papers.

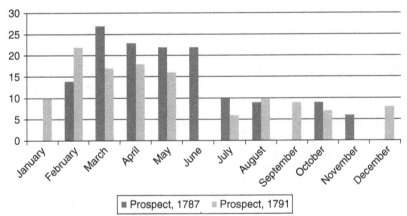

FIGURE 2.11. Number of days each month the primary mill was operating at Prospect (Jamaica) in 1787 and 1791.
Source: Prospect Plantation Journals, 1787–1793, 0627-0019.

spectrum was the length of the harvest at Prospect and at Pleasant Hill in Jamaica. The planters on these estates appear to have tried to end the bulk of the harvest and ship their product before the storm season to avoid risky shipping. (see Figure 2.10 and 2.11). Yet, in some years, the crop – because of excessive rain, insufficient labor, or a particularly large volume of cane – was not finished before the storm season, and they continued to harvest periodically through the rest of the year, starting and stopping the mill for a few days each month whenever it seemed dry enough. These crops were kept on hand for shipping either after the hurricane season was over or with the bulk of the crops the next spring. Sugar harvests were not normally shipped between August and December. The cost of insuring a cargo was very high in these months.[114]

The harvest on a cane plantation was demanding because of the pace and the hours required, but the work required less physical strength than holing or dunging. Whereas cane holing could be done only by the most physically able members of the first gang, and holing gangs were normally between thirty and fifty slaves, cane cutting could be done by a greater number of slaves. Cane cutting gangs were not uncommonly over fifty slaves. Even though digging cane holes required extreme physical exertion, cane cutting and harvesting may have required as much or more of a labor investment per acre. The work logs from Prospect record how many days it took to harvest a specific acreage or quantity of cane. On average, it took forty-eight slaves to cut an acre of canes in a day in 1786, approximately thirteen to twenty-three work days more than it took to dig cane holes. In terms of the total yield, slaves spent an average of thirty-seven work days harvesting each hogshead of sugar. Although harvesting an acre took more total work days than holing, planters were able to use people in harvesting who were too physically weak to dig cane holes. Not all of the slaves at work in the Prospect harvest were actually cutting cane. Many were following the cane cutters to bundle and transport canes to the mill or collect field trash. Some even spent their days working at the mill.

In total, slaves at Prospect (a monocropping estate) spent a much greater proportion of their work days cutting canes than did slaves at Newton or Seawell (multicropping estates). During 1796–1797, when drought plagued the Barbadian sugar harvest, the Newton and Seawell field workers spent only 4–6 percent of their time cutting canes and clearing the fields. Even if one includes all cane harvesting tasks and the time spent working at the mill, the boiling house, and the distillery, the field hands at Newton and Seawell spent no more than 10 percent of their work days harvesting canes that year. Because cotton was more resistant to drought, the field hands at Seawell actually spent more time in the field picking cotton (8 percent) than cutting canes (4 percent). The next year, with a bumper crop, the proportion of time spent on all harvesting tasks rose to 20 percent of the field

---

[114] Pleasant Hill Boiling House and Crop Books, MS8441, MS11496, Slebech Papers.

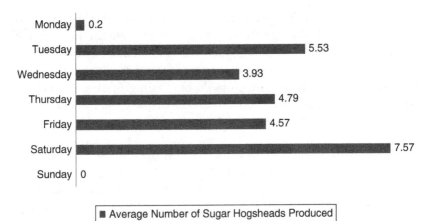

FIGURE 2.12. Average daily production totals from the York Plantation boiling house (Jamaica) for the crop of 1791.
Note: This harvest lasted from February 7 to May 18.
Source: York Boiling House Account Book for the Crop of 1791, Section 3/H, Gale-Morant Papers, University of Exeter Library.

hands' work days at Newton. Even in an exceptionally good harvest year, the Newton slaves only spent half as much time harvesting as the Prospect slaves. In 1787 and 1791, the slaves at Prospect spent between 40 and 44 percent of their work days harvesting.

At York Plantation in Jamaica, there was a distinct rhythm to the harvest work week, and slaves were often forced to work in the mills past the break of dawn on Sunday morning. Over the course of York's fourteen-and-a-half-week harvest in 1791, the average number of sugar hogsheads produced was far greater on Saturday than on any other day of the week (see Figure 2.12). The Saturday totals were almost certainly higher because the mill continued to operate until late in the day on Sunday in order to finish canes that had been cut during the week. It is possible that slaves at York were driven harder to cut an even greater amount of cane on the last day before they would rest, but slaves were already being driven at a maximal pace and it would be hard to attribute such a vast difference in daily production totals to simply greater efforts. Mills on most sugar plantations were in operation from shortly after the canes began to be cut, but the milling and boiling of a crop continued long into the early morning of the next day, indicating that the speed with which the crop could be harvested was much faster than the speed with which it could be milled. The weekly rhythm of harvest work at York was also notable in that the mill rarely operated on Mondays, after the day off. This

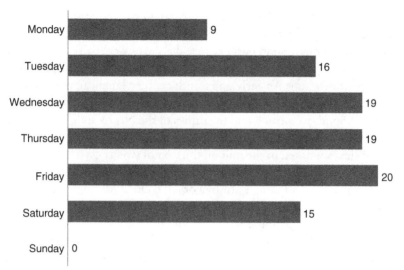

FIGURE 2.13. Days of the week in which the Newton Mill was in operation for the crop of 1798.
Source: Newton Work Log, 1797–1798, MS 523/110, 123, Newton Family Papers.

may have been a planned break to ease the night labors of slaves, or the overseers may have felt no need to start the mill until a sufficient number of canes had been cut. On average, the water mill at York produced 27.4 hogsheads a week, despite the absence of production on Mondays. Remarkably, the York mill production was even greater than the average of 20–25 hogsheads a week that the Jamaican planter and manual writer John Dovaston estimated was the top speed of production for a Jamaican water mill.[115] At Newton, as at York, the mill operated less on Monday than on any other day of the week (Figure 2.13). However, unlike York Plantation, there was also less Saturday work in the mill at Newton than on most days of the week (Figure 2.13). The volume of canes on a multi-cropping estate such as Newton was lower than at York, and it wasn't necessary to keep the mill operating as often.

Whereas Sunday was a rest day on Chesapeake estates, and it was usually a rest day on Barbadian estates, Sundays in Jamaica became,

---

[115] John Dovaston, "Agricultura Americana or Improvements in West-India Husbandry Considered Wherein the Present System of Husbandry Used in England is Applied to the Cultivation or Growing of Sugar Canes to Advantage" [1774], Codex Eng 60, vol. 2. John Carter Brown Library.

increasingly, a seventh day of forced labor – in part because planters ran the mill into the early morning on Sunday and sometimes began again on Sunday afternoons, and in part because the slaves were driven, sometimes under the driver's lash, to grow an ever-increasing share of their provisions during their own time An early nineteenth-century Jamaican planter noted that "On many plantations the mill, in crop-time, is not stopped till a late hour on a Sunday morning and the duties of the Negro are renewed at an early hour on Sunday evening."[116] At Jamaica's Pleasant Hill, in 1786, a crew of slaves worked in the mill on thirteen of twenty-two Sunday afternoons during the cane harvest, beginning normally at five or six o'clock in the evening and continuing until five or six o'clock Monday morning.[117] On two other weekends, a crew of slaves worked at the mill from six o'clock Saturday evening through noon on Sunday. In other words, sometimes the mills in Jamaica were stopped for only four hours on the slaves' customary day off. On an early nineteenth-century Jamaican estate, Duckensfield Hall, the planters started the mill even earlier (at four o'clock) on Sunday afternoons during the harvest.[118] Work in the cane fields was the only chore that slaves were not forced to do on a Sunday. A few Barbadian plantations probably adopted the same approach to working for a portion of Sunday during the harvest but, given the lower volume of cane being cut and the multicropping strategies, most Barbadian plantations were probably like Newton and Seawell, where the mill was never put into operation on Sundays. The manager, however, admitted that the slaves sometimes stayed in the sugar works until late in the evening on Saturdays.[119] In Virginia, planters appear to have more fully respected a slave's right to Sundays and, when they required slaves to work on a Sunday, they would commonly reward those slaves with extra time or money.[120]

The Chesapeake grain harvests were much shorter in duration than Caribbean sugar harvests, and the time demands imposed by the nature of sugar cane (a quickly decomposing crop) in a hot and humid environment were not present to the same degree in grain harvesting. The wheat

---

[116] Gilbert Farquhar Mathison, *Notices Respecting Jamaica in 1808, 1809, 1810* (London: J. Stockdale, 1811), 40.
[117] Pleasant Hill Boiling House and Crop Book, 1786, MS11496, Slebech Papers.
[118] "An Account'g of Duckensfield Hall Estate Negroes" [November–December, 1806], Codex Eng-183, John Carter Brown Library.
[119] "Report on the Buildings at Newton," MS 523/290, Newton Family Papers.
[120] Ira Berlin, *Many Thousands Gone: The First Two Centuries of Slavery in North America* (Cambridge: Belknap Press of Harvard University Press, 1998), 134.

harvest was, like the sugar harvest, highly organized; they both relied on an interdependence of gang labor. Cradlers, who were normally men, mowed the wheat while less capable hands followed and gathered the crop in the same way in which secondary gangs followed cane cutters at harvest and collected the crop. There was more of a gendered division of labor in the wheat harvest than in the sugar harvest, and the task of mowing wheat was understood to be more skilled and specialized than the task of cutting canes. Overall, the demands of wheat and corn cultivation appear to have been greatest outside the harvest. The percentage of monthly labor required to tend wheat was higher during the months in which slaves were plowing and harrowing wheat and corn than it was during the harvest (see Figure 2.4).[121]

The total number of cash crop harvest days could vary widely from one plantation to the next or from one year to the next, particularly on sugar plantations. The harvest at Prospect and at Pleasant Hill was much longer than the grain harvest at Mount Vernon or even at other sugar plantations such as Newton, Seawell, or Somerset Vale. The mill was running at Pleasant Hill and at Prospect for more than 140 days of the year. The mill at Newton operated for less than 100 days a year during a bountiful crop, and during a bad year the Newton mill operated for only twenty-one days. The mill at Somerset Vale operated for only sixty-one days a year in 1776–1777 (Figure 2.14). The difference was largely a question of multicropping versus monocropping sugar planting strategies. However, even on a multicropping sugar estate such as Newton during an abysmal crop, the harvest still took longer than most Chesapeake wheat harvests. On the Mount Vernon quarters in 1797, the wheat harvest took no more than twenty-one days and usually less.

CONCLUSION

Whether on Chesapeake or Caribbean plantations, field hands toiled through long, backbreaking, and often monotonous days. Although the number of days worked tended to be constant in each season throughout the Americas, the working hours varied from one season to the next – with the amount of available daylight and, in Barbados and Jamaica, with the amount of night work. Work hours tended to be greater in Jamaica than elsewhere because of longer harvest seasons and because the planters were more likely to demand work from their slaves on the one customary day off

---

[121] Morgan, *Slave Counterpoint*, 170–175.

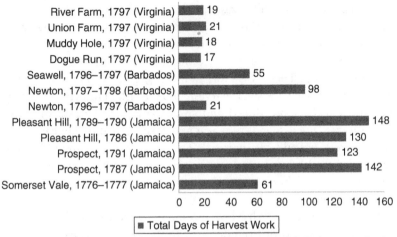

FIGURE 2.14. Total number of cash crop harvesting days each year in Barbados, Jamaica, and Virginia.
Note: The numbers at Seawell and at Somerset Vale include days spent cutting and milling canes and days spent harvesting secondary cash crops. Seawell slaves spent twenty-eight days harvesting cotton in 1796–1797 and twenty-seven days on canes. At Somerset Vale, slaves spent twenty-two days picking coffee and thirty-nine days harvesting canes. At the height of the harvest, the mill often operated on Sundays for part of the day. These Sundays have not been included. The numbers for the outlying Mount Vernon farms include only days spent harvesting wheat and corn. Because the Mount Vernon farm reports were taken weekly, the number of days spent harvesting on the outlying farms required some estimates based on the total number of work days and tasks recorded during the week and the proportion of workers involved in the harvest.
Sources: Pleasant Hill Boiling House and Crop Books, MS 8441, MS 11496, Slebech Papers; Newton Work Logs, 1796–1798, MS 523,110, 123, Newton Family Papers; Mount Vernon Farm Reports, 1797; Somerset Vale Work Logs, 1776–1780, Codex Eng 180; Prospect Plantation Journals, 1787–1793, 0627-0019.

each week: Sunday. The organization of labor in the field and the intensity of labor – meaning the degree of physical exertion required in daily chores – also varied with the seasons. Without question, the work in the Caribbean, in large part because of the labors of cane holing and the amount of time slaves' worked with dung, was more brutal and demanding than any work in the Chesapeake. The sugar harvest, despite its long hours, was less of a drain for slaves because it did not require as much backbreaking toil.

Although the amelioration movement paid lip service to easing the labors of slaves, planters would only change the kinds of crops that they grew, the techniques they forced the slaves to use, or the way they divided labor if they believed it would make the plantation function more smoothly and efficiently, more profitably. A growing diversification of agriculture in the late eighteenth century in both the Chesapeake and the Caribbean may have made slaves' labors more demanding by eliminating slack periods in the labor cycle. More provisions were grown in the Caribbean after the mid-eighteenth century and especially after the American Revolution, and many planters adopted secondary crops and other economic endeavors such as distilling or fishing, shifting plantations from monocropping operations to multicropping operations.

Despite movements toward self-sufficiency and the diversification of plantation production, there were estates – mostly in Jamaica – that continued to focus on monoculture, on generating vast revenues from a single cash crop while purchasing whatever provisions, supplies, and building materials were necessary for an estate. The contrast between work routines on a near monoculture sugar estate such as Prospect and work routines on multicropping sugar plantations such as Newton, Seawell, and Somerset Vale were almost as great as the contrast between large Chesapeake grain plantations, such as Mount Vernon, and multicropping sugar estates. In some ways, such as the emphasis on corn production with regular gang labor, Newton, Seawell, and Somerset Vale looked more like Mount Vernon than like Prospect or Pleasant Hill. The range of possible plantation production strategies in the late eighteenth century was striking, and these schemes were changing from year to year, adapting to circumstances. Plantation managers, in their labor and land allocation decisions, were remarkably responsive to both external factors (such as market price or war-induced shortages in supply) and internal factors (such as soil quality or the available labor and livestock supply). What the land could support in a particular environmental setting was probably more of a limiting factor in plantation management strategies than what work the slaves could be forced to perform.

In the late eighteenth century, certain changes in slave agriculture became entrenched, transforming the way plantations operated. Throughout the Chesapeake and the Caribbean, planters started raising more livestock to replace some of the slaves' labors with animal power, but the livestock were also raised for their dung, and distributing this manure was one of the most demanding daily tasks for slaves, especially in the Caribbean; in total, the introduction of livestock may have made the daily labor requirements more intense. The plow eased the labors of slaves in the Chesapeake, but it also led to more cultivated acreage to tend and required slaves to more fully clear the fields of stumps and root systems to allow for the plow. By the end of the eighteenth century, planters in the Chesapeake were demanding that their slaves learn the skills necessary to perform multiple jobs, including tending a vast array of cash, provision, and fodder crops, while fishing, clearing new ground, and raising more stock. Through diversification, they were eliminating slack periods in labor demand, and they were attaining higher productivity levels per slave than ever before. Given the increasing productivity levels in sugar agriculture and the evidence of planters encroaching on slaves' Sundays, it appears that Caribbean slaves were also being driven harder in the late eighteenth century, particularly in Jamaica. In Barbados, and on some Jamaican estates, the diversification of plantation production within individual plantations meant that the island's planters were expecting more constant efforts from the slaves throughout the year. Although planters in the islands and on the mainland espoused humanitarian reform and searched for methods and tools to save labor, the labor saved would always be invested elsewhere. Efficiency, improvement, and reform often meant an intensification of work for the slaves.

3

Lockstep and Line

Gang Work and the Division of Labor

The division of labor in the field was a critical site of investigation and experimentation for eighteenth-century plantation improvers. Many hoped that the successful organization of a gang would be one of the keys to both maximizing labor and improving the health of their workers. The principal system of field labor organization in Jamaica, Barbados, and Virginia was gang labor. Overseers and drivers divided the cultivation chores among the slaves on the basis of their experience and their physical and, to a lesser extent, mental capabilities. Field slaves under this system worked collectively on a single task or a set of tasks from sunup to sundown under the direction of a work leader, normally a driver. They were identified collectively as a "gang," their individual identity subsumed to the working unit.

Work in the gang system was closely supervised and, in its archetypal form, it was conducted in a rhythmic pace designed to maximize the efficiency of motion and keep the laborers working in unison together, discouraging stragglers. Once they were assigned to a gang, slaves became units of production, interchangeable numbers contributing to a whole. Individuals or small groups could be drawn from the gang to work on other tasks, but the bulk of field slaves would normally be ganged and assigned duties for the entire working day. Each slave in a gang was expected to work at the same pace and accomplish the same amount of labor. In contrast to the kind of task system that emerged in the Lowcountry, gangs were not given work quotas for the day and were allowed free time after they had finished. Gangs could be subdivided or multiple gangs could be amalgamated into one work group, depending on the tasks required from day to day. Planters often organized labor to ensure that multiple gangs worked interdependently with each other, specializing on portions of a task. On estates with multi-tiered gangs, a slave's movement through the gangs became part of a process of apprenticeship. Gang labor was productive but it was also psychologically oppressive and physically demanding, to the point that it has never been consistently employed as a tool of labor management with free laborers.

Gang labor was not a static form of labor organization. Planters, especially in the era of improvement, were continually debating, experimenting, and developing ideas about how to organize and direct their gangs. As a form of labor organization, ganging evolved over time, and there was a significant difference between gang work on large estates in the Chesapeake and gang work in the Caribbean. The archetype of the gang labor system appeared on sugar plantations, but, even on sugar plantations, the planters and overseers approached this form of labor organization in a variety of ways. Jamaican plantations, because they were larger, tended to have more gangs and more drivers than Barbadian estates. Larger sugar plantations had a greater division of labor among the gangs than smaller estates. Some planters used gangs to encourage labor specialization, and they gathered together a particular group of slaves for holing or weeding.

Large Chesapeake plantations, which were divided into smaller farm quarters, tended to use only one gang on each quarter, and Chesapeake slaves on these quarters did more independent labor than their sugar plantation counterparts. There were not enough slaves or gangs on the Mount Vernon quarters to have gangs specialize on different tasks or to develop and deploy interdependent gang labor to improve efficiency for particular tasks. There was no tobacco grown at Mount Vernon by the end of the eighteenth century, which meant that the work groups could be larger. Tobacco cultivation required more care and precision than most crops. Tobacco workers needed close supervision, which kept the number of slaves in a tobacco gang to less than twenty and ideally less than a dozen. The work groups on most of the Mount Vernon quarters were larger than a dozen slaves. The elimination of the staple crop of tobacco led to a greater reliance on gang labor.

To avoid generalizations about gang labor and to understand the evolving nature of ganging and its many variants, it is critical to explore the decision-making process that planters and overseers underwent in designing labor systems. Their ideas drew on larger Enlightenment themes such as the search for universal rules and processes and the belief that economic progress and efficiency would entail a better life for the slaves. The emphasis planters placed on designing the most effective gangs reflected their belief that discipline was the key to both moral and economic reform on slave plantations. Field labor organization was a key issue in late eighteenth-century discussions about plantation management. It was a point of intersection between the movement to improve the efficiency and productivity of plantation agriculture and a humanitarian reform movement that strove to improve the conditions of slavery. Agricultural improvement manuals, striving to find the best mode of coercing and compelling maximum labor efforts, debated the ideal method of organizing and directing slave labor in the field. As part of an increasing belief in the superiority of free labor and its incentives to labor, a few Caribbean sugar planters, where the gang system was pervasive, began to experiment with task labor, usually using collective tasking.[1] Although the demands of a crop often encouraged certain system of labor organization and dictated, to some extent, the size and spatial dimensions of an estate, the system of labor organization was never simply determined by the crops being grown.

This chapter examines the division of labor into gangs on large plantations in Jamaica, Barbados, and Virginia. It explores the nature of those gangs and the decision-making process behind their formation. It looks at the differences in labor allocation among the gangs on plantations with multiple gangs and on the ways in which planters could strive for specialization and interdependent work among the gangs. It also determines how many gangs most plantations used and how the number of gangs and the size of each gang changed with the season or the task.

GANG HIERARCHY

On Caribbean sugar plantations, the division into gangs was as much a hierarchical classification and organizational system for the laborers as a description of how they labored. Gangs collapsed the individual features of a slave's identity into one single work identity. Plantation managers found it best to conceptualize slaves as belonging to separate gangs in order to divide tasks on the basis of a slave's work capacity or special skills. Ganging became so pervasive in the region that planters grouped transport workers, such as mulemen, slaves working at the mill, and even tradesmen into gangs under the supervision of a work leader.[2] A St. Kitts work log, for example,

---

[1] Philip D. Morgan, "Task and Gang Systems: The Organization of Labor on New World Plantations," in Stephen Innes, ed., *Work and Labor in Early America* (Chapel Hill University of North Carolina Press, 1988), 191, 201–202; William Dickson, *Mitigation of Slavery in Two Parts* (Miami, FL: Mnemosyne Pub. Inc., [1814] 1969), 9.
[2] Ibid., 195.

differentiated between the field gangs and the "Mill Gang."[3] "Gangs" often referred to a group of slaves who were particularly adept at certain tasks, enabling labor specialization. A sugar plantation with between 150 and 400 slaves normally used two to three adult field gangs and a children's gang.[4] Variations in the number and size of adult gangs were determined more by plantation size than by regional differences among the islands. Because Jamaican plantations tended to be larger than Barbadian ones, they usually had more gangs and more workers in each gang.

When it came to assessing their labor force, planters and overseers tended to think of their primary field gang as if it was a single entity whose strength waxed and waned. It was a faceless laboring body, a mass comprised of many "hands." The notion of the gang as a single entity shaped the ways in which planters thought about labor allocation. In later years, as sugar planters began to experiment with tasking, they never seriously considered individual tasking as an option; if planters considered tasks at all, they thought about assigning tasks to the gang as a whole, a unitary body.[5] When plantation managers talked about the "strength" of the first gang, they meant the amount of labor that could be expected from the gang in a given day, and the strength of the gang was a constant concern.[6] A St. Kitts attorney, in 1797, feared that the "effective Strength" of the working gang on the estate he managed was "by no means equal to what it was" because even though the number of slaves had not changed, "many of the working Negroes are getting old & feeble." Rather than being concerned that there was an insufficient number of slaves in the gang, he worried that the effective collective strength of the gang had diminished because of weak individuals. He asked the owner to purchase "Ten or a dozen young females" to keep up the strength of the gang.[7] He seems to have emphasized females in particular to encourage fertility in this field gang, conceptualizing

---

[3] Clement Caines, *Letters on the Cultivation of the Otaheite cane: the manufacture of sugar and rum; the saving of melasses; the care and preservation of stock; with the attention and anxiety which is due to Negroes: To these topics are added, a few other particulars analogous to the subject of the letters; and also a speech on the slave trade, the most important feature in West Indian cultivation.* London: Messrs. Robinson, 1801, 246 [insert]. This work log insert is not available in all editions. There is an insert in the copy at the Library Company of Pennsylvania.

[4] Peter Marsden, *An Account of the Island of Jamaica* (Newcastle: S. Hodgson, 1788), 31.

[5] Morgan, "Task and Gang Systems," 191, 201-202.

[6] Catherine Harding to William Gale, 15 March 1782, Section 1/D, Gale-Morant Papers

[7] Robert Thompson to William D. Shipley, 22 June 1797, Bodrhyddan Papers, in Clare Taylor, ed., *West Indian Planter Attitudes to the American and French Revolution as Seen in Manuscripts, in the National Library of Wales* (Aberystwyth: University College of Wales, Department of History, 1978), 308-311.

it again as a unitary organism capable of its own reproduction and growth. Sugar planters strove to make the production of a gang uniform throughout the years to be better able to organize and allocate labor and project production schemes.

Ideally, the first-gang slaves were the ablest and the most productive workers on the plantation. Slaves normally entered the first gang at the end of their teens or in their early twenties. The first gang was also referred to as the "strong gang" or the "Great Gang." Planters often described this group as the "working gang."[8] First-gang slaves were assigned the most important, most pressing, and most physically demanding tasks. Some planters would try to encourage a sense of pride in being a member of this gang and offered incentives to slaves who could remain in the group. It was proper, one plantation manual suggested, "to distinguish them with greater indulgencies" than the rest of the laborers. Extra "time allotted to their own use" or "extraordinary food" would suffice.[9] Others, such as the Barbadian planter Dr. H. E. Holder, disagreed with the common practice of giving first gangs any special treatment, perhaps fearing that this would cause overseers to neglect the second-gang hands and injure their health.[10]

The emphasis that sugar overseers and planters placed on carefully dividing the strongest laborers from the rest was closely connected to the physical demands of key tasks in the sugar cultivation cycle. First-gang workers were strong enough that overseers could force them to hole for canes, cut canes, or turn and throw out dung. Cane holing requirements and the demands of that individual task may have had an important impact on the development of gangs on Caribbean sugar plantations. First-gang workers were sometimes referred to as the "holers."[11] Barbadian cane-holing techniques, which were very labor intensive but helped to conserve the soil and protected against hurricanes, were perfected in the late seventeenth century at about the same time at which Barbadian planters were working out the system of ganging.[12] William Belgrove, in his 1755 plantation manual, claimed to be copying Henry Drax's treatise on plantation

---

[8] Robert Thompson to William D. Shipley, 22 June 1797, Bodrhyddan Papers, in Taylor, ed., *West Indian Planter Attitudes*, 308–311.

[9] David Collins, *Practical Rules for the Management and Medical Treatment of Negro Slaves in the Sugar Colonies* (London: J. Barfield, 1803), 177.

[10] Dr. H.E. Holder to Sir Henry Fitzherbert, October 26, 1815, in Fitzherbert Collection, E23929. See also Patrick Kein, *An Essay upon Pen-Keeping and Plantership* (Kingston, Jamaica: His Majesty's Printing Office, 1796), 20.

[11] Collins, *Medical Treatment of Negro Slaves*, 179.

[12] David Watts, "Origins of Barbadian Cane Hole Agriculture," *Journal of the Barbados Museum and Historical Society* 32.3 (May 1968), 143–151; Russell R. Menard, *Sweet*

management from 1679; he quoted Drax as saying that the manager should divide the slaves "into two Gangs, the abelest and best by themselves for Holeing and the stronger Work, and the more ordinary Negroes in a Gang for Dunging, & c."[13] Belgrove's more detailed description of gang divisions does not appear in the original copy of Drax's instructions, which has been preserved in the Bodleian Library. However, the original version of the instructions do suggest forming separate planting and dung-carrying groups of slaves who would work interdependently during the planting of cane. The word "gang" was not used in Drax's instructions, and there was no discussion of which slaves should form each group but the description of interdependent work groups, creating a near assembly-line process, was one of the hallmarks of the archetypal gang labor that emerged in the eighteenth century.[14] It is possible that Belgrove was quoting a revised version from later in the seventeenth or early eighteenth century that had been kept in Barbados and no longer survives.[15] It is more likely, however, that Belgrove added these comments about labor division himself. The ganging system was still being developed in the 1670s. By 1755, when Belgrove revised Drax's instructions, planters were beginning to insist that more careful divisions of labor and labor specialization, especially during holing, were one of the keys to productivity. By the middle of the eighteenth century, specialized jobbing gangs were hired from off the plantation specifically to dig cane holes.[16] Although it is not entirely clear when the holing specialization developed, the division into hierarchical gangs based on a slave's physical ability was clearly a product of the brutal demands of holing, and it was part of a process of labor specialization.

The first gang was the spine of the plantation, and planters strove to have as many able-bodied laborers as possible in that gang.[17] Most estates had one large group of the strongest slaves working together on one or two chores for the day. If the task changed, it was normally after the midday break. First gangs ranged in size from about thirty to more than one-hundred slaves.[18] The Jamaican planter Bryan Edwards thought that

Negotiations: Sugar, Slavery and Plantation Agriculture in Early Barbados (Charlottesville: University of Virginia Press, 2006), 96–98.

[13] William Belgrove, *A Treatise upon Husbandry or Planting* (Boston: D. Fowle, 1755), 65.
[14] Peter Thompson, "Henry Drax's Instructions on the Management of a Seventeenth-Century Barbadian Plantation," *William and Mary Quarterly* 3rd ser., 86.3 (2009), 590.
[15] Ibid., 568n, 582–604.
[16] Lowthers Plantation Accounts, 1756, MS 43507, Papers of the Duke of Cleveland.
[17] B. W. Higman, *Slave Populations of the British Caribbean, 1807–1834* (Baltimore: Johns Hopkins University, 1984), 164, 170.
[18] Caines, *Cultivation of the Otaheite Cane*, 246 [insert]; Inventory of the Codrington Plantations, May, 1783/C/COD/44, Codrington Papers, C Series.

Gang Work and the Division of Labor

on a "well conditioned plantation" the first gang would consist of one-third of all slaves. Indeed, Barbadian and Jamaican plantation inventories and work logs suggest that between 20 and 40 percent of all slaves worked in the first gang.[19] The early nineteenth-century ameliorationist Dr. David Collins insisted, contrary to standard practice, that the strongest gang should "not be more than one-sixth part of your whole number."[20] His ideal proportion was so low because he thought that too many slaves were forced to work beyond their capacity with the primary gang. He envisioned a more careful division of labor and more distinct labor specialization as a key element in amelioration.

Although the first-gang workers were ideally the strongest and most able hands, managers would often simply lump together all of the mature adults into the first gang. Such a process was more common on plantations that used a large number of African-born laborers. It was more difficult for both overseers and the enslaved drivers to judge the capabilities of these unknown slaves when it came to labor division. Creolization fostered more appropriate labor divisions. Sometimes, the great gang on an estate became large enough that overseers divided it into subsets for heavier tasks that required close supervision, such as holing. In such cases, managers would differentiate between the stronger and weaker hands. The Barbadian attorney and agricultural reformer Philip Gibbes thought it was common in a first gang with eighty-five workers to have about fifteen "inefficient people."[21] They were able, he believed, to accomplish about as much as second-gang slaves. These were the people on the margin between the first and second gangs. They were listed with the first gang, but they probably worked separately whenever the tasks became too demanding.[22] At Newton, these slaves on the margin between the first and second gang were known as the "infirm gang," and on a St. Kitts plantation, they were

---

[19] See for example Newton Work Logs, 1796–1798, Seawell Work Log, 1796–1797 and Seawell Work Log, 1798 "Report on the [Newton] Negroes," "Report on the Negroes of Seawell Plantation," MS 523/110, 111, 122, 123, 288, 292, Newton Family Papers; Prospect Plantation Journals, 1787 to 1793, 0627-0019; Drax Hall Slaves and Livestock from 1804 Inventory, Z9/11/5, Barbados Department of Archives; Inventory of the Codrington Plantations, May 1783; *Minutes of the Society for the Improvement of Plantership in the Island of Barbados* (Liverpool: Thomas Kaye, 1811), 13; York Slave Inventory, 1782, 3/c, Gale-Morant Papers.
[20] Collins, *Medical Treatment of Negro Slaves*, 176–177; Bryan Edwards, *The History Civil and Commercial of the British Colonies in the West Indies*, 2 vols. (Dublin: Luke White, 1793), vol. II, 128.
[21] *Society for the Improvement of Plantership*, 13.
[22] Newton Work Log, 1796–1797, MS 523/110, Newton Family Papers.

known as the "feeble" gang within the big gang.[23] Likewise, Thistlewood, the Jamaican overseer, referred to fifteen of the slaves under his charge as his "cripple gang."[24]

Two adult gangs was the norm on sugar plantations. Beneath the first or strong gang were the slaves thought of as belonging to the "inferior" or "middling" gang. Second-gang workers were those slaves who were strong enough for field work but not ready to consistently perform the most demanding chores, such as holing. They were usually just beyond or just entering their physical prime.[25] The second gang was usually one-quarter to one-half the size of the great gang.[26] Twenty to thirty-odd slaves was common for this gang.[27] Contemporaries occasionally suggested that the second gang was a good place for "women far gone with child" or "convalescents" who "are not sufficiently recovered to return to their station among the strong gang."[28] One planter calculated that it would take the second-gang workers three days to accomplish as much as it took the first gang to do in two days.[29] Second-gang slaves often worked interdependently with the first gang. If too many first-gang members were forced to miss work or if the first gang lacked sufficient strength, some plantation manuals suggested that planters could make "occasional draughts" from the "middle gang."[30] It served as a reserve force.

The size of the adult gangs at the top of the Caribbean gang hierarchy and the number of gangs deployed could vary over the course of the year. The ability to effectively supervise and coerce labor and the need to control the rhythm and pace of work were the factors limiting the size of a gang. More gangs meant higher supervision costs. Drivers were almost always the most valuable slaves, and they were difficult to obtain. The physical landscape also played a significant role in determining the ideal size of a

---

[23] "Report on the [Newton] Negroes," MS 523/288, Newton Family Papers; Caines, *Letters on the Cultivation of the Otaheite Cane*, 264 [insert].

[24] Thomas Thistlewood Diary, April 24, 1752, Monson 31/3.

[25] Collins, *Medical Treatment of Negro Slaves*, 180; "Report on [Newton] Negroes"; "Report on the Negroes of Seawell Plantation"; H. T. De la Beche, *Notes on the Present Condition of the Negroes in Jamaica* (London: T. Cadell in the Strand, 1825), 7.

[26] Newton Work Loga 1796–1798 and Seawell Work Logs 1796–1797 and 1798, "Report on the [Negroes] at Newton" and "Report on the Negroes at Seawell," MS 523/ 110, 111, 122, 123, 288, 292; Prospect Plantation Journals, 1787–1793, 0627-0019; *Society for the Improvement of Plantership*, 13.

[27] *Society for the Improvement of Plantership*, 5; Caines, *Cultivation of the Otaheite Cane*, 51.

[28] Edwards, *History, Civil and Commercial*, vol. II, 121; Collins, *Medical Treatment of Negro Slaves*, 180.

[29] *Society for the Improvement of Plantership*, 13.

[30] Collins, *Medical Treatment of Negro Slaves*, 179.

plantation's gang. It was more difficult to maintain a constant rhythm and pace across rocky hillsides, and it was easier for drivers and overseers to see a large gang on a broad and open expanse of land than it was to see a gang on uneven or sloping ground.

Although Caribbean field workers were conceptually grouped together into their respective gangs in plantation inventories or in the correspondence of managers, they were often divided into smaller work groups or squads when they were in the field. Individuals were also moved back and forth over the course of the year between squads and gangs, especially if they were recovering from illnesses or pregnancies. Sometimes each separate subgroup would work with the controlled rhythmic pace of gang labor and with a driver to ensure productivity. Sometimes their labors were not closely supervised. The larger the plantation, the more likely the first two gangs would be divided in daily practice into these additional subgangs or squads. On a plantation in St. Kitts, there were two field gangs – the "Big Gang" and "Little Gang." Yet, in early May 1801, when the primary tasks were both harvesting and digging cane holes at the same time, the slaves who normally worked with these two gangs were divided in daily practice into as many as six different work squads: "Big Gang – able, Big Gang – feeble, Little Gang, [Cane] Cutters, [Cane] Tiers, Mill Gang."[31] Likewise, the first gang at Newton, from 1796 through 1798, included between eighty-nine and ninety-eight slaves. It was difficult for drivers and overseers to supervise such a large group on the same task. If the task allowed for the controlled motion and pace of gang labor, managers would be hard pressed to make that many individuals with different abilities and limitations work with the same rhythm. The entire Newton first gang never worked together. The largest number of workers employed together on a task in these years was seventy-nine. Together, they spent a day tending to Guinea corn. It was a hardy crop that did not require strict supervision or backbreaking labor. On most days at Newton, the primary work group within the first gang had between fifty and seventy-five slaves working together. The remaining slaves did duty as watchmen or worked individually or in small squads on tasks such as tending to stock, where they were not under the driver's lash or subject to the rhythmic and controlled pace of gang labor. It is not clear whether the same slaves were always chosen to specialize in these chores or whether slaves were rotated through these positions.

[31] Caines, *Cultivation of the Otaheite Cane*, 247 [insert].

Some of the vast Jamaican sugar plantations used many gangs in daily practice. In 1779, Parnassus in Clarendon Parish had 457 slaves. Of that total there were 147 adult field hands and a remarkable eight drivers to supervise them. Among the drivers were probably one or two slaves who led child gangs, and it is possible that some of these drivers were too ill or disabled to work, but the number of drivers suggests that the adult field workers on the estate were regularly divided into at least five or six gangs or subgangs.[32] Despite the tendency toward large plantations and a greater degree of gang divisions on Jamaican estates compared to Barbadian estates, not all Jamaican estates regularly used multiple gangs. At Braco Estate – a large estate in Trelawny, Jamaica, with approximately 370 slaves in 1796 – the overseers used only two adult gangs. The size of the two gangs varied significantly. During the harvest, the great gang was cutting and there were only forty-six to forty-eight slaves employed at that task. At other points in the cultivation cycle, they had as many as ninety slaves grouped together in the great gang.[33] Smaller estates almost always used only one or two adult field gangs. For example, at the other end of the spectrum from an estate like Parnassus, with its many gangs, was Jamaica's Somerset Vale. There was little in the way of gang division at Somerset Vale, which grew a mix of sugar and coffee. It was a small estate with 115 slaves and fifty-nine field adult hands (forty-two of whom were women). Occasionally, some of "the weak hands" were put to work on separate tasks but, through most of the year, "all hands" – meaning all adult field workers – performed the major tasks. Because of the economies of scale in sugar production, few sugar plantations had fewer than fifty adult field workers. This meant that most sugar plantation workforces could be divided into at least two adult gangs – the weaker and the stronger workers or the first and second gangs – during holing, manuring, or cane cutting. At Vere Plantation, a small sugar plantation in Jamaica in 1779, there were seventy-nine slaves, including fifty-eight field hands. Such a group could and was probably worked as an individual unit but there were also two drivers, suggesting that there was some division into stronger and weaker hands during part of the year on even the smallest sugar estates.[34]

---

[32] Parnassus Plantation Slave Inventory, 1779; Jamaican Accounts, 1779, box 13, item 2.1/6 and 16, Wilberforce House Museum.

[33] Braco Estate Work Journal, 1796, in M. Craton, J. Walvin, and D. Wright, eds., *Slavery, Abolition and Emancipation: Black Slaves and the British Empire* (London: Longman, 1976), 110.

[34] Vere Plantation Slave Inventory, 1779; Jamaican Accounts, 1779, box 13, item 2.1/10 and 20, Wilberforce House Museum.

Although planters with fewer than fifty slaves were unlikely to try to grow sugar, if they had at least thirty able-bodied slaves they were likely to hire them out as a single "jobbing" gang to do tasks such as holing on other sugar estates.[35]

Overseers on medium-sized Barbadian estates, like their Jamaican counterparts, normally organized their field workers into two adult gangs. The number of adults in the first gang varied. With as many as ninety-eight slaves in 1797, the Newton first gang was much larger than the average first gang on the island. The sixty slaves in the first gang at Seawell in 1796–1797 was a normal size. At Drax Hall, there were sixty-nine workers in the first gang.[36] In 1783, there were two Codrington plantations in Barbados. They had fifty-one and thirty-five first-gang hands, and sixteen and nine second-gang hands, respectively. In both cases, about a third of the slaves on the estate worked in the first-gang. The thirty-five first-gang hands on the smaller Codrington estate was close to the minimum size of a Caribbean first gang.[37]

The gangs at the bottom of the hierarchy on sugar plantations consisted, for the most part, of young children doing light work with a female supervisor. Ideally, planters hoped, she would be "a careful Old Woman."[38] These predominantly child gangs were often known in Jamaica as "grass gangs," and in Barbados they were sometimes known as the "hogsmeat gang." Their primary task was to gather grass for the stock. They were not usually associated with the field hands. At Newton and Seawell, they did almost nothing but gather fodder for the stock.[39] An early nineteenth-century Jamaican planter suggested that these slaves were usually from six to nine years old.[40] Sometimes, depending on the health of the child or the strength of the plantation's force of field hands, children were allowed a longer time to physically mature in the grass gang. At Newton, a boy

---

[35] John Stewart, *An Account of Jamaica and Its Inhabitants* (London: Rees and Orme, 1808), 146.
[36] Drax Hall Slaves and Livestock from 1804 Inventory, Z9/11/5, Barbados Department of Archives.
[37] Inventory of the Codrington Plantations, May 1783/ C/COD/44, Codrington Papers, C series.
[38] William Dickson, *Letters on Slavery: To which are added, addresses to the whites, and to the free Negroes of Barbadoes; and accounts of some Negroes eminent for their virtues and abilities* (Westport: Negro Universities Press, [1789] 1970), 12; Belgrove, *Treatise upon Husbandry or Planting*, 65.
[39] Newton Work Log, 1796–1797, MS 523/110, Newton Family Papers.
[40] De la Beche, *Notes on the Present State of the Negroes*, 7.

named Thomas was kept in the grass gang until he was fourteen years old.[41] On larger estates, these younger children, if they were old enough, were put into a gang just beneath the second gang, sometimes called "the small gang" and forced to perform slightly more arduous tasks "with small hoes adapted to their size."[42] At Prospect, the third gang was referred to as both the "small gang" and the "children's" gang.[43] The labors of this gang were less regimented than that of others. According to the Jamaica planter Bryan Edwards, children's gangs were generally given "some such gentle exercise" in the field.[44] Yet, the evidence suggests that children's labors were not that gentle. One of the subadult skeletons in the Newton cemetery had a herniated lumbar disc, extremely rare among children or adolescents and indicative of demanding physical labor at a young age.[45]

The sugar plantation gang hierarchy fostered labor discipline and efficient labor allocation, but it was also a multi-tiered process of apprenticeship for younger field hands. Service in the lower ranks of this hierarchy, ideally, helped workers develop the knowledge, strength, and skills necessary to join the first gang, creating, as one plantation manual argued, a "perpetual succession of recruits, gradually trained and habituated to labour."[46] Such a process was part of an increasing recognition that field labor required skill and expertise. Discipline was also becoming more pronounced in the sugar fields, and most improving planters agreed that their slaves had to be habituated to increasing degrees of discipline. From the age of four or five, slaves were incorporated into the lowest tiers of the gangs "to preserve them from habits of idleness."[47] The growing emphasis on work as morally redemptive helped planters reconceptualize the gang system as a vehicle for moral reform. Service in the second gang was the final and most critical stage in the apprenticeship, and, according to one Barbadian plantation manual, planters should treat the "small people" of the second gang with "the greatest attention" to see that they became maximally productive as

---

[41] "Report on the [Newton] Negroes," Seawell Work Log, 1798, MS 523, 122, 288, Newton Family Papers.
[42] Collins, *Medical Treatment of Negro Slaves*, 180.
[43] Prospect Plantation Journal, 1785, 0627-0017; Prospect Plantation Journals, 1787–1793, 0627-0019.
[44] Edwards, *History, Civil and Commercial*, vol. 2, 121.
[45] Kristrina Shuler, "Health, History, and Sugar: A Bioarchaeological Study of Enslaved Africans from Newton Plantation, Barbados, West Indies" (Ph.D. dissertation, Southern Illinois University, Carbondale, 2005), 303.
[46] Collins, *Medical Treatment of Negro Slaves*, 182.
[47] Edwards, *History, Civil and Commercial*, vol. II, 121.

first-gang slaves.[48] To train the second-gang hands, the Barbadian planter Philip Gibbes thought it was essential that the second gang's driver be "a person of experience" who could "instruct the young negroes how to manage their hoes and to weed land and to dig holes in a proper manner."[49] The second gang was much smaller than the first, allowing the driver to more closely supervise the work done by these younger slaves.

There were some tasks that second gangs did much less often than first gangs, and there were some tasks that second gangs never did. First gangs were always chosen to cut canes, throw out dung onto the field, and dig cane holes. Second gangs almost never did these tasks. Second-gang hands spent far more time weeding and more time gathering, tying, and transporting trash than did firstgang hands. At Prospect Estate, in 1787, for example, second gang hands spent 50 percent of their work days weeding and cleaning canes compared to just 12 percent of workdays spent weeding and cleaning by first-gang hands. In 1791, the second gang spent 23 percent of its time weeding and cleaning compared to 1 percent of time spent on such work by first-gang slaves. Second-gang Prospect slaves spent twice as much time (22 percent compared to 11 percent) molding canes and nearly ten times as much time tending to the cane-hole banks, ensuring that the ridges were kept up around the holes to prevent erosion. Second-gang Newton slaves also spent more time tending to the growing canes (including such activities as molding and weeding) than their first-gang counterparts. In 1796–1797, the second gang at Newton spent 23 percent of its time on such tasks compared to only 4 percent of workdays spent by the first gang on such tasks. The slaves laboring in the second gang at Newton also spent more time in the sugar works than did first-gang slaves. While the first-gang slaves cut canes, sometimes as many as half of the second-gang slaves were sent to the works to assist with milling, boiling, and distilling. In total, from 1796 through 1798, the second gang spent 10 percent of its time in the works compared to the first gang's 6 percent. Tasks such as feeding the canes into the mill were less demanding and less skilled than wielding a harvesting knife among the cane stalks.

On sugar plantations that grew secondary cash crops, such as coffee or cotton, or provisions, the gangs immediately beneath the great gang spent far more time, proportionately, on these crops than the first gang did. The

---

[48] Edwin Lascelles et al., *Instructions for the Management of a Plantation in Barbadoes. And for the Treatment of Negroes, etc., etc., etc.* (London: [s.n.], 1786), 26.

[49] Philip Gibbes, *Instructions for the Treatment of Negroes, etc., etc., etc.* 2nd ed., with additions (London: Shepperson and Reynold's 1788), 16; see also Lascelles et al., *Management of a Plantation in Barbadoes*, 22; Higman, *Slave Populations of the British Caribbean*, 193.

"weak" at Somerset Vale were the slaves who were sent to bill coffee. At Seawell, where the management juggled cotton and canes, the overseers assigned most of the necessary cotton labor to the second gang. Just as the great gang was the holing gang, the second gang was normally the cotton gang. Compared to the first gang, the second gang at Seawell spent a much larger share of its cash crop working days on cotton (24 vs. 11 percent). They were not required to cut canes, but, during the harvest, they did pick and gin cotton. At Newton, from 1796 through 1798, the second gang spent 33 percent of its time on provision crops compared to 23 percent of the time spent by first-gang slaves. Likewise, at Seawell, in 1796–1797, the second-gang hands spent slightly more time on provisions than first-gang workers (34 percent compared to 29 percent). On all plantations, the second gang always performed tasks that were not only less physically demanding but also tasks that had the least impact on revenues.

To further encourage productivity and efficiency, planters and overseers in multi-tiered Caribbean gang systems sometimes used the gangs together on a task, dividing a cultivation chore into component parts that were more suitable for each gang while the gangs worked interdependently as a collective unit. This specialization and the synchronization of gangs was part of what made estates with multiple gangs more productive. Breaking a task down into its smaller component parts, which were steadily repeated throughout the day, made field work like assembly-line factory work. Interdependent labor appears to have been most common during the cane harvest. As the strongest gang cut canes, the secondary gang would follow closely behind to bundle the loose canes for transport to the mill and then return to tie together the trash for fueling the boiling house fires or for feeding the mill.[50]

Sugar planters may have also tried to employ interdependent gang labor at other points in the year. During planting, for example, the secondary gangs on some estates would precede the first gangs, dropping a cane plant in each cane hole for the first gang workers, who would dig a little deeper in the hole, place the plants horizontally, and cover them with dirt.[51] Late eighteenth-century plantation manuals encouraged readers to further maximize production by relying even more heavily on interdependent labor and

---

[50] William Clark, *Ten Views of the Island of Antigua* (London: T. Clay, 1823), plate III.
[51] Clark, *Ten Views of the Island of Antigua*, plate IV; see also John Dovaston, "Agricultura Americana or Improvements in West-India Husbandry Considered Wherein the Present System of Husbandry Used in England is Applied to the Cultivation or Growing of Sugar Canes to Advantage" [1774], Codex Eng 60, vol. 2. John Carter Brown Library.

more intricate divisions of labor. A 1786 Barbadian manual, for example, insisted that sugar planters should "proportion your second gang to the number of negroes employed in throwing out dung, so that the former may follow and cover up the dung as fast as the latter throw it out."[52] If planters used or advocated interdependent labor, it was normally with jobs that required the first gang's expertise or physical strength, such as throwing out dung, cutting canes, digging cane holes, or planting.

Having multiple gangs work interdependently together in one field not only made the cultivation process more efficient through task specialization and synchronization, it also reduced supervision costs and made it easier for drivers and overseers to maintain labor discipline. By tying the second gang's labors to the first gang's labors, planters could better dictate a constant working pace through two gangs at once, thus improving discipline. The stronger and more able first-gang workers would set a pace that the second-gang hands had to try to match. Interdependent labor in the same field meant that the second gang could better observe the labors of the first, but they also became accustomed to the pace of labor in the first gang, which greatly enhanced the apprenticeship aspects of multi-tiered gang labor. Having enough slaves on an estate to take advantage of a multi-tiered gang system and the interdependent synchronization of labor helped to create economies of scale on large plantations. The degree of specialization on an estate, the amount of interdependent gang labor, and the extent to which slaves were divided into gangs or subgangs increased during cane holing, planting, dunging, and harvesting. In weeding, provision cultivation, livestock work, and other aspects of plantation maintenance, planters rarely relied on interdependent or specialized labor. The tasks may not have been as easily reducible to repetitive component parts.

Plantation manuals advocated the synchronization of gangs, and most planters strongly encouraged it, especially in a post-*Wealth of Nations* era when managers throughout the British Atlantic were becoming more receptive to ideas about comparative advantages in labor specialization and to the benefits of proper labor division.[53] In daily practice, however, planters may not have relied as heavily on such synchronization as the improvers would have hoped. Work logs suggest that slave gangs often worked interdependently – especially when it came to cutting canes – but

---

[52] Lacelles et al., *Management of a Plantation*, 9.
[53] Adam Smith, *An Inquiry Into the Nature and Causes of the Wealth of Nations* (New York: The Modern Library, 1937 [1776]).

not as consistently as they could have. At Braco Estate, in Jamaica in 1796, the gangs were divided during the harvest into the "Great Gang or cutters" and the "Small Gang or tyers," suggesting the extent to which the overseers on that estate relied on synchronization of the first two gangs' chores.[54] Likewise, at Duckensfield Hall, in Jamaica in 1806, when the harvest began in December, on all but one day in which the first gang cut canes, the second gang spent the day gathering and bundling the canes on the same field.[55] Newton, in 1797–1798, stands as somewhat of a contrast. The first gang cut canes on ninety-three work days. Second gang hands did trash work or tied canes, presumably on the same field, on only twenty-three of those days. It is not clear who gathered and bundled canes and carried them to the mill on the other days. The slaves who were cutting may have stopped periodically to do the work themselves, allowing them a chance to rest their backs, weary from hours of being bent over cane stalks. Alternatively, some of the second-gang hands recorded as working "at the Mill" – sometimes as many as eight or one-quarter of the gang – may have been journeying to and from the field to bundle canes and transport them to the mill. On almost every harvest day, there were slaves assigned to work "with carts," who were probably doing most of the transport work.[56] At Prospect, the second gang very rarely assisted the first gang by tying trash during the harvest, but on some days the first gang was described as cutting the canes and tying the stalks on the same day. The slaves in Prospect's great gang, like their Newton counterparts, may have taken a break from cutting to tie cane stalks or collect trash, or a separate squad may have been carved from the first gang to undertake the task. Normally, a half-dozen men or slightly more would be assigned to work as mulemen during the Prospect harvest, gathering and transporting the canes over the mountainous cane fields back to the mill. Despite the apparent advantages of interdependent labor and the synchronization of multiple gangs, it may not have been easy to orchestrate this system in daily practice on some landscapes. The rocky, mountainous, and uneven fields of northeastern Jamaica, where Prospect lay, would have made both the pace of labor and the interdependent synchronization of gang labor more difficult to achieve. Essentially, plantation reformers may have envisioned and sought more interdependent gang labor than they could realistically achieve. Although most plantation improvers sought to compel their slaves

---

[54] "Braco Estate Work Journal, 1796," 110.
[55] Duckensfield Hall Estate Papers, Codex Eng-183, John Carter Brown Library.
[56] Newton Work Logs 1796–1798, MS 523/110, 123, Newton Family Papers.

to work both longer and faster, productivity gains in the Caribbean during this era owed more to the planter's control of the slaves' time than it did to the planter's ability to better dictate the slaves' working pace.

In contrast to the multiple gang divisions on Caribbean estates, Chesapeake workers were rarely organized into more than one gang on even the largest plantations. In part this was because large Chesapeake estates were divided into smaller farm "quarters." The number of adult workers on these individual quarters (a dozen to two dozen at most) was never large enough to justify two gangs. Planters who grew tobacco moved small units around to temporary quarters to cultivate the crop. Tobacco exhausted the soil quickly, forcing planters to relocate their fields often and rely on long periods of fallowing. At Mount Vernon, more than 8,000 acres in size by the time of his death, the quarters remained in effect even after Washington stopped growing tobacco. The five separate quarters at Mount Vernon were a way to divide the estate into more manageable units of cultivation. Field workers at Mount Vernon were associated with a quarter rather than a numbered and hierarchically ordered gang. This kind of organization made the work unit synonymous with the smaller enslaved community (i.e., the Muddy Hole gang or the Union Farm gang) rather than a first or second gang. There were effectively five Mount Vernon gangs – one on each farm quarter – but the division of labor was a product of the spatial dimensions of the estate and the division into five farm units, rather than a deliberate attempt on the part of the overseers and managers to differentiate between the capabilities of individual slaves. There were not enough workers on each farm to necessitate any further divisions for the sake of organization. Whereas skilled slaves moved throughout Mount Vernon's five farms, the day-to-day worlds of field hands on each quarter had narrower boundaries. As a work unit, they stayed in one place.

Although field hands in the Chesapeake were normally not divided into multiple numbered gangs for the sake of organization and physical classification, they were distinguishable from the skilled slaves, the domestics, and the children or the elderly, and they did often work collectively on tasks with a supervisor. They also worked in small squads on some days, or they worked in pairs. Less often, a single slave would spend the day alone. The pace of labor and the degree of synchronization among the gang changed with each task. Sugar plantation gangs had much more regimentation and supervision, but Chesapeake field hands were also closely watched. Chesapeake planters and overseers believed, as the Mount Vernon manager put it, that "The Negroes will slight and neglect their work unless they are

Closely attended to."[57] More supervisors meant higher costs, and the owners of highly organized Caribbean sugar plantations with vast revenues were better able to bear the cost of supervising multiple gangs than were Chesapeake managers.[58]

There was only one point in the Chesapeake cultivation cycle during which labor was divided to take full advantage of the interdependent potential of multiple gangs based on the physical abilities of the slaves. During the wheat harvest, while semiskilled hands mowed the wheat, subsidiary workers, generally younger or less physically capable slaves, were assigned to keep pace with them and collect the cut wheat.[59] It was also the closest that a Chesapeake overseer came to employing two separate gangs at any point during the cultivation cycle. In this sense, the labors of Chesapeake gangs were never as specialized as their counterparts on sugar plantations, but there were also no tasks on Chesapeake farms that, like cane holing or manuring on sugar plantations, could only be done by an elite force of field workers.

THE EFFICIENCY AND PRODUCTIVITY OF GANGS

As a gang, a group of slaves worked together on the same task – ideally at the same pace – from sunup to sundown. The gang system robbed slaves of autonomy and individuality in order to maximize production. Overseers used multiple gangs to help dictate the pace of labor, better supervise and discipline the workers, and create an economy and repetition of motion that would coerce the workers into greater exertion. William Dickson, a Barbadian, described a gang at work holing a field. "The holes are dug, with hoes, by the slaves, in a row, with the driver at one end, to preserve the line. They begin and finish a row of these holes as nearly, at the same instants, as possible."[60] In most tasks, slaves lined up in a long row and moved progressively, as a synchronized unit, across the field. According to a Jamaican observer, these

---

[57] William Pierce to George Washington, August 27, 1797, in W. W. Abbot, ed. *The Papers of George Washington*, 57 vols. Retirement series. (Charlottesville: University of Virginia Press, 1976), vol. 1, 321.

[58] Lorena S. Walsh, "Slave Life, Slave Society, and Tobacco Production in the Tidewater Chesapeake, 1620–1820," in Ira Berlin and Philip D. Morgan, ed., *Cultivation and Culture: Labor and the Shaping of Slave Life in the Americas* (Charlottesville: University Press of Virginia, 1993), 172–199.

[59] Philip D. Morgan, *Slave Counterpoint: Black Culture in the Eighteenth-Century Chesapeake and Lowcountry* (Chapel Hill: University of North Carolina Press, 1998), 171–174.

[60] Dickson, *Letters on Slavery*, 23.

rows "extended to a great distance" across the field.⁶¹ This monotonous repetition, synchronized movement, and forced pace was as psychologically demanding as it was physical. To combat the monotony and to attain the ideal pace of labor that would carry them through a day with the least amount of coercive abuse from the driver or overseer, slaves would sing through the day, controlling the working pace through the rhythm of the song.⁶² The singing harmonized community action and strengthened the slaves' spirit.

Slaves in a gang attained a kind of collective labor skill. Working as a unit, they developed a rhythm for accomplishing certain tasks, but it took time to develop an ideal pace. The longer the core members of a gang stayed together, and the more exposure they had to the first gang's labors before joining them, the more likely they were to develop a stronger sense of collective timing. This experiential learning added to the much greater value of creole slaves, especially those who were born on the plantation. Caribbean planters acknowledged the increased efficiency and skill of a set gang of slaves. Large planters, with sufficient resources, often hired a gang of thirty to fifty slaves from outside the estate – a "Jobbing" gang – to do the most demanding chores. Usually, men such as local overseers without sufficient capital to buy a mill and land to grow sugar bought enough slaves to assemble a jobbing gang and rented that gang out to sugar estates. Rather than hire individual slaves to assemble a gang, planters would hire this entire gang to do the particular job. Jobbing gangs were normally hired to hole or, less often, to dung a set number of acres at a piece rate per acre. In late eighteenth-century Barbados, holing was normally done at the rate of approximately £3 per acre, and in Jamaica, where the land tended to be more steep and rugged and less fully cleared and labor was more scarce, holing was done at £6–£7 an acre.⁶³ Contemporary estimates suggest that it took approximately thirty-three slaves a day to hole an acre of land.⁶⁴ Planters could have hired and assembled thirty-three

---

⁶¹ Marsden, *Account of the Island of Jamaica*, 29.
⁶² Collins, *Medical Treatment of Negro Slaves*, 191; Walter Jekyll, *Jamaican Song and Story* (London: D. Nutt, 1907), 157–189; Shane White and Graham White, *The Sounds of Slavery: Discovering African American History Through Songs, Sermons, and Speech* (Boston: Beacon Press, 2005).
⁶³ Heather Cateau, "The New 'Negro' Business: Hiring in the British West Indies, 1750–1810," in Alvin O. Thompson, ed., *In the Shadow of the Plantation: Caribbean History & Legacy* (Kingston, Jamaica: University of the West Indies Press, 2002), 105.
⁶⁴ Dickson, *Mitigation of Slavery*, 263. In St. Kitts, James Ramsay noted that it took thirty slaves a day; James Ramsay, *An Essay on the Treatment and Conversion of African Slaves in the British Sugar Colonies* (Dublin: T. Walker, C. Jenkin, R. Marchbank, L. White, R. Burton, P. Byrne, 1784), 119; *Society for the Improvement of Plantership*, 12.

individual field workers at a day rate to do the work instead of paying the piece rate. Once hired, that slave could have been put to any task the planter wished. Given the standard rate of hire each day for individual slaves, a Barbadian planter could have hired enough individuals to assemble a gang at a rate of approximately £1.65 a day (instead of £3), and in Jamaica it would have cost approximately £3.02 to hire enough individual slaves (instead of £6–£7) to hole an acre of land.[65] In other words, the piece rate for jobbing gangs was approximately twice as much as it would have cost to hire a sufficient number of individual adult slaves by the day to do the same task.

There were four important reasons why planters paid such a substantial premium for gang labor. First, the tasks for which jobbing gangs were normally hired – cane holing and throwing out dung – were demanding enough on the health of slaves that planters were paying a premium to preserve the health of their permanent labor force. The premiums were being paid for wear and tear on the jobbing gang. Second, planters paid more to avoid the logistical difficulties of finding, hiring, and assembling thirty-five individual slaves. Third, a jobbing gang came complete with a driver – a particularly valuable and knowledgeable slave who could dictate an appropriate labor pace. These jobbing gang drivers may have been even more skilled than regular plantation drivers at directing cane holing because, as part of a jobbing gang, they spent more time than plantation slaves digging cane holes – essentially, labor specialization. Fourth, and most important, planters preferred to hire a complete gang over individual slaves because that gang had already attained the rhythm and efficiency that came with working as a unit for an extended period of time – collective skill.

REFORMING AND IMPROVING GANGS

During the era of improvement, plantation manuals insisted that more attention needed to be paid to the appropriate division of gangs. There was significant tension in the improvement movement when it came to discussions of gang labor. Planters wanted to depersonalize slaves and make them into interchangeable and faceless units of production in order to aid

[65] I have converted the currency to a decimal system for this calculation. My rate of hire for slaves per day and per acre is drawn from Dickson's estimates as well as from the 1780s, from a combination of annual financial abstracts from Newton, Seawell, Mount Alleyne, and Turner's Hall. See bibliography for the location of these manuscripts; for rates of hire on different islands, see Dickson, *Mitigation of Slavery*; for Jamaica, see Cateau, "New Negro Business," 105.

quantification and make plantation work more predictable, but, when it came to gang labor, many reformers were arguing that this process had gone too far and that planters needed to pay more attention to the individuality of their workers in order to best divide and group their labor. The efficiency and high productivity of the gang system depended on the manager properly assessing each worker's skill, experience, and physical prowess. Philip Gibbes was a prominent Barbadian manager and attorney and a member of the Barbadian Society for the Improvement of Plantership. As the author of a popular plantation manual that went through three editions, he insisted that "One of the most important parts of management is a judicious division of negroes into gangs. The application of their labour to works suited to their strength and ability requires the strictest attention."[66] To better organize the gangs, the Barbadian Society for the Improvement of Plantership insisted that planters could and should rely on the advice of the principal slaves on the estate to determine who would be best for each gang. On "every plantation," the Society insisted, "there are leading people with powers to distinguish."[67] Deciding who should work in each gang was never an easy task. The slowest and weakest members of the gang would inevitably exhaust themselves in the struggle to keep pace. After describing a gang of slaves driven to hole a field with efficiency and precision, Dickson, a proponent of amelioration, noted that the problem with such labor was that "this *equal* task must be performed, in *the same time*, by a number of people who, it is *next to impossible*, should all be *equally strong and dexterous.*"[68] Many planters began to stress that the strictest attention to labor division was the key to increasing productivity, maintaining discipline, and keeping slaves alive.

Treatises on plantation management attacked the division of labor based on age alone as being not only inefficient but unhealthy. Dr. David Collins, the author of an 1803 plantation manual, thought that field hands were too often divided by age rather than ability, "power being inferred from age." Consequently, the gang never achieved an ideal working pace. Either the pace was too slow because "the weaker negroes" would "retard the progress of the stronger ones," or the pace would be too fast and the less able hands would be driven into the sick house. Collins was convinced that sugar slaves would have lower rates of mortality and morbidity if the managers would simply adhere to better principles of labor division. Too often, too

---

[66] Gibbes, *Treatment of Negroes*, 2nd ed., 10.
[67] *Society for the Improvement of Plantership*, 22.
[68] Dickson, *Letters on Slavery*, 23.

many slaves were grouped into the great gang based on their age alone and were required to do the most demanding labors. Collins, like many reformers, maintained that planters needed "a greater number of sections or gangs," despite the extra supervision costs.[69]

A few ameliorationists suggested that the monotony of gang labor might be improved by continuing to work with controlled and supervised motion but establishing production quotas each day and offering the gang the incentive of free time once the quotas were met.[70] The increasing interest in this task system reflected the growing late eighteenth-century belief in the importance of incentives to labor that was part of the emergence of a belief in the superiority of free labor.[71] Collins thought that the system of task labor as it was applied "in many parts of the continent of America" was useful and noted that the application of this task "ought to be done" wherever possible, but he thought that the "many well-meaning speculative men in England" who were suggesting the introduction of task labor to the Caribbean were somewhat naïve.[72] He doubted that task labor would work well on a sugar estate because the sugar slaves had to be divided into gangs in order to distinguish which slaves were capable of certain tasks (such as holing), and the strength of the gang fluctuated enough that it was impossible to expect a standard amount of labor from a gang each day. Because of the great variations in soil and weather conditions on even the smallest plantations, Barbadian Philip Gibbes argued like Collins that "It is impossible to prescribe any rule for the quantum of labour, which a gang of negroes should perform in a day."[73] A Jamaican planter agreed, suggesting that the task system would lead to widespread standardized production quotas that would be "a very great and manifest injustice" because there were enormous variations in the abilities of different gangs and in the landscape and soil of each plantation.[74] Essentially, planters argued that because each individual adult was different and because the strength of the gang changed too often, a standardized task could be as oppressive a labor system as the overseer's effort to divide slaves into gangs based on his perception of their physical abilities and force them to work at one standardized pace. Most planters seem to have not even considered the

---

[69] Collins, *Medical Treatment of Negro Slaves*, 176.
[70] Edwards, *History, Civil and Commercial*, 147.
[71] Drescher, *The Mighty Experiment: Free Labor Versus Slavery in British Emancipation.* (New York: Oxford University Press, 2002).
[72] Collins, *Medical Treatment of Negro Slaves*, 178.
[73] Gibbes, *Instructions for the Treatment of Negroes*, 2nd ed., 12.
[74] "Review of American Husbandry," xvi–xxx.

idea that slaves could be assigned individual tasks or that they could work separately. Tasks could only be given to the gang as a whole – collective tasking – which suggests how naturalized gang labor had become on sugar plantations. Caribbean planters were willing to enter into discussions about production quotas, but most had difficulty envisioning field slaves as anything but gang workers, collective entities.

SEXUAL DIVISION OF LABOR

Although gang labor divided slaves on the basis of their physical abilities into multiple groups, planters and overseers did not usually use gangs to divide men from women in the field. In Barbados, some evidence suggests that gang divisions were used until the middle of the eighteenth century to divide men from women during the cane holing season, at least conceptually. In Belgrove's version of Drax's seventeenth-century instructions to his manager, the manager was supposed "constantly to Gang all the Negroes in the Plantations in the Time of Planting" by putting "All the Men Negroes into two Gangs...by themselves, for Holeing and for Stronger Work" and the "Women Negroes also into two Gangs." These instructions do not appear in the surviving copy of Drax's instructions at the Bodleian Library, so it is hard to tell when this system emerged. At Lowther Estate, in Barbados in 1756, the men may have been divided from the women along the lines of what Belgrove suggested. There were 128 slaves at Lowther that year. The estate's slave inventory records a male driver supervising more than twenty-one male field hands, and, in a separate section, a female driver with eighteen female field hands. The two drivers indicate that two gangs were operating at Lowther but not whether there was a mix of males and females in each gang. Whether these divisions into separate gangs on the basis of sex were simply conceptual classification schemes or whether these divisions actually applied in field labor is unclear.[75]

To ensure that a sufficient number of laborers with equal ability could be found on a single estate, Caribbean planters increasingly maintained that the "stoutest and most able slaves," should, "without any regard being had to their sex," do the most demanding tasks.[76] In fact, there may have been less of an emphasis placed on a sexual division of field labor toward the

---

[75] Belgrove, *Treatise upon Husbandry or Planting*, 65; P. Thompson, "Henry Drax's Instructions," 582–604; Menard, *Sweet Negotiations*, 96; "Inventory of Negroes, Cattle & Horses on the Estate of Sir James Lowther Baronet in Barbadoes...31 December 1756," MS 43507, British Library.

[76] Collins, *Medical Treatment of Negro Slaves*, 176.

end of the eighteenth century than there had been in the early eighteenth century. There are "many women," Collins insisted, "who are capable of as much labour as men; and some men, of constitutions so delicate, as to be incapable of toil as the weakest women."[77] By the turn of the nineteenth century, the vast majority of field workers on sugar plantations were women. Women labored alongside men in regimented gang lines at the most difficult tasks on the plantation.[78] Women and men were hired at the same rate by plantations in need of extra labor, suggesting that planter's thought that there was little difference in their abilities. In Barbados, some planters acknowledged that there were differences in, at least, physical size between their male and female field hands, especially when they were purchasing tools. For example, Barbadian plantation ledgers sometimes recorded the purchase of "women's hoes."[79]

Although Chesapeake planters also used slave women in the field for the same tasks as men, the switch to grain and to plow agriculture and the increasing size of the slave population brought more labor divisions on the largest plantations, particularly sexual divisions among the field hands. Some of the tasks involved in cultivating wheat, such as mowing with a scythe, required skills that planters preferred to have the men learn. Men also did more of the plowing, perhaps because of the upper body strength required to keep the plow steady.[80] Men took most of the specialized and semiskilled occupations, and their labors became more varied, whereas women, ever wielding the hoe, continued to work more often on the most basic and monotonous of jobs in the field.[81]

Physical ability, age, and skill were the factors Caribbean planters considered most important in dividing slaves into gangs in the late eighteenth century, but it would be an exaggeration to argue that there was no sexual division of labor in the sugar fields. Men were usually but not

---

[77] Ibid.
[78] Richard Dunn, "Sugar Production and Slave Women in Jamaica," in Berlin and Morgan, eds., *Cultivation and Culture: Labor and the Shaping of Slave Life in the Americas* (Richmond: University Press of Virginia, 1993), 49–72; Solomon Northup, *Twelve Years a Slave* (Baton Rouge: Louisiana State University Press, [1855] 1968), 117, 123.
[79] Hannays Plantation Accounts, 1795–1796, Shilstone Library, Barbados Museum and Historical Society; "An Abstract of the Crop and Expenses of Turner's Hall Plantation for the property of Sir Henry Fitzherbert Bart for the year 1830," E20711, Fitzherbert Papers.
[80] Morgan, *Slave Counterpoint*, 171–175.
[81] Lorena S. Walsh, "Land Use, Settlement Patterns and the Impact of European Agriculture, 1620–1820," in Philip D. Curtin et al., eds. *Discovering the Chesapeake: The History of an Ecosystem* (Baltimore: Johns Hopkins University Press, 2001), 243.

exclusively chosen as work leaders, and some chores were more often assigned to women. At Somerset Vale, in the late 1770s, the forty-two women and seventeen men worked together as a gang throughout most of the year, but when there was building or construction work, such as sawing or splitting shingles for a new trash house to be done, the majority of the men were removed from the gang to undertake those jobs while the women remained in the field. When the women worked alone, they were almost always forced to do weeding or cleaning crops.[82] At Newton and Prospect, the first and second gangs were sometimes carved into more specialized female gangs. Most Barbadian planters agreed that there would always be a smaller group of "inefficient people" within the first gang. At Newton, this group was comprised of eleven adult women; they were identified in the July 1796 census as "the infirm gang."[83] They may not have always worked alongside the more physically able slaves, but they were potentially productive enough to be associated with the first gang. In 1796–1797, these women were probably among those workers who were regularly carved from the main gang to work as an independent squad led by a woman named Molly. Molly, fifty years old, was the mother of the first-gang driver Dickey-Budd.[84] Her association with Dickey-Budd undoubtedly helped her secure the position as this work squad's leader.

Molly's squad had between six and thirty-one workers in it throughout the year. Most commonly, there were twenty-one to twenty-three people in it. Her gang included all the infirm women from the first gang and, perhaps, women who were pregnant or recovering from pregnancy. Indeed, given that the supervisor was a woman, and most supervisors among adult field hands were male, this squad of slaves might have been entirely female. This separate gang suggests some sexual division of labor but these divisions had porous boundaries. Molly's group was not always working separately, there were no specific tasks from which they were always excluded, and, even on days when slaves worked with Molly, there would have been at least twenty-four other women who remained working with the rest of the men in the first gang.

On the days that Molly's squad was separated from the main body of the gang (46 percent of all possible working days), they performed predominantly provision work and weeding.[85] Molly's gang spent two days

---

[82] Somerset Vale Logs, 1776–1780, Codex Eng 180.
[83] "Report on the [Newton] Negroes," MS 523/288, Newton Family Papers.
[84] Ibid.
[85] Newton Work Log, 1796–1797, MS 523/110, Newton Family Papers.

"digging up banks and distance" between the cane holes.[86] This was as close as this group came to doing a task that required more exertion or precision. During the cane harvest, there was never a group working "with Molly" but that does not mean that her charges were all cutting canes. On any day in which the main body of the Newton gang cut canes, between eleven and twenty-one first-gang slaves worked "with carts," "at the mill," "in the boiling house," or "in the distilling house." Jobs at the mill and boiling house at Newton included carrying canes and feeding them to the mill, and overseers often reserved these jobs for less efficient workers or for women. William Clark, in his *Ten Views of the Island of Antigua* noted that after the canes were left near the mill, they were carried into the mill by "the labour of the Negro-girls."[87] Some of Molly's female crew probably worked at the mill or at the boiling house during the harvest.

At Prospect, in 1785, there was also a gang working under the direction of a woman: "Jubar's gang." Jubar was an older woman and a mother. She had a young child who died in November of 1785 while she led the gang.[88] From a total of approximately ninety to one-hundred field workers of all ages and abilities, seven to twenty-two were drawn to work under Jubar on nearly every day of the year. It is not clear from which group these slaves were drawn or who they were. Some of them were probably the inefficient slaves from the first gang. Given their leader, most of them were probably women. On days in which Jubar's gang worked together, there was also a great gang working and a small gang with only fourteen slaves. On the few days in which Jubar's gang was not recorded in the logs, the small gang would grow to include more than thirty slaves, incorporating most of Jubar's charges and possibly Jubar herself. Like Molly, Jubar led her gang in lighter tasks, predominantly weeding and cleaning crops.[89] Yet, Jubar also led her gang in cane holing for three days in 1785. Given her sex and planters' bias toward using men as drivers for first-gang tasks, this was remarkable. A combination of gender ratios and the tremendous labor requirements of cane holing forced planters to overlook European gender norms and employ their women in cane holing and in every field task performed by male slaves, but they could easily have avoided using women as supervisors for field work. The fact that Jubar led a gang in cane holing, if only for three days, suggests that Caribbean planters could overlook the

---

[86] Ibid.
[87] Clark, *Ten Views of the Island of Antigua*, plate IV.
[88] Prospect Plantation Journal, 1785, 0627-0017; Prospect Plantation Journals, 1787–1793, 0627-0019.
[89] Ibid.

sex of the slaves, sometimes even for the most arduous jobs, in order to choose the best and most experienced work leaders for the task at hand.

As a nonessential task requiring little strength or skill, weeding was almost always the work that less capable hands were asked to perform. Although, second-gang hands at Newton and Seawell were almost never assigned to dig cane holes or plant or cut canes, they did a major share of the weeding and cleaning (from 24 to 30 percent of their work days) – more than first-gang workers. They were not, however, as specialized in weeding as the groups led by Molly or by Jubar. In total, three-quarters of work days "with Molly" were spent weeding various crops. On days when Molly's gang was not working, the first gang spent only 1 percent of its time weeding.[90] Likewise, Jubar's gang spent the vast majority of its time in 1785 (80 percent of work days) "cleaning" canes, which meant, primarily, weeding but also clearing dead stalks, debris, and pests. Molly and Jubar's gangs were what many sugar planters, particularly in Jamaica, referred to as the "weeding gang."[91] At Phillipsfield and Pleasant Hill, there were also separate specialized "weeding gangs" working on their own.[92] Fewer than ten slaves worked in these gangs. Like Molly's and Jubar's gangs, these were probably female-dominated gangs. In 1789, when Jubar died, a man name Reynold took over the leadership of her weeding gang, indicating that the weeding gang was predominantly but never exclusively female.[93]

Women were the majority in most Caribbean field gangs at the close of the eighteenth century, but they were normally denied roles as the leaders of the most productive gangs. Some women, such as Molly and Jubar, were chosen to lead smaller squads, but most of the jobs they supervised were deemed not vital to the cash crop regime – such as weeding, cleaning, or tending provisions. The slaves never worked with Molly and rarely worked with Jubar on field tasks that required a greater degree of exertion or skill, such as digging cane holes, cutting canes, or planting canes. A male driver was almost always chosen to oversee these tasks. Female-led gangs tended to be weeding gangs doing mostly weeding work. Weeding was women's work, and planters trusted in women to lead weeding gangs.

---

[90] Newton Work Logs, 1796–1797, MS 523/110, Newton Family Papers.
[91] Thomas Roughley, *The Jamaica Planters' Guide; or, a System for Planting and Managing a Sugar Estate or Other Plantation in that Island and throughout the British West Indies in General* (London: Longman, Hurst, Rees, Orme, & Brown, 1823), 401.
[92] Pleasant Hill Work Log, March 15 to March 20, 1790, MS8492, Slebech Papers; Phillipsfield Work Log, March 15 to March 20, 1790, MS8491, Slebech Papers.
[93] Prospect Plantation Journals, 1787–1793, 0627-0019.

CONCLUSION

The one constant in all plantation ganging systems was the length of the working day in the field – sunup to sundown. For a gang slave, there was no incentive to hasten the completion of the day's chores. Other than those commonalities, there were major differences between the system of ganging employed on a large, diversified Chesapeake farm and the system that drove Caribbean sugar production. Militaristic precision was a key aspect of gang labor on a Caribbean sugar estate. Gang labor on sugar plantations was multi-tiered, highly disciplined, and there was a much more extensive division of labor and more interdependent work than there was in the Chesapeake. Sugar gangs were organized to achieve the greatest degree of labor specialization possible, and sugar slaves were grouped according to their ability to perform the most demanding tasks.

With the growth of the amelioration and agricultural improvement movement, Caribbean agricultural reformers began to advocate even greater and more precise divisions of labor, suggesting that more gangs be divided. More gangs, however, would require more drivers, and good leaders were never easy to train or acquire. Although most planters began to focus on improving ganging systems, others, believing that incentives to labor would increase efficiency and production, started entertaining the idea of using task labor in sugar production, offering slaves the incentive of free time to encourage labor. Task labor changed the way some sugar planters operated in the early nineteenth century, but its effects were limited. Most planters insisted on continuing to use gang labor, and, when they adopted tasking, it was as a limited hybrid task and gang labor system – collective tasking.

The demands of a crop played an important role in determining the kinds of ganging that would form on an estate. Laboring on some crops required more supervision than on others. The most significant and demanding task in sugar cultivation was cane holing. The regimentation and economy of motion that accompanied the most extreme form of gang labor may have been most useful during cane holing, the most brutal of all tasks on a sugar plantation. Cane holing in the Barbadian style – which was adopted in the late seventeenth century – might have encouraged the division into gangs to determine who was capable of holing, and the task itself might have encouraged the kind of disciplined lockstep motion that accompanied the most extreme forms of gang labor. The grid pattern that most planters adopted in cane holing helped encourage the synchronization of movement in a gang and a consistent pace.

Gang Work and the Division of Labor

Caribbean gang labor was as much a hierarchical system of classification as a description of how slaves labored. When overseers drew up work logs, they organized slaves conceptually into gangs in order to allocate tasks. The gang alignment indicated the value of that slave's labor as a resource, and the work logs showed what that resource was being spent on or how much of the resource was lost to sickness, runaways, or pregnancies. Slaves in each gang did not always labor collectively. Sometimes smaller squads, such as Molly's gang, were formed from the larger group, the gang was split to undertake different tasks, or individual slaves would be drawn from the collective to do an array of smaller chores, such as minding cattle, running errands in town, or nursing pregnant slaves.

On large estates in the Chesapeake, there was normally only one gang on each quarter. There were few tasks on a Chesapeake estate that were so much more arduous than the rest that they required extensive divisions of labor based on the physical abilities of the worker. Tobacco required skill and close supervision, and the rhythmic pace of gang labor helped with the intensive demands required during the wheat harvest. The wheat harvest was the only point during the year at Mount Vernon in which there was a division into more than one gang on any of the quarters. During the harvest, some slaves mowed wheat while others followed and collected the crop – a kind of interdependent gang labor division similar to the harvesting of cane. It was the only point in the year in which Chesapeake gang organization looked even remotely like the gang system on a sugar plantation. In general, Chesapeake gangs were small, normally fewer than two dozen slaves. There were no economies of scale in wheat or tobacco production that were comparable to sugar, and the crops were less labor intensive, meaning that the density of laborers on Chesapeake estates was lower than in the Caribbean. Chesapeake planters and overseers did try to encourage a rhythmic pace and an economy of motion in their gangs. A headman would set a pace that the others would follow, but the style of labor in Chesapeake gangs never matched the militaristic discipline that characterized labor on most collective tasks in the archetypal sugar gangs.

Although gang labor was the primary system of field labor organization and allocation used in Barbados, Jamaica, and Virginia, the contrasts between gang labor on a Caribbean sugar estate, such as Prospect in Jamaica, and a Chesapeake mixed-farming unit, such as Mount Vernon, were stark. Chesapeake gang labor was more loosely organized and less extensively divided than in the Caribbean. Chesapeake slaves worked collectively but in much smaller groups than on sugar plantations. Gang labor on sugar plantations was highly disciplined and closely supervised; it often relied on interdependent labor among the gangs, and it was part of an extensive division of labor. Although slaves in all systems of ganging worked from sunup to sundown, the physical and psychological demands of ganging were most severe on sugar plantations, and the extensive divisions of labor and the labor discipline on sugar plantations shaped the working world and the lives of the slaves more significantly than the system of gang labor shaped the lives and work of slaves in the Chesapeake.

4

Negotiating Sickness

Health, Work, and Seasonality

Sick or otherwise, enslaved workers in the Chesapeake and the Caribbean toiled through the vast majority of the year, missing remarkably few days to illness. The slaves were undoubtedly battered and exhausted from overwork, particularly in the sugar islands, but they were kept at their labors. To keep slaves in the field for more days each year, planters increasingly stressed the need to police the boundaries between real and feigned illness. Slaves, in return, struggled to resist the increase in working days. Acting as if they were too ill or injured to work could give them a day of respite. David Collins, the St. Vincent physician and author of an early nineteenth-century guide for managing sugar slaves, observed that "when labour presses, all [slaves] would be ill to escape the field," but he also warned his readers that "no care of the planter, however laudably exerted, can prevent his having many sick people on his hands."[1] Plantation labor, especially in the Caribbean, was simply too draining, and planters had to accept there would always be a few slaves too sick to make it into the field. Collins was also admitting that planters would never know for sure if some slaves were too sick to work.

The meaning or significance of sickness and its identification and treatment became a point of tension in plantation management strategies. Healthier slaves, many planters argued, were more productive and reproductive workers, but every day that a planter allowed the slave to rest in the sick house was an idle day, a day of lost labor. In the closing decades of the eighteenth century, planters in Virginia, Barbados, and Jamaica engaged in a

---

[1] David Collins, *Practical Rules for the Management and Medical Treatment of Negro Slaves in the Sugar Colonies* (London: J. Barfield, 1803), 231, 236.

common struggle to minimize the time slaves spent sick and maximize labor output while still adhering to what they saw as ameliorationist principles of management. Slaves fought to protect their own health, and they resisted being forced to work through illness and injury.

"Health" and "sickness" are terms that must be used with caution. They are ambiguous terms, especially in a discussion of plantation life. A slave who was sick enough to be removed from the workforce could have been suffering from a wide range of maladies (broken bones, mental illnesses, infections, viruses, etc.), and a working slave was not necessarily a well slave. It would be wrong to characterize the vast majority of underfed and overworked slaves in the fields each day in the Caribbean or the Chesapeake as healthy. Health and sickness are relative rather than absolute concepts. Rates of increase or decrease among slave populations can be used as indicators of their collective health, but they are not the sole indicators. There was an array of other physical and even psychological factors involved in a slave's mental and physical well-being. It can be said, however, that Caribbean sugar slaves were, generally, less healthy than their better-fed and less intensely worked counterparts in the Chesapeake.

Virginian slave populations achieved positive natural reproductive growth by the end of the first decade of the eighteenth century. The Chesapeake quickly became the healthiest slave society in the Americas. In the last half of the eighteenth century, the Virginian slave population grew naturally at a rate of approximately 2–3 percent a year.[2] Caribbean sugar plantations, in sharp contrast to Chesapeake grain plantations, exacted a nightmarish toll. Death, disease, and disability ravaged the slave populations. Jamaican slaves, like most sugar slaves, were never self-reproducing. In the eighteenth century, they decreased by somewhere between 2 and 3.5 percent annually.[3] In terms of achieving natural increase before emancipation, Barbados became unique among the Caribbean sugar islands, but slave deaths exceeded births and the population decreased by about 2 percent per annum through most of the last half of the eighteenth century.[4] The health of a plantation's slaves was most closely connected to the demands of work. Slaves on Jamaican coffee plantations and livestock pens had better reproductive rates than slaves on

---

[2] Philip D. Morgan, *Slave Counterpoint: Black Culture in the Eighteenth-Century Chesapeake and Lowcountry* (Chapel Hill: University of North Carolina Press, 1998), 81.

[3] Kenneth Kiple estimates between 3 and 3.5 percent; see Kiple, *The Caribbean Slave: A Biological History* (New York: Cambridge University Press, 1984), 106. A sample of 10,350 slaves living on fourteen sugar plantations in Jamaica between 1779 and 1809 showed a rate of natural decline of 1.94 percent. For the records used in this sample, see Figure 4.3.

[4] Kiple, *Caribbean Slave*, 106.

sugar plantations, suggesting that work trumped the environment as a factor in the health of enslaved populations. Sugar was the most demanding of the staple crops for slaves to produce.[5] Chesapeake tobacco cultivation also placed considerable demands on the health of slaves, but it was not nearly as devastating as sugar. The switch to wheat and corn and mixed farming over the course of the eighteenth century improved working conditions for slaves. Wheat and corn were among the least demanding crops to produce.

This chapter focuses on the relationship between plantation work, health, and seasonality. It begins by exploring how planters introduced more discipline and supervision into plantation health care to coerce and compel even more labor from slaves. To assess the amount of annual labor time lost to illness and the health implications of particular working conditions, this chapter determines how many days the average slaves spent sick, and it identifies whether age or sex played a role in how many days slaves missed work because of illness. It determines the ways in which sickness was connected to seasonal rhythms and work routines. It concludes by exploring the effects that weather and climate had on working conditions, the concerns that planters had about weather and health, and the degree to which they responded to these concerns in their strategies for allocating labor.

THE DISCIPLINE OF PLANTATION HEALTH CARE

Improving planters tried to curb slaves' freedoms to improve their health, and they closely supervised them to discourage the slaves' from faking or exaggerating an illness or injury. Every element of a planters' medical management of his workers was geared toward maximizing the amount of work slaves could perform without having to rely too excessively on imports. For most planters, letting a slave recover from illness or injury was less a matter of benevolent management and more a matter of exchanging the present value of a slaves' work for greater future value. Permitting a sick slave to occasionally miss a day or half a day, one Jamaican insisted, would "obviate the loss probably of many days."[6] Wood, the manager at Newton, agreed with such a policy, and he insisted that the slaves' long-term health was one of his chief concerns, although he complained that it was "it is

---

[5] Ibid.
[6] Patrick Kein, *An Essay upon Pen-Keeping and Plantership* (Kingston, Jamaica: His Majesty's Printing Office, 1796), 24.

impossible to tell when a person is sick or not."[7] To solve the dilemma, Wood forced sick slaves back to work as soon he found "their digestion good & their appetite keen."[8] Likewise, to avoid an unnecessary loss of labor, the author of an 1801 plantation manual argued that a planter should dwell on "the disgusting appearance of the [sick] Negroes...How nasty they look..." in order to compel them to heal and return to work.[9] In contracts with overseers, George Washington stipulated that they "be very careful of the Negroes in sickness," but he was certain that slaves feigned sickness, and he read the work logs returned by his overseers with a keen eye to ensure that slaves, unless they were exceptionally ill or injured, never missed work for more than a week.[10] For Washington, "Nobody can be very sick without having a Fever" and real pain "will appear by its effects." Otherwise, slaves were being "lazy" and "deceitful," and they should be working.[11] There was constant tension between the planter's desire to be ameliorative in his management and his fear that the slave would win the struggle for time through deception, by seeming to be something other than what they were.

Sick slaves in Jamaica, Barbados, and Virginia were sometimes sent to recuperate at a designated site, but the nature of such sites varied widely. On large Caribbean estates, sick or injured slaves were normally confined to a hospital or infirmary, sometimes called a "Sick House" or, in Jamaica, a "Hot House." This was a separate building normally located in the plantation yard near the mill – to enable better supervision. The term "Hot House" might have originated among the slaves. According to one nineteenth-century Jamaican planter, every plantation had a "hot-house, as the negroes are pleased to call it." Some eighteenth-century Jamaican estates had separate "Warm & Hot Houses" for slaves with different maladies. It is not clear which buildings were reserved for which maladies.[12] According

---

[7] "Report on the Buildings at Newton," MS 523/290, Newton Family Papers.
[8] Sampson Wood to Thomas Lane, September 8, 1797, MS 523/324, Newton Family Papers.
[9] Clement Caines, *Letters on the Cultivation of the Otaheite cane: the manufacture of sugar and rum; the saving of melasses; the care and preservation of stock; with the attention and anxiety which is due to Negroes: To these topics are added, a few other particulars analogous to the subject of the letters; and also a speech on the slave trade, the most important feature in West Indian cultivation* (London: Messrs. Robinson, 1801), 152.
[10] Articles of Agreement with William Garber, December 10, 1788, in Twohig, ed., *Papers of George Washington*, Presidential Series, vol. 1, 172.
[11] George Washington to William Pearce, March 22, 1795, in Fitzpatrick, ed., *Writings of Washington*, vol. 34, 153.
[12] H.T. De La Beche, *Notes on the Present Condition of the Negroes in Jamaica* (London: T. Cadell in the Strand, 1825), 25; "Mr. Richard Beckford's Instruction to Messrs. John Cope, Richard Lewing and Robert Mason, Westmoreland, 10 April, 1754," Monson 31.86, Thistlewood Papers; William Hilary, *Observations on the Changes of the Air and the*

to the Newton manager, plantation hospitals were "for slaves who are not very sick, but either in reality or from pretence not fit to work."[13] Slaves with more severe, long-term, and debilitating illnesses were kept in their houses and, essentially, removed from the plantation workforce. Likewise, slaves with permanently crippling injuries were not normally kept in the infirmaries. Unless they were complete "invalids" or so old that they had become "superannuated," they were assigned nonfield tasks better suited to their capacity, such as guard duty. In Virginia, with naturally reproducing slave populations and, consequently, planters who were less concerned about promoting life and reproduction, a designated building for sick slaves was less common. Only the largest estates had the resources or revenues for a hospital or a large enough slave population to justify the existence of a hospital but, even on these estates, there was rarely a specific building for sick slaves. At Mount Vernon, smaller groups of slaves worked on quarters spread across an estate that was more than fifteen times the size of a large sugar plantation, making the construction of a single large, centralized, and fixed building for the sick less practical. Instead, Virginian slaves tended to be confined to their houses.

Hospitals were not common on Caribbean estates until after the middle of the eighteenth century. Plantation hospitals – designed to control, discipline, and punish as much as they were designed to heal – were physical manifestations of the growing concern with both amelioration and improvement. They were dark and dreary places that grouped slaves with a wide variety of maladies, from musculoskeletal complaints to infectious diseases, into a small space. In 1796, the new manager at Newton described the sick house as "a horrid unhealthy hole."[14] An advice guide for planters noted that plantation hospitals were "rather a disgusting scene, charged with unpleasant odors, and occupied by offensive objects."[15] There was little in the way of furniture in most sick houses. Slaves lay on the floor. Some of the infirmaries had cupboards for medicine. In the Phillipsfield hot house, there was only "1 Old Chair."[16] Most sick houses had chamber pots for the slaves.[17] Building materials were scarce and expensive, especially in the

---

Concomitant Epidemical Diseases in Barbadoes (London: L. Hawes, W. Clarke, and R. Collins, 1759); Matthew Lewis, *Journal of a West India Proprietor: Kept During a Residence in the Island of Jamaica* (London, J. Murray, 1834), 122, 342; Kein, *Pen-keeping and Plantership*, 24.

[13] See "Report on the Buildings at Newton," Newton Family Papers.
[14] Ibid.
[15] Collins, *Medical Treatment of Negro Slaves*, 254.
[16] Inventory and Valuation of Nathaniel Phillips Estates, 1789, MS11523, Slebech Papers.
[17] Annual Abstract, 1772, 1785, 1793, E20696, E20682, E20700, Fitzherbert Papers.

Leeward and Windward Island, so the space in a plantation hospital was often limited. In 1796, the sick house at Seawell in Barbados was 576 square feet.[18] This meant the amount of space available for sick slaves at Seawell ranged from less than thirty-six to eighty square feet per day, depending on how many people were in the sick house. Such conditions must have encouraged the growth of bacteria and the spread of contagious diseases and parasites.

Sick houses were designed so that slaves could rest and recover until they could work again, but they also maintained discipline and order among nonworking slaves. Just as eighteenth-century English workhouses served to correct the indolence of the poor, plantation hospitals punished slaves for being unable to work. In fact, the conditions in sick houses were so undesirable that slaves were kept in infirmaries under lock and key. Slaves, the Newton manager explained, were "confined" to the sick house "till they profess themselves ready to go to work again."[19] The windows and doors in sick houses, if there were any, were kept tightly shut to prevent slaves from leaving during the day or night.[20] According to one plantation manual, sick house windows should be "fortified with bars, or jealousies to prevent the escape of the negroes."[21] With little fresh air and tightly packed quarters, a hospital under the hot Caribbean sun must have been muggy and suffocating – literally a "hot house." Hospitals were designed not only to heal but to discipline and punish, to compel slaves to want to work instead. According to Collins, "It is not the sick only, but, sometimes, negroes in health," who were sent to the hospital because their "offenses are too light to require the dungeon."[22] In the hospital, Collins explained, "they suffer a privation of amusements and are forthcoming to their labour."[23] At both Pleasant Hill and at Phillipsfield in Jamaica, there were a "Pair [of] Stocks" in the "Hot House."[24] Overseers probably used these stocks to keep the most resistant slaves from escaping the infirmary. Stocks were also used to render a slave immobile during treatments.[25]

---

[18] "Report on the Land of Seawell Plantation," MS 523/291, Newton Family Papers.

[19] "Report on the Buildings at Newton," MS 523/290, Newton Family Papers.

[20] Jerome S. Handler, "Plantation Slave Settlements in Barbados, 1650s to 1834," in Alvin O. Thompson, ed., *In the Shadow of the Plantation: Caribbean History and Legacy* (Kingston, Jamaica: Ian Randle, 2002), 139–140; "Report on the Buildings at Newton."

[21] Collins, *Medical Treatment of Negro Slaves*, 255.

[22] Ibid., 265; see also Alexander Barclay, *A Practical View of the Present State of Slavery in the West Indies* (London: Smith, Elder & Company, 1827), 322.

[23] Collins, *Medical Treatment of Negro Slaves*, 265.

[24] Inventory and Valuation of Nathaniel Phillips Estates, 1789, MS11523, Slebech Papers.

[25] Collins, *Medical Treatment of Negro Slaves*, 265.

Ameliorationists believed that imprisoning slaves in a sick house would discourage feigned illness because slaves "abhor confinement, which disables them from attending to their own little concerns."[26] One plantation manual recommended that a slave who entered the hospital at any time during the work week, "however slight his complaint may be," should be forced to remain through Sunday until the following Monday morning, to keep slaves from attending any festivities or traveling and to discourage fakers by depriving them of their one given day.[27] For a slave, choosing between toiling in the fields and drawing attention to (or feigning) sickness to stay in the infirmary would not have been easy. Most slaves probably reported to the sick house not when they felt sore or weak but when they were too ill or injured to work at all.

SICKNESS RATES

Jamaican slaves tended to be on the plantation sick rolls more often than Barbadian or Virginian slaves, corresponding with the higher rates of population decline in Jamaica. At Prospect, in Jamaica, in 1787, the plantation was less than four years old, and the majority of the slaves were recent imports still adjusting to the climate, the disease environment, and the workload. The initial work of clearing, settling, and cultivating a sugar plantation was exceptionally demanding. The sickness rate for the entire workforce that year was devastatingly high. Prospect slaves missed work because of health problems for an average of forty days per person year in 1787. However, this average includes slaves in all occupations. Of the 117 laborers at Prospect in 1787, about eighty were adult field workers.[28] Their labors were more demanding than those of nonfield workers, and they suffered more from exposure to the weather. It is impossible to be precise with the Prospect sickness data but the evidence suggests that the average number of sick days per field slave at Prospect was closer to fifty days each year.

Sickness rates per slave at Prospect did not remain consistently high. Annual levels of disease and injury could vary greatly on sugar plantations. The annual rate of sickness among the total Prospect workforce fell from an average of at least forty days per worker in 1787 to about fourteen days

[26] Ibid., 261.
[27] Caines, *Cultivation of Otaheite Cane*, 148.
[28] Prospect Plantation Journals, 1787–1793, 0627-0019.

in 1791.[29] For the average field worker, it was probably closer to twenty-one days in 1791, but this was still much lower than six years earlier. The "seasoning" process had ended for the new Africans, and the brutal work of clearing and preparing land on a new plantation was, for the most part, over. At the same time, lower sickness rates were not always the product of better health among the slaves. Threats, force, confinement, and the whip also played important roles in keeping the slaves from reporting to the plantation hospital. Prospect's planters in the 1780s and 1790s were trying to combat a declining workforce and maintain sugar yields. Keeping slaves in the field rather than in the sick house was one way to address an inadequate labor force, but ignoring illness and injury eventually brought diminishing returns in labor productivity and, eventually, death. For the Prospect slaves, of course, less days in the sick house meant more unremitting and exhausting toil, consistent with the increasing amount of labor in the improvement era.

Annual sickness rates per slave were lower on well-established plantations than they were on newly formed Jamaican plantations, but not by much.[30] At Pleasant Hill, thirty of approximately 360 workers were in the sick house each day in the first week of June, 1789. That sickness rate would have been equal to twenty-one annual sick days per slave. In mid-March, 1790, twenty-four people were in the sick house, approximately the same rate of sickness. In early June, 1789, the sickness rate would have been equivalent to more than forty-five days per slave each year. In mid-March of 1790, the sickness rate among all workers was similarly high. It would have translated to thirty-nine sick days per slave per year.[31] With approximately the same number of slaves in the sick house on both estates in July 1789, the overseer reported that "The Negroes still continues [sic] in pretty good health."[32] As with Prospect, the overall sickness rates per slave at Pleasant Hill and Phillipsfield were almost certainly lower than the rates of sickness among field hands. In fact, on most days, the "hot house" or plantation hospital was probably dominated by field workers, exhausted from toiling in the canes. Assuming that three-quarters of the slaves in the sick house were adult field slaves, then sickness rates among the adult field hands at Phillipsfield and Pleasant Hill in 1789–1790 ranged from approximately twenty-six to forty-nine days per year, and the surviving records are from

---

[29] Ibid.
[30] MS 8489–MS 8492, Slebech Papers.
[31] MS 8489–MS 8492, Slebech Papers.
[32] Thomas Barritt to Nathaniel Phillips, July 24, 1789, MS8343, Slebech Papers.

the harvest season, normally the healthiest time of the year. The planters at Pleasant Hill and Phillipsfield appear to have been losing approximately 16 percent of their field workers on any given day during the harvest, which must have exacerbated the chronic labor shortages on the estates. Yet, they reported that the slaves were in good health. Clearly, matters could get much worse on a Jamaican sugar estate.

The evidence suggests that Barbadian slaves spent much less time in the plantation hospitals than their Jamaican counterparts. Contemporaries agreed that the conditions of slaves in Barbados were better than elsewhere and that treatment was somehow milder.[33] The work of cultivating sugar in Barbados may have been less laborious than it was in Jamaica because the Barbadian terrain was not as steep and rugged. The trade winds also kept temperatures cooler in Barbados than on many of the islands, making the climate more pleasant. A visitor to Barbados in 1774 noted that Barbados was "reckoned the most healthy Island in the West Indies."[34] During 1796–1797, field workers at Newton and Seawell were in the sick house for an annual average of between twenty-one and twenty-five days, with little difference between first- and second-gang slaves or between the plantations. The manager for both estates was new that year, and this may have inflated the number of sick days. Slaves were better able to deceive a new manager about the extent of their illnesses or infirmities. The next year, the field workers at Newton were in the sick house for an average of only fourteen days each, more than a week less than in the previous year. During both years, children in the third gang were almost never in the sick house, presumably a reflection of their much lighter labors, although they might also have been allowed to recuperate outside of the sick house.

Most of the workers at Newton and Seawell spent even less days in the plantation hospital. In 1796–1797, the mean number of sick days per first gang-slave (twenty-three) was actually much higher than the median (fourteen) because a few individual slaves were sick for several months of the year. The total number of sick days for the ninety individual slaves who worked regularly with the first gang ranged from zero days for eight individuals to 146 days for an older woman named Rosey who worked with the first gang (see Appendix B, Table A18). The median number of

---

[33] Richard B. Sheridan, "Why the Condition of the Slaves was 'less intolerable in Barbadoes than in the other sugar colonies,'" in Hilary Beckles, ed., *Inside Slavery: Process and Legacy in the Caribbean Experience* (Kingston, Jamaica: The University of the West Indies Press 1996): 31–50.

[34] Nicholas Cresswell, *The Journal of Nicholas Cresswell, 1774–1777* (New York: MacVeagh, the Dial Press, 1924), 37.

total sick days among first-gang hands at Newton appears low for what most scholars would expect to see from a sugar plantation, especially given the brutal demands of sugar. In 1797–1798, the slaves harvested an even larger crop of sugar than the previous year, and they spent less time in the sick house. In fact, the most typical experience for first-gang Barbadian slaves was to spend no more than a handful of days sick each year. Several people at Newton worked from sunup to sundown for over 300 days in a single a year, breaking only for Sundays and holidays.

Not surprisingly, given the less demanding work routines and the dominance of creole slaves in Virginia, Mount Vernon's sickness rates were also very low, but it is interesting to note that they were comparable to the sickness rates among Barbadian sugar slaves. At Mount Vernon, in 1797, field hands missed an average of nineteen days per year, with a range of from fifteen days at the Mansion House to twenty-seven days at Dogue Run. Much like at Newton and Seawell, a few Mount Vernon slaves were sick for lengthy periods of time, raising the average significantly. The median number of days spent sick among Mount Vernon hands was only twelve. The majority of Mount Vernon workers were in the fields for more than 290 days in 1797 (see Appendix B, Table A19).

The makeup of the slave community played a particularly important role in determining the rates of sickness. The slaves at Newton and Seawell in 1796–1797 were, like the Mount Vernon hands in 1797, almost entirely creole. At Prospect, in 1787, African-born slaves were the vast majority, with many still undergoing seasoning, and the average number of sick days reached forty-one days per year, approximately double the average in Barbados and Virginia. Creole slaves were more productive and more valuable not only because they were more experienced and skilled but also because, with more immunity to the disease environment, they missed work because of illness less often, and, given the additional training and experience they possessed, they were less likely to be injured. The proportion of creole slaves on the plantation may have been as significant a factor as the physical demands of the work routines in sickness rates. Overall, given the long hours and arduous labor, the number of days slaves missed because of sickness was strikingly low in Barbados, Virginia and, in some years, in Jamaica, but sick days tended to be a bit higher in Jamaica.

SEASONALITY AND SICKNESS

The cane harvest was widely recognized among Caribbean planters as being the healthiest season of the year. During the harvest, slaves, allowed to eat some of the maturing cane, were better nourished, thus improving their resistance to disease. "The meagre and sick among the negroes," Bryan Edwards claimed, "exhibit a surprizing alteration in a few weeks after the mill is set in action."[35] Benjamin Moseley was so amazed by the difference in the health of the slave population during a sugar harvest that he suggested that sugar-canes might have healing properties. Maturing canes, he thought, had an almost magical effect on the health of slaves. "I have often seen old, scabby, wasted negroes, crawl from the *hot-houses*, apparently half-dead, in crop-time," he explained, "and by sucking canes all day long, they have soon become strong, fat and sleaky."[36] Moseley went so far as to suggest the possibility that "if canes were always ripe," the slaves "would never be diseased."[37] Matthew Lewis, the gothic novelist and owner of Jamaican estates, agreed that harvest season was when the slaves were "most healthy and merry."[38] A Caribbean physician encouraged planters to buy new slaves "in crop-time" because they were "much more likely" to survive at that time of year.[39] Planters immersed in Enlightenment discourses that stressed the universal benefits of progress and work found easy evidence in the harvest that the increasing work hours and productivity could foster better health among the slaves. Big harvests, they imagined, would produce strong and fat workers. Although planters may have exaggerated the benefits of the harvests to their slaves, the slaves, often undernourished, undoubtedly benefited from the additional calories they received from sucking cane stalks and drinking the rum that was distilled during the harvest.

The cane harvest brought long hours and a frenzied pace. There was a limited window of opportunity for cutting cane to maximize the quantity and quality of its juice, and, once cut, cane lost its sucrose content quickly. It had to be immediately milled. Slaves at Prospect worked as much as 330 hours in a single month at the peak of the harvest. Newton slaves worked even more hours during a single month in the 1798 harvest. Given the time constraints of the harvest, managers were probably less willing to

---

[35] Bryan Edwards, *The History Civil and Commercial of the British Colonies in the West Indies*, 2 vols. (Dublin: Luke White, 1793), vol. II, 216.
[36] Benjamin Moseley, *A Treatise on Sugar: With Miscellaneous Medical Observations*, 2nd ed. (London: John Nichols, 1800), 142.
[37] Ibid., 141.
[38] Lewis, *Journal of a West India Proprietor*, 63.
[39] James Grainger, "An Essay on the More Common West-Indian Diseases," in J. Edward Hutson, ed., *On the Treatment and Management of the More Common West- India Diseases (1750–1802)* (Kingston, Jamaica, 2005), 11.

allow slaves to remain in the sick house at this time of year, and the slaves were likely even more motivated than usual to avoid the sick house in order to share in consuming some of the maturing canes. At Seawell, the time constraints and the workload during the harvest were even greater. The cotton harvest corresponded with the cane harvest, and slaves worked to both pick cotton and cut and mill cane, alternating between the two from day to day.

The sugar harvest may have brought health benefits, but it also brought physical risks. Skeletal evidence from the Newton cemetery shows evidence of a remarkably high number of lower limb infections, consistent with the kind of deep lower limb lacerations field workers on a sugar plantation might have suffered from their cane knives while cutting canes. Modern sugar workers wear shin guards to avoid these injuries.[40] Tired slaves cutting at the frenzied pace and long hours that the early modern cane harvest demanded would have been particularly susceptible to these cuts. Without shin guards, skill with a blade and experience alone would be their only protection. Slaves were also subject to industrial accidents during the harvest. A Jamaican overseer told a horrified Lady Nugent, during her tour of a plantation works in 1802, that tired slaves sometimes got their fingers stuck in the mill and the only way to save the slave was "to sever the whole limb." A "hatchet" was kept close and "always ready" for this purpose.[41] Another Jamaican planter thought that such accidents tended to "happen in the Night when the Negroes are drowzy."[42]

The relationship between health and the harvest was not always as simple and direct as planters imagined. There is some evidence to support lower sickness rates at the beginning of the sugar harvest, but there is also evidence showing higher sickness rates later in the harvest. In 1797, the harvest at both Newton and Seawell began in February. That was the month of the year at Seawell when the fewest slaves were sick, and at Newton the sickness rates were also lower in February than in most other

---

[40] Kristrina Shuler, "*Health, History, and Sugar: A Bioarchaeological Study of Enslaved Africans from Newton Plantation, Barbados, West Indies*" (Ph.D. Dissertation, Southern Illinois University, Carbondale, 2005), 305; on the working conditions for modern cane workers see Alec Wikinson, *Big Sugar: Seasons in the Cane Fields of Florida* (New York: Knopf, 1989).

[41] Philip Wright ed., *Lady Nugent's Journal of her Residence in Jamaica from 1801–1805* (Kingston, Jamaica: University of the West Indies Press, 2002), 63.

[42] John Dovaston, "Agricultura Americana or Improvements in West-India Husbandry Considered Wherein the Present System of Husbandry Used in England is Applied to the Cultiation or Growing of Sugar Canes to Advantage" [1774], Codex Eng 60, vol. 2. John Carter Brown Library.

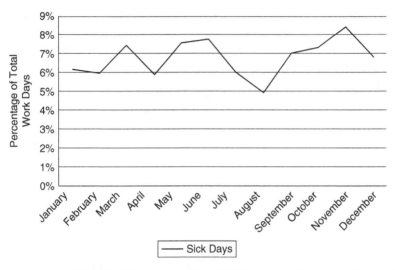

FIGURE 4.1. Monthly sickness rates for all field hands at Newton and Seawell, 1796–1798.
Source: Newton Work Logs, 1796–1798; Seawell Work Log; 1796–1797, MS 523/110,111, 123, Newton Family Papers.

months of the year. At Seawell, the cotton harvest began in January, before cane cutting, and the sickness rate was devastatingly high that month. However, when the slaves started cutting cane, sickness rates dropped significantly, from 11 percent of work days in January to 6 percent in February. Yet, during the 1798 harvest at Newton, there were more slaves in the sick house in May than at any other point in 1797–1798, and this was right in the middle of a particularly prosperous and long cane harvest (see Figure 4.1). In 1787, the sickness rates at Prospect, in Jamaica, were almost always higher than they were at Newton and Seawell, but they were also much more constant throughout the year (see Figure 4.2). Nevertheless, the evidence does point toward slightly lower sickness rates at Prospect in January at the beginning of the harvest than during the rest of the year. For the remainder of the harvest, Prospect sickness rates rose before falling again. Although the consumption of canes and cane juice at the beginning of the harvest may have reduced the number of sick slaves through a combination of incentive and better nourishment, the fatigue that came with night work and an increased pace during crop probably led to rising sickness rates during the harvest, especially during a long harvest.

Provisioning cycles may have made food more difficult to acquire in the summer months (particularly in the late summer months) on Caribbean

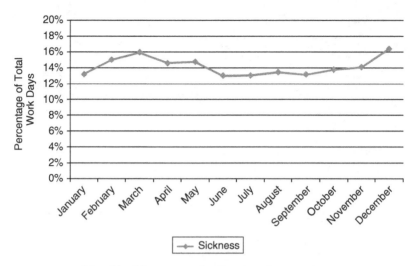

FIGURE 4.2. Monthly sickness rates for Prospect slaves, 1787.
Note: The evidence in this graph includes sickness rates for both field and nonfield workers on the estate. Evidence on sickness rates for field hands alone is unavailable.
Source: Prospect Plantation Journals, 1787–1793, 0627-0019.

sugar estates, but these were not consistently unhealthy months at Newton, Seawell, or Prospect. Skeletal evidence indicates that Newton slaves suffered from periodontal diseases, consistent with bouts of starvation, but it is impossible to tell when this might have happened.[43] The historian J. R. Ward found evidence of significantly higher mortality rates in the late summer between 1751 and 1789 in the Caribbean, which he attributed to the lack of food. From 1783 through 1832, he found no evidence of higher mortality at this time of year, suggesting, he argues, that food shortages became less common or less consequential with amelioration.[44] Some estates may have continued to suffer from shortages in these months. Gilbert Mathison, a Jamaican planter in the early nineteenth century, thought that there was "general scarcity throughout the island" in "June, July, and August, when provisions are planted, but are not sufficiently matured to be gathered in."[45] Yet, the number of slaves in the sick house at Prospect each month in 1787 fell during June, July, and August before rising in the fall

[43] Shuler, "Health, History and Sugar," 285.
[44] J.R. Ward, *British West Indian Slavery, 1750–1834: The Process of Amelioration* (New York: Oxford University Press, 1988), 150–151.
[45] Gilbert F. Mathison, *Notices Respecting Jamaica in 1808, 1809, 1810* (London: J. Stockdale, 1811), 32.

(see Figure 4.2). If we assume that inadequate provisions contributed to disease and illness, the particularly low sickness rates from June through August are surprising, but they concur with Ward's findings in this era. At Newton, the logs record the amount of corn given to each slave, and the amount remained constant throughout the year from 1796 through 1798, but the late summer months had the lowest sickness rates at Newton and Seawell during the same period. The major work for August at Newton and Seawell was weeding and, given that the food allocation remained constant during this period, this light work may account for the low sickness rates in August. Overall, by the 1790s, the postharvest or summer months on Caribbean estates appear to have been a period of lower than normal sickness rates, and the low-intensity labor at this time of year may have made it easier for slaves to avoid the hospital.

It was not during the summer but during the fall when both mortality and morbidity levels on sugar estates tended to be highest. Sickness in the Caribbean was, according to Dickson, "most prevalent during the periods of holing, dunging and planting," which was most commonly done from September through December.[46] Digging cane holes and distributing dung were widely recognized as the two most demanding tasks on sugar plantations, and the two tasks were often combined. Most planters forced slaves to put dung in the holes immediately after they finished digging and again after planting.

Sickness rates rose in October, November, and December at Prospect, and the high levels in October and November correspond with rising sickness rates at Newton and Seawell at this time of the year. October had the highest sickness rate of any month at Seawell, and sickness was high on both estates in November. The higher sickness rates on these plantations in October, November, and December were probably connected to the work routines at this time of year. The spike in October at Seawell and in November on both Barbadian estates can be clearly explained by the major chores in those months. Slaves spent the vast majority of October at Seawell and November on both estates turning and distributing dung.[47] October and November were also the months of the year with the most precipitation in Barbados, so the wet dung would have been even heavier. At Prospect, in 1787, the slaves dug most of the cane holes from September through

[46] Dickson, *Mitigation of Slavery, In Two Parts* (Miami, FL: Mnemosyne Pub. Inc., [1814] 1969), 434.
[47] Newton Work Logs, 1796–1798; Seawell Work Log, 1796–1797, MS 523/110, 111, 123.

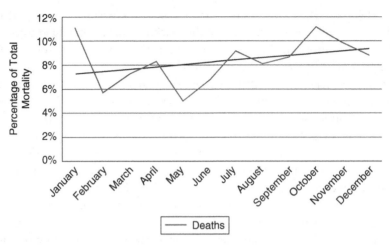

FIGURE 4.3. Seasonal mortality rates on Caribbean sugar plantations, 1779–1809.
Note: Sample size = 579 deaths.
Data have been drawn from increase and decrease of stock accounts and from work logs from sugar plantations. Only sources that systematically recorded deaths throughout an entire year were included in the sample.
Sources: Plantation Records in Jamaica from Prospect, Phillipsfield, Pleasant Hill, Gale's Valley, York, Tredways, Vere, Friendship, Windsor, Sutton's, Parnassus, Old Plantation, Caymanas, and Hope. Plantation records in Barbados from Newton, Seawell, and Turner's Hall. For the location of these records, see bibliography.

December, and sickness rates rose slightly, especially by December, toward the end of this grueling stint (see Figure 4.2).

Increase and decrease accounts from sugar plantations can be used to reconstruct the seasonal mortality rates among slaves in Barbados and Jamaica, and they clearly indicate that the most deadly season for sugar slaves was from October through January (see Figure 4.3).[48] The very high mortality rates in October and November match the rising sickness rates at Prospect, Newton, and Seawell during the same time of the year – with the exception of December at Newton and Seawell. The cane holing and dunging months were clearly the most brutal months of the year for field workers. The evidence also shows that the death rates continued to be high in January after the cane holing and dunging season. Slaves were continuing to suffer from the effects of that work, but the harvest traditionally began in January and, after a month of harvesting, mortality rates fell sharply again. However, as with sickness rates, mortality began to rise in

[48] Ward, *British West Indian Slavery*, 150–151.

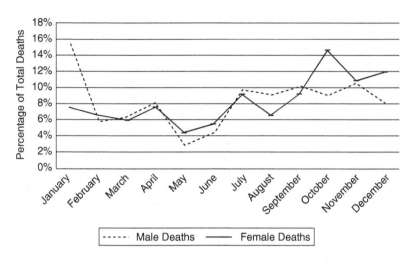

FIGURE 4.4. Seasonal mortality by sex on Jamaican sugar plantations, 1779–1798. Sample size = 207 male deaths and 184 female deaths.
Note: Data have been drawn from increase and decrease of stock accounts from multiple Jamaican plantations. Data are unavailable for Barbadian plantations.

March and April as the harvest progressed (see Figure 4.3). Overall, there was a clear trend showing fewer deaths during the dry season, when slaves were harvesting, and more deaths during the rainy season, when they were cane holing and dunging. The demands of tasks such as manuring may have weakened the slaves' immune system and encouraged illness. The rainy season also brought mosquitos, which were vectors for often fatal diseases such as malaria.[49] Yet, it is significant to note that white mortality rates in the sugar islands did not rise significantly during the rainy season, suggesting that mosquitos alone cannot be to blame and that some aspect of work or living conditions was the decisive difference in seasonal mortality between whites and blacks.[50]

There were distinct differences between men and women in seasonal mortality rates (see Figure 4.4). The men were much more likely to die in January than in any other month of the year. It is difficult to explain this phenomenon by work alone. The male slaves may have survived better

---

[49] John Robert McNeill, *Mosquito Empires: Ecology and War in the Greater Caribbean* (New York: Cambridge University Press, 2010).
[50] Amanda Thornton, "Coerced Care: Thomas Thistlewood's Account of Medical Practice on Enslaved Populations in Colonial Jamaica, 1751–1786," *Slavery & Abolition* 32.4 (Fall, 2011), 548–550.

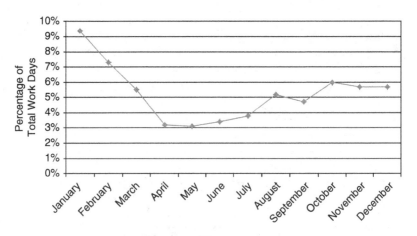

FIGURE 4.5. Monthly sickness rates for Mount Vernon field hands, 1797–1798.
Note: For January through April, this graph combines available data from two years of farm reports (1797 and 1798). Data for the months of May through December are drawn only from the 1797 reports.
Source: Mount Vernon Farm Reports, 1797–1798.

during the cane holing and dunging season only to succumb by January, but what seems more likely is that new African men bought at the beginning of the harvest to help with the harvest were dying during the initial deadliest months of the seasoning process. Women's mortality rates were at their highest by far in October and November, at the height of the holing and dunging season. The field gangs had a female majority, and field slaves were probably most likely to die during October and November because of the work at that time of the year. Moreover, the particularly backbreaking labor of dunging and holing done during these months was probably harder on women than it was on men.

There were also significant seasonal variations in both sickness and death rates on Virginian plantations. Winter, in particular, was the season of death and sickness in Virginia. In Mount Vernon quarters, sickness was highest in January, at 12 percent, and lowest in April and May, at 3 percent (see Figure 4.5). Overall, the number of days slaves missed work because of sickness was highest in fall and winter and, with the exception of a short spike in July and August, lowest in the spring and summer. The high levels of sickness at Mount Vernon in the fall and winter and the low rates in the summer correspond to a significant degree with the death rates among both blacks and whites, which other scholars have found in Virginia in the seventeenth and eighteenth century. This suggests that mortality and morbidity in the Chesapeake were more closely linked to the changing weather and the availability of food than to the plantation work regime.[51] Mosquitos also infected Chesapeake slaves with malaria from August through early October, but the impact of these vectors seems to have been minimal.[52] There was only a slight rise in sickness levels during this period (see Figure 4.5).

Seasonal variations in work routines had a more significant impact on the slaves' health in Jamaica and Barbados than the weather, but the effects of hard work on sickness rates were, not surprisingly, less significant in Virginia. There were no sudden spikes in the physical intensity of work routines on Virginian plantations to rival the holing and dunging season on a sugar estate. Sickness and death rates in Virginia appear to have been highest when the work demands and the number of work hours were at their lowest. Winter work in Virginia was, for the most part, less demanding, but the cold winter weather probably brought frostbite, as well as rheumatic and arthritic aches in the bones of weary slaves, which would have kept them from the field. As slaves grouped together to keep warm, they might have more easily communicated diseases. Food supplies, especially of fresh fruits and vegetables, were at their lowest in Virginia in January, and this could have led to both greater sickness and higher death rates. Mount Vernon slaves might have even suffered from subacute or chronic scurvy in these months. The greatest share of work in January involved building and repairing fences and, because there were no pressing crop concerns, overseers were probably more willing to allow slaves to rest and recover from illness or injury.

Sickness rates at Mount Vernon were lowest in April, May, and June, and they rose steadily from May onward. The number of hours worked each day in the spring and early summer were significantly higher than in the winter because of the increase in daylight hours, but sickness rates were still much lower. The short wheat harvesting season in July and August produced a slight rise in sickness rates, which may have been caused by the increased pace of labor or the increased number of work hours per month that came with longer summer days. Unlike on a sugar plantation, there was not a sudden spike in caloric intake on grain plantations to offset the increased pace of labor. Overall, the wheat harvest, normally lasting two

---

[51] Darrett B. Rutman, Charles Whetherell, and Anita Rutman. "Rhythms of Life: Black and White Seasonality in the Early Chesapeake," *Journal of Interdisciplinary History* 11.1 (Summer, 1980): 37.

[52] Lorena S. Walsh, *Motives of Honor, Pleasure and Profit: Plantation Management in the Colonial Chesapeake, 1607–1763* (Chapel Hill: University of North Carolina Press, 2010), 618.

to three weeks, was short enough, compared to a three- to six-month cane harvest, that it did not have a significant effect on sickness or mortality.

WOMEN, WORK, AND HEALTH

Sugar planters were normally confident that women could accomplish the most demanding tasks on the plantation. Indeed, women in the first and second gangs on a sugar plantation worked alongside men in every major task in sugar cultivation, regardless of how arduous those tasks were. However, given the higher mortality rates for women during holing and dunging season than at other times of the year, and the much higher mortality rates for women than men at that time of the year, the work in the cane fields appears to have been more physically demanding or draining for women than it was for men. Indeed, women on sugar plantations also spent more time in the sick house than did men. Both archaeological and historical evidence suggests that sugar cultivation ravaged women's bodies.

Skeletal evidence from Caribbean plantations demonstrates how much more demanding field work was for enslaved women than it was for enslaved men. There were high rates of muscle and tendon injuries, herniated discs, and degenerative joint conditions in both men and women, indicating intense physical labor for both groups, but women were more likely than men to have signs of wear and tear and tendon and muscle injuries in every joint. This was due to in part to there being more women than men involved in field work, but it was also a sign that sugar cultivation (such as holing and hauling manure) was much more physically demanding for women. Whereas women tended to have degenerative joint changes or signs of torn tendons throughout their bodies, men tended to have degenerative joints or signs of muscle and tendon tears in the upper body, particularly in the shoulders. This suggests that women faced a wider array of daily work activities than men. Men were less likely than women to have muscle tears, but the men's tears were more likely to be severe. These men with severe tears may have been craftsmen working in jobs that required sudden bursts of heavy lifting, such as masonry.[53]

At Newton, there was little difference between the first and second gang in average sick days, but there were significant differences in the averages between men and women in these gangs, particularly in the first gang. First-gang men were sick for an average of just sixteen days per year in 1796–1797, but the average for women was twice that, at thirty sick days

[53] Shuler, "Health, History and Sugar," 259, 278–279, 301–309, 319–321.

per slave each year. The average sick days per year for second-gang women ranged from twenty-one to twenty-seven, and for men the average number of sick days was no less than eleven and no more than seventeen days. The discrepancy between sickness rates among men and women in both gangs is striking. Some first-gang women spent very lengthy periods of time in the sick house, inflating the averages for their cohort slightly. Rosey, for example, spent half a year in the sick house. The highest number of sick days for a man in the first gang was much lower (seventy-seven for a man named Cuffey). Excluding the outliers, Rosey and Cuffey, there were still remarkable contrasts in the average number of sick days per slave in the first gang, fourteen for men and twenty-seven for women.

Despite the amelioration movement and the rise of pronatalist policies, the vast majority of planters lumped the pregnant with the sick. However, the immediate effect of pregnancy does not appear to have been a significant factor in the difference between men and women in the amount of time spent sick. Ten women gave birth while in the first gang in 1796–1797. Pregnant women were often recorded as "sick" for a month or more before eventually "lying-in." Undoubtedly, the effects of pregnancy also played a role in sickness rates. Women were forced to return too quickly to labor, and that alone probably drove them into the sick house and created chronic health concerns. Yet, even if one excludes all women who gave birth or miscarried at Newton, the average annual number of sick days among first-gang slaves at Newton was still nearly twice as high for women (thirty-one) as it was for men (sixteen). In fact, the difference between men and women was slightly greater if one excludes pregnant slaves.[54] These higher sickness rates help to explain why planters were willing to create separate, predominantly female weeding gangs like the gang working at Newton with Molly. This was lighter work, that would ease the labors of the weaker women for at least part of the year.

Despite the demanding work being done by female-majority gangs on sugar estates, an increasing focus on reproduction and fertility on sugar plantations in the late eighteenth-century made some planters more attentive to the particular strengths and weaknesses of women's bodies and constitutions. At least one planter, at the turn of the nineteenth century, was beginning to question whether women were as capable of hard sugar labor. Mathison thought that, overall, the chores that slaves were asked to perform were "within the limits of fair and good regulation" but, he

---

[54] Newton Work Log, 1796–1797, Seawell Work Log, 1796–1797, and "Report on the [Newton] Negroes," MS 523/110, 111, 288, Newton Family Papers.

suggested, "perhaps young females are too much subjected to hard labour at an early and critical period of their lives." He worried that this put a check on their fertility.[55]

Caribbean planters did not often divide men from women in field work – aside from occasionally sending a few women to work in separate weeding gangs – but some reformers strove to achieve sexual divisions in the sick house. In his guide to managing slaves, Collins argued that a sick house should consist of separate rooms for men, for women, and for slaves with "dangerous diseases" and, he continued, "care should be had that the sexes have no direct communication with each other."[56] It is unlikely that many plantations had the revenue, size, building supplies, or workforce to achieve such an ideal setting in the hospital, but sexual division in the sick house may have been a pervasive concern. When Wood arrived at Newton and Seawell in the mid-1790s, he complained that the Newton sick house needed renovations because, among other problems, "men and women are most indecently mixed together."[57] In the final decade before emancipation, at least one author claimed, probably unrealistically, that "every hospital" in the British Caribbean had "separate apartments for the men and the women."[58] This certainly had more to do with moral conventions than with any health issues.

No evidence survives to indicate whether there were different sickness rates between men and women on other Jamaican or Barbadian estates, but at Mount Vernon, women and men spent an almost identical number of days sick per year (18.4 days for woman and 19.2 days for men). If anything, men were sick slightly more often than women. Just as the rigors of certain field chores for women help explain the high sickness rates among Newton field women, so a less strenuous laboring regime at Mount Vernon probably helps account for its male and female equity in sickness rates.

WORK AND PREGNANCY

Pregnant slaves were "most difficult to manage," complained James Thomson, the author of a treatise on Jamaican medicine published in 1820. In the last decade before the slave trade ended, and in the years leading up to emancipation, many planters adopted pronatalist policies and some

[55] Mathison, *Notices Respecting Jamaica*, 34–35.
[56] Collins, *Medical Treatment of Negro Slaves*, 252.
[57] "Report on the Buildings at Newton."
[58] Barclay, *The Present State of Slavery*, 322.

went as far as to exempt pregnant women from heavy labor for months before and after birth. They were removed from the great gang, placed in the second gang, and sometimes allowed to stop working entirely within four months of letting the overseer know that they were pregnant. New mothers would not be expected to return to work until their infants had been weaned.[59] Although the ameliorationist movement promoted reproduction, and these pronatalist policies appear to have improved conditions for some pregnant women, many, if not most, planters remained reluctant to lose the labor of their female slaves for any more time than was absolutely necessary, creating tension between plantation productivity and slave reproduction. Thomson's observations on pregnant women reflected such frustrations. He reacted to the new pronatalist policies by arguing that the exemption of pregnant women from labor was a kind of "Indulgence" that was "totally misplaced."[60] He insisted that "Nature does not require such exemption from exercise during that state." Lengthy rests would only inculcate "habits of idleness."[61] Idleness was the enemy of every planter interested in increasing the total quantity of labor, and much was done in plantation management with the justification that it would help inculcate habits of industry, which were in turn associated with civility and progress. Thomson's attitude helps to explain why sugar planters were unable to significantly increase fertility after the abolition of the slave trade. Until the rise of pronatalist strategies at the end of the eighteenth century, the vast majority of planters offered little in the way of rest to pregnant slaves. "When I first went to Barbadoes [in 1772]," Dickson claimed, "I was particularly astonished to see some women far gone in their pregnancy, toiling in the field."[62] Pregnancy was an inconvenience because, until slave prices began to rise in the late eighteenth century, it was cheaper to buy a "saltwater slave" from Africa than it was to raise one.

Planters viewed pregnancy on sugar plantations as a form of sickness keeping women from their labors. They also referred to a woman's menstruation as "their monthly sickness," a condition that threatened their productivity.[63] When they could no longer labor, pregnant women were

---

[59] Kenneth Morgan, "Slave Women and Reproduction in Jamaica," *History* 91 (2006), 238.
[60] James Thomson, *A Treatise on the Diseases of Negroes, As they Occur in the Island of Jamaica: With Observations on the Country Remedies* (Jamaica: Alex Aikman, 1820), 112.
[61] Ibid.
[62] Dickson, *Letters on Slavery: To which are added, addresses to the whites, and to the free Negroes of Barbadoes; and accounts of some Negroes eminent for their virtues and abilities* (Westport: Negro Universities Press, [1789] 1970), 12; Dickson, *Mitigation of Slavery*, ix.
[63] Thomson, *Treatise on the Diseases of Negroes*, 112.

usually confined to the hospital, where they were subject to the same discipline and punishment as other sick slaves. At Newton, ten of approximately sixty women who served regularly in the first two gangs gave birth during the year covered by the 1796–1797 logs.[64] Several of these women were "sick" for a few days or weeks immediately before "lying-in." On average, these women were allowed only thirty-five days – including lying-in days, sick days, Sundays, and holidays – for giving birth and recovering afterward. The number of days ranged from twenty-five for Jubah to fifty-three for Peggy Hester. Peggy may have had a difficult pregnancy because the overseer listed her as "sick" for more than five weeks straight before nearly two weeks spent "lying-in." Forcing a woman to toil at heavy labors in the cane fields with the first gangs after an average of only five weeks of rest to give birth, including the time before and after birth, must have been devastating to her health. Furthermore, the quick return to work no doubt had an impact on both the mortality rates among infants and fertility rates among women.

The time the manager allowed to pregnant women at Newton was remarkably low, but at Mount Vernon the women were rushed back to work even sooner. Fifteen of the fifty-five field women for whom data were available at Mount Vernon gave birth in 1797 (a higher fertility rate than at Newton). These women were allowed an average of only twenty-six days each (including all sick days before and after and all Sundays and holidays) to give birth and recover before returning to their labors – nine days less than the average at Newton. The range was from a seemingly impossible seven days for Patt at Union Farm to thirty-eight days for Darcus at Muddy Hole. Perhaps the time lost to pregnancy for Patt was inaccurately recorded or her pregnancy ended early because of a miscarriage. Excluding Patt, the average time allowed to Mount Vernon women for pregnancy was still only twenty-seven days. The Mount Vernon women returned to work more quickly than at Newton because the work itself was much less demanding than it was in the Caribbean. Virginian managers could make pregnant slaves do one of a wide range of light tasks around the farm until they had recovered. It is nonetheless striking that such short rests did not create more serious health problems for the women at Mount Vernon.

The seasonal rhythms of plantation life shaped almost every aspect of a slave's life, including the likelihood and timing of conception for women. A sample of 270 births on Barbadian and Jamaican slave plantations shows significant seasonal variations in birth rates (see Figure 4.6). Remarkably,

---

[64] Fifty-three of the women were of child-bearing age (aged 15 to "40 odd").

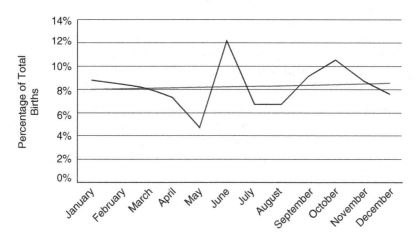

FIGURE 4.6. Seasonal birth rates on Jamaican and Barbadian sugar plantations, 1779–1809. Sample size = 344 births. Data have been drawn from increase and decrease of stock accounts and from work logs. Only sources that systematically recorded births throughout an entire year were included in the sample.
Source: Plantation Records from Prospect, Phillipsfield, Pleasant Hill, Gale's Valley, York, Tredways, Vere, Friendship, Windsor, Sutton's, Parnassus, Old Plantation, Caymanas, Newton, Seawell, and Turner's Hall.

the lowest birth rate (in May) was only a month apart from the highest rate (in June). Some factor or combination of factors discouraged conception in August and promoted it in September. The scarcity of food on sugar estates in the late summer was probably the key to the low conception rates in August; and presumably the harvesting of estate provisions then caused the spike the following month. Birth rates were slightly lower than average in July and August, nine months after the cane holing season reached its peak, suggesting not surprisingly that the intensity of holing and dunging kept conception rates down. The reason for steadily rising birth rates in September, October, and November can be more readily explained. They correspond with the onset of the cane harvest nine months earlier, and the additional nourishment during the harvest probably encouraged conception. Clearly, the long hours of harvest labor did nothing to discourage conception. The high birth rates in October do correspond with the high mortality among women at that time of year, suggesting that there may have been more women dying during childbirth at that time of year, but there was not a similar increase in female mortality during June, the month with the highest birth rate. The cane holing and dunging in October was probably particularly brutal work for women in the late stage of pregnancy or recovering from childbirth. Women who became pregnant early in the harvest faced the danger of having to give birth during the cane holing and dunging season. The seasonal rhythms of the plantation exacerbated the death rates among women because the fertility that the harvest encouraged meant that women would be close to giving birth during the season with the most demanding and backbreaking labors. Despite the growth of pro-natalist policies in the final decades before the closing of the slave trade, most planters would be unwilling to excuse pregnant women from these brutal field chores for long enough to safeguard their health or the health of the newborn.

AGE AND SICKNESS

Age was a determinative factor in the sickness rates of workers, but there was not always a simple correlation of old age with sickness. Certainly, old age, if a slave lived that long, brought an array of health concerns. The ages that planters recorded for slaves in inventories were estimates and were thus not entirely reliable, but they were usually accurate within a decade. The ages of slaves beyond their prime were probably overestimated because decades of labor had worn them down and made them appear older than they were. Planters would also want to avoid suggesting that overwork had worn a slave down. Age was a more acceptable culprit. Age became as much a description of a slaves' physical ability as it was a precise chronological marker. A slave named Gunner at Mount Vernon offers an extreme but illustrative example of the inaccuracy of age recordings. In 1781, he was described as being a valuable brickmaker about forty-five years old.[65] Eighteen years later, he was "Passed Labour" and living at the Mansion House, and he was, according to Washington's will, ninety years old.[66] His work had worn him down, and he appeared older than he was. Despite the brutal conditions of slavery and the fact that most slaves died young, there are many examples of slaves who appear to have been laboring until an advanced age and, not surprisingly, the oldest examples seem to be from Virginia. At Mount Vernon, in 1797, there were slaves in their seventies working in the field and, at Newton and Seawell, there were many slaves in their sixties working with the first gangs. Yet, in contrast, there seem to have been very few Jamaican field hands working with the

---

[65] Fitzpatrick, *Writings of Washington*, vol. 22, 14n.
[66] Mount Vernon Slave Inventory, June 1799 in Abbot, ed., *The Papers of George Washington, Retirement Series*, vol. 4 (Charlottesville: University Press of Virginia, 1999), 528–540.

field gangs beyond their fifties. The oldest woman in the field at Pleasant Hill and Phillipsfield in 1789 was fifty-five, and the oldest man was fifty-two. Beyond that age, Jamaican sugar slaves tended to become "invalid," or they were assigned to other nongang tasks. A Jamaican watchman, for example, was often "a worn-out negro."[67] Planters only valued slaves for their physical contributions and, according to the managerial staff of a plantation, years of overwork left the slave "worn-out" like an old tool.

Given the demands that decades in the field could place on a body, one might expect that the older a slave was, the more time he or she would spend in the sick house, but this was not always the case. In the first gang, there were two slaves in their sixties – the oldest of the crew, long past their prime – and nine slaves in their fifties. These older Newton slaves spent surprisingly little time in the sick house. At Newton, it was actually first-gang slaves in their late teens, the youngest slaves in that gang, who spent the most time in the sick house (see Figure 4.7). These adolescents may have had difficulty adapting to the demands of work and to the pace of labor in the first gang. As they grew stronger and more accustomed to first-gang work, and as they learned survival techniques to avoid exhaustion or being singled out by the overseer's whip, they spent less days in the sick house. The skeletal evidence from Newton plantation shows significant activity related changes and infections in skeletons of adolescents, confirming that the transition from childhood to the adult gangs was very demanding for sugar workers. One of the adolescent skeletons from Newton actually had a herniated disc, a very rare finding among adolescents.[68] At the same time, the quantity and quality of nutrition that children received as they entered the gangs probably increased, somewhat offsetting the demands of transitioning to a gang. Enslaved children tended to be shorter than their free counterparts throughout the Americas until they entered the workforce, where they probably had access to more protein. In the eighteenth and nineteenth centuries, adult slaves born in the Americas were as tall as freeborn peoples in the Americas.[69]

In 1796–1797, seven of the eleven first-gang Newton slaves over the age of fifty were women. Most of these older women spent part of the year

---

[67] William Beckford, *Remarks upon the Situation of Negroes in Jamaica* (London: T & Egerton, 1788), 19.
[68] Shuler, "Health, History and Sugar," 321.
[69] Philip R.P. Coelho and Robert A. McGuire, "An Exploratory Essay on the Impact of Diseases upon the Interpretation of American Slavery," in John Komlos and Joerg Baten, eds., *The Biological Standard of Living in Comparative Perspective* (Stuttgart: Franz Steiner, 1998), 183.

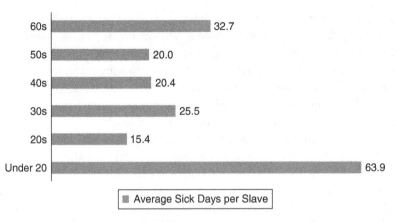

FIGURE 4.7. Average annual sick days by age category among first-gang workers at Newton, 1796–1797.
Note: No age was given for Rosey, who was sick for 146 days. Her totals have not been included in this graph. However, Rosey was also referred to as "Old Rosey," suggesting that she was over the age of sixty.
Sources: Newton Work Logs, 1796–1797 and "Report on the [Newton] Negroes," MS 523/110, 288, Newton Family Papers.

working separately in "the infirm gang" (also known as "Molly's Gang") on tasks that required less strength, manual dexterity, or speed, such as weeding. This may have kept these older women's sickness rates down.[70] The men continued to be driven at the same pace and on the same tasks as the bulk of the first gang. At Newton, the existence of an infirm gang for women, especially older women, with no male counterpart, underscores the particularly strenuous nature of sugar work for women. Clearly, as much as they hoped to make slaves into depersonalized and interchangeable units of production in their work log calculations, planters and their overseers were forced in daily practice to recognize the range of individual abilities in the gang.

At Mount Vernon, the evidence suggests a simple and more predictable correlation between age and illness among field hands (see Figure 4.8). Although the Mount Vernon records were approximate rather than exact, they offer strong evidence of an age-related trend in sickness. Essentially, the older a slave became, the more time he or she spent out of the workforce because of illness or injury. On average, those field slaves over the age of seventy who were still working missed nearly eight times as much work

---

[70] "Report on the [Newton] Negroes," MS 523/288, Newton Family Papers.

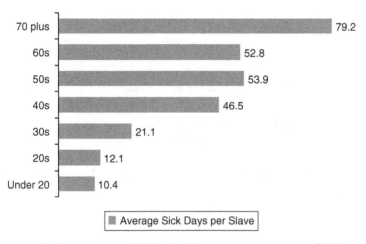

FIGURE 4.8. Average annual sick days by age category among field hands at Mount Vernon, 1797.
Source: Mount Vernon Farm Reports, 1797.

to illness and injury as the adolescents working with the field hands. Yet, it is remarkable that these slaves were working at all. It is a testament to the lighter nature of labor in the Chesapeake compared to the sugar islands.

Regardless of how old a slave was or the malady with which he or she was afflicted, Washington had trouble tolerating the inefficiency, poor discipline, and deception that, he thought, accompanied sickness. He insisted that the elderly be made to do whatever they could possibly do. When Old Frank, a man who was believed to be over seventy years old, missed too many days of work for sickness in 1793, Washington wrote to ask, "what is the matter with Old Frank, that he is always (almost) on the Sick List?"[71] The months each year that these old slaves spent in the sick house were not indicative of Washington's tolerance for the complaints of the elderly. Instead, they were clear signs of the lasting effects on health of the decades they had spent in the field. Continuing to labor at that age was, presumably, even more of a constant struggle than it was for young slaves (see Figure 4.8). Given that there were more older slaves continuing to labor in the field at Mount Vernon than there were on a sugar estate, and that these slaves were often sick, the amount of time lost to sickness among field workers in their prime at Mount Vernon was much lower than the amount of time lost to sickness on Caribbean sugar estates.

[71] George Washington to Anthony Whiting, January 27, 1793, in Fitzpatrick, ed., *Writings of Washington*, vol. 32, 319.

BLAME IT ON THE RAIN: HEALTH, WORK, AND WEATHER

Planters often cast weather as one of the chief culprits in poor health and mortality. Anxieties about weather are common in agricultural settings, but they were amplified on eighteenth-century plantations in the British Atlantic because plantation owners and managers adhered to climatic and seasonal theories of disease. They worried endlessly about too much or too little precipitation, high winds, and, in Virginia, where temperatures were more variable, excessively cold or hot weather. They wrote about the weather whenever they reported on their plantations; they tracked changes in the air and assessed the impact of rain and wind on both the land and on the bodies of their slaves. By the end of the eighteenth century, sugar planters, in particular, were arguing that wet weather and working in the rain was a critical factor in the high mortality and low fertility rates of their slaves.

Eighteenth-century medical theories were attentive to the impact of the environment on bodies. Bodies were shaped by changes in the air. Airborne agents of disease, known as *miasmas*, were responsible for creating unhealthy environments. Moisture, warm weather and decaying matter produced noxious miasmas and encouraged putrefaction. Compared to more temperate climes, such as Virginia's, bodies in the tropics were thought to be less susceptible to fevers but more prone to deadly fluxes. Climatic theories were increasingly racialized. Blacks, it was said, were suited to hot climates. Physicians and planters, however, claimed that wet weather and humid conditions in the tropics were dangerous for both whites and blacks. Medical theorists believed that the change in air during torrential downpours destroyed the balance in healthy bodies. William Hilary, who wrote one of the most influential tracts on tropical medicine while living in Barbados, blamed sudden rainfalls for death and disease among the slaves. Hilary explained that when the weather changed suddenly "from very dry to very wet, Dysentaries [sic] became very frequent and epidemical." Sudden changes in the air, particularly in temperature, were upsetting to the constitution, but one of the greatest dangers with rain in the tropics, most physicians agreed, was that it stopped people from freely perspiring.[72] Hilary theorized that the heavy rains "too suddenly stop the Discharge by Perspiration and Sweat, which in this warm Climate are

---

[72] Hilary, *Observations on the Changes of the Air*, 26.

usually very great," which resulted in "the Humours" being "too suddenly turned upon the Bowels."[73] The St. Vincent physician Collins agreed that "a greater degree of cold when united with moisture" will "close the pores of the skin" and "check the perspiration, which descends in torrents when negroes are in health, and at work." This sudden clogging of the pores, Collins maintained, caused "fluxies and dropsies, two of the worst diseases, and almost the only fatal ones" on Caribbean plantations.[74] Too little sweat encouraged fevers, but too much encouraged fluxes. Ideas about the effect of climates on bodies filtered down to the day-to-day management of enslaved populations and became interwoven with vernacular medical practices and with the ameliorative strategies of managers.[75]

The rainy season in the Caribbean begins in June or July and continues through the end of November, with the heaviest rains coming in October and November. Precipitation in October tends to be four to five times greater than during the driest months. Sugar planters often observed that the months with the most rain were the deadliest season of the year. Mortality was higher in the rainy season, and the greatest number of deaths among the workers came in the wettest month of the year: October. Most sugar planters expected the height of the rainy season to be deadly. In November of 1798, a Barbadian manager was surprised to note that the slaves "look extremely well at present, & enjoy very good health for this season of the year, as it is a season that has been fatal to many persons both white & black." They were healthy, the manager insisted, because he had done everything he could to keep them out of the rain.[76]

Greater mortality during the wet season encouraged planters to believe that the rain itself was deadly, but the wet weather alone was probably not killing slaves. There were other more significant factors. First, there tended to be less ripe homegrown provisions available during these months. Second, planters all agreed that the most backbreaking chores were cane holing and hauling baskets of dung to the field, and holing and manuring were normally done during the wet season. In other words, the most exhausting chores were done with inadequate provisions in the rain, and

---

[73] Ibid.
[74] Collins, *Medical Treatment of Negro Slaves.* 58.
[75] Frederick Sargent II, *Hippocratic Heritage: A History of Ideas about Weather and Human Health* (New York: Pergamon Press, 1982); Mark Harrison, *Medicine in an Age of Commerce and Empire: Britain and its Tropical Colonies, 1660–1830* (New York: Oxford University Press, 2010), 27–88.
[76] Edward Clarke to John Brathwaite, November 1, 1798, C/COD/46, Codrington Papers, C series.

the wet weather made the dung even heavier to carry. The damp weather also brought mosquitos, vectors for deadly diseases.

Planters and physicians recognized that rain was not the sole cause of slave mortality, but they assigned it a prominent role among the possible factors. They agreed that part of the problem with tropical rains was not the precipitation itself but the "crude and waterish" provisions that sprung up during the rainy season. Slaves grew sick because they would "voraciously devour" these unripe provisions. James Grainger, a Caribbean physician, argued that "great care" had to be taken when "purchasing Negroes in wet months" because they tended to grow ill after eating too many waterish and inferior provisions.[77] In 1782, a Jamaican overseer complained that violent storms and "uncommon heavy seasons" had caused "a General destruction of the provision grounds" and "Sickly times with the Negroes." This overseer thought that it was not just the ruined provisions but also the "the heavy violent rains" that had made the slaves sick; the rain itself brought disease. As soon as the rains stopped, he noted, the slaves "regained their health."[78]

Improving planters began to advocate protecting slaves from the rain, especially in the tropics. They were most adamant from the 1770s onward, and Barbadians appear to have been especially concerned about meteorological adjustments, even though there was less rain in Barbados than in Jamaica. In 1786, a Barbadian plantation manual, written in collaboration by several leading planters, maintained that on the "bad days, during the rainy season," the slaves "should be employed about some work within doors" and on regular "damp and rainy mornings," an overseer should "be indulgent to those who come late into the field."[79] In 1788, the Barbadian Philip Gibbes, in his own sugar plantation manual, warned that it was "injurious" to work slaves "in the rain."[80] In 1798, the attorney for the Codrington Plantation in Barbados tried to convince the Society for the Propagation of the Gospel, which owned the estate, that he was treating the slaves with humanity. His evidence was that he had kept the slaves out of the rain during the harvest. "I make it a point," he explained, "never to expose them to rain if it can be avoided by any means ... let the consequence

---

[77] Grainger, *Essay on the More Common West-India Diseases*, 11.
[78] John Kelly to Chalenor Arcedeckne Esq., March 19, 1782, Vanneck-Arc/ 3A/ 1782/9, Simon Taylor Papers.
[79] Edwin Lascelles et al., *Instructions for the Management of a Plantation in Barbadoes. And for the Treatment of Negroes, etc., etc., etc.* (London: [s.n.], 1786), 24.
[80] Philip Gibbes, *Instructions for the Treatment of Negroes, etc., etc., etc.*, 2nd ed. with additions (London: Shepperson and Reynold's, 1788), 13.

be what they will."[81] In the early nineteenth century, the owner of Turner's Hall in Barbados was adamant in his instructions to his attorney. He insisted that "Negroes [were] never to work in the rain."[82] Some Jamaican planters may have even hoped that taming the landscape itself would improve the health of slaves. The Jamaican planter Edward Long noted in 1774 that the rains that lashed the new frontier of Portland Parish, where Prospect would eventually be situated, "would undoubtedly decrease ... as they have done in the other districts, if any considerable part of this wilderness was cleared, and room given for a free passage to the wind and vapors."[83] Paradoxically, to improve the slaves' health, planters would first have to subject them to the brutal labor of logging and clearing mountainous plantation lands.

Some planters seem to have believed that the rain would not only harm a slave's constitution but that slaves would be less tractable in their character or more disobedient during wet weather. The Codrington attorney was pleased to observe that the slaves had "behaved amazingly well during that dreadful heavy weather that we experienced," but he explained that it was because he had kept them out of the rain and had made a particular effort not to "distress them."[84] It is not clear whether the slaves shared the planters' anxiety about wet weather, but Collins complained that "you will in vain admonish a negro" for wearing wet clothes or exposing him- or herself to open air, suggesting that perhaps slaves did not blame the rain for their health problems.[85]

Ameliorationists often argued that slaves needed to be kept dry in the field *and* in their quarters. A Barbadian planter, in a letter to an associate, warned that insufficient attention was paid to maintaining slave housing so that, over time, "the House lets in the Rain, becomes damp & unwholesome, the Negroes grow Sickly ... not from Tyranny and oppression, but from the Neglect & indolence of an easy, good humoured Manager."[86] Likewise, a Jamaican plantation manual cautioned its readers to "choose airy, dry situations for houses" and ensure that the dwellings were "perfectly water tight" because "the inclemencies of weather, generate the most malignant diseases."[87] Work logs show that planters forced slaves to

---

[81] Edward Clarke to John Brathwaite, November 1, 1798, C/COD/46, Codrington Papers, C Series.
[82] H. E. Holder to Henry Fitzherbert, October 26, 1815, E23929, Fitzherbert Collection.
[83] Edward Long, *History of Jamaica*. (Montreal: McGill-Queen's University Press, 2003), 170.
[84] Edward Clarke to John Brathwaite, November 1, 1798, C/COD/46, Codrington Papers, C series.
[85] Collins, *Medical Treatment of Negro Slaves*, 135.
[86] "Notes on Housing for Negroes," E20777, Fitzherbert Collection.
[87] Kein, *Pen-Keeping and Plantership*, 23.

repair their houses as part of their regular gang labors, suggesting that planters would not trust the slaves to repair them on their own.

The rain became a point of particular tension in plantation management because, although planters sought to keep slaves alive, they also saw benefits to working in the rain. In, *Letters to a Young Planter*, written in 1785, Gordon Turnbull insisted that planters "should not expose the slaves to be often wet, nor oblige them to remain long in the field under heavy rains."[88] Yet, in contradiction, he also suggested that the demanding and time-consuming chore of distributing dung on the fields "should be done in rainy weather, that the salts in the dung may sooner be carried down into the soil."[89] The combination of the decaying matter, warm tropical weather, and moisture would, according to miasma and putrefaction theories, have been particularly lethal. The rain-soaked dung in the baskets would have also been much heavier to carry. Wet dung baskets weighed nearly twice as much as dry ones.[90]

As ideal as it might have seemed, it was simply not practical to keep sugar workers out of the field every time it rained. Sugar, as a tropical grass, can only be grown where there is sufficient rain to nourish it. Collins, for example, "wished ... that negroes could be kept altogether from working in the rain" but he admitted that "circumstances do not admit of it."[91] Most planters sought coping strategies. Seasoned slaves, for example, could work in the rain, but "New Negroes" should avoid working too many hours during the rainy season until they were accustomed to the climate.[92] Sick slaves should be kept out of the rain, but healthy ones would be fine.[93] Some planters suggested that it was best to focus on bolstering slaves' constitutions and raising their spirits during the work day. The conventional opinion was that rum should be given to slaves either before or after a wet work day to prevent chills and improve morale.[94] A prominent Barbadian planter went further, arguing that "light portable sheds" could be used "to protect negroes from rain."[95] The Jamaican overseer, Thistlewood, constructed rain sheds to shelter the slaves and gave the field slaves a

---

[88] Gordon Turnbull, *Letters to a Young Planter; Or Observations on the Management of a Sugar Plantation* (London: Stuart and Stevenson, 1785), 57.
[89] Ibid., 7.
[90] Dickson, *Mitigation of Slavery*, 164.
[91] Collins, *Medical Treatment of Negro Slaves*, 194.
[92] Beckford, *Situation of Negroes in Jamaica*, 33.
[93] Thomas Barritt to Nathaniel Phillips, April 28, 1795, MS9202, Slebech Papers.
[94] William Belgrove, *A Treatise upon Husbandry or Planting* (Boston: D. Fowle, 1755), 67; Edwards, *The History, Civil and Commercial*, 131.
[95] Gibbes, *Instructions for the Treatment of Negroes*, 2nd rev. ed., 22.

"dram" of rum each after a wet day.⁹⁶ Collins saw the rain as dangerous, but he disagreed with the idea of keeping slaves from the rain. Instead, he offered a rogue solution, suggesting that slaves "should be taught to labour most in the rain" to ensure that they avoided chills and kept sweating. Work became a physical cure. The slaves could put on dry clothes and work less vigorously when the rain ended. The slaves, he admitted, "would not very well relish" such a plan, but it was in their best interests.⁹⁷ The rain was dangerous, all agreed, but just what to do about it was a contentious point. Should planters keep their slaves from the rain altogether, give them rum to improve their morale, or simply compel them to work harder when the rain fell?

In addition to working contingency plans for the weather into their management strategies, planters consistently recorded the weather in their work logs as part of the revolution in plantation accounting techniques.⁹⁸ Logs often tracked both weather conditions and work routines. These weather records reflected a larger Enlightenment project of weather recording. Weather observers sought to better characterize the weather of a particular climate and forecast future weather by determining the natural patterns undergirding changes in the air.⁹⁹ With work logs, planters hoped to deduce weather patterns so that they could anticipate them in the future and allocate work accordingly.

How often did managers actually stop work or give the slaves new chores when the rain fell? A Barbadian ameliorationist thought that "foul weather," on average, probably kept slaves from work at least six days each year, but he hoped planters would accept that that needed to be increased to keep

---

⁹⁶ Thomas Thistlewood Diary, March 31, 1752, Monson 31/3.
⁹⁷ Collins, *Medical Treatment of Negro Slaves*, 194.
⁹⁸ M. J. Mepham, "The Scottish Enlightenment and the Development of Accounting," in R. H. Parker and B. S. Yamey, eds. *Accounting History: Some British Contributions*. (Oxford: Clarendon Press, 1994), 268-293; P. Cohen, *A Calculating People: The Spread of Numeracy in Early America* (Chicago: The University of Chicago Press, 1982).

Peter A. Coclanis, "Bookkeeping in the Eighteenth-Century South: Evidence from Newspaper Advertisements," *South Carolina Historical Magazine* 91.1 (1990), 21-33; Richard K. Fleischman and Thomas N. Tyson, "Cost Accounting during the Industrial Revolution: The Present State of Historical Knowledge," *Economic History Review* 46.3 (August 1993), 503-517; Paolo Quattrone, "Is Time Spent, Passed or Counted? The Missing Link between Time and Accounting History," *Accounting Historians Journal* 32.1 (2005), 185-208; and B. S. Yamey, "Scientific Bookkeeping and the Rise of Capitalism," *Economic History Review* 1.2-3 (1949), 99-113.
⁹⁹ Jan Golinski, *British Weather and the Climate of Enlightenment* (Chicago: University of Chicago Press, 2007).

slaves healthy.[100] Work logs from 1796 to 1798 from Newton and Seawell show not a single day of work was lost to weather over the course of two years.[101] In part, this was because these two estates were located in the southeast, the driest region of the island. There was, however, sufficient rain in both years to harvest a crop, indicating that slaves did work through the rain. It is possible that certain tasks at Newton and Seawell were modified or changed because of the weather, but the managers never mentioned it.

The work logs from the 1780s and 1790s at Prospect, an average-sized plantation in the wet and densely wooded mountains of Portland Parish in northeastern Jamaica, show, again, that wet or stormy weather rarely meant an end to the slaves' toil, despite the schemes of improving planters and physicians. Average annual rainfall in the area around Prospect is approximately 40 percent higher than what is considered ideal for sugar cultivation, nearly twice what it would have been at Newton and Seawell. Prospect's enslaved workers were continually subject to wet conditions. Work was stopped during extreme rainstorms, and tasks were occasionally changed because of the rain, but the slaves also dug cane holes, harvested, and carried manure in rainy weather. In 1785, while the estate was still being cleared, slaves were in the field on every work day, regardless of the weather. The hurricane that tore through the island in late August of that year hit Prospect on a Sunday, the slaves' traditional day of rest, so that not one day's work was lost. The slaves spent the week afterward repairing houses and mending provision grounds. In 1787, work was stopped for only two days because of rain, and the slaves continued to perform the most demanding chores while wet.

The enslaved workers at Prospect almost always worked through the rain, but managers did in some circumstances factor the weather into their decisions about what chores to assign. In 1791, for example, fifty-eight rainy days were recorded at Prospect.[102] Work was stopped or slowed down on eight-and-a-half of those days. On some days, slaves were kept "in their Houses" on "Account of the Rain" but it is not clear whether this was because the rain was severe enough to impede their work or because the overseer believed the downpour threatened the slaves' health. When the cane harvest was halted one day after the midday break because of "a Deluge of Rain," the health of the slaves was probably less of a concern

[100] Dickson, *Mitigation of Slavery*, 433.
[101] Newton Work Logs, 1796–1798, Seawell Work Log, 1796–1797 and 1798, MS 523/110, 111, 122, 123.
[102] Prospect Plantation Journals, 1787–1793, 0627-0019.

than the water-logged canes springing from the cane knives and grinding poorly. On four of those eight-and-a-half days, slaves were kept in the field, but their work were slowed so much by rain that "Little or Nothing" was done.[103] That they were kept in the fields even if they were not producing suggests that the overseer was not swayed by ameliorationist policies regarding weather. Complete work stoppages and work slowdowns due to rain at Prospect in 1791 represented a total loss of potential labor over the entire year of only 3 percent. Although the slaves worked through most rainy days, and worked on every major task in the rain at some point, cane cutting was the task that was most often halted by wet weather. Overseers stopped the harvest and the mill whenever there was rain for more than a day. The cane cutting gang on those days would stay out in the rain and bundle together cut canes and other field trash. The other work gangs would join them. Keeping the gangs together during a rainfall, when visibility was often lower, allowed the drivers the opportunity to better supervise and discipline their charges. When the weather became too severe during planting, the slaves were often directed to cut pasture lands to feed the cattle. There is no indication that wet weather ever stopped the slaves at Prospect from digging cane holes or manuring. Rain would have both aided and hampered the process of cane holing. Wet soil was easier to penetrate, but it was also heavier, and the holes could easily collapse or fill in during a downpour. Rain never stopped the Prospect slaves from weeding, hoeing, molding, banking, trashing, or tying canes. These were tasks that were done more often on rainy days than on dry days.[104]

Weather conditions halted or slowed work slightly more often on Virginian plantations than it did in the Caribbean. William Cabell, in his agreements with overseers in the 1770s, insisted that slaves were not be forced to work at "unreasonable times, such as in the Night, or in Rains or Snow."[105] The overseers seem to have followed those orders. The weather conditions were also severe enough at times that there was little that the planter and his slaves could do but wait, particularly during a heavy snowfall. Resting in such cases was more of a necessity than a choice. Snow during the winter of 1791–1792 was especially heavy and, in mid-February, Cabell noted that "we have done no work in our plantation for 5 Weeks this day from the depth of the snow & the severity of the weather." It was

---

[103] Ibid.
[104] Prospect Plantation Journals, 1787–1793, 0627-0019.
[105] William Cabell Common Place Book [1774], Mss5:5C1117: 4, Virginia Historical Society.

another week before the snow melted enough for much work to be done.[106] Virginian rain or snowstorms were less destructive and dangerous than Caribbean hurricanes or tropical rainstorms but, as the evidence from Cabell's plantation suggests, snowstorms and cold weather had the potential to halt or slow work for a longer period of time. Rain could also halt or slow work for lengthy periods on a Virginian plantation. In July, 1794, Cabell noted that "the ground so wet that we cannot work it & has been so a fortnight." The slaves might have done other chores during that period, such as repairing fences, but they could not do any of their primary field labors. A week later, the weather was improving, but he complained that it had been "very wet for 41 daies, & the greatest part of the time the ground too wet to work."[107] It is very unlikely that Cabell's slaves were allowed to completely stop working for a month and a half straight. When a heavy rain soaked the ground at James Francis Mercer's Marlborough Plantation, the overseer noted that it kept the slaves from seeding rye, but the wet weather gave them an opportunity to kill "thousands of worms Which must have destroyed many hundreds of plants of Tobo. had not this timely relief been given to them."[108]

Rain or snow at Mount Vernon in 1797 caused work to be modified, but such weather rarely halted work. Slaves on most of the quarters worked through all seasons and in all climatic conditions. At Union Farm, not a single day of work was lost to weather. The average number of annual days lost per slave to weather at Muddy Hole, Dogue Run, and at the Mansion House ranged from 0.3 to 1.8. At River Farm, an average of 9.6 work days per slave were lost to rain and snow. This was the highest number of days lost to weather on any quarter. It was also the only Mount Vernon farm on which work was completely stopped for snow that year. Why so many more days were lost to weather at River Farm is unclear. The terrain may have made it difficult to work under bad weather conditions. The higher number of days lost to weather at River Farm brought the average number of days lost to weather among all Mount Vernon field hands to 3.8, which was still a negligible amount over the course of the year. It may be that 1797 was a mild year for weather, but it is more likely that Washington's own insistence on maximizing work and efficiency meant that his farm managers found a way for slaves to do something at all times, regardless of the weather

---

[106] William Cabell Common Place Book [1791–1792], Mss5:5C1117: 9, Virginia Historical Society.
[107] Ibid.
[108] Solomon Betton to John Francis Mercer, September 6, 1791, Mercer Family Papers, section 33, Mss1 M5345, a223–232, Virginia Historical Society.

conditions. The diversity in production at Mount Vernon and the emphasis on self-sufficiency offered a broad range of possibilities for work under any weather conditions. Whether it was Barbados, Jamaica, or Virginia, the ambitious schemes of improving planters, such as protecting slaves from the rain, were rarely adopted if they posed too great a threat to production.

CONCLUSION

Nicholas Cresswell spent time traveling throughout the Chesapeake and the Caribbean in the 1770s. He said little of the conditions of slavery in Virginia but, after witnessing the labor of sugar hands in Barbados, he noted that the sugar slaves surely must go to "a better place" when they die "for they have a hell on earth."[109] Virginian slaves on mixed farms and grain plantations worked most of the year and were subject to the emotional trauma of enslavement but they lived, compared to their Caribbean counterparts, remarkably healthy lives. Slave populations in Jamaica were never able to sustain themselves, and in Barbados, a naturally reproducing slave population did not emerge until the final decades before the close of the slave trade. Barbados had an older and more creolized slave population at the end of the eighteenth century and, accordingly, better balanced sex ratios, which may have improved their reproductive rates. The sickness rates in Jamaica, Barbados, and Virginia appear to have mirrored the reproductive trends of the slave population. Plantations in Jamaica tended to have the highest rates of decline and the highest number of days lost to sickness, whereas slaves on Barbadian and Virginia plantations had very low sickness rates and better reproductive rates among the slaves. However, low levels of sickness did not always indicate a healthy slave population. Ill and injured slaves were regularly forced to work, and resistant slaves sometimes feigned illness to avoid work.

The work required on the plantation was the major factor in the differences in fertility and mortality among the slaves in the Chesapeake and the Caribbean. Slaves in Barbados and Jamaica worked more hours per year on more demanding tasks and under more severe and rigorous discipline than did slaves in Virginia. The regimented, closely supervised, and brutally efficient system of gang labor that was used on Caribbean sugar plantations was not so fully applied or utilized in Virginia. The corn and wheat harvests were shorter in Virginia, and there were less time

---

[109] Cresswell, *Journal of Nicholas Cresswell*, 39.

constraints in the processing of grain than there were in the processing of sugar, so the slaves were not made to continue work through the night. Plowing on grain plantations required significant upper-body strength, but the chore did not destroy the slaves in the way that cane holing did on sugar plantations. Sugar, by the eighteenth century, required substantial manuring on many older plantations, and the terrain was rocky enough and the destination (a single cane hole) specific enough that the planters often preferred the labor of slaves to cattle in carting that manure. It was a brutal task and it, like holing, increased sickness rates among the slaves. Virginian planters were also relying heavily on manure to revitalize soils, but the cleared and flat terrain and the abundance of livestock made it easier to transport that dung.

The seasonal rhythms of sickness point toward a close relationship between work and health. Sickness and mortality rates tended to rise on sugar plantations during seasons when sugar slaves were holing or manuring, and conception rates fell. In contrast, the sugar harvest, despite the long hours, lowered mortality rates and encouraged conception, and sickness rates fell at the beginning of the harvest before the long hours took their toll and sickness rose again. In Virginia, sickness rates appear to have been more closely tied to the weather and the availability of provisions. Sickness rates rose at Mount Vernon during the coldest seasons and when the demands and hours of work were at their lowest. On sugar plantations, sickness and mortality rates rose during the wettest seasons, but this was also the season in which the most demanding work of holing and manuring was done. Planters, drawing on pervasive eighteenth-century medical theories about weather and climate, blamed the rain as much as they did the work for fatalities during the rainy season, but the evidence suggests that it was the work that had a more detrimental effect on the health of sugar slaves, particularly the women who worked in the fields.

In an era of amelioration and improvement, the focus was on keeping slaves healthy and reproducing in order to extract as much labor as possible from them and keep the costs of labor replacement low. This created some tension in the policies of planters with regards to acknowledging or treating sick or pregnant slaves. Pregnant women in both Virginia and the Caribbean were forced back to work with little time to rest, and old slaves were kept in the field until they became too crippled by labor or until they died. Healthy slaves were kept working through most of their illnesses and injuries. Planters wanted to improve the lot of slaves, but in the cheapest way possible, and they flinched more at the loss of labor than they did at the loss of life. Virginian planters were not as often forced to sacrifice the health of the slave population to obtain more labor because they were not as chronically short-handed as sugar planters and the work on a Virginian estate was less demanding. In the sugar islands, there was a constant tension between short- and long-term labor gains. The precise timing required in the sugar cycle and the chronic labor shortages with which planters operated made them opt for the short-term gains of labor often enough that, especially in Jamaica, they continued to drive slaves to their graves and continued to rely on importing new laborers until the end of the slave trade. On the mainland and in the islands, planters did all they could to keep slaves at work through sickness and health, rain or shine. For the most part, they were successful.

5

Labor and Industry

Skilled and Unskilled Work

A Grenada sugar planter argued, in 1785, that enslaved tradesmen and supervisors "ought to be particularly encouraged, and invested with some authority over the rest of the negroes."[1] Likewise, the Barbadian ameliorationist William Dickson contrasted enslaved field workers with tradesmen and supervisors, noting that, "comparatively," the elite slaves lived "in ease and plenty."[2] Bryan Edwards, a prominent Jamaican plantation owner, agreed that enslaved tradesmen were "in general vastly better lodged and provided" than field hands.[3] In Virginia, Washington sometimes threatened to punish his elite slaves by stripping them of their status and having them "severely punished" by making them a "common hoe negro."[4] Planters often stressed the distinctions between their field workers and more elite slaves, and they struggled to police the boundaries between these classes of slaves. In daily practice, those distinctions often broke down.

Jack, an enslaved carpenter, offers a more nuanced understanding of the overlap between skilled slaves and field hands. Jack worked at Seawell, a large Barbadian sugar and cotton plantation. Jack was about thirty years old in 1796, and he was Seawell's lone carpenter. The son of "Great

---

[1] Gordon Turnbull, *Letters to a Young Planter; Or Observations on the Management of a Sugar Plantation* (London: Stuart and Stevenson, 1785), 42.

[2] William Dickson, *Letters on Slavery: To which are added, addresses to the whites, and to the free Negroes of Barbadoes; and accounts of some Negroes eminent for their virtues and abilities* (Westport: Negro Universities Press, [1789] 1970), 6.

[3] Bryan Edwards, *The History Civil and Commercial of the British Colonies in the West Indies*, 2 vols. (Dublin: Luke White, 1793), 135.

[4] George Washington to Anthony Whiting, May 19, 1793, in Fitzpatrick, ed. *The Writings of George Washington: From the Original Manuscript Sources, 1745–1799.* 39 vols. (Washington, DC: Government Printing Office, 1931), vol. 32, 463.

Phebe," Jack was born and raised on the plantation.[5] He was one of Phebe's five remaining children, all grown men. Phebe's sons were unusually privileged. Whereas more than three of every five men at Seawell worked with the field gangs, only one of Phebe's five sons worked as a field hand. Jack's eldest brother Frank was a ranger, the headman on the estate. Dick Mingo and Peter, Jack's other two older brothers, worked together as Seawell's coopers.[6] Jack occasionally worked alongside them. His younger brother, Alee, was the only brother working full-time in a field gang. Jack had been a field slave until he was at least eighteen years old, and he was working throughout the year with the first gang in 1784. At some point before 1796, Jack was trained in carpentry, perhaps to replace the aging and "infirm" carpenter Joe, who was in his sixties by the 1790s.[7]

Jack continued to work in the field, regularly, after learning his trade. Carpenters were among the most valuable of all craftsmen in the West Indies. Maintaining the sugar works during the fast pace of the sugar harvest was critical. If a windmill sail was broken or a mill shaft was malfunctioning, the harvest stalled. Freshly cut canes become dry and brittle quickly, and profits would be lost. Although it was tempting for an overseer to assign a carpenter to field labor when his skills were not required, at least two Barbadian plantation manuals cautioned against this practice.[8] No such warnings were ever given about keeping masons or coopers from the field. Carpenters required the kind of fine motor skills and manual dexterity that could be ruined by injuries sustained in the field. Despite the threat of injury, his value, and the advice of contemporary plantation manuals, Jack spent a large share of his year either in field labor or cutting bushes to feed the lime kiln. In fact, from 1796 through 1797, Jack spent almost as much time in the field (36 percent) as he did working on tasks that required his craft skills (39 percent). He was too sick to work for only a single day that year. Not only did he join the field hands to cut canes during the harvest, he also assisted with tasks that were not essential for cash crop production, such as planting and breaking corn or cutting yam plants. He would have been accustomed to

---

[5] "Report on the Negroes of Seawell Plantation," MS 523/292, Newton Family Papers.
[6] "Report on the [Newton] Negroes," MS 523/288, Newton Family Papers.
[7] Seawell Slave Inventory, June 7, 1784, and "Report on the Negroes of Seawell Plantation," MS 523/278, 292.
[8] Philip Gibbes, *Instructions for the Treatment of Negroes, etc., etc., etc.*, 2nd ed., with additions (London: Shepperson and Reynold's 1788), 22; Edwin Lascelles et al., *Instructions for the Management of a Plantation in Barbadoes. And for the Treatment of Negroes, etc., etc., etc.* (London: [s.n.], 1786), 30.

field work from his younger days with the field gangs. He was a Jack-of-all-trades.

Jack's experience as both an enslaved carpenter and a field worker, presumably in rank and file alongside the first gang, raises important questions about how stark the division was between skilled and unskilled rural slaves in their daily labors. Although there was a hierarchy operating on large slave plantations that accorded more rank and status to tradesmen and supervisors than to field workers, there was also significant overlap in their daily work routines and porous boundaries between the two categories of workers. Distinctions between skilled and unskilled workers were as much a cultural and social construction as they were a product of the kinds of labor undertaken each day. The division between skilled and unskilled slaves was based not just on the intrinsic nature of their daily labors or on the kinds of training and expertise required for the job but also on planters' gendered assumptions about who was eligible to be a skilled worker, as well as other cultural attitudes that plantation managers held about the nature of work.

This chapter examines the work routines of skilled workers and explores the differences between skilled and unskilled workers and work. It contrasts skilled workers on sugar plantations, where the proto-industrial processing equipment required highly specialized workers, with the skilled workers at Mount Vernon, where diversified crop production and an excess of labor created very different working conditions. Using work log evidence, this chapter compares and contrasts the annual work routines of coopers, masons, and carpenters in Barbados, at Newton and Seawell, with the same tradesmen in Virginia, at Mount Vernon. Such detailed evidence is not available for Jamaica but, wherever possible, the analysis will be extended to that island. Ultimately, the frequency with which they were subjected to gang labor, the prestige accorded to the occupation, the degree of bargaining power their craft accorded them, and the amount of individual control over the labor process were the key distinctions in day-to-day labor between field slaves and the slaves whom planters considered to be skilled and elite.

SKILLED WORK ON PLANTATIONS

Eighteenth-century political economists, as part of an emerging free labor ideology, argued that slavery was either always inefficient or, at least, incompatible with skilled craftsmanship and with technological or industrial development. Stage-based or evolutionary theories of social development bolstered arguments about the incompatibility of slavery with progress by dismissing labor systems such as slavery or serfdom as relics of earlier stages of development. These theoretical frameworks encouraged contemporary theorists and subsequent generations of scholars to conceptualize slavery as a fundamentally distinct kind of labor system. Adam Smith, in his *Wealth of Nations* – although his position was full of contradictions and qualifications – was the most prominent figure among theorists postulating that slavery was less efficient than free labor. The absence of incentive in slavery was the key for Smith. Men must own slaves to domineer, he argued. If profit was the primary concern, they would always choose free labor because it was more versatile and productive. At the same time, he explicitly acknowledged the tremendous profits being made by Caribbean planters.[9] Other Enlightenment thinkers were more nuanced in their position on the profitability of slavery or its compatibility with progress. James Steuart, in *Inquiry into the Principles of Political Economy* (1757), differentiated between manual "labor" and skilled work or what he called "industry." Slaves were the best option where simple manual work was needed, but "industry" required thoughtful work, and such labor had to be free to be effective. Slavery produced careless and mindless workers who had no incentive to either learn a craft or practice it with dexterity.[10]

The standard ideological position of the late eighteenth-century British Atlantic was that slaves were best used only for the simplest manual labor and with the most basic tools. This argument was buttressed by racist assumptions about the innate flaws of African labor forces. In a similar vein, both eighteenth-century theorists and planters argued that slavery did not encourage the invention of labor-saving devices, such as new tools, and that it bred sloth among the master class as well as among the slaves. Accordingly, slavery was, in this tradition, incompatible with anything beyond the simplest manual labor and with technological development.[11]

Historians, echoing such theorists, have often agreed that slaves could not be taught the skills needed for skilled or industrial work, in part because anything other than the simplest manual labor required too much attentiveness on the part of the laborer, and there was too much potential for sabotage when one used slave labor around machines. The argument that slavery retarded technology, although no longer dominant in the literature, continues to have some academic weight, despite ample evidence to the

---

[9] Seymour Drescher, *The Mighty Experiment: Free Labor Versus Slavery in British Emancipation* (New York: Oxford University Press, 2002), 9–33.
[10] Ibid., 16–17.
[11] Drescher, *Mighty Experiment*, 9–33.

contrary.[12] Other scholars have maintained that plantation owners had to deliberately avoid introducing labor-saving tools, devices, or machinery (and that they might have deliberately tried to slow the pace of labor) to ensure that the slaves always had something to do, even during "down time" in the crop cycle because the labor demands of an estate were determined by the increased pace during the harvest.[13] This kind of argument underestimates the range of activities in which a slave could be employed and the degree to which planters could diversify production to even out the seasonal highs and lows in labor demands. In some of the sugar islands with the most brutal labor regimes, attorneys and overseers wrote repeatedly to absentee owners complaining that they were shorthanded in labor and pleading for capital for fresh supplies of Africans. Restrictions on the use of technology or new tools on slave plantations, where they existed, were the product of planters' assumptions about slaves' capacities rather than anything intrinsic in the institution. In fact, by the end of the eighteenth century most planters were looking to adopt labor-saving devices and schemes, and they were increasingly looking to their slaves to accomplish the skilled work of the plantation. There was always tension between the use of slave labor in skilled positions and the theories that planters espoused about slaves being unable to accomplish such tasks. Some planters reconciled the tension

---

[12] Carl Bridenbaugh, *The Colonial Craftsmen* (New York: New York University Press, 1950), 17; William A. Green, "The Planter Class and British West Indian Sugar Production, before and after Emancipation," *Economic History Review* 26.3 (August, 1973), 448–463; Lucille Mathurin Mair, "Women Field Workers in Jamaica during Slavery," in Brian L. Moore, ed. *Slavery, Freedom and Gender: The Dynamics of Caribbean Society* (Kingston, Jamaica: The University of the West Indies Press, 2001), 188–189.

[13] Richard Dunn, "Servants and Slaves: the Recruitment and Employment of Labor," in Jack P. Greene and J.R. Pole, eds., *Colonial British America: Essays in the New History of the Early Modern Era* (Baltimore, 1984), 174–175; Michael Craton, *Searching for the Invisible Man: Slaves and Plantation Life in Jamaica* (Cambridge: Harvard University Press, 1978), 226. Recent scholarship has tended to discount such claims. See for example J. R. Ward, "The Amelioration of British West Indian Slavery, 1750–1834: Technical Change and the Plow," *New West-Indian Guide* 63.1–2 (1989), 41–58; J.R. Ward, *British West Indian Slavery, 1750–1834: The Process of Amelioration* (New York: Oxford University Press, 1988); Alex van Stipriann, "The Suriname Rat Race: Labor and Technology on Sugar Plantations, 1750–1900," *New West Indian Guide* 63.1–2 (1989), 94–117; John Bezis-Selfa, "A Tale of Two Ironworks: Slavery, Free Labor, Work and Resistance in the Early Republic," *William and Mary Quarterly* 56.4 (1999): 677–700; Richard B. Sheridan, "Changing Sugar Technology and the Labour Nexus in the British Caribbean, 1750–1900, with Special Reference to Barbados and Jamaica," *New West Indian Guide* 63.1–2 (1989), 60–92; Glenn A. Crothers, "Agricultural Improvement and Technological Innovation in a Slave Society: The Case of Early National Northern Virginia," *Agricultural History* 75.2 (Spring 2001), 135–161; R. Keith Aufhauser, "Slavery and Technological Change," *The Journal of Economic History* 34.1 (March 1974), 36–50.

by hiring white tradesmen when they felt the job was too complicated. Ultimately, however, slaves proved themselves more than capable of skilled work or of using new labor-saving tools, and the planters recognized the economic benefits that came with relying on skilled slaves rather than free white tradesmen.

Compared to most other eighteenth-century agro-businesses, sugar production and processing was very technologically sophisticated; some scholars have gone so far as to describe sugar plantations as proto-industrial or as "a synthesis of factory and field."[14] Sugar production was capital intensive agriculture that required extensive labor division and specialization, especially in the sugar works during the harvest.[15] Craftsmen proficient at coopering, masonry, and carpentry were needed throughout the year on every sugar plantation and, during crop season, planters needed slaves with expertise at several stages in sugar and rum processing, such as a mill boatswain (the man in charge of the mill), boilers, clarifiers, and a distiller.

In contrast, not even the largest Chesapeake plantations required significant capital expenditure on processing equipment for the staple crops. The majority of Chesapeake plantations in the late eighteenth century were small-scale enterprises with fewer than twenty slaves. Larger estates tended to be divided into "quarters" – smaller units, each with a small working gang of between ten and twenty-five slaves. There were not significant economies of scale in tobacco or corn production. There may have been some economies of scale in wheat production.[16] Chesapeake mixed farms and plantations were less obviously a synthesis of factory and field or proto-industrial businesses. However, if one privileges the role of labor management and work culture as key elements in the process of early industrialization, then it is possible to see the Chesapeake plantations as participating in the process of industrializing. Despite the absence of capital intensive processing equipment in Chesapeake agriculture, most large planters were training enslaved specialists and craftsmen or teaching their slaves new technologies by the late eighteenth century.

Approximately one in ten slaves in the Chesapeake worked as a tradesman or driver, a higher proportion than on sugar plantations in Barbados or Jamaica – in part because sugar was a more labor intensive crop requiring

---

[14] Sidney Mintz, *Sweetness and Power: The Place of Sugar in Modern History* (New York: Penguin Books, 1985), 46–52.
[15] Craton, *Searching for the Invisible Man*, 223.
[16] James. R. Irwin, "Slave Agriculture and Staple Crops in the Virginia Piedmont" (Ph.D. Dissertation, University of Rochester, 1986), v, 4.

a greater number of field workers.[17] The surplus of labor in the late eighteenth- and early nineteenth-century Chesapeake forced planters to diversify production and be creative in their uses of slave labor.[18] Washington was among the top two dozen largest slaveholders in the Chesapeake and, at Mount Vernon, he had one of the highest slave-to-land ratios of all the large plantations.[19] By the summer of 1799, the population had grown so large at Mount Vernon that Washington complained, "I have more working Negroes ... than can be employed to any advantage in the farming system."[20] Although Washington's situation was more extreme than most, large planters throughout the Chesapeake were forced to consider a range of new employments for their slaves. Slaves, even in rural areas, tended to occupy a wider range of craft positions than their counterparts in rural Barbados and Jamaica. In addition to carpenters, coopers, and masons, there were a variety of other rural craft specialists in the region, including (but not limited to) boat builders, shoemakers, tanners, distillers, bakers, and blacksmiths.[21] Over the course of their lives, Chesapeake slaves became remarkably versatile and skilled at multiple trades.[22] On large estates, a greater proportion of slaves tended to be skilled than on small estates. Some of the largest plantations, such as Mount Vernon, strove to train and maintain enough craftsmen to be almost entirely self-sufficient. At Mount Vernon, 22 of the 317 slaves were tradesmen or drivers (7 percent of the population). If one includes the spinners and knitters and a shoemaker – and the only reason not to include them would be that these occupations were rare on a Caribbean sugar plantation – then thirty-one slaves were recorded as regular trade workers or drivers (10 percent of the population).[23]

---

[17] Philip D. Morgan, *Slave Counterpoint: Black Culture in the Eighteenth-Century Chesapeake and Lowcountry* (Chapel Hill: University of North Carolina Press, 1998), 211.

[18] Richard Dunn, "After Tobacco: The Slave Labour Pattern on a Large Chesapeake Grain-and-Livestock Plantation in the Early Nineteenth Century," in Kenneth Morgan and John J. McCusker, eds., *The Early Modern Atlantic Economy* (New York: Cambridge University Press, 2000), 344.

[19] Lorena S. Walsh, Slavery and Agriculture at Mount Vernon," in Philip J. Schwarz, ed. *Slavery at the Home of George Washington* (Mount Vernon: Mount Vernon Ladies Association, 2002), 48.

[20] George Washington to Robert Lewis, August 18, 1799, in Fitzpatrick, ed., *Writings of Washington*, vol. 37, 338.

[21] Morgan, *Slave Counterpoint*, 212.

[22] Ibid., 218.

[23] Mount Vernon Slave Inventory, June, 1799 in Abbot, ed., *The Papers of George Washington, Retirement Series*, vol. 4 (Charlottesville: University Press of Virginia, 1999), 528–540.

There was some variation in the standard ratio of craftsmen and drivers to total population on sugar plantations in Barbados and Jamaica – normally between one in twelve and one in twenty. Craftsmen and sugar specialists, along with the primary supervisors (gang drivers and rangers), were known on British Caribbean sugar estates as slaves "with offices" or as "Head Negroes."[24] These slaves formed the slave elite on a sugar plantation. A typical late eighteenth- or early nineteenth-century sugar planter strove to have at least two drivers, a cooper, a mason, and a carpenter on the estate, but the bare minimum appears to have been at least two enslaved drivers. Smaller estates could hire enslaved or free craftsmen when they needed them. On Barbadian and Jamaican sugar plantations, approximately 6–8 percent of the slaves served as tradesmen or drivers.[25]

In the late eighteenth century, plantation managers responded to the economic challenges that came with war, declining soil fertilities, the rising cost of slave labor, and an expanding plantation frontier by trying to improve the self-sufficiency and productivity of their plantations, which meant training a growing number of skilled laborers. Training slaves to assume the skilled positions that had initially been occupied by white workers allowed planters to achieve better returns on slave labor and lowered the costs of production.[26] By the last quarter of the eighteenth century, most of the craft work on large plantations in Barbados, Jamaica, and Virginia was done by enslaved laborers.[27] The growing specialization of slave labor and the increasing number of slave craftsmen on both sugar plantations and mixed-farming units in the Chesapeake was actually running counter to a general trend toward the deskilling of labor and the erosion of craft status and bargaining power occurring among many European artisans during the early stages of the Industrial Revolution.

[24] Edwards, *History, Civil and Commercial*, 143.
[25] A sample of eight Jamaican sugar plantation inventories from 1779 shows 107 tradesmen and 33 drivers among 1,988 slaves – equaling 7 percent of the population This sample is drawn from the inventories of Tredways, Friendship, Windsor, Parnassus, Old Plantation, Caymanas, Vere, and Sutton's. For the location of these records, see bibliography. Other sources suggest similar numbers; see Harry J. Carman, *American Husbandry* (New York: Columbia University Press, [1775] 1939), 426–427, M. Craton, *Sinews of Empire: A Short History of British Slavery* (London: Anchor Press, 1974), 208; Prospect Plantation Journals, 1787–1793, 0627-0019; B. W. Higman, *Slave Populations of the British Caribbean, 1807–1834* (Baltimore: Johns Hopkins University, 1984), 552–558; Justin Roberts, "Working Between the Lines: Labor and Agriculture on Two Barbadian Sugar Plantations, 1796–1797," *William and Mary Quarterly* 63.3 (2006), 560.
[26] Craton, *Searching for the Invisible Man*, 223.
[27] Robert W. Fogel, *Without Consent or Contract: The Rise and Fall of American Slavery* (New York: Norton, 1989), 43.

Planters chose promising boys from among both the domestics and field gangs to be trained as tradesmen.[28] These apprenticing craftsmen were increasingly trained by other slaves.[29] When the Virginian planter, William Lee, switched to less labor intensive grain cultivation schemes, he found himself with an abundance of laborers. He asked the overseer to "have promising young Fellows" – elsewhere he called them "geniuses" – sent to become apprentices at "every useful trade viz House Carpenters, Joiners, Wheelwrights, sawyers, Bricklayers, Smiths, Shoemakers, Weaver & c."[30] Lee's request suggests that at the heart of the association of skilled work with male slaves was an assumption about male superiority in mental acuity as much as physical strength. Such assumptions drew in part on Aristotelian traditions – which gained significant cultural force over the course of generations – suggesting that men derived their intellectual ability from their dry and hot constitution, whereas women, cold and wet, were considered inconsistent and incapable of mastering intellectual tasks or skilled trades.[31]

Stereotypical assumptions about the mental and physical suitability of particular ethnic groups for specific trades or labors were common throughout the Atlantic world in the last half of the eighteenth century. Planters made assumptions about ethnic differences within a broader racial group. They consistently differentiated between the "intelligent creole" slave and the "ignorant uninstructed African" slave. The latter, they assumed, was better suited to field work. Skin color enhanced this conceptual distinction. Mulattoes were also much more likely than American-born slaves to be chosen as craftsmen.[32] In fact, it was almost unheard-of for planters to assign a slave they identified as a mulatto to the field. Planters also associated particular African ethnicities with field work, skilled work, or domestic

---

[28] Higman, *Slave Populations of the British Caribbean*, 192; Richard Dunn, "A Tale of Two Plantations: Slave Life at Mesopotamia in Jamaica and Mount Airy in Virginia," *William and Mary Quarterly* 34.1 (1977), 51; Richard Dunn, "'Dreadful Idlers' in the Cane Fields: The Slave Labor Pattern on a Jamaican Sugar Estate," *Journal of Interdisciplinary History* 17.4 (1987), 804.

[29] Edwards, *History, Civil and Commercial*, vol. 2, 78–79; Minutes of the Meeting of Codrington Attorneys, August 30, 1770, C/COD/39, Codrington Papers, C series.

[30] William Lee to [PHS?], May 30, 1778, William Lee's Letterbook, section 116, Mss1 L51 f 417; William Lee to [Richard Lee], July 12, 1782, William Lee's Letterbook, December 1780–June 1783, Section 119, Mss1 L51 f420, Virginia Historical Society.

[31] Daryl Hafter, *Women at Work in Preindustrial France* (University Park : Pennsylvania State University, 2007), 55.

[32] Dunn, "'Dreadful Idlers' in the Cane Fields," 807–808; Gilbert Farquhar Mathison, *Notices Respecting Jamaica in 1808, 1809, 1810* (London: J. Stockdale, 1811), 29; Higman, *Slave Populations of the British Caribbean*, 197–198; Morgan, *Slave Counterpoint*, 216.

work. There were a wide range of stereotypes about different African groups and their suitability for different kinds of work or their common health problems. These stereotypes were often contradictory or inconsistent. One of the most consistent was about Gold Coast slaves – planters often called them Coromantees, named after a Dutch fort on the Gold Coast. These slaves were said to make the best field workers but, supposedly, they were more bellicose and dangerous.[33] The Jamaican John Dovaston argued that Gold Coast slaves were "the best for the field [because] their disposition is dull and stupid and only fit for Labour." Dovaston drew a distinction here, as Steuart had, between dull and menial "labor" and the finesse of" industry."[34] Some slaves, according to these ethnic stereotypes, were completely unsuited for laborious field work. Planters maintained, for example, that slaves from the Congo were "totally unfit for laborious occupations," but they made excellent "domestic servants and tradesmen."[35] Laborious tasks were reserved for particular groups of slaves.

SKILLS AND FIELD WORK

Field and craft work have been too often depicted as polar opposites; field work continues to be represented as unskilled drudge work (labor), whereas craft work is portrayed as skilled and dexterous (industry). It is easy to exaggerate any distinction between skilled and unskilled work. Skilled work is the synchronization of the mind, the hand, and the other senses in the production of something. Knowledge of a craft is the ability to use those skills to solve problems with a particular type of material. Carpenters, for example, were problem solvers with wood, and masons were problem solvers with stone. Craftsmen were distinct in that they required an apprenticeship, a process by which expertise and knowledge of their specialty in production was achieved. By broadening or being more creative in the definition of an apprenticeship or the ways in which craft expertise can be acquired and refined, it becomes possible to conceptualize

---

[33] Barry David Gaspar, *Bondsmen and Rebels: A Study of Master-Slave Relations in Antigua* (Durham: Duke University Press, 1993), 89–91.

[34] John Dovaston, "Agricultura Americana or Improvements in West-India Husbandry Considered Wherein the Present System of Husbandry Used in England is Applied to the Cultiation or Growing of Sugar Canes to Advantage" [1774], Codex Eng 60, vol. 2. John Carter Brown Library.

[35] David Collins, *Practical Rules for the Management and Medical Treatment of Negro Slaves in the Sugar Colonies* (London: J. Barfield, 1803), 42; Edwards, *History, Civil and Commercial*, vol. 2, 72.

a wider range of occupations as being skilled work or craft work, and clear distinctions between skilled and unskilled work become less tenable. On slave plantation, the divisions between skilled craft workers and unskilled field workers were less stark than they might appear at first glance.

Working in the field required a degree of expertise and skill and sometimes a kind of problem-solving ability with crops and the soil. Learning how to wield tools in the field effectively and learning what was required for various crops demanded a degree of expertise. At what angle should a cradle scythe be held as a slave swung it to cut grains? Where exactly should one make the first cut on a sugar cane at harvest? What was the ideal pace or working cadence required in a field gang? Skeletal evidence suggests that field workers on a sugar plantation were forced to perform fine motor manipulations more often than slaves working on other physically demanding crops, such as rice. Field slaves throughout the Americas had severe degenerative changes in their spines, but sugar slaves were more likely than their counterparts on South Carolina rice plantations to have degenerative changes in smaller joints, such as their wrists and elbows. Rice slaves showed more degenerative changes in their shoulders and hips.[36] The degenerative changes in sugar slaves' wrists and elbows were probably the result of years of careful movements made against hard soils during cane holing on precisely measured fields. Planters recognized that it could take time to become skilled in the use of field tools. The author of an unpublished sugar plantation manual warned that when new African-born slaves "begin to handle the hoe, you cannot expect them to be handy at it unless Some of them have used it in their own Country, which is not often Most wise."[37] The Caribbean gang labor system, with its progressive steps through hierarchical layers of gangs and its training in increasingly complex, demanding, and essential tasks was a kind of field apprenticeship.

The acquisition of skills in the field could take years, and this expertise was, to some extent, tied more fully to a particular plantation's land than the knowledge of a craft. Slaves learned not only how to cultivate certain crops but how to best cultivate the specific soils of their plantation. According to the attorneys at the Codrington estates in Barbados, "no Slaves either of the African kind or those brought from other parts of the Island are equal in

---

[36] Kristrina Shuler, "Health, History, and Sugar: A Bioarchaeological Study of Enslaved Africans from Newton Plantation, Barbados, West Indies" (Ph.D. Dissertation, Southern Illinois University, Carbondale, 2005), 309.

[37] Dovaston, "Agricultura Americana," vol. 2.

value to such as are upon a Plantation, tho' in appearance they may be ... as much."[38] Creole field slaves were considered to be worth about one- to two-thirds more than a slave who had just arrived from Africa.[39] The expertise that slaves gained from working for decades in the fields on one particular plantation meant more than simply greater levels of productivity from these slaves; it also meant that that individual slaves were less likely to be sold or moved away from their family or community because their cultivation skills were less valuable on other estates. For example, although there were a few African-born workers at Newton and Seawell in 1796, not a single slave had been born on another plantation in Barbados. Once born or brought onto a plantation, field hands did not tend to be traded or sold to other plantations because their knowledge was grounded, literally, in the soil of the plantation they started on.

Drivers were not only supervisors; they were also among the most skilled of the field hands. They knew better than anyone on a plantation how to best cultivate its crops. Such expertise could take decades to acquire and perfect. Drivers in the Chesapeake had less responsibility than their Caribbean counterparts, and they were not usually referred to as drivers. They were more like work leaders or foremen than drivers. They normally worked alongside the other slaves. Chesapeake slaves were not normally promoted to the position of foreman until at least their late twenties.[40] On sugar plantations, drivers were rarely promoted until their thirties.[41] A slave had to have at least ten years of experience with the most able and adept field workers before being promoted to the position of driver or foreman. When a Virginian planter, Francis Gildert, wrote to ask his fellow planter William Lee about purchasing "a negro Man under Thirty who perfectly understands making Tob[acc]o," Lee warned him that "it will be difficult to find such a one as I do not recollect having known one of that age who has sufficient experience to be trusted with the direction of making good Tob[acc]o." Lee told Gildert to be more realistic and instead look for a man who was "not above 50 Years of age."[42] Tobacco required

---

[38] Letter from Codrington Attorneys, August 20, 1778, C/COD/41, Codrington Papers, C series.
[39] Arthur Young, *Political Essays Concerning the Present State of the British Empire* (London: Strahan and T. Cadell in the Strand, 1772), 282.
[40] Morgan, *Slave Counterpoint*, 216.
[41] This author has found only one Jamaican or Barbadian slave inventory with a head driver younger than thirty; "Report on the [Newton] Negroes," MS 523/288, Newton Family Papers.
[42] William Lee to Colonel Francis Gildert, October 9, 1787, Section 121, William Lee's Letterbook, Mss1 L51 f422, Virginia Historical Society.

more skillful cultivation than most major staple crops in the Americas, but the essential point to be taken from Lee's response was that slaves developed a proficiency in cultivating specific crops that could take decades to develop, especially if they were to become field supervisors. According to Alexander Barclay, a long-time resident of Jamaica, "the welfare of a plantation depends mainly on a good driver."[43] Caribbean planters protected their drivers by exempting them from night work during the sugar harvest.[44] Caribbean plantation inventories show that the driver was almost invariably as valuable as any slave on the estate. In 1789, at Pleasant Hill, in Jamaica, the driver Leapold was almost past his physical prime at forty-five years of age, and he was "Ruptured" but, despite his advancing age and his hernia, he was valued at £160, whereas prime male field hands in their late twenties and early thirties were valued at only £100.

Among the field hands, plowmen were exceptional in that planters understood such labor to be skilled. Mastering a plow was not substantially different from mastering some of the other tools used in field work; yet, planters saw plowmen as separate from the rest of the field hands and, as an occupation, plowing was masculinized. Some sugar planters were concerned that plowing required too much intelligence, attentiveness, and dexterity to be practiced by slaves. Essentially, as a tool, the plow demanded too much skill.[45] In 1798, a St. Kitts planter, Patrick Blake, with perhaps some hyperbole, suggested in an article in Arthur Young's *Annals of Agriculture* that it would take "seven years to teach a negro how to handle a plow."[46] Blake probably had in mind the standard seven-year apprenticeship to a trade in many contemporary European guilds, invoking the argument, in a post-*Wealth of Nations* era, that slaves were incapable of becoming master tradesmen or of learning new technologies.[47] To incorporate the plow in sugar cultivation on his Jamaican plantation, Bryan Edwards chose to train "two Negroe Boys with sufficient dexterity" as plowmen in the same way that he would have done if he was training a cooper or a carpenter.[48]

---

[43] Alexander Barclay, *A Practical View of the Present State of Slavery in the West Indies* (London: Smith, Elder & Company, 1827), 40.
[44] H. T. De La Beche, *Notes on the Present Condition of the Negroes in Jamaica* (London: T. Cadell in the Strand, 1825), 7.
[45] Ward, "Amelioration of British West Indian Slavery," 47.
[46] Patrick Blake, "Culture of Sugar in the West Indies," in Arthur Young, ed., *Annals of Agriculture*, 31(1798), 363.
[47] John Rule, "The Property of Skill in the Period of Manufacture," in Patrick Joyce, ed., *The Historical Meanings of Work* (New York: Cambridge University Press, 1987), 100–101.
[48] Bryan Edwards, "Notes on Long's Jamaica," Codex Eng-87, John Carter Brown Library.

The vast majority of plowmen in the plantation Americas were men.[49] To some extent, the association of plows with male slaves was related to physical differences between the sexes. Wherever the plow was introduced in European agriculture, the occupation of plowman tended to be almost exclusively reserved for men, which was probably connected to what historian Michael Roberts called an "inherited association of men with stock-keeping."[50] Plows did require more upper-body strength than most field work, to keep the plow steady, but planters did not shy from assigning other brutally demanding field tasks, such as cane-hole digging, to their female laborers, and many women were capable of plowing. At Mount Vernon, there was a slave woman named Daphne who "ploughs very Well, and is a good hand at any work."[51] On nineteenth-century cotton plantations in the Deep South, women, according to the testimony of the ex-slave Solomon Northup, "plowed fields as frequently as the men."[52] Given that women were clearly capable of plowing, the association of plows with skilled men was as much a social and cultural construction as it was a response to any real sexual differences in strength or stature.

Tools, such as the plow, were central to the planters' conceptualization of the boundaries between skilled and unskilled work and to their understanding of the capacity of enslaved workers to perform skilled work. Even though his Mount Vernon slaves developed a remarkably diverse array of skills and wide-ranging agricultural expertise, George Washington worried that the invention of any kind of "complicated" agricultural "machinery" was "useless" because it would be worked only by "ignorant and clumsy hands" on a slave plantation.[53] Most planters agreed. According to an Antiguan planter, "nothing has yet been found so completely suited to the Disposition of the Slaves as the hand hoe." To him, the hoe – which field hands, especially women, were ever wielding – was simply an extension of the body, requiring no finesse or thought.[54]

---

[49] Lorena S. Walsh, "Plantation Management in the Chesapeake, 1620–1820," *The Journal of Economic History* 49.2 (June, 1989), 405.

[50] Michael Roberts, "Sickles and Scythes: Women's and Men's Work at Harvest Time," *History Workshop Journal* 7 (1979), 8.

[51] Mount Vernon Slave Inventory, June 1799.

[52] Solomon Northup, *Twelve Years a Slave* (Baton Rouge: Louisiana State University Press, 1968 [1855]), 123.

[53] George Washington to Charles Vancouver, November 5, 1791, in Fitzpatrick, ed., *Writings of Washington*, vol. 31, 410.

[54] *British Parliamentary Papers*, 1789, Part III, Antigua, No. 42; see also, Ward, "Amelioration of British West Indian Slavery," 47.

Some planters thought of plowmen as being exceptionally adept in the use of all field tools, particularly new tools. Patrick Kein, a Jamaican planter and overseer, thought that plowmen were central to the improvement of agriculture because they could transmit new agricultural knowledge and techniques to the field hands. A "skillfull ploughman," Kein argued, could be assigned to teach groups of specialized field slaves, working separately from the first gang, "the dexterous use of the spade and all other necessary tools." In other words, Kein was envisioning the plowman as a master craftsman who would train a special work group of skilled field hands. Not surprisingly, he thought that men should compose this group, and he contrasted the output of these new skilled male field hands using new techniques and tools with the traditional output of female slaves. Using new tools and techniques, "four negro men," he explained, "will load a cart with earth or dung in less time than twelve women can do with baskets according to the old custom."[55] Other planters, such as the Jamaican planter Nicholas Robson, contrasted the "ease and speed" of a spade (a new tool) to the "laborious action" of a hoe (the customary tool); yet, despite its benefits, Robson was concerned that the spade would be too difficult a tool to introduce to all slaves at once.[56] He recommended that "a few of the more sensible negroes" on a sugar plantation be chosen and trained in the use of new agricultural implements such as the spade. A small cadre of slaves, he thought, could be "wholly employed in handling and using the spade," becoming specialists in the field.[57] The Jamaican William Beckford maintained that young slaves "take the hoe [for field hands], the adze [for coopers], the hammer [for masons], or the plane [for carpenters]" into their hands with excitement and ease and became well skilled at whatever was asked of them.[58] Whether artisan or field hand, the tool was symbolic of the trade, and planters associated old laborious field tools (such as hoes and baskets) with women and new, more efficient, and dexterous field tools (such as spades and plows) and craft tools (such as the hammer or the adze) with men.

On large Chesapeake estates growing grains, some field hands, other than the plowmen, appear to have been considered particularly able, dexterous,

---

[55] Patrick Kein, *An Essay upon Pen-Keeping and Plantership* (Kingston, Jamaica: His Majesty's Printing Office, 1796), 56.
[56] Nicholas Robson, *Hints for a General View of the Agricultural State of St. James in the Island of Jamaica* (London: John Stockdale, 1796), 13.
[57] Ibid.
[58] William Beckford, *Remarks upon the Situation of Negroes in Jamaica* (London: T & Egerton, 1788), 14.

and specialized, a step above the common hand, although their primary tasks were not that different from the work done by a first-gang hand in the Caribbean. These Chesapeake slaves, normally men, were called "ditchers," and, as their occupation title suggests, they dug ditches throughout the estate, primarily for irrigation or drainage. The essential task of digging ditches on a Chesapeake estate did not differ significantly from the trenching and cane holing done by slaves on Jamaican or Barbadian sugar plantations. In fact, first gangs on sugar plantations were sometimes, like "ditchers," called "holers" or the "holing gang" because digging cane holes was their primary and most demanding task.[59] They were, in a sense, being recognized as specialists in cane-hole digging. The attitude toward the skill required for such labor, the organization of labor, and the laborers themselves was the key difference between a Caribbean holing gang and a Chesapeake ditching gang. Whereas cane holes and trenches were dug in the Caribbean by large gangs (with a female majority) led by a driver, Chesapeake ditchers were all men, they worked in small units, and their primary task was regarded as a kind of semiskilled labor.

The diversity of the daily tasks done by Mount Vernon suggests that Washington and his managers saw the ditchers as more versatile and independent than common field hands. All four of the regular ditchers were men ranging in age from their early twenties to their late fifties. They were sick for an average of only ten days a year in 1797, compared to nineteen days for field hands.[60] They spent more time than common field hands on tasks that required solitary labor and very little supervision – although they did sometimes work as a small squad. They also spent a greater share of their time on tasks that would have been seen as requiring more dexterity and intelligence than simple menial labor. They spent the majority of their time working in the fields, but only 9 percent of their time was spent actually doing the task (digging and cleaning ditches) that defined their occupational status. Ditchers spent approximately the same proportion of each year (one-tenth) ditching as first-gang Caribbean "holers" spent digging cane holes (see Appendix B, Table A20, and Chapter 2). The ditchers actually spent slightly more time each year building fences (11 percent) than digging ditches (9 percent). The Mount Vernon ditchers spent 15 percent of their work days at the mill and distillery, whereas field hands on the outlying farms spent only 2 percent of their work days there. Most of the ditchers' time at the mill and distillery was spent doing repair work, tasks normally

[59] Collins, *Medical Treatment of Negro Slaves*, 178.
[60] Mount Vernon Farm Reports, 1797.

done by carpenters or masons. Compared to the field hands, the ditchers also spent more of their work time fishing (7 percent compared to 0.6 percent) and more of their time toiling at the brickyard (4 percent vs. 0.2 percent). They also spent much more of their time cutting wood (11 percent vs. 1.3 percent) and making hay (20 percent vs. 0.1 percent) than the common field hands. Cutting wood was an independent task, whereas making hay may have been a lighter task designed to relieve them after the more demanding physical work of ditching. They spent much less time than the field hands on the staple wheat crop (2 percent vs. 14 percent) and on most of the other agricultural crops. Mount Vernon ditchers also traveled more than the regular field workers among the various quarters and outside of the estate lands. Washington became irritated when his ditchers were used as common laborers. He wrote his manager, in 1793, to insist that "the Ditchers" not be used as "jobbers" on the outlying farms because each farm had a sufficient laboring "force ... of its own" to accomplish all of the necessary agricultural work "except ditching."[61]

In a post-*Wealth of Nations* era, planters understood labor division and specialization to be keys to increasing efficiency. Ditching was a kind of field specialization that came to be considered a craft, but it is important to recognize that specialization and skilled or craft work are not always the same thing. In fact, they can be entirely at odds. The process of industrialization disaggregated the work of the traditional craftsmen, dividing the production into multiple specialized tasks done independently but contributing to the entire product in order to improve efficiency. Specialized labor can involve a very limited kind of skill, or it can be generally unskilled. Historian Haim Burstin notes that groups of unskilled workers in Paris in the eighteenth century "controlled separate tasks, often exclusively." Porters, for example, were unskilled laborers, but they became specialists in hauling a particular type of good.[62] In terms of their status and the autonomy granted to them, Washington treated his specialized ditchers as elite slaves, and he reserved the task, as he did trades work, for men.

The dichotomy that planters created between menial field work and skilled craft work had a significant gendered component. They implicitly, and sometimes explicitly, acknowledged that field work, beyond being simply "laborious" or menial, required expertise and dexterity. Yet, in

[61] George Washington to Anthony Whiting, January 27, 1793, in Fitzpatrick, ed., *Writings of Washington*, vol. 32, 319.
[62] Haim Burstin, "Unskilled Labour in Paris at the End of the Eighteenth Century," in Thomas Max Safley and Leonard N. Rosenband, eds., *The Workplace Before the Factory: Artisans and Proletariats, 1500–1800* (Ithaca: Cornell University Press, 1993), 71.

virtually all cases, they chose to train men for the few available spots as craftsmen on an estate and they left women to fill the positions as field hands. They believed that men had the mental acuity to accomplish the tasks and women did not. Indeed, the majority of field hands in Barbados, Jamaica, and Virginia were women. Field work may have been so often identified as common and unskilled drudgery because it was, for the most part, understood to be women's work.[63] In other words, the conceptual lines drawn between skilled and unskilled labor, which were somewhat artificial and always blurry, were reinforced by the sexual division of labor.

SKILLED WOMEN

Enslaved women developed knowledge of particular crafts, but female craft work was not normally essential to the production of the primary plantation crops, and it was not as highly valued by managers as male craft work. In the early nineteenth-century British Caribbean, only 7 percent of all artisans were females, almost exclusively textile workers.[64] No more than 1 percent of enslaved adult women on sugar plantations in Barbados or Jamaica worked as textile workers. At Mount Vernon, these female craftsmen were much more common. In 1797, a total of sixteen female slaves (and two male slaves) worked at some point with the spinners and knitters. In other words, in 1797, approximately 6 percent of all slaves or 19 percent of adult women at Mount Vernon worked at some point with the spinners and knitters.[65] Fourteen women and one crippled man worked with the spinners and knitters for the entire year.

The annual work routines of the Mount Vernon textile workers demonstrate the ease with which these female craftsmen, although they were the most highly specialized of all craft workers on an estate, could move from their craft to the house or to the field – although moving to the house was more common for them than moving to the field. As a group, more than half of their time was spent spinning wool or flax, and a fifth of their time was spent knitting (see Appendix B, Table A21). The female textile workers spent much more time than other craft workers as domestics (11 percent of all work days). They moved to the house when the raw materials for

---

[63] The same process has been observed by labor and gender historians in other contexts. For example, see Hafter, *Women at Work*, 3–4, 54, and Ruth Oldenziel, *Making Technology Masculine: Men, Women and Modern Machines in America, 1870–1945* (Amsterdam: Amsterdam University Press, 1999).
[64] Higman, *Slave Populations of the British Caribbean*, 192.
[65] Mount Vernon Slave Inventory, 1799.

spinning were in short supply, when their equipment was damaged, or simply when more slaves were needed in the house. Washington's managers may not have thought of the female textile workers as being as versatile or as valuable as the other slaves. The spinner and knitters spent 1 percent of their work days in 1797 doing "nothing" when there were no materials available for textile work. It was rare for Washington to tolerate slaves doing nothing. However, the amount of time lost among textile workers because of a shortage in materials was comparable to the amount of time that field workers spent doing nothing because of bad weather.

Alse was one of the enslaved textile workers at Mount Vernon. She was around forty years old in 1797. She was married to a free black man named Charles Freeman, and she had three children.[66] In December 1797, she became pregnant again and continued with her textile labors.[67] Although she had worked primarily as a house servant when she was younger, she had been trained to work as a spinner by 1786 at the latest.[68] Alse spent the vast majority of her work days in 1797 either spinning (48 percent) or sewing (32 percent). When she was spinning, she could spin between five and six pounds of yarn in a week, depending on what type of yarn it was. When she sewed, she would sew between four and six entire suits of clothes or between nine and eleven shirts in a week. Like the rest of the textile workers, she was subject to production quotas but, unlike some of the others, she almost always achieved them. She was not the most productive spinner, but she seems to have had a particular aptitude for sewing, and she was more productive at that than most of her peers, which may be why she spent more time sewing and less time spinning than her fellow textile workers. Occasionally, she would be called on to sew particular items for Martha Washington. Martha may have liked Alse or her work more than that of some of her peers. Alse was primarily a spinner but she also filled in as a house servant at the Mansion House. She spent 19 percent of her work days as a domestic, greater than the average among spinners and knitters. It offered some variety to her work schedule but being continually under the master's eye undoubtedly had its drawbacks. Alse missed fifteen days

---

[66] Ibid.
[67] Mount Vernon Farm Reports, 1797.
[68] List of Tithables in Fairfax County, July 1774, in W. W. Abbot and Dorothy Twohig, eds., *The Papers of George Washington: Colonial Series*, vol. 10, March 1774– June 1775 (Charlottesville: University of Virginia Press, 1995), 137–138; Mount Vernon Slave List, February 18, 1786, in Donald Jackson and Dorothy Twohig, eds., *The Diaries of George Washington*, vol. IV, 1784–June 1786 (Charlottesville: University Press of Virginia, 1978), 277–283.

of work to sickness, slightly less than the annual average of nineteen days for field hands and much less than the annual twenty-four average sick days among spinners and knitters.[69] Although the vast majority of her year was spent as a domestic or as a spinner and knitter, she also acted as a caretaker for her own family. In December 1797, around the time she became pregnant, she was allowed two days to attend to her "Sick Husband."[70]

Some of the spinners and knitters, such as Alse, became domestics when necessary and others, such as Matilda, became field hands, demonstrating how fluid the boundaries were between occupations at Mount Vernon.[71] Matilda was in her late thirties or early forties in 1797.[72] Her husband, Boson, was a ditcher.[73] Matilda was the most consistently productive of all the spinners. Unlike Alse and some of the other textile workers, Matilda did not knit, sew, or work in the house. She was a specialist. She spent every working day that year indoors spinning either wool or tow yarn. She was sick more often (thirty days) than most of her peers. In March 1798, she was sent to join the field workers. In 1799, she was still working in the field. There was no explanation for the change in Matilda's occupation, and it seems odd given her productivity. It was not the first time, however, that she had been sent to the field. In 1786, Matilda had been sent to assist with weeding at Dogue Run, and, in 1793, Matilda had been sent to the field when there was a consistent shortage of "raw materials" for the spinners and knitters.[74] Her move to the field in 1797 might have been punitive, or it might simply have been that there was another raw material shortage and Matilda's skills were deemed more valuable in the field.

Matilda was not the only woman at Mount Vernon to serve as a textile worker and a field hand. Whereas Matilda made the switch from the shop to the field at a young age, Doll made the switch from the field to the shop as she grew older. When Washington found that she was missing too much time, regularly, to sickness at Ferry Farm, he asked that Doll be brought to the Home plantation and taught to knit so that she could join the spinners

[69] Mount Vernon Farm Reports, 1797.
[70] Ibid.
[71] Ibid.
[72] Mount Vernon Slave Inventory, 1799.
[73] Ibid.
[74] George Washington to Anthony Whiting, January 6, 1793, in Abbot, ed., *The Papers of George Washington, Presidential Series*, vol. 11, August 1792 to January, 1793 (Charlottesville: University of Virginia Press, 2002), 594–599, and Anthony Whiting to George Washington, January 16, 1793, in Abbot, ed., *The Papers of George Washington, Presidential Series*, vol. 12, January–May 1793, 11–12.

and knitters.[75] Some slaves moved back and forth regularly from the field to the textile shop. Delia, for example, was "equally good at the Spinning Wheel or Hoe, but has been kept chiefly at the farm."[76] Again, in this description of Delia, the tool became the symbol of the trade, and mastery of multiple tools was evidence of the slave's utility.

SKILLED MEN

Field workers were sometimes understood to be skilled workers, and, despite their elevated and privileged status, plantation craftsmen were never entirely excluded from the drudgery and demands of field labor. In Barbados, the Newton and Seawell tradesmen were, fittingly, jacks-of-all trades, versatile and adaptable laborers in almost every facet of plantation production. Sometimes they performed tasks suited to their specific skills. The coopers filled and trimmed hogsheads, the masons built houses or plastered the dungeon, and the carpenter repaired the plantation works.[77] These tradesmen also did a remarkable amount of less specialized work, and the coopers and masons labored both individually and collectively on the same basic tasks – such as making fences or railings – often enough that they seemed, at times, interchangeable. Labor maximization was the planters' operating principle, and labor allocation became a question of opportunity cost. When the manager felt it was more advantageous to have an extra able-bodied worker in the cane fields, cultivating provisions, even digging rocks out of the ground, the tradesmen's specific skills became a secondary consideration. On these days, the craftsmen usually performed the same labors as the first gang, presumably in rank and file alongside them. Cabbenah, a Newton mason, was used even more regularly in the field. He was identified as "a Field Negroe and Mason." For part of 1796–1797, he worked as the third mason, but, for most of the year, he seems to have been at work with the first gang. According to one Barbadian plantation manual, the average island estate should have "fourty able people in the roll of the first gang, exclusive of constant watchmen and principal tradesmen," suggesting that tradesmen and watchmen commonly accompanied the first gang in their labors.[78] Tradesmen on sugar plantations clearly performed a significant amount of field work, but they may have gained some working

---

[75] George Washington to Anthony Whiting, November 4, 1792 in Abbot, ed., *The Papers of George Washington, Presidential Series*, vol. 11, 330–334.
[76] Mount Vernon Slave Inventory, 1799.
[77] Higman, *Slave Populations of the British Caribbean*, 171.
[78] Lascelles et al., *Management of a Plantation in Barbadoes*, 5.

privileges in day-to-day labor allocation that distinguished them from regular field hands. The Newton and Seawell tradesmen, for example, cut canes and performed a wide range of field tasks from weeding to provision work, but they never dug cane holes or hauled dung. Cane holing and dunging were the most physically taxing tasks. The Newton and Seawell tradesmen, because of their special craft skills and their versatility, were simply too valuable to risk in such work.

Some of the field work done by Newton and Seawell artisans might have actually been preparatory work for masonry. A significant number of work days – 3 percent for Jack the carpenter and 4 percent for the masons and coopers – were spent "picking" or "pecking" rocks (see Appendix B, Table A22). They may have been clearing rocks from the field for easier cultivation. According to the manager's plans for the year, Newton laborers would be put to work clearing rocks and spreading dung on some of the nonagricultural lands whenever there was time to improve the soil depth and quality.[79] They might also have been quarrying, hauling, and dressing stone for the masons. Higman notes that it is unclear if Caribbean masons and carpenters had to gather the raw materials for masonry and carpentry, or if this work was done by field hands.[80] If this is how the rocks cleared from fields at Newton and Seawell were used, then the task of hauling stones was not done exclusively by masons or field hands but, rather, by all classes of tradesmen, as well as by the field hands. Somewhat surprisingly, the coopers spent more time than the masons at the task.

Although Caribbean tradesmen clearly performed a significant amount of field work, they also gained working privileges in day-to-day labor allocation that helped set them apart from field hands. Ordered to cut canes and perform various field tasks, such as weeding or provision work, the carpenter and the other Newton and Seawell tradesmen never dug cane holes or distributed dung. Overseers were willing to use tradesmen in the field, but cane holing and dunging were widely understood to be the most damaging to the health of slaves. Tradesmen – because of their special craft skill, their versatility, and their status in the slave community – were simply too valuable to risk in such work. Barbadian tradesmen also seem to have been given additional rewards when they performed their own trades. William Dickson noted that enslaved "artificers, *when working at their trades*" were given "a *bit*, or near 6d. ster. *per* day."[81] The additional

---

[79] "Report on the [Newton] Lands," MS 523/289, Newton Family Papers.
[80] Higman, *Slave Populations of the British Caribbean*, 171.
[81] Dickson, *Letters on Slavery*, 14 [italics added].

monetary reward on days when they performed their artisanal work was both an incentive to keep slaves attentive in their more detailed craft labors and an effort on the part of managers to maintain a conceptual boundary between skilled and unskilled work and thus reinforce status hierarchies on the estate – difficult to do when a worker moved so seamlessly from trade work to field work on a daily basis.

It is not clear whether the work routines of Jamaican tradesmen were similar to those in Barbados or if Jamaican tradesmen were used in the field to the same extent. Detailed evidence on the day-to-day work routines of Jamaican tradesmen over an entire year has not been found. At Duckensfield Hall, a large Jamaican estate, in November and December of 1806, the coopers and carpenters did not work with the field hands even during the harvest. They spent most of their time at "Sundry Jobs." The carpenters also built a mule pen, and the coopers made hogsheads and headed sugar casks. The coopers also spent time out of the shop performing heavier skilled work; for a week, they were "digging the foundation" of a house – a task that would normally be associated with masons, but there were no masons on the estate.[82] Although the Duckensfield Hall tradesmen did not join the field hands when the harvest began in December, it is reasonable to assume that some Jamaican tradesmen assisted with cane cutting during the harvest for the same reasons (time constraints, labor intensive harvest production, and value of harvest field labor, for example) that they cropped in Barbados.

The work routines of the majority of Jamaican carpenters were undoubtedly different from their Barbadian counterparts in at least one significant way. Jamaican plantations had more readily available wood than did Barbadian estates. Barbados was almost completely deforested by the end of the eighteenth century. Specialized sawyers commonly appeared on the inventories of Jamaican estates, but they were essentially nonexistent in Barbados.[83] On Jamaican estates without a specialized sawyer, the task of gathering and preparing wood was left to the carpenter. On average, these Jamaican carpenters would have spent far more time than their Barbadian counterparts gathering and sawing raw materials for their trade

At Somerset Vale, a small mixed sugar and coffee estate in Jamaica in the 1770s, labor specialization was difficult to achieve and there was little

---

[82] Duckensfield Hall Estate Papers, Codex Eng-183, JCB.
[83] Higman, *Slave Populations of the British Caribbean*; for examples of sawyers on Jamaican estates, see Sutton's Slave Inventory, 1779, box 13, item 2.1/8 and 18; Old Plantation Slave Inventory, 1779, box 13, item 2.1/7 and 17; and Parnassus Plantation Slave Inventory, 1779, box 13, item 2.1/6 and 16, Wilberforce Museum.

distinction each day between skilled and unskilled workers. There were no more than sixty adult field hands, not enough for specialization or for extensive division into more than two gangs.[84] During cane holing, all of the able-bodied men and women dug holes. However, when construction or carpentry work was needed, select men were removed from the main gang and assigned to the task while the women generally weeded or did nonessential field tasks. For most of December and January of 1776–1777, for example, the estate work logs reported that "10 Men [were] Sawing & Splitting Shingles for [the] Trash House" while the "rest of the Negro's [were] Clean'g & Supply Cane" or performing similar tasks. It is noteworthy that not only were the women excluded from construction or carpentry work, they also never performed the most essential cash crop labors without men.[85]

Although production was more diversified at Mount Vernon than it was in Barbados, the Mount Vernon tradesmen tended to be slightly more specialized than their Barbadian counterparts. Whereas Mount Vernon tradesmen spent 78 percent of their work days on craft labors in 1797, the Newton and Seawell tradesmen – even if one includes the time spent hired out – spent only 62 percent of their time on craft labors from 1796 through 1798 (see Figures 5.1 and 5.2). Hiring was one of the most significant

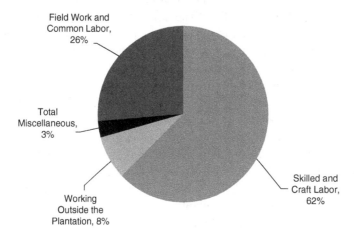

FIGURE 5.1. Labor activities of all Newton and Seawell Tradesmen, 1796–1798. *Source*: Newton Work Logs, 1796–1798, Seawell Work Log, 1796–1797, MS 523/110, 111, 123, Newton Family Papers.

---

[84] Slaves at Somerset Vale, Codex, Eng 181.
[85] Somerset Vale Logs, 1776–1780, Codex Eng 180.

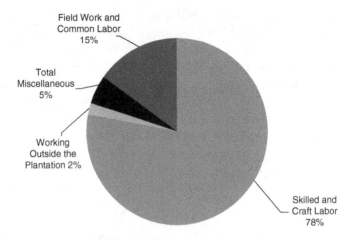

FIGURE 5.2. Labor activities of all Mount Vernon tradesmen, 1797.
Source: Mount Vernon Farm Reports, 1797.

differences between the Mount Vernon and the Newton and Seawell tradesmen. Whereas the Barbadian tradesmen were hired out to surrounding plantations to perform their trades whenever their skills were not in demand at home, Washington never hired out his tradesmen because it interfered with their family lives. The difference in hiring practices meant that Newton and Seawell tradesmen spent 8 percent of their time working away from the plantation, compared to only 2 percent of all working days at Mount Vernon. Washington's tradesmen only left the estate to run errands or collect goods from town.

The Mount Vernon carpenters were not as essential to ensuring the production of the primary crop as the carpenter at Seawell, but they were more specialized. Jack, the Seawell carpenter, spent more than a third of his time performing common labor and working with field hands. In contrast, his Virginian counterparts spent only 13 percent of their time on such tasks (see Appendix B, Table A22). Nevertheless, even at Mount Vernon, the carpenters were unable to avoid heavy manual labor and field work. Almost 8 percent of their work days were spent hauling timber from the surrounding woods and sawing it. Although the Mount Vernon carpenters spent less time performing heavy manual labor than Jack, they spent slightly more time (4 percent vs. 2 percent) of their time cultivating crops alongside the field hands – both harvesting and plowing grain.

Just as the Newton and Seawell tradesmen took up cane knives and joined the field gangs to cut canes during the sugar harvest, the Mount

Vernon carpenters snatched up cradles for mowing wheat and became field workers at the height of the grain harvest. In the middle of June, two of the six Mount Vernon carpenters cut hay, oats, and wheat, and were joined by three more carpenters the following week. The harvest was the most labor intensive time of year on a grain plantation, and all hands were needed. Much like on a sugar plantation, it became more advantageous to use a Chesapeake carpenter in the field during the harvest than to have him perform his trade. Essentially, the harvest on grain and sugar plantations became a leveling experience as slaves who were considered elite, such as the male tradesmen, put down their craft tools and joined the field hands to get the crops harvested. Domestics and nurses or caretakers also joined the field hands for the harvest, especially on smaller estates. At Somerset Vale in 1787, Rose, was "a very usefull negro in Crop time" but spent most of her time looking after slave children.[86]

Outside of the grain harvest, the Mount Vernon carpenters spent the vast majority of their time laboring at tasks that required the specific talents of their trade. Approximately 83 percent of the time, the carpenters worked as tradesmen – closer to 90 percent, if one considers the sawing and hauling of wood as part of their trade (see Appendix B, Table A23). They spent most of their time maintaining barns (especially Washington's prized sixteen-sided barn at Dogue Run), building or repairing carts and cart wheels, and maintaining plows and field tools. Some of the carpenters had subspecialties. Isaac, for example, was normally asked to build and maintain the plows. Washington praised "the character [Isaac] had of being skilled in making of these, and other impliments of husbandry," and he hoped that other carpenters would learn from him.[87] Yet Washington was also frustrated by the amount of time the carpenters spent repairing carts and plows "for it is inconceivable that Isaac always and Joe frequently should be employed in making and repairing Ploughs and Carts; abuse, more than the use of these things, must be the cause of it."[88]

Although the Mount Vernon carpenters spent the vast majority of their time working at tasks that required the talents of their specific craft, there were a wide range of activities that fit this description (see Appendix B, Table A23). The Mount Vernon carpenters also spent a large share of their work days (12 percent) building and maintaining the new "wheat

---

[86] Slaves at Somerset Vale, Codex, Eng 181.
[87] George Washington to William Pearce, March 29, 1795, in Fitzpatrick, ed., *Writings of Washington*, vol. 34, 161.
[88] George Washington to James Anderson, December 21, 1797, in Abbot, ed., *Papers of George Washington: Retirement Series*, vol. 1, 526.

machines" (presumably threshing machinery) with which Washington hoped to experiment. On rainy days and in bad weather, they worked on small jobs in the shop or made and dressed shingles. Not all of their craft work was specifically carpentry. Among the Mount Vernon carpenters was a man named Davy, who spent most of the year working with the group but a portion of the year making flour barrels with the coopers. Sometimes, rather than work in the shop or the field, a carpenter was called to the house. One of the carpenters worked as a domestic for two-and-a-half weeks in 1797 at the Mansion House. The ease with which Mount Vernon carpenters could move from one trade to another, such as from carpentry to cooperage, or from the shop to the field to the house, demonstrates the remarkable array of craft skills that slaves could attain over a lifetime, as well as the flexibility and versatility of slave labor.

The two Mount Vernon coopers were even more specialized than the carpenters, spending almost 90 percent of their time on craft work. However, they also spent a slightly greater share of their time (9 percent vs. 4 percent of work days) working with the other field hands cultivating crops (see Appendix B, Table A24). Not surprisingly, during the harvest, the coopers were called on to cut wheat and oats. Somewhat surprisingly, the coopers spent additional time outside of the harvest working on tasks in the field that were not normally considered high priority or labor intensive. They spent fourteen days cleaning the meadow, which was similar to the less essential provision cultivation tasks assigned to tradesmen at Newton and Seawell. In 1797, they were the only tradesmen at Mount Vernon who were assigned to such a nonessential field task. The Mount Vernon coopers spent 69 percent of their time coopering. With respect to the time spent at their craft, they were among the most specialized of all the Barbadian and Virginian artisans for which detailed information exists. They spent more than three times as many work days as the Newton and Seawell coopers on tasks that involved their specific skills as coopers, and, unlike the Newton and Seawell coopers and masons, the coopers at Mount Vernon rarely worked with other skilled slaves on a task.

Whereas the Newton and Seawell masons spent the least amount of time of all the tradesmen on those estates performing field work and other unskilled labors, the Mount Vernon brick layers spent the most amount of time in field work or on ruder unskilled tasks, such as hauling stone. Bricklaying is, essentially, a branch of masonry. As construction work, masonry and bricklaying required great physical power. Friedrich Engels, when differentiating between trades in nineteenth-century England, described bricklaying (or masonry) as "simple, less exact work ... a question more of strength than skill."[89] The work routines of the masons at Mount Vernon lend credence to his observation. Hauling stones to the mill and the distillery required 16 percent of all the work days of the Mount Vernon brick layers (see Appendix B, Table A25). This task offers an excellent example of the way in which craft labors and more menial work could overlap. Hauling stone to a worksite was a brutally heavy and backbreaking task, demanding great physical exertion and, seemingly, little skill. It required more of the Mount Vernon masons' work days than any other task outside of the work associated with brickmaking. Yet, far from being simply general labor, it was part of a mason's special duties, essential to his craft. Choosing the right stones required knowledge and training. When he needed stone quarried for a new dam at Golden Grove, Jamaican attorney Simon Taylor chose to hire a "good" free white mason rather than using an enslaved mason, because he wanted to ensure that the selection of stones was done correctly. Taylor intended to put newly purchased African slaves to work hauling stones under the mason's direction, the kind of unskilled task, he believed, that new arrivals could easily perform. Moreover, using newcomers in this way, he explained, would allow him to build the dam "at the Smallest Estate Expence" because the opportunity costs of using creole or seasoned plantation slaves, who were already skilled at field work, would be too high.[90]

Even if this task of hauling stone is considered part of their craft work, the Mount Vernon masons still spent more time on jobs that were not associated with a trade and more time in the field than did the coopers and carpenters on the estate. They spent 12 percent of their work days alongside the field hands. Overall, a mason's work at Mount Vernon was much more diverse than that of the other tradesmen. The masons not only spent more time in the field, but also in conveying boats to town, running errands, and fishing, than the other tradesmen. Remarkably, they spent 18 percent of their work days either hauling or mending the fishing nets, suggesting that fishing became almost as much a craft for them as bricklaying or masonry.

Although they served in the field and were assigned to heavy work for a significant amount of the year, slave craftsmen on a large Chesapeake estate such as Mount Vernon may have actually been more specialized than free rural craftsmen in the Chesapeake. Craft work in the rural Chesapeake

---

[89] Freidrich Engels, *The Condition of the Working Class in England* (New York: Oxford University Press, 1993), 104.
[90] Simon Taylor to Chalenor Arcedeckne, September 24, 1786, Vanneck-Arc/ 3A/ 1786/17, Vanneck-Arcedeckne Papers.

was much less institutionalized than craft work in Europe, which was dominated by the guild system and more careful and demanding apprenticeships. Free carpenters in the rural eighteenth-century Chesapeake tended to work as "farmer-carpenters" rather than on their trade alone. There was not enough work available in the rural Chesapeake to keep a carpenter employed year round, so the majority of these craftsmen worked as farm laborers or grew crops on their own lands and as hired carpenters when there was more work available. It was easy to pursue these dual occupations in grain farming because grains, for the most part, were only labor intensive crops during the harvest.[91] At Mount Vernon, the size of the estate and the year-round guaranteed and captive labor force allowed managers to allocate slaves to more specialized tasks.

THE MYSTERIES OF SKILL: THE BOILER AS A CASE STUDY

Before the early to mid nineteenth-century technological developments in sugar processing made their craft obsolete, the head boiler was the craftsman who was most invaluable to sugar production. Boilers were the masters of the sugar works. They were difficult to replace. Early modern labor historians Leonard Rosenband and Thomas Safley argue that "the artisan's power existed in the mysteries of skill," as well as in "their control over technique and technology."[92] Not surprisingly, plantation manual authors demonstrated remarkable fascination with the mysteries of the boiler's craft. A boiler's knowledge was more kinesthetic than any of the other slave craftsmen. Their skills were less readily taught or transferable. Instead, their skills were experiential. Boilers were human thermometers, gauging the exact point at which a temper (such as lime) should be added to the sugar, as well as the right temperature for the fire and the precise points at which the sugar should be moved into the next vessel for further processing. Under the system known as the "Jamaica Train," granulating sugar was generally moved as it boiled through five successive kettles of different sizes. Boilers would watch the ladles with which sugar was stirred to help them

---

[91] Jean B. Russo, *Free Workers in a Plantation Economy: Talbot County, Maryland, 1690–1759* (New York: Garland Publishing, Inc., 1989); Peter C. Marzio, "Carpentry in the Southern Colonies during the Eighteenth Century with Emphasis on Maryland and Virginia," *Winterthur Portfolio* 7 (1972), 229–250.

[92] Leonard Rosenband and Thomas M. Safley, "Intro," in Rosenband and Safley, eds., *The Workplace before the Factory: Artisans and Proletarians, 1500–1800* (Ithaca: Cornell University Press, 1993), 4.

make these decisions. According to the Jamaican planter and overseer, Patrick Kein, boilers would "arrive by long habit, to some degree of judgment by the eye only, from its appearance on the back of the ladle" and they "also attend both by the eye and ear, to the rattling of a ladle of sugar on the lead [boiling containers]."[93] When they judged the sugar to be nearly ready, they would take "proof." They would dip a "pan-stick" into the "tache" (a large vessel for boiling sugar) and take some sugar from the stick between their thumb and forefinger, examining its consistency. Some planters allowed their boilers to examine the ladle by eye rather than by touch, because the latter was simply too painful.[94]

Because a boiler's skills were tactile, sensory, and experiential, they could not be easily taught to new workers. Indeed, Kein called the "knowledge of boiling sugar ... almost impossible to teach" except through experience.[95] The Jamaican planter I. P. Baker agreed that "it is wonderful, what long Experience will do."[96] The process, Kein insisted, "cannot be expressed in words precisely."[97] Learning to be a boiler was a very painful and hazardous process. The heat and humidity in the boiling house were so intense that, according to one observer, the occupation was "the most unhealthy of any to which a negro can be applied."[98] Many boilers struggled through their labors with badly blistered thumbs from testing the boiling sugar.[99] Moreover, moving from a diurnal to a predominantly nocturnal existence must have required significant adjustment in the circadian rhythms of a young boiler.

Despite the drawbacks of the craft, a boiler's unusual and essential talents gave him significantly more leverage in the master-slave relationship than most slaves. A boiler could use this bargaining power to his advantage or to effect change on the plantation. Some boilers served as drivers out of crop, making them even more indispensable to plantation production and solidifying their role as leaders in the slave community.[100] The Jamaican overseer Thomas Thistlewood reported as early as 1751 that "some negroe

---

[93] Kein, *Pen-Keeping and Plantership*, 71.
[94] I. P. Baker, *An Essay on the Art of Making Muscovado Sugar Wherein a New Process is Proposed* (Kingston, Jamaica: Joseph Weatherby, 1775), 34.
[95] Kein, *Pen-Keeping and Plantership*, 71.
[96] Baker, *Essay on the Art of Making Muscovado Sugar*, 34.
[97] Kein, *Pen-Keeping and Plantership*, 73.
[98] Collins, *Medical Treatment of Negro Slaves*, 186.
[99] Kein, *Pen-Keeping and Plantership*, 74; see also Baker, *Essay on the Art of Making Muscovado Sugar*, 34.
[100] York Plantation Slave Inventory, 1782, 3/C, Gale-Morant Papers, and "Report on the Negroes of Seawell Plantation."

Sugar Boilers purposely will make no sugar to get the overseer turn'd out when they don't like him."[101] As with certain craftsmen, such as weavers, whose labors became mechanized during the process of industrialization in Europe, boilers eventually lost their status in nineteenth-century Louisiana and Cuba when instruments were developed that would do the same job of gauging the ideal temperature and consistency in sugar production.

As planters tried to exert more control over all processes of sugar production, they had to come to terms with the boiler's unusual position. His work could not be easily quantified or measured. "Negro-Boilers have no Rule at all," complained Baker as he tried to understand and improve the craft.[102] For planters concerned with outlining constant rules of plantation management, the boiler's mysterious skill was difficult to accept. According to Baker, who was trying to find a way to impose scientific methods in the boiling house, it was far too unpredictable an environment for making experiments and developing clear rules and systems. He suggested putting the cane syrup on a small pane of clear crown glass and taking it outside the boiling house to examine it because "this method is used by Chemists to try evaporated Solutions of all other Salts, it may seem therefore somewhat strange it has not been long adopted in the Boiling House." For Baker, science should trump art; and, in the process, the boiler's magical powers would be curtailed.[103]

Patrick Kein, a resident planter and former overseer, claimed to have traveled throughout Jamaica in August and September of 1768 and found, to his frustration, that "none of the overseers that had the least knowledge ... in making sugar" but only because there seemed to be "no other mode of making good sugar but one, which I called the touch," by which he meant a boiler's skillful ability to gauge the consistency and temperature of the sugar as it was processed. Boiling by "the touch" referred specifically to the process of feeling the sugar between thumb and forefinger. Not all boilers relied on the touch. Some boilers tried to gauge the consistency and temperature by sight, sound, and smell alone, preferring to examine the sugar on the ladle without touching it.[104] Kein had to concede that the boiler's skills were, in some respects, not only irreplaceable but also much beyond the ken of most overseers and therefore difficult to supervise. He admitted "candidly" that he learned how "to make sugar from a Papaw [an African from the Bight of

---

[101] Thomas Thistlewood Diary, March 18, 1751; Monson 31/ 2.
[102] Baker, *Essay on the Art of Making Muscavado Sugar*, 34.
[103] Ibid., 35, 37.
[104] Kein, *Pen-Keeping and Plantership*, 71; see also Samuel Martin, *An Essay upon Plantership*, 4th ed. (London: Samuel Chapman, 1765), 46.

Benin] negro" rather than a planter or overseer, and he could not master the craft. "[T]hat eye art," he complained, "I have attended with all diligence" but he "could never acquire that critical exactness" that a master boiler possessed.[105]

Planters struggled with authority issues in the sugar works, trying to identify a compromise between the boiler's authority and their own. Sampson Wood, the Newton and Seawell manager, seems to have resolved this tension by keeping his office in the boiling house both in and out of crop. "The Boiling House," he assured the owner, "has been my constant residence all day as soon as light would permit work to be done."[106] Other planters may have been quick to incorporate clock time in the boiling house, in order to feel more confident about exerting labor discipline in a realm that was often not their own. According to Clement Caines, the author of *Letters on the Cultivation of the Otaheite Cane*, it was "prudent not to interfere" too much in the boiling house because, after years of experience, "Negro boilers must be more perfect in their business, than any white man can pretend to be."[107] At the same time, Caines contradicted himself by recommending that the boiler be constantly supervised and, if a planter saw a fault in the end product, he should consult the boiler and make recommendations for alterations. In the end, however, struggling for balance between positive control and negative interference, he warned planters that they must proceed cautiously with any recommendations they might make to the boiler because "the degree to which an alteration should take place, it is right to leave to them."[108]

THE THREAT OF THE FIELD

In their daily work routines, slaves strove to avoid being sent to the field. Fieldwork required certain skills, but it involved more exhausting physical labors, a loss of autonomy, and, in the long-run, a loss of elite status. Washington was certain that a Mount Vernon carpenter named James

---

[105] Kein, *Pen-Keeping and Plantership*, 71.
[106] Sampson Wood to Thomas Lane, October 15, 1797, MS 523 / 322, Newton Family Papers.
[107] Clement Caines, *Letters on the Cultivation of the Otaheite cane: the manufacture of sugar and rum; the saving of melasses; the care and preservation of stock; with the attention and anxiety which is due to Negroes: To these topics are added, a few other particulars analogous to the subject of the letters; and also a speech on the slave trade, the most important feature in West Indian cultivation* (London: Messrs. Robinson, 1801), 99, 101.
[108] Ibid.

deliberately cut himself at the beginning of each harvest to avoid joining the field hands.[109] Slaves sometimes claimed ignorance of field work in order to avoid it. A Caribbean attorney, Michael Keane, tried twice at public auctions in 1788 to sell a man in his prime named Cuffy with no success. Keane complained that if Cuffy "had been a field negroe," he would have fetched a good price. Keane tried to market him as a field slave, but Cuffy had other plans: "he himself declaring that he never worked at any labour but Cooking."[110] Because Cuffy insisted that he had never been a field hand, the price bid at both auctions "was so infinitely below his appraised Value" that Keane "could not think of letting him go."[111] Potential buyers would have feared that Cuffy simply did not have the experience or skills that planters sought in a field hand. Keane, desperate to sell or gain from Cuffy, struggled to decide what to do with him. Surprisingly, he did not suggest sending Cuffy to the field on his own estate, perhaps because Cuffy had indeed never actually worked in the field, and Keane thought it would be impossible to put him to such work so late in life. Instead, "I will try & do the best I can with him," Keane explained to the owner, "tho' I have no other use for him than putting him to a Trade for which he is rather old."[112]

Sometimes craftsmen were sent to the field as a specific form of punishment. When Washington became annoyed with the production of his spinners and knitters, he insisted that they start meeting their quotas "otherwise they will be sent to the several Plantations, and be placed as common laborers."[113] He seems to have meant that they would make the move on a more permanent basis. Likewise, Washington threatened to punish a bricklayer by placing him "under one of the overseers as a common hoe negro."[114] Significantly, work was linked to a particular type of tool – the hoe – which was, in turn, associated throughout the plantation Americas with women's work. West African cultural traditions that dictated that field work was women's work helped make this association stronger and

---

[109] George Washington to William Pearce, March 20, 1796, in Fitzpatrick, ed., *Writings of Washington*, 502–503.
[110] Michael Keane to John Crosbie, Esq., November 25, 1788, Letterbook of Michael Keane, 1787–1790, Mss1 K197 a 1, section 1, Virginia Historical Society.
[111] Michael Keane to John Crosbie, Esq., December 4, 1788, Letterbook of Michael Keane, 1787–1790.
[112] Ibid.
[113] George Washington to Anthony Whiting, December 23, 1792, in Fitzpatrick, ed., *Writings of Washington*, vol. 32, 277.
[114] George Washington to Anthony Whiting, May 19, 1793, in Fitzpatrick, ed., *Writings of Washington*, vol. 32, 463.

made field work seem even more emasculating and punitive for a male craftsman. As much as field work might have been a punishment, some craftsmen may have occasionally preferred working in a group, appreciating the anonymity of field work to the isolation of craft labor. When one of Landon Carter's tradesmen was sent to the field, he told his owner how pleased he was to join the field hands and take up the hoe.[115]

The key advantage to learning an individual trade or developing a skill outside of the field was that it gave a slave the opportunity to escape the gang system – even if only intermittently. The monotony and controlled motion of gang labor and the constant threat of the driver's whip made collective work in the field more psychologically and physically brutal than artisanal occupations. Washington warned his spinners that if they were sent to the field, they would be "under the Overseer's thereat."[116] Free blacks occasionally worked as craftsmen on plantations, but they would not hire themselves out as field workers, especially on a sugar plantation. Knowledge of a craft allowed the artisan a degree of autonomy in the workplace that common field workers were rarely able to attain – especially on sugar plantations. Slave artisans might have also taken some personal pride in their specialized skills. In addition to increased opportunities for traveling beyond the plantation, pilfering tools, additional privileges, and elevated wages or rewards, craft occupations offered slaves an opportunity for independent control over the labor process and a sense of individuality, rather than the mindless subversion of their will to a driver.

CONCLUSION

In an era of industrialization, when European craftsmen were beginning to lose their craft status and control over their labor process, a growing number of slaves on large estates in Barbados, Jamaica, and Virginia were becoming skilled trade workers or supervisors. Yet these enslaved rural tradesmen rarely specialized, as a European guildsman would, on trade work alone. The boundaries between shop and field were porous over a slave's lifetime and in day-to-day work. The combination of a fixed labor force and the seasonal rhythms of agricultural production – which created periods of greater and lesser labor demands – meant that versatile slaves

---

[115] Morgan, *Slave Counterpoint*, 236.
[116] George Washington to Anthony Whiting, December 23, 1792, in Fitzpatrick, ed., *Writings of Washington*, vol. 32, 277.

became more valuable and productive slaves. In essence, planters saw slave workers as interchangeable units, but they had to take into consideration an individual's skill set, and they made decisions about laboring allocations with opportunity costs in mind. The planter's understanding of a slave's skill set drew heavily on assumptions about age, ethnicity, and gender. When the advantages to be gained from using an artisan in the field outweighed the advantages of assigning him or her craft work, he or she was sent to the field. Crop time, because of its intensive labor demands, was a leveling experience on both sugar and grain plantations. Every able-bodied laborer – from the shop and, often, from the house – was called upon to join the harvest on both grain and sugar plantations. Slaves could move often during a single year from trade work to field work or other heavier physical labors requiring less dexterity or finesse.

Craft workers at Mount Vernon, Newton, and Seawell spent a significant amount of time working in the field or at nontrade labors. Yet certain distinctions were maintained in the working environment between skilled and field hands on these plantations. Sugar plantation tradesmen worked in the fields but never at digging cane holes or hauling manure baskets; tradesmen at Mount Vernon, as well as at Newton and Seawell, tended to be entrusted with more individual labors than the average field hand.

Men and creole slaves (especially mulattoes) were most likely to be assigned a trade or a supervisory role. Planters masculinized skilled work – which they believed required dexterity, intelligence, and ingenuity – and technological innovation. Women's work was unskilled work that, given the female majority in field gangs, made field tasks seem more clearly unskilled. Skilled or specialized occupations in the field (such as plowing or ditching) came to be associated with men, despite ample evidence that women could perform these tasks. These choices had as much to do with gendered assumptions about ability as they did with natural differences between the sexes.

There were different degrees of skill and specialization on any plantation, and not all field tasks were menial. Over many years, field workers developed significant expertise with individual crops, and planters appear to have recognized these abilities in their field hands. Compared to trade work, the expertise of a field hand was tied more firmly to a particular estate because it involved knowledge of the fields, soils, and weather conditions of that estate. The extent to which trade work ("industry") was skilled and field work ("labor") was unskilled was exaggerated by planters and continues to be confused by historians. The expertise and knowledge that field hands developed was highly valued – if not always explicitly acknowledged – by planters. There were porous boundaries between field and nonfield work in the daily work routines of plantations in the Chesapeake and the Caribbean. Tradesmen were often called on to do field work or less specialized labor. Planter's perceptions of their slave's skills and their decisions about who could be skilled drew heavily on assumptions about age, ethnicity, and gender. The division of labor and the masculinization of skilled work both fostered and supported status and privilege hierarchies in the slave community. "Skilled" workers formed a slave elite, and the skills that planters saw in their slaves came to be embodied in the worker as much in as the work.

6

Working Lives

Occupations and Families in the Slave Community

Turner's Hall, a Barbadian sugar plantation, had the largest surviving stand of woods in the island, fifty acres. Some of it served as a plantain grove for the slaves. When a bondsman working as the "Watch to the Wood" in the late 1750s was suspected of not only eating too many of "the Plantains himself, but [also] suffered them to be stolen," the new overseer, Samuel Rollstone, chose to replace him.[1] "I found it absolutely necessary," Rollstone explained to the owner, "to put someone there that I could place some confidence [in]."[2] The watchman, however, had been at his post a long time, and he refused to relinquish it. Being a watchman meant that he worked long, lonely, and isolated hours, often through the night, but the position also gave him a significant degree of freedom at work, the opportunity to avoid field work, and more access to provisions, which he or his kin could pilfer. As well, for favors or coins, he might turn a blind eye to other thefts. The Turner's Hall watchman held an "office" that allowed him to guarantee more provisions for himself and his kin. He could enjoy a higher quality of life than a common laborer, but he had to be careful not to be too obvious in what he stole or allowed to be stolen lest he be caught. He may have developed an identity or a measure of self-esteem based on his post or even a sense of proprietary claim to the largest surviving stand of wood in the island.

Rollstone set out to find the "great Villain," but the old watchman had already heard about his impending removal and, "being highly displeased,"

---

[1] Financial Abstracts, 1778, E20688; Samuel Rollstone to William Fitzherbert, July 12, 1756, E20511, Fitzherbert Papers.
[2] Samuel Rollstone to William Fitzherbert, July 12, 1756, E20511.

he had hidden in the woods.[3] The overseer entered the woods on that July day in 1756 without knowing that the watchman had a gun, given to him by the previous overseer to scare away birds. Not surprisingly, the slave kept his possession of the gun secret when the new overseer arrived.[4] Even if he had no plans to rebel or resist, a gun could be a valuable acquisition for hunting, and it could be sold or shared among kin. He probably hoped the gun would be forgotten in the change of management. Furious with Rollstone, the watchmen "lay in wait" and tried to shoot the new overseer but he missed.[5] Rollstone left the old watchman in the woods but sent a new one to replace him. The old watchman returned that night with the gun to his post "in the Plantan walk, and there seeing the [new] fellow shot him dead upon the spot, about 12 of the Clock at night." The killer ran. Rollstone sent the constable after him, and the old watchman, "finding he should be taken, He with the same Gun destroyed himself and this for no other Punishment for his villainy than displacing him from his office. And putting one who is that I could have more dependence on."[6] What sort of community dynamics lurked beneath the surface of these events, and what was the relationship between the old watchman and his replacement? Why was the old watchman so desperate to protect his occupation? Why did he stay in the woods so close to the estate after shooting at his overseer? Although the old watchman's motivations remain a mystery, the story raises important questions about occupations, individual identity, and community relationships on a slave plantation; it demonstrates the degree to which slaves might have struggled to attain and maintain a particular work assignment, and it hints at the complex array of human relationships on a plantation.

As the creation of work logs demonstrates, managers strove to reduce the people working on the estate to interchangeable units of production: little more than "hands," extensions of the master's will. There was constant tension between this project and the benefits that might be gained from understanding the individuality of slaves. Behind the numbers were human faces, and managers, as much as they might have liked to exercise complete control, were constantly forced to contend with the humanity and individuality of their laborers. Far from simply labor resources or

---

[3] Ibid.
[4] Ibid.
[5] Gad Heuman, "Runaway Slaves in Nineteenth-Century Barbados," in Gad Heuman, ed., *Out of the House of Bondage: Runaways, Resistance and Maroonage in Africa and the New World* (London: Frank Cass, 1986), 106.
[6] Samuel Rollstone to William Fitzherbert, July 12, 1756, E20511.

flexible capital units, slaves were people with their own weaknesses and strengths, desires, aspirations, and idiosyncrasies.

The workers on any large plantation were enmeshed in an intricate web of kin-based and community relationships. The people working side by side through the long days, sharing time in plantation hospitals, and helping (or catching) each other steal food, had lived for many years, often decades, on a single estate. This was especially the case in late eighteenth-century Barbados, which was becoming a predominantly creole slave society, and in Virginia, which had an almost exclusively creole slave population. There were extensive and extended kinship networks on large estates, sometimes consanguine and sometimes fictive, beyond these immediate families. The networks that slaves participated in spread beyond the boundaries of individual estates to surrounding plantations, creating local neighborhoods among the slaves. Geographic boundaries, such as mountains, valleys, rivers, or ocean fronts helped form and solidify these plantation neighborhoods. The relationships within the community of a large slave plantation were just as dynamic and complicated as in any community. Slaves could share affective bonds, develop allegiances, and harbor enmity toward each other. Occupations and the privileges granted by the master within the working world played a critical role in individual identities, in community formation, and in the relationships between slaves.

Although the successful formation of slave communities has been construed as a kind of collective resistance to enslavement, it is important not to paint too romantic an image of cohesiveness, solidarity, or egalitarianism within a slave community. From the 1970s to the late 1990s, historiography on the master-slave relationship was powerfully shaped by sociopolitical and moral pressures.[7] It stressed the slaves' agency but, in doing so, it tended to overemphasize successful slave resistance and the autonomous and unified nature of slave cultures and communities.[8] Relationships on a slave plantation were more complex than a simple

---

[7] Stanley Elkins, *Slavery: A Problem in American Institutional and Intellectual Life* (Chicago: University of Chicago Press, 1959); Robert L. Douglas, "Myth or True: A White and Black View of Slavery," *Journal of Black Studies* 19.3 (1989), 343–360; Philip D. Morgan, *Slave Counterpoint: Black Culture in the Eighteenth-Century Chesapeake and Lowcountry* (Chapel Hill: University of North Carolina Press, 1998), xii; Nathaniel Huggins, "The Deforming Mirror of Truth: Slavery and the Master Narrative of American History," *Radical History Review*, 49 (1991), 29. On the sociopolitical implications of this problem, see Daryl Michael Scott, *Contempt and Pity: Social Policy and the Image of the Damaged Black Psyche, 1880–1996* (Chapel Hill: University of North Carolina Press, 1997).

[8] See, for example, John Blassingame, *The Slave Community: Plantation Life in the Antebellum South* (New York: Oxford University Press, 1979); M. Mullin, *Africa in America: Slave*

contest between the evil oppressors and the heroically resisting oppressed, and, rather than drawing distinctions between the slave's world and the master's world, it is important to understand not only the constant interplay between the two but also possible internal tensions and divisions within the slave communities themselves. Community, in this sense, means the ways in which people interact with each other and the relationships they form within the context of a shared space and a shared existence. Scholars have downplayed the hierarchies that developed within slave communities in order to represent slave communities as unified and thus more effective in their resistance to their oppressors.[9] The formation of a community, with its own mores, hierarchies, relationships, and standards, can be read as a kind of accommodation or adaptation to circumstance, but the particular relationships and hierarchies that develop within a community need not be viewed as a positive or negative development.

Resistance does not have to be at the core of discussions about plantation slavery if scholars are willing to conceptualize a plantation as encompassing more than just two identities – master and slave. Power dynamics on slave plantations were multifaceted. Sometimes slaves struggled against the master, and sometimes they struggled with each other. Hierarchy within the slave community allowed for the kind of leadership that would enable organized resistance against the master, but that same hierarchy could also foster inequalities and oppressive relationships among the slaves. Issues of power, influence, and control were part of not just master-slave negotiations but also part of the relationships that slaves formed with each other.

The hierarchy and power dynamic within the slave community and slave identities were closely tied to the slaves' occupations.[10] In large part, the study of slave work and occupations has been kept separate from the study of slave community. Scholars have tried to maintain a conceptual distinction between the master's world and the slave's world in order to better

Acculturation and Resistance in the American South and the British Caribbean, 1736–1831 (Chicago: University of Illinois Press, 1992); on the problem with such depictions, see David W. Blight, "The World the Slave Traders Made: Is There a Postrevisionism in Slavery Historiography?" *Reviews in American History* 19.1 (1991), 37–42; Jon F. Sensbach, "Charting a Course in Early African-American History," *William and Mary Quarterly* 50.2 (1993): 401–402; Mintz, "Slave Life on Caribbean Sugar Plantations: Some Unanswered Questions," in Stephen Palmie, ed., *Slave Cultures and the Cultures of Slavery* (Knoxville: University of Tennessee Press, 1995), 17.

[9] Blassingame, *Slave Community*; for a contrasting view, see William Dusinberre, *Them Dark Days: Slavery in the American Rice Swamps* (New York: Oxford University Press, 2000), 84, 90.

[10] Michael P. Johnson," Work, Culture and the Slave Community: Slave Occupations in the Cotton Belt in 1860," *Labor History* 27.3 (1986), 325–355.

depict unified and autonomous slave communities and strong and viable slave cultures. This chapter brings those two worlds together more fully by exploring how occupations in the working world overlapped with the formation of slave families and communities. It also examines how community and family ties and working roles shaped resistance, and, finally, it explores the phenomenon of short-term work absences as a kind of labor negotiation strategy, an institutional pressure valve, and a way – through taking the time to visit other estates – to maintain extraplantation slave communities and kinship networks.

WORK AND COMMUNITY

The spatial dimensions of a plantation and its surrounding neighborhood and the labor requirements of the staple crop had a significant impact on the formation and internal dynamics of a slave community. The labor intensive nature of sugar and the organization of the plantation around a central mill – with limitations on the distance at which canes could be successfully cultivated away from the mill – fostered a large and concentrated community. Whereas slaves on large Chesapeake plantations were spread across the multiple farm quarters, creating several smaller pockets of community within a larger neighborhood, slaves on sugar plantations lived and worked together in a more confined space, especially on tiny islands such as Barbados. Although the number of slaves on Jamaican plantations was, on average, larger than the number on Barbadian estates, the near absence of both woodlands and provision grounds in Barbados made the density of slave communities on Barbadian estates more pronounced than in Jamaica. The vast majority of Barbados was cleared and cultivated, and the terrain was much flatter than in Jamaica. The Barbadian landscape made it easier for slaves to travel to other estates and extend their community networks beyond the bounds of the plantation to surrounding neighborhoods, but the same terrain made it more difficult for slaves to run away and more difficult for them to have separate provision lands. Compared to Jamaica, the smaller ratio of blacks to whites in Barbados and, especially, in Virginia also made it difficult for slaves to create a large and autonomous slave community.[11]

[11] B. W. Higman, "Physical and Economic Environments," in Verene Shepherd and Hilary Beckles, eds., *Caribbean Slavery in the Atlantic World: A Student Reader* (Kingston, Jamaica: Ian Randle Publishers, 2000), 365–389; B. W. Higman, "Economic and Social Development of the British West Indies From Settlement to ca. 1850," in Stanley

On sugar plantations, the specialization of labor in sugar processing and the harsh and regimented discipline of gang labor fostered the creation of a class of enslaved workers with more significant privileges and higher status than most common laborers. These slaves were sometimes identified as being "with office."[12] "Officers" were the most valuable workers on slave lists and inventories, and they assumed leadership roles in the working world. Drivers, tradesmen, head stock keepers, and sugar processors were slaves "with offices." Among these "officers," the first-gang driver, the sugar boiler, the head carpenter, and the head cattle keeper were normally the highest ranking and the most valuable slaves. In Barbados, some plantations had a headman, ranking above the first-gang driver, called a ranger.[13] Common field hands, the majority of whom were women, never held offices.

When women held offices, the link between their office and their occupation was as much a social distinction as it was an occupational distinction. It denoted higher social status and, perhaps, the special privileges that the planter had bestowed on her. Although field workers could not hold office, some other women could. A woman's occupation, however, did not guarantee that she would garner an "office" on the plantation. In 1782, at Newton, for example, there were seven women with offices.[14] Three of them were "corn beaters": specialists in pounding the corn that was fed to slaves. There were no corn beaters without offices, and corn beaters did not work with the gangs in the field. Their task does not seem to have required significant training or expertise, and it is not clear why these occupations would entitle the women to an elevated rank. Perhaps, as food providers, they earned community respect; or, perhaps the recognition of leadership qualities allowed them to secure their appointment to an essentially honorific position. There were four other women who served as elite slaves with offices. They were all domestics. Not all domestics held equal rank. Four enslaved women working as domestics were identified as being with office, but there were also two female domestics without offices. Likewise, in other years at Newton, caretakers, such as a sick nurse, were often but not always granted this elite status as officers.[15] In 1774, one

L. Engerman and Robert E. Gallman, eds., *The Cambridge Economic History of the United States* (New York: Cambridge University Press 1996), 297–336; L. S. Walsh, Plantation Management in the Chesapeake, 1620–1820," *The Journal of Economic History* 49.2 (June, 1989), 393–406.

[12] Newton Slave List, 1782, MS 523/282, Newton Family Papers.
[13] See "Report on the [Newton] Negroes," MS 523/288, Newton Family Papers; see also Drax Hall Slave List, May 8, 1820, Z9/11/8.
[14] Newton Slave List, 1782, MS 523/282, Newton Family Papers.
[15] Newton Slave List, 1774, MS 523/274, Newton Family Papers.

of the women with office had an economically insignificant and unusual occupation. According to the overseer, "Old Nanney takes care of the Mulattoes."[16] The term "with office" was not applied universally to all female workers in a particular occupation. Instead, it indicated that a slave held a leadership role and a set of privileges accompanying that role.

Managers invested elite slaves, such as those slaves "with office" in the British Caribbean or tradesmen and work foremen in the Chesapeake, with authority over other slaves and granted them privileges that ensured that they had a higher standard of living than common laborers. Compared to a field hand, a privileged slave had the opportunity and the skills necessary to acquire more goods and provisions and build a larger house.[17] Unequal property, power, and privilege created something akin to class divisions within the slave community. Resident Barbadian planter and attorney Philip Gibbes, in his treatise on slave housing, advocated longer houses with multiple partitions for "Negroes of the first distinction." Gibbes argued further that "Framed Houses" should be given "only to the Principal Negroes" because "the inferior Negroes will not take care of them."[18] A mid eighteenth-century Barbadian plantation manual recommended that drivers and boilers be given double the normal allowance of fish each week.[19] Likewise, archaeological evidence in the Chesapeake shows that high-status slaves probably had access to more meat and to better cuts of meat.[20] At Turner's Hall, in 1782, the "Principal Negroes" were paid an allowance to buy food from domestic sources when "there was no corn to spare."[21] The assumption was that they would share that food, however they saw fit, with dependents.

Wealth production among slaves, and the unequal distributions that attended it, some scholars maintain, were primarily a product of the slaves' successful work efforts on their own time and on their own plots of land.[22] Such a view is limited because it fails to account for the privileges and resources masters granted to their slaves. In terms of a slave's accumulation of property, what mattered was not only a slave's desires, ingenuities, work

---

[16] Ibid.
[17] Dylan Penningroth, *Claims of Kinfolk: African-American Property and Community in the Nineteenth-Century South* (Chapel Hill: University of North Carolina Press, 2003), 45–110.
[18] Philip Gibbes, "Notes on Housing" (ca1785), E20777, Fitzherbert Papers.
[19] William Belgrove, *A Treatise upon Husbandry or Planting* (Boston: D. Fowle, 1755), 66.
[20] Diana C. Crader, "Slave Diet at Monticello," *American Antiquity* 55.4 (October, 1990): 690–717.
[21] Turner's Hall Financial Abstract, 1782, E20692, Fitzherbert Papers.
[22] Larry E. Hudson, *To Have and to Hold: Slave Work and Family Life in Antebellum South Carolina* (Athens: University of Georgia Press, 1997).

efforts, and abilities but also the resources (including material goods and provisions but also time, land, and energy) available to him or her. The claim that a slave's wealth was largely a product of his or her own ingenuity is most compelling in a region where the task system predominated, such as in the South Carolina Lowcountry.[23] Ostensibly, slaves under the task system could work harder at their tasks, finish them early, and gain more time for their own productive efforts. In the gang labor system, which predominated in both Virginia and the sugar islands, the amount of time available for slaves to cultivate grounds, raise livestock, or grow their own foods was limited because work was scheduled from sunup to sundown.

In Barbados, the slaves had virtually no land to produce their own food and thus even less opportunity to gain a surplus. Rather than being forced to work on Sundays like their Jamaican counterparts, Barbadian were free to use their day off for resting and visiting. In this sense, in Barbados, any differences in wealth were far more dependent on the privileges and goods granted by the master than on the slaves' willingness to work their lands. Recent archaeological investigations of slave plantations confirm that enslaved Barbadians had less access to foods and goods and were more dependent on their masters' provisioning than were their counterparts on other Caribbean sugar islands.[24] Barbadian masters normally granted exceptional goods and privileges to elite slaves. At Newton, only a few slaves were given any extra land other than the small space around their huts. Yet, during 1796–1797, the head cooper George Saers was given a day off to work his own ground, indicating not only the privilege of extra time that came from being a head cooper but, more importantly, that Saers, unlike most of his fellow Barbadian bondsmen, had provision grounds of his own to tend.[25]

It cannot be assumed that slaves with access to land in places such as Jamaica or Virginia automatically worked it for gain. Dylan Penningroth argued that, in the mainland South, with abundant land resources, "slave's independent economies were founded on an economy of time rather than an economy of land."[26] In most places in the Americas – with the

---

[23] Ibid.
[24] Thomas C. Loftfield, "Creolization in Seventeenth-Century Barbados: Two Case Studies," in P. Farnsworth, ed., *Island Lives: Historical Archaeologies of the Caribbean* (Tuscaloosa: University of Alabama Press, 2001), 207–233.
[25] Newton Work Log, 1796–1797.
[26] Penningroth, *Claims of Kinfolk*, 47; for examples of the rich literature on slaves' productive efforts on their own time, see the essays in "Part III: The Slaves Economy," in Ira Berlin and Philip D. Morgan, eds., *Cultivation and Culture: Labor and the Shaping of Slave Life*

possible exception of land-poor islands such as Barbados – time was, as Penningroth suggests, a more limiting resource than land in the slaves' productive efforts. An even more critical resource than time, however, was energy. Often undernourished or malnourished, and always overworked, slaves rarely possessed surplus energy. Slaves, especially in field gangs, regularly worked to the point of exhaustion. In the late eighteenth and early nineteenth century, many planters, trying to coerce more productive efforts from their slaves, began to shift more of the responsibility for growing food over to the slaves at the same time as they strove to intensify their work efforts during the week. This was particularly the case in Jamaica, where land resources were abundant. This effort to extract more labor from slaves, even if was to produce provisions in their own grounds, was not always easy to achieve. Many planters turned to using drivers on Sundays in the slaves' own provision grounds to compel greater labor efforts (see Chapter 1). The planters believed that slaves were often too lazy to work on their own. In reality, with the hours of work increasing, field workers probably lacked the energy they needed to cultivate their grounds.

An economy of energy operated among plantation slaves, and it was closely tied to a slave's occupation. That occupation determined, in large part, how much energy a slave had to apply to his or her own productive activities during time granted to him or her. The work week of a cooper, for example, was demanding but less physically arduous than the work week of a field hand. The backbreaking and never ending monotony of field tasks must have left slaves physically and psychologically exhausted, especially slaves working lockstep in a line in the grueling gang labor systems on sugar plantations. A tradesman would have had more energy reserves than a gang slave to work his provision grounds or raise stock on his days off and, consequently, he had more opportunity to improve the material conditions of his life. This difference in energy levels between a tradesmen and a field hand was more pronounced on sugar plantations than on Chesapeake estates because field cultivation on sugar plantations was more backbreaking and demanding, but also because, during a good harvest year, there could be nearly 500 additional hours of labor for sugar workers each year.

in the Americas (Charlottesville: University of Virginia Press, 1993), 203–299; R. A. McDonald, *The Economy and Material Culture of Slaves: Goods and Chattels on the Sugar Plantations of Jamaica and Louisiana* (Baton Rouge: Louisiana State University Press, 1993).

Slaves' opportunities to accumulate wealth varied significantly, depending not only on the system of labor being used or a slave's occupation but also on the size and nature of their kinship group and the proportion of creoles in the slave population. Groups of slaves could adopt collective strategies to overcome time and energy deficiencies. They could draw on family and extended kin, pooling their resources, or, they could force other slaves to work their grounds. Wealth could be passed from one generation to the next among slave families, helping to maintain elite status within particular kinship networks. The higher the proportion of field hands in a kinship group, the less resources (especially energy) that those slaves had for their collective productive efforts. Creole families could pool and pass on property, and slaves born on an estate had a longer period of time to accumulate wealth over the course of their lives. Some elite creole slaves amassed a surprising amount of wealth over their lifetimes, and they struggled to keep that wealth within their families. At Turner's Hall, for example, in the 1750s, an "an Old Carpenter Fellow ... at his death left a considerable sum of Money to the Value of 32 or 33 pounds to his son." He left it "in Trust however to another Negro to be deliverd to his Son, when he should arrive to an age, capable of makeing a proper use of it."[27]

Trying to build wealth was always a precarious process for a slave. Any possessions a slave had that were tied to an estate, such as a particularly productive plot or chickens or hogs, could be lost the moment a slave died or was sold or moved. Slaves could mitigate against this danger by laying claim to property among families or households rather than stressing individual possession, but there were other more difficult obstacles to wealth accumulation among slaves. In theory, slaves had no legal property rights and little way of proving their claims. Their possessions were allowed them by custom rather than by law, and they could be snatched away by masters in a moment or stolen by other slaves or poor whites. The old carpenter's life savings, for example, were stolen by an overseer shortly after his death, but the plantation attorney was very critical of the overseer's actions when they came to light, insisting that the slaves' customary right to amass money or goods be honored.[28]

Wealth and privilege were distributed and held unevenly within slave communities, but it is another thing altogether to say that these wealth divisions produced noteworthy differences in social status among slaves. The contrast in wealth or quality of life between masters and slaves or even

---

[27] Samuel Rollstone to William Fitzherbert, July 12, 1756, E20511, Fitzherbert Papers.
[28] Ibid.

white plantation staff and slaves was so dramatic that one could conclude that the collective experience of oppression was more important to a slave's identity and to community formation than any wealth inequalities among them. Yet the wealth inequalities produced by the occupational hierarchy and, to some extent, by the different prospects of creole and African slaves, could foster oppressive community dynamics, especially on sugar plantations. Caribbean managers often observed class hierarchies, fraught relations, and even forced labor within slave communities. At the Jamaican estate of Blue Mountain, the plantain walk was destroyed by the 1787 hurricane, and the remaining provisions were inadequate to sustain the slaves. The managers failed to purchase enough to keep the slaves fed, and the slaves took matters into their own hands. William Sutherland, the plantation attorney, learned that the "better sort" of slaves, who were all skilled artisans and work leaders, responded by establishing new provision grounds and had the "poorer sort" work those grounds, giving them some of the produce in return but, as Mary Turner notes, "the [slaves'] system broke down," and the estate managers ended up having to intercede and give the poorer slaves more provisions to sustain them.[29] Likewise, in Barbados, Gibbes, in his treatise on housing, insisted that the principal slaves on an estate needed large enough houses "to lodge some Inmate, whom the Master of the House receives to do the drudgery of the Family."[30] In Jamaica, Simon Taylor advocated separating newly purchased African-born slaves – "New Negroes" – from the rest of the slaves lest they "be destroyed by the Old Negroes making them their Slaves."[31] The Jamaican planter William Beckford agreed that new slaves were often placed with old slaves "who will teach them how to live and cultivate," but the principal drawback of this system was that the older slaves would force labor from the newer ones and abuse them.[32]

That some slaves oppressed or required labor or tribute from others should not be shocking. Legal status is far from the only mechanism of coercion in forced labor. Moreover, both Africans and creoles had been raised in slave systems and were accustomed to slavery, dominance, and a

---

[29] Mary Turner, "Chattel Slaves into Wage Slaves: A Jamaican Case Study," in Turner, ed., *From Chattel Slaves into Wage Slaves: The Dynamics of Labor Bargaining in the Americas* (Bloomington: Indiana University Press, 1995), 34.

[30] Philip Gibbes, Notes on Housing [ca 1788], E20777, Fitzherbert Papers.

[31] Simon Taylor to "Sir," Chalenor Arcedeckne, June 11, 1782, Vanneck-Arc/ 3A/ 1782/28.

[32] W. Beckford, *Remarks upon the Situation of Negroes in Jamaica* (London: T & Egerton, 1788), 27–28. See also B. Edwards, *The History Civil and Commercial of the British Colonies in the West Indies*, 2 vols. (Dublin: Luke White, 1793), 119–120.

hierarchical order. At the least, the comments planters made about oppressive relationships between "New Negroes" and established plantation slaves supports the argument that there were significant status divisions, wealth inequalities, and separate identities between African and creole slaves. Yet, these planter observations must not be taken at face value. Managers may have been projecting their own system of social hierarchies onto the slave community; they may have misunderstood a more benign mentorship or tribute relationship between old and new slaves, or they may have been justifying slavery by pointing to the degree of oppression that could exist among slaves without the protection of the master, and, in an era of abolitionism and ameliorationist sentiment, they may have been simply displacing guilt.

The manager at Newton and Seawell, Sampson Wood, mapped the community hierarchy in a census, which he prepared in July 1796. An unusually detailed and uniquely organized list, it offers insight into the key principles operating in the ranking of slaves within the community. It was more thorough in description than the standard slave inventories produced at Newton and at other estates in this era, but it did not identify the monetary value of individual slaves. Its organizational principles were not strictly alphabetical, age-based, or value-oriented. Instead, it seems to have been drawn according to a kind of rough ranking of slaves' influence and position within the plantation community, which was loosely related to a slave's age, value, and occupation. Longevity and experience played a prominent role. Preeminent in this census was Saboy, "the former overseer or driver of the first gang." He was elderly, but he cannot have been very valuable because he was "retired now and does not work."[33] His place at the top of the list might have been honorific. He seems to have been the headman of the estate, presumably because of his knowledge and influence. Age and experience counted for much in Saboy's and others' rankings. The second man on the list, Demurron, was a mere field hand who was very old – "superannuated" – but he had been born at Newton and had lived there all his life. He had not worked in fifteen years.[34] His influence in the slave community was significant enough to have him placed directly above a fifty-year-old man, a retired clayer named Sambo, and also above the plantation's current driver. Although first-gang drivers normally headed standard slave inventories, the new first-gang driver at

---

[33] "Report on the [Newton] Negroes."
[34] Newton Slave List, May 24, 1776, MS 523/270; Newton Slave List, 1782, MS 523/271; "Report on the Newton Negroes," Newton Family Papers.

Newton, a young mulatto in his thirties named Dickey-Budd, was eighth on this list. Nevertheless, his occupation was important enough that he was ranked ahead of many older slaves. Women were recorded separately from men, and the female domestics were kept separate from female field hands. The field hands tended to be recorded from eldest to youngest – the opposite of most slave inventories, which focused on a slave's value – indicating, again, that the census was taking into account a kind of ranking of hierarchy in the slave community.

The key factors in the Newton ranking were a blend of age, experience, birthplace, family relationships, and occupation. The most critical factors were age and occupation, current or former. It is not clear whether the occupations of slaves dictated their place in the slave community or whether the relative power and influence of slaves in the slave community dictated the occupations they were assigned by overseers and managers. A feedback loop may have been operating. Hierarchies in the slave community were both created by slaves and imposed by managers. In this sense, the process of community building and the establishment of leaders was part of the constant negotiation between master and slaves, a continual interplay between the slave's world and the working world.

WORK AND FAMILY

Plantation owners encouraged the formation of family groups, especially in the Caribbean in an era of amelioration, in which the focus was on stopping the continual decline in the slave population.[35] The most prominent Jamaican attorney, Simon Taylor, for example, tried to foster marriages by purchasing women whenever the sex ratios on the estates he managed became too imbalanced. In 1794, he bought "20 Young Ebo Women for Wifes," for a group of slaves on a plantation he managed because the owner "had a great many more Men than Women." Ibo (Ebo) women had a reputation for fertility.[36] Some sugar planters granted privileges to slaves who formed families on the estate, which not only encouraged coresident family formation but also fostered more differences in wealth between slaves who had spouses on the estate and slaves who did not.[37] A Barbadian plantation manual, for example, recommended that male slaves with a

---

[35] Ward, *British West Indian Slavery*, 176.
[36] Simon Taylor to Chalenor Arcedeckne, 18 January, 1794, Vanneck-Arc/ 3A/ 1794/2.
[37] J.R. Ward, *British West Indian Slavery, 1750–1834: The Process of Amelioration* (New York: Oxford University Press, 1988), 176.

house and a wife on the estate should be given an extra half day off each month to plant their ground and care for their family.[38] Although a half day a month might seem insignificant, free time was precious to a slave, and a half day to a slave receiving just four Sundays a month meant a 13 percent gain in the amount of free time he or she would be guaranteed each month, comparable to an extra day off every two weeks for a modern office worker. Having a spouse on the estate also gave slaves more opportunities to be productive on nonworking days. They saved the time needed to visit other estates, and they could divide their labors in tending to their own grounds if they had them or raising stock or engaging in other forms of production that could be marketed for gain. Planters sought to promote marital relationships among their own slaves. Wood complained that the Seawell slaves were not as intermarried as they were at Newton, which meant that the Seawell slaves too often left the plantation to visit their spouses.[39] At Mount Vernon, Washington insisted that slaves ask his permission before they marry off the estate. At least one slave, a man working as a domestic, asked him for his consent.[40]

Few plantation records are detailed enough in the eighteenth century to allow for a closer examination of the relationship between families and occupations. However, the unusually rich records from Mount Vernon, Newton, Seawell, and, to a lesser extent, Turner's Hall offer some indication of how particular families came to control privileged and leadership occupations, and how the knowledge of particular trades could be controlled by a slave family and passed down from one generation to the next. These records are unique in that they purport to show slave households and the relationships within those households.[41] Comparable records from Jamaica prior to the abolition of the slave trade have not survived. The evidence indicates that elite family groups in the slave community tended to control most of the supervisory and skilled positions, and that elite slaves formed larger coresident families within the bounds of the plantation than did field workers. The difference in status and in successful

---

[38] Edwin Lascelles et al., *Instructions for the Management of a Plantation in Barbadoes. And for the Treatment of Negroes, etc., etc., etc.* (London: [s.n.], 1786), 25.
[39] "Report on the Negroes of Seawell Plantation," MS 523/292, Newton Family Papers.
[40] Mary Thompson, "'They Appear to Live Comfortable Together': Private Lives of the Mount Vernon Slaves," in Philip J. Schwarz, ed., *Slavery at the Home of George Washington* (Mount Vernon: Mount Vernon Ladies Association, 2001), 80.
[41] Ward, *British West Indian Slavery*, 176; B.W. Higman, "The Slave Family and the Household in the British West Indies, 1800–1834," *Journal of Interdisciplinary History* 6.2 (Autumn, 1975), 261–287.

coresident family formation between privileged slaves and common laborers was more pronounced in Barbados than in Virginia. Without much land available for their own production, elite occupations were the key to a Barbadian slave family's wealth accumulation because those elite occupations brought more privileges and goods from the planters and their managerial staff.

At Newton and Seawell, slaves who worked outside of the field were more likely to be married and have children on the estate. Whereas almost 50 percent of the elite men (such as the drivers, watchmen, stock keepers, and tradesmen) had spouses living on the estate, only 15 percent of men in the field had a wife living on the plantation. The men at Newton and Seawell who were able to attain an occupation outside the gangs also had more living children on the plantation than did the fifty-six slaves who were strictly field hands (0.94 compared to 0.32). Upward mobility in a plantation's occupational hierarchy was harder for women than for men, and being a female domestic at Newton and Seawell did not seem to significantly increase a woman's chance of finding a husband on the estate. Of all the adult women on the two estates, 24 percent were married to a man within the plantation, but domestics and sick nurses were not much more likely (25 percent) to have a husband on the estate. Having a privileged domestic position and the possessions that often accompanied it did, however, significantly increase the likelihood that the women would have living children on the estate. On average, the female domestics and sick nurses had nearly three times as many living children as the women working in the field (2.7 compared to 1.1). Working in the sugar fields made it not only harder to conceive a child, but it was probably more difficult for field women to obtain the resources they needed to keep their children alive.

The difference in marriage rates between privileged slaves and field workers at Mount Vernon was not as pronounced as it was at Newton and Seawell, and it was more likely for Mount Vernon slaves to be married. Whereas 54 percent of men working in the field at Mount Vernon were married, only a slightly higher proportion of elite slaves were married – 62 percent. The ability of married slaves or enslaved families to collectively pool their resources was also constrained by the geography of the estate. Although there were more married couples at Mount Vernon than there were at Newton and Seawell, the Virginian estate was more than fifteen times larger than those Barbadian plantations. The division of the property into five separate farm quarters meant that many married couples, even though both individuals were Mount Vernon slaves, lived separately day to day because they worked on different quarters. Nevertheless, the large number of marriages at Mount Vernon meant that it was still more likely that a married slave would live with his or her spouse and children (38 percent of adults) than it was at Newton and Seawell (28 percent of adults).[42] Somewhat surprisingly, at Mount Vernon, the women working as domestics or in skilled work, such as spinning or knitting, were actually less likely than women in the field to be married, but this corresponds with the evidence of no greater likelihood of marriage among Newton and Seawell domestics than among field hands.[43]

At Turner's Hall in Barbados, the elite slaves were far more likely than field hands to be part of large kinship groups. The large kinship groups of elite slaves would better support cooperative strategies of survival (such as a pooling of resources). The 165 Turner's Hall slaves recorded in a 1780 census were divided into sixty-two households or kinship groupings.[44] Only twenty-six of the slaves had no kinship ties. These slaves appear to have lived alone. None of the tradesmen and only one of the three drivers (the second-gang driver) lived alone. The vast majority of the slaves who lived alone were field gang workers. The average size of a household at Turner's Hall was 2.4 slaves, ranging in size from 1 to 8. There were only eight coresident marriages on the estate. Notably, even though the majority of the men at Turner's Hall were gang slaves, only one of the eight married men worked in the field. The other married men were drivers, rangers, boilers, clayers, tradesmen, and watchmen.[45]

Some slave kinship groups were remarkably successful at attaining elite positions and privileges for their members. At Newton, Doll's family was such an exceptionally elite group that its members were recorded separately in the 1796 slave census. Old Doll, the matriarch of the family, was in her sixties. She had been born at Newton. She had worked as a midwife and as a healer. In 1796, the manager noted that she "does nothing," but she and her family members acted as healers and caretakers whenever necessary for both managers and slaves. The new manager noted that they had helped him through an illness.[46] Doll's family had gained and manipulated the

---

[42] "Report on the [Newton] Negroes," MS 523/288, Newton Family Papers; Mount Vernon Slave Inventory, June, 1799 in Abbot, ed., *The Papers of George Washington, Retirement Series*, vol. 4 (Charlottesville: University Press of Virginia, 1999), 528–540. ; Higman, "The Slave Family," 269.
[43] Mount Vernon Slave Inventory, 1799.
[44] Turner's Hall Slave List, 1780, E20753, Fitzherbert Papers.
[45] Ibid.
[46] Karl Watson, *A Kind of Right to be Idle: Old Doll, Matriarch of Newton Plantation* (Cave Hill, Barbados: University of the West Indies Press, 2000).

favor of the managers, probably because of the matriarch's skill as a healer, and they used their proximity to the house to their advantage. The new manager, Sampson Wood, noted that they were "indulged" because of their "former Services" but did not allude to what those services entailed. By 1796, they had attained "a kind of right to be idle."[47] Wood, frustrated with this unusual family, complained, "I wish they would take themselves off to a distance" because they were "so dead an expense to the Estate without the least profit."[48] There were twenty-one slaves recorded as members of Doll's family. Although some of the children picked grass to feed the livestock, none of the slaves worked with the field gangs. The males were all domestics, tradesmen, or apprentices to trades, and the females, for the most part, did "nothing" at all except make clothing occasionally or care for the sick. In other words, their labors were invisible to the plantation economy and worthless to the master. Previous overseers had tried to "put them into the field by way of degradation and punishment" but the last overseer "very properly" removed them from the gangs "for they were absolutely a nuisance in the field and set the worst example to the rest of the Negroes."[49]

The experiences of Old Doll's family were very unusual, but they suggest the extent to which being a skilled and supervisory slave, a sick nurse, or a domestic could give slaves more regular contact with white managers, which the slaves could use to gain trust and favors and acquire provisions and goods. At Newton, Billy Thomas, a grandson of Old Doll who "was in great confidence with his Master and trusted with everything," stole the keys to storehouses on the estate when the overseer was asleep. He was described as an "agent and assistant" in "pilfering" for Doll's family.[50] He and the rest of the family used their trust and their access to the master to steal enough goods to make their houses "perfect Shops for dry goods, Rum, Sugar and other commodities."[51] Clearly, proximity to the master and to the house could vastly increase a family's chances of accumulating possessions. This was not necessarily a wealth shared among the slave community at large, but instead it was kept among a specific kinship group. When the grandson was finally caught in the act and reported, it was by two slaves – a watchman and a mill boatswain – who were not from Old Doll's family, indicating that other slaves on the estate were unsympathetic to the pilfering. The boy was put to death,

---

[47] "Report on the [Newton] Negroes," MS 523/288, Newton Family Papers.
[48] Ibid.
[49] Ibid.
[50] Ibid.
[51] Ibid.

Occupations and Families in the Slave Community 255

demonstrating the limits of this unique family's power and influence.[52] The example of Doll's family suggests that, rather than solidarity in the slave community, the primary organizational unit at Newton was the kinship group.

At Mount Vernon, the slaves living around the Mansion House enjoyed the greatest quality of life and attained the most privileged positions on the plantation. Proximity to the owner, Washington, and his managers vastly increased the chance that a child would become an elite slave. Moving away from the house and the master decreased a woman's chance of securing good occupations for her children. Betty, a fifty-four-year-old cook at Union Farm with no husband in 1799, was the mother of at least seven children, including a mulatto named Marcus, suggesting, perhaps, an intimate relationship with one of the plantation managers.[53] Betty started her working life in the 1770s, as a house servant at the Mansion House, before being moved, perhaps as punishment, to work in the field at Union Farm at some point between 1774 and 1786 – probably closer to 1786.[54] Her three eldest boys Godfrey, Hanson, and Marcus – the last and youngest born in 1785 – became semiskilled or skilled slaves. Godfrey was a carter at the Mansion House. Hanson was a distiller, and Marcus, the mulatto (who changed his own name from Bill Langston), was a tradesman.[55] Clearly, at some point, Betty's sons were being favored for privileged positions. Yet, after 1786, when she had been permanently moved to Union Farm, the two boys she bore then, Gideon and John, were sent to the field, working alongside their sister Lucretia and their mother until she became a cook.[56] The decision to make Betty work as a

---

[52] Ibid.
[53] Mount Vernon Slave Inventory, June, 1799; Mount Vernon Slave List, February 18, 1786, in; Donald Jackson and Dorothy Twohig, eds., *The Diaries of George Washington*, vol. IV, 1784–June 1786 (Charlottesville: University Press of Virginia, 1978), 277–283.
[54] Lists of Tithables, in Abbot, ed., *The Papers of George Washington: Colonial Series* vol. 6, September 1758–December 1760 (Charlottesville: University of Virginal Press, 1988), 217, 282, 428; Lists of Tithables, in Abbot and Twohig, eds., *The Papers of George Washington: Colonial Series* vol. 7, January 1761– June 1767. (Charlottesville: University of Virginia Press, 1990), 45, 139, 227–228, 313, 376–377, 442–443, 515–516; Lists of Tithables, in Abbot and Twohig, eds., *The Papers of George Washington: Colonial Series* vol. 8, June 1767–December 1771 (Charlottesville: University of Virginia Press, 1993), 104, 220–221, 356–357, 479; Lists of Tithables, in Abbot and Twohig, eds., *The Papers of George Washington: Colonial Series* vol. 9, January 1772– March 1774 (Charlottesville: University of Virginia Press, 1994), 54–55, 238–239; Lists of Tithables, in Abbot and Twohig, eds., *The Papers of George Washington: Colonial Series* vol. 10, March 1774– June 1775 (Charlottesville: University of Virginia Press 1995), 137–138.
[55] Mount Vernon Slave Inventory, 1799.
[56] Ibid.; Mount Vernon Slave List, 1786.

cook was almost certainly related to her earlier work as a house servant at the Mansion House. In 1799, Betty's other surviving daughter, Mary, was an eleven-year-old who had been separated from her mother and was working with the field hands on a different quarter altogether, at Muddy Hole.[57] It is not clear why she was separated from her family at Union Farm. The differences between the elite positions attained by Betty's older sons and the common field roles attained by her younger children illustrate the importance of domestic work and proximity to the house in determining whether a family was able to secure privileged positions for its members. After she left the Mansion House farm, Betty and her youngest children all became field workers. Like tradesmen, domestic workers were accorded privileges and had opportunities that were simply unavailable to common laborers.

At Seawell, there was one clearly elite family. Although the privileges they attained never rivaled those granted Doll's family, they ranked at the top of the community. This Seawell family was headed by an African-born woman named Great Phebe, who worked in the overseer's house. It was unusual for African-born women to be domestics. Creoles and mulatto slaves were more likely than Africans to work in the house or in skilled and supervisory positions, whereas Africans were far more likely to have spots in the field. Great Phebe was an exception, a testament to her individual abilities. Africans were a clear minority at Seawell. The estate's population was nearly reproducing itself, and the managers rarely needed to resort to importing labor. By 1796, there were only eleven Africans remaining among the 182 slaves at Seawell.[58] Great Phebe was in her fifties. She had been moved to the house later in life. In 1784, she had been the estate's "Sick Nurse."[59] As a healer, she could, like Old Doll, have easily attained a significant degree of respect and influence in the slave community. Working as a domestic allowed her, like Betty and the women in Doll's family, to overhear the conversations of white managerial staff, thus gaining access to knowledge networks.

Not surprisingly, Phebe's sons became an elite class of slaves on the plantation. In 1796, her five surviving children were all men, including Jack the carpenter (see Chapter 5). Only one of Phebe's five sons worked as a field hand.[60] The rest, like Jack, assumed positions as tradesmen and

---

[57] Mount Vernon Slave Inventory, 1799.
[58] "Report on the Negroes of Seawell Plantation," MS 523/292, Newton Family Papers.
[59] Newton Slave Inventory, 1784; MS 523/277, Newton Family Papers.
[60] B. W. Higman, *Slave Populations of the British Caribbean, 1807–1834* (Baltimore: Johns Hopkins University, 1984), 585–586.

supervisors. The eldest, Frank, who was in his thirties, was a ranger, which made him the headman on the estate. Two of his younger brothers, Dick Mingo and Peter, also in their thirties, spent their days working together as coopers.[61] They had been working together in that trade since at least 1784.[62] Jack, the second youngest, was about thirty years old, and, by 1796, he was the carpenter at Seawell. Alee, the youngest brother, in his late twenties, was the only field worker in the family. Three of the five brothers – Frank, Jack, and Dick Mingo – were married to women on the estate, a higher ratio than usual. Doe, a young man in his twenties, was not part of Great Phebe's immediate family, but he split his time between working as a domestic with her in the house and as a cooper with her sons. He may have been treated as part of an extended kinship network.[63] Four of five of Phebe's children avoided field labor, and their mother's role as a domestic and as a former sick nurse most likely helped keep them out of the gangs.

The occupation of sick nurse, which links Great Phebe's family to Old Doll's family, was a key position for women on sugar plantations, and it may have helped give their families a status at the top of the slave community and the most privileged work roles. Nothing comparable occurred at Mount Vernon. Both Phebe and Old Doll acted as sick nurses at points in their lives, and Old Doll acted as the estate midwife. Likewise, at Turner's Hall, two of the most elite or privileged families on the estate, Great Robin's family and Rose's family, boasted sick nurses. In his prime in 1780, Great Robin was the headman on the estate, a ranger, and the head sugar boiler. His wife, Marriah, worked on the estate as a sick nurse "under" the older head nurse named Old Rose. Their eldest child, a "young" woman named Nanny, worked as a domestic. Their other two daughters and two sons – along with Robin's two nephews, who lived in his household – were still too young to be assigned occupations. As children or perhaps toddlers, they spent their days collecting grass for the stock. There was only one female domestic at Turner's Hall, which was an absentee estate in 1780, and it is not surprising that a daughter of the headman on the estate and one of the plantation's sick nurses was chosen to be that domestic, thus avoiding field work.[64] The head sick nurse at Turner's Hall, Old Rose, had been purchased at some point. She was grouped in a family unit with two other

---

[61] "Report on the [Newton] Negroes," MS 523/288, Newton Family Papers.
[62] Seawell Slave Inventory, June 7, 1784, MS 523/278, Newton Family Papers.
[63] "Report on the [Newton] Negroes," MS 523/288, Newton Family Papers.
[64] Turner's Hall Slave List, 1780, E20753, Fitzherbert Papers.

purchased slaves, an old and a middle-aged woman, and with Rose's three children. There is no indication that the other two purchased slaves were related to Rose or to each other, but they were considered part of the same "family." They may have been fictive or extended kin. Their family was the first recorded in the slave list, seemingly suggesting its prominence in the plantation community. Rose's three sons were all mulatto. Her eldest son, Mulatto Joes, worked as a smith, the only one on the estate. The other two boys were too young to have a trade but were probably not destined for field labor.[65]

Economic historians of slavery have argued that slaves were less likely than free workers to pass their trades down from one generation to the next.[66] A more detailed study of individual plantations suggests that this may be overstated. At Newton, Seawell, and Mount Vernon, enslaved families came to dominate specific trades as knowledge passed from one generation to the next and was shared among siblings. In the 1790s, at Seawell, two of the three coopers were brothers. Likewise, two of the three masons were brothers. At Newton, there were three men working as coopers and four boys assisting the coopers, presumably as apprentices. Five of the seven were related to Old Doll, including the head cooper, George Sear. The Newton managers in this case may have wanted to encourage productivity by maintaining family relationships during the work day. They may have also found it easier to leave the training of slaves to their family members.[67] Younger slaves in an enslaved family commonly took other family members' names and learned their occupations. In the 1780s, for example, Great Toby worked as a smith at Newton alongside his son, also a smith, also named Toby (Little Toby).[68] At Seawell, in 1796, Jeffry and his brother Tom worked as masons, and they were both brothers of Thit, the first-gang driver and head boiler. Jeffry was probably kin to another Jeffry, who was the ranger and headman in the field at Seawell twelve years earlier. The older Jeffry had died by 1796, when kinship groups were first recorded. If the Jeffrys were in fact related, it would help to explain how Thit, who was undistinguished and no more valuable than the many "negro boys" at Seawell in 1784, rose to the role of lead driver twelve years later. Both fathers and mothers passed on their trades. Among Old Doll's family at Newton, the women seem to have taught each other the art of

---

[65] Ibid.
[66] Robert W. Fogel and Stanley L. Engerman, *Time on the Cross: The Economics of American Negro Slavery* (Boston: Little & Brown, 1974), 150.
[67] Johnson, "Work, Culture and the Slave Community," 339.
[68] Newton Slave Inventory, [1780s?], MS 523/274, Newton Family Papers.

healing, working as sick nurses.[69] At Mount Vernon, Betty Davis taught her daughter Delphia how to spin yarn, and they spent 1797 working together indoors near the Mansion House among Washington's spinners and knitters.[70]

Proximity to the planter or to his white managerial staff could help a slave family to continue to secure privileged occupations for its members, but there were also many elite enslaved parents who were unable to keep their children from the field. At Mount Vernon, Isaac, the head carpenter who had also served time as an overseer, was married to Kitty, a milk maid. They were both in their forties or fifties. Remarkably, they had nine living daughters in 1799 and no sons. One of Kitty's daughters, Alley, was trained and worked as a knitter but only because she was "lame." Kitty had worked with the spinners and knitters in the early 1790s; she may have taught her daughter how to knit. None of Alley's sisters worked in the house or in the dairy with their mother. Those who were old enough to cultivate crops worked in the field together. In 1797 and early 1798, at least four of the sisters worked alongside each other among the six to ten field hands at the Mansion House.[71] Unless they were mulattos, there were very few opportunities for women to avoid the field. If Kitty had had a boy, he might have worked as a carpenter with his father.

Most enslaved kinship groups fell somewhere between the extremes of Doll's elite and unusually privileged family and the common field slaves living on their own at Turner's Hall. At Seawell, Great Jubbah's family held more of a middling status than Thit and his two brothers or Great Phebe's family. Great Jubbah, a former field hand in her sixties, was working as a cook for the "little negroes" in 1796. Unlike Great Phebe, she was a creole, born and raised at Seawell, but only two of her four surviving sons had escaped the drudgery of field work. One, Little Nick, was a mason, and Little Harry was the second-gang driver. Her other sons, Cudjoe and Knocko, were first-gang field hands, common laborers like their mother. Compared to Great Phebe's sons or Thit and his brothers, Great Jubbah's children were less successful at securing skilled and supervisory positions but there is little indication in the records as to why. Managers may have rewarded certain families with these privileged positions, or they may have

---

[69] "Report on the Newton Negroes," MS 523/288, Newton Family Papers.
[70] Mount Vernon Slave Inventory, 1799; Mount Vernon Slave List, 1786; Mount Vernon Farm Reports, 1797–1798.
[71] Mount Vernon Farm Reports, 1797–1798; Mount Vernon Slave Inventory, June 1799; Mount Vernon Slave List, 1786; List of Negros Clothes, 1792, Mount Vernon Ladies Association Archives.

tried to match occupations and trades to whatever hierarchy of power and influence they perceived in the slave community.

In contrast to the families headed by matriarchs such as Phebe and Doll, Saboy's family at Newton offers an example of a family headed by an elite elder male and, despite his importance to the managers, Saboy seems to have been unable to help his family members avoid the field. Saboy was the first slave listed in the 1796 census, suggesting that he held significant power and influence in the plantation hierarchy – at least in the eyes of the new manager. Saboy had been the driver of the first gang, but he was no longer valuable as a day-to-day laborer. The manager noted that Saboy was "very old" and was effectively "retired."[72] Although he no longer worked, his experience was still an important asset to the estate. He was most likely still consulted regularly by managers, overseers, and other drivers about aspects of cultivation, possible innovations, or even matters of labor organization, allocation, and discipline. Yet, despite his elite role, Saboy's wife, Nanney, was still working in the first gang in her sixties. She was among the oldest first-gang female workers. Saboy's daughter Haron was a first-gang field hand in her forties, and his three eldest sons – Moses, Bango, and Sam – in their twenties and early thirties, worked in the first gang. Sam was known as a "mulatto" despite being recorded as the child of Saboy and Nanney. Neither of Sam's parents were described as mixed race. Saboy probably acted as the father of a child whose biological father was one of the white managerial staff. Sam was the only one of Saboy's or Nanney's children referred to as a mulatto. It was very unusual for a mulatto to be given a field position, and it seems likely that Sam's biological father had either never had or no longer had any influence in the management of the plantation. Saboy's youngest son, Adam, a teenager, was a cattle boy in 1796 – a common position for young men before moving to the field gangs.[73] Indeed, by November 1797, Adam was working with the second gang.[74] Although it is surprising that Saboy's privilege did not allow him to obtain better positions for his family than common field hands, perhaps having his family able to be together each day and, for many years, under his direction in the field could be deemed a kind of reward. Given that field work required skill and that it could even be labeled a kind of craft, it is also possible that the planters at Newton deliberately placed the children of the first-gang driver in the field because they anticipated that they might

---

[72] "Report on the [Newton] Negroes," MS 523/288, Newton Family Papers.
[73] Ibid.
[74] Newton Work Log, 1797–1798, MS 523/122, Newton Family Papers.

have either inherited Saboy's skill and knowledge or that they would be more apt at field work because they had more direct access to their father's expertise.⁷⁵

The reasons that a certain family shared elite status or dominated privileged positions are never easy to decipher. The records are too limited to allow for anything more than speculation. At Newton, for example, the first-gang driver was a mulatto named Dickey-Budd, in his thirties. The manager noted that he was "a most excellent servant." Dickey-Budd's mother, Molly, was a field hand in her fifties, but she often led a separate smaller group of less capable first-gang slaves, known as "the infirm gang." Dickey-Budd was given an elite position because he was a mulatto. His father was probably one of the plantation's former white managerial staff or tradesmen. Together, Molly and her son had significant control over the other first-gang hands. Moll's only other surviving child, a daughter named Ester Cam, worked with the second-gang hands in 1796–1797 but was moved to the first gang toward the end of 1797, after turning eighteen. Compared to other second-gang hands, Ester Cam missed an unusually high number of days to sickness in 1796–1797 (thirty-one), and one could speculate that the overseers were more tolerant of Ester Cam's illnesses and allowed her more rest because of her family relationships.⁷⁶ Why Molly was a gang leader is less clear than why her son was a driver, but the relationship between their family connection and their dual leadership roles seems more than coincidental. Molly might have been granted a leadership position as a result of her relations with a previous white staff member – which produced her son. Alternatively, Dickey-Budd, as gang leader, might have been able to exercise some of his own influence as first-gang driver and have his mother given her position. Dickey-Budd, as a mulatto, was more likely to have a privileged position. Perhaps he was chosen as a first-gang leader rather than a tradesman or domestic because his mother was such a capable field worker and a leader. Managers might have assumed that she could teach him some of the craft.

Overall, elite slaves were more likely to have large families on a plantation, and the families who attained the most privileged occupations on an estate shared certain characteristics. They were more likely to be headed by a domestic worker or sick nurse, they were more likely to have a driver or a ranger among them, they were more likely to share knowledge of a particular trade that could be transmitted to younger generations, and they were

---

⁷⁵ Johnson, "Work, Culture and the Slave Community," 342.
⁷⁶ Newton Work Log, 1796–1797, MS 523/110, Newton Family Papers.

more likely to have had close contact, often sexual, with masters or other white staff. These factors did not guarantee that the family would remain elite or that parents could secure privileged spots for their offspring, but they improved the chances that the members of that kin group or household could avoid field work. The key difference between the islands and the mainland was that sick nurses may not have had the same significance on Chesapeake plantations, and the difference in status and opportunities between privileged slaves and common laborers was not as exaggerated on large Chesapeake estates as it was on sugar plantations.

WORK, COMMUNITY, AND RESISTANCE

Despite the hierarchy within the slave community, slaves shared common interests and experiences, and they could and sometimes did exercise unified resistance against the master. Slaves would join together in protest against working conditions or the treatment of a driver or overseer, and they took advantage of every opportunity, as limited and difficult as these were, to negotiate better conditions for themselves. In 1795, Sir John Gay Alleyne, the attorney for Turner's Hall in Barbados, had heard about the ill treatment of slaves by the estate's current overseer, a drunk. Yet he was more concerned about the slaves taking advantage of a new overseer than he was about the overseer's conduct. He warned against "making a rash change in the Person of the Manager" at the estate. In his experience, such a change "has been too often attended with disagreeable Consequences in the ... Tempor of the Gang of Slaves." They would, he warned, "try their strength upon any weakness the New Manager may Discover in his Conduct with a view to the advantage of the Estate also."[77] The slaves persisted in trying to get the overseer removed, and several Turner's Hall slaves left the plantation to report to the attorney the details of the ill treatment they were receiving. The attorney finally agreed that, especially with regards to provisions, the overseer's actions seemed like "madness" and the man was dismissed.[78] Such collective group protests against a particularly abusive overseer were not uncommon, particularly on sugar plantations. In 1774, slaves at the Codrington estates in Barbados, finding their overseer to be too harsh "went in a body from thence to Lodge the complaint with John A[lleyn]e of the unusual cruelty they had received." Alleyne listened to the slaves and suggested to the owners that the overseer

[77] John Gay Alleyne to Henry Gally, July 16, 1795, E20572, Fitzherbert Papers.
[78] John Gay Alleyne to Henry Gally, October 20, 1795, E20573, Fitzherbert Papers.

be removed.[79] On December 31, 1752, at the onset of the harvest, the Jamaican overseer Thistlewood reported that two enslaved women, Bella and Abigail, returned home from a visit to the plantation's owner. They had "been there to complain" about him. Not surprisingly, given the clock time-consciousness that increasingly dominated eighteenth-century sugar plantations, Thistlewood was careful to note the time they returned: "abt. 1pm."[80] Refusing to labor was the most significant bargaining tool a slave possessed. Labor stoppages or desertions could destroy the timing of crop cultivation. On a sugar plantation, especially during the harvest, that loss of labor could be disastrous. The headmen or officers on an estate, such as the boilers, played key roles in protests and in efforts at gaining stronger footing in negotiations between master and slave.

Work protests could range from large-scale desertions to individual absences, but smaller-scale absences were not usually an explicit protest against work conditions or deliberate resistance against the institution of slavery. Runaways have been a key topic in the historiography of slave resistance. The literature has tended to collapse the distinctions between short- and long-term runaways and to underestimate the massive imbalance in volume between *petit* and *grand maroonage*.[81] Most of the scholarly work on runaways has focused on runaway advertisements and, in the antebellum United States, runaway slave narratives.[82] Runaway advertisements (which tended to be posted several weeks or even months after a slave had left an estate) and runaway slave narratives (which were written by successful escapees) offer an incomplete and imbalanced view of runaways. Most short-term runaways went unrecorded in newspapers, being both commonplace and brief enough in duration to be unremarkable. Work logs help to complete the picture by showing the surprising frequency with which short-term absences – lasting only a handful of days at most – occurred. In terms of costs or a threat to production, these short-term runaways or absences did not have a significant impact on the business operation of plantations, but they offer some fascinating insights into other aspects of plantation life and labor organization.[83]

---

[79] Richard Hind to Society for the Propagation of the Gospel, July 20, 1778, C/COD/42, Codrington Papers.
[80] Thomas Thistlewood Diary, December 31, 1752, Monson 31.3.
[81] See, for example, Alvin O. Thompson, *Flight to Freedom: African Runaways and Maroons in the Americas* (Kingston, Jamaica: University of the West Indies Press, 2006).
[82] Gad Heuman, "Introduction," in Gad Heuman, ed., *Out of the House of Bondage: Runaways, Resistance and Maroonage in Africa and the New World* (London: Frank Cass, 1986), 1.
[83] Loren Schweninger, "Counting the Costs: Southern Planters and the Problem of Runaway Slaves, 1790–1860," *Business and Economic History* 28.2 (1999): 267–275.

What the work absences suggest is not a large number of "runaways" seeking permanent freedom but, instead, the existence of both an institutionalized pressure valve and extensive extraplantation community networks. When physical and psychological exhaustion had reached the point at which a slave could no longer face the daily drone of labor or when a slave sought the time needed to visit kin on other estates, he or she took the day off.[84] As far as planters were concerned, these slaves' whereabouts were temporarily unknown, and their absence was recorded as if they were a stray mule or a missing tool.

Sampson Wood, the Newton manager, in a letter to the plantation owner, complained that too many of the slaves would "some times take a day or two without leave."[85] The logs note when these slaves were "absent." There were no permanent absences or extended flights from Newton or Seawell between 1796 and 1798. There were significantly more total days of absence at Newton in the first year (fifty-six) than in the second year (twelve). Complete evidence is only available at Seawell for one year. The Newton slaves may have been testing their new manager during his first year on the plantation, taking advantage of a change in the management to establish more advantageous standards in labor bargaining with the manager. The vast majority of absences on these two plantations (82 percent) lasted only a day or two (see Appendix B, Table A26).

Second-gang workers, the majority of whom were in their teens, tended to be absent for longer durations than first-gang workers, and the three slaves who spent the most time absent in total on the two estates were all in the second gang. The longest absence, nine days, was by a Newton slave named Dublin in July 1796. Dublin was an adult working with the second gang, which was unusual, but the manager considered him to be one of the "diseased negroes" because he was missing a thumb.[86] Because of this extended July disappearance, he was gone more than any other slave on the two estates between 1796 and 1798. The second and third highest number of absences came from two of Seawell's second-gang hands: Thomas (with six total days) and Cate (with five total days). Thomas and Cate had both been moved into the second gang from the grass gang very recently. Cate, who was also known as "Kitty," had been moved into the second gang at an unusually young age. She was only eleven years old, the youngest member of the second gang. Thomas was the youngest of the

[84] Newton Work Log, 1796–1797, MS 523/110, Newton Family Papers.
[85] "Report on the [Newton] Negroes," MS 523/288, Newton Family Papers.
[86] Ibid.

five surviving children of Great Sarey – a woman in her fifties, whose condition had deteriorated to the point at which she "does little." He was about fifteen when he ran away and, somewhat surprisingly, he had still been working with the third-gang grass pickers as late as July 1796. He would have been by far the oldest member of that children's gang. His five elder sisters all worked as first-gang field slaves, and Thomas, if he lived and stayed healthy, was almost certainly bound for a life of field service. Thomas and Cate actually disappeared together at one point on a Monday in mid-December 1796. Cate came back on the Wednesday and Thomas returned on the Thursday. One can only speculate as to why some second-gang hands ran away for longer durations and more frequently, but it is significant to note that the absence of these two newest members of the second gang corresponds with the high annual sickness rates for the youngest members of the first gang. Thomas and Cate, like the young first-gang slaves in the plantation hospital, might have been struggling to adapt to the increasing discipline and physical demands that came with their progression through the gangs. Heuman found that younger slaves ran away for longer periods of time.[87] Likewise, the longest duration of absences at Newton and Seawell tended to be among the youngest slaves in the second gang.[88]

Absences were not normally large group protests. Approximately two-thirds of the time, the slaves ran away alone for the day (see Appendix B, Table A.27). Occasions on which multiple slaves took the day were rare, but on March 9, 1797, six first-gang Newton women left for a single day. About 60 percent of first-gang members were women, so it is not clear whether there was a gendered significance to their absence. Why were six slaves absent together? Was it coincidence? Was this a form of collective labor protest? If so, one might have expected a mention of it in the plantation records. Perhaps, just as plausibly, they left the plantation to attend an event in town or on a nearby estate, such as a funeral. That their absence merited no comment from the overseer seems to imply its humdrum, everyday character rather than any political statement.

Individual absences were common on both estates, and harsh punishments were rare. What is remarkable is how readily plantation managers seemed to have tolerated work absences. Rather than just one or two recalcitrant slaves, there were at least forty-five and as many as seventy-six different field hands from the two plantations listed as absent for a day or

---

[87] Heuman, "Runaway Slaves in Nineteenth-Century Barbados," 103.
[88] Seawell Work Log, 1796–1797, MS 523/111, Newton Family Papers.

more between April 1796 and October 1798. Given that the combined field hand population on the two estates from 1796 through 1798 was, at its highest, approximately 210 slaves, it appears that one-fifth to one-third of all field hands ran away for at least a day during these two and a half years. On only one occasion was an absent slave "locked up" as punishment when he returned. This unnamed Seawell slave left for a single day in April 1797 and was locked up for 7.5 days after returning. Although slaves might have received a beating or a whipping on their return, the manager never commented on it and whatever physical punishment they received was not severe enough to send them to the sick house because, in almost all cases, they were working with the rest of the gang the day after their absence ended. Managers may have turned a blind eye to these absences unless they became too common, recognizing that they were part of a process of labor negotiation and that punishment might rob them of more work than they had lost that day. Indeed, although the Newton and Seawell manager complained about the absences on these estates, he posed no plan for punishment and insisted that he would rely more on confinement than the whip when he decided he wanted to punish a slave.[89]

The timing of absences during the work week was predictable, and the weekly pattern offers significant insight into the slaves' motivations for leaving. Individual absences tended to cluster around or bracket a Sunday, so that slaves were either claiming or being given successive days off – the equivalent of a long weekend – before returning to their labors. It was especially common for a slave to disappear on Sunday and return on Tuesday or Wednesday (see Figure 6.1). Supervision was more lax on a Sunday, and it was easier for a slave to abscond. Slaves took successive days off to get the travel time needed to go to town or to visit kin on other plantations.[90]

Planters recognized that their estates were part of a "neighborhood" of plantations.[91] Slaves traversed these larger neighborhoods during their working days and on their own time. There was little a planter could do to prevent nighttime and Sunday journeys around the neighborhood. There was simply not enough supervision. A Jamaican attorney, for example, worried that "the Negroes in the Neighborhood are very sickly with a variety of dangerous Complaints." The estate he managed had not yet

---

[89] "Report on the [Newton] Negroes," MS 523/288, Newton Family Papers.
[90] Philip D. Morgan, "Colonial South Carolina Runaways: Their Significance for Slave Culture," in Gad Heuman, ed., *Out of the House of Bondage: Runaways, Resistance and Maroonage in Africa and the New World* (Totowa, N.J.: Frank Cass & Co. Ltd., 1986), 69.
[91] Thomas Barritt to Nathaniel Phillips, February 25, 1795, MS9201, Slebech Papers; see also Thomas Barritt to Nathaniel Phillips, January 16, 1795, MS9201, Slebech Papers.

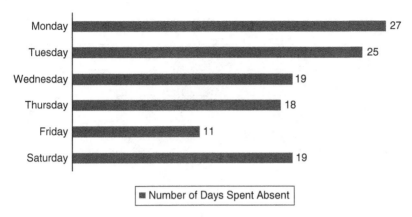

FIGURE 6.1. Day of the work week on which absences occurred. Total absent days: 119.
Note: This includes all absences from work in the first set of 1796–1797 Newton and Seawell work logs, from the entire fourteen months of the 1797–1798 Newton work log, and from the ten surviving months of the 1798 Seawell log.
Sources: Newton Work Logs, 1796–1798; Seawell, Work Logs, 1796–1798.

suffered, but he was struggling to prevent it by giving "particular directions that none of our People go through" other estates as they traveled. He also insisted that no slaves from other estates "be allowed coming here, to prevent the infection as much as possible." Ultimately, he realized he was fighting a losing battle. The slaves would not stick to the roads alone. "I am afraid," he admitted, "they will not all of them attend to the Orders."[92] Many slaves traveled at night, making it nearly impossible for managers to police plantation boundaries. Thistlewood was sometimes alarmed by the night traffic through the plantation he was overseeing in Jamaica. In October 1752, he noted in his diary that "for Severall Nights Past" there had been "an abundance of Negroes passing and repassing all Night long."[93]

Although the dataset for the number of recorded absences at Newton and Seawell is small, there appear to have been significant seasonal variations in absences. Somewhat surprisingly, there were no absences in the month of October in 1796 or 1797 on either estate (see Figure 6.2). It is conceivable that the onset of the heavy rainy season in the fall encouraged slaves to stay sheltered on the estate in October, but during the peak November rains, the number of absences rose again in those first two

[92] Thomas Barritt to Nathaniel Phillips, February 25, 1795, MS 9201, Slebech Papers.
[93] Thomas Thistlewood Diary, October 24, 1753, Monson 31.3, Thistlewood Papers.

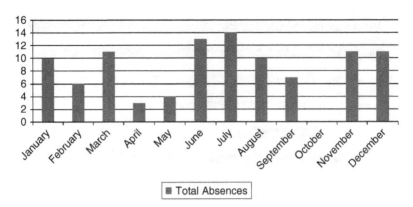

FIGURE 6.2. Total days of absence at Newton and Seawell, 1796–1798. Total absent days: 100.
Note: This chart draws only on logs that cover, approximately, a full year. Data are taken from the 1796–1797 Newton and Seawell logs and from the 1797–1798 Newton log from August 1, 1797 to July 31, 1798.
Sources: Newton Work Log, 1796–1798; Seawell Work Log, 1796–1797.

years. The fall was the season for throwing dung, a horrendous task that slaves might have wanted to avoid. Yet, the threat of an impending task does not normally appear to have factored into their decision making. The Newton and Seawell logs show no correlation between the likelihood of absences and the tasks performed by the majority of the gang on the day of the absence or on the day before. Heuman found that the least popular months for runaways in Barbados were February and May, during the harvest.[94] Absences at Newton and Seawell were also lower in this period, but they were not as low as in October. Slaves were probably more likely to stay on an estate during the harvest because they were allowed to eat some of the maturing cane. This tendency to not run away or be absent during the sugar harvest stands in sharp contrast to an increased number of runaways that scholars have found in certain areas of North America, such as in North Carolina, during the harvest. The difference may point toward the distinctive nature of the sugar harvest and the sugar cultivation cycle. Labor was much less intense during the sugar harvest than at other points in the sugar plantation cycle, and planters often commented on the health and happiness of their slaves during the harvest.[95]

---

[94] Heuman, "Runaway Slaves in Nineteenth-Century Barbados," 103.
[95] Marvin L. Michael Kay and Lorin Lee Cary, "'They are Indeed the Constant Plague of Their Tyrants': Slave Defence of a Moral Economy in Colonial North Carolina, 1748–1772," in

Food was scarcest in Barbados in the late summer months. The couple of months after the crop ended were known among the slaves in Barbados as the "hungry-time" or the "hard-time."[96] Long-term runaway attempts in Barbados as a whole rose in July and August.[97] With the sugar crop over and the corn crop not maturing until September, it may be that Barbadian slaves were sometimes left undernourished and forced to scrounge for sustenance. They may have taken the day to find food for themselves or to get food for or from kin on neighboring estates. The greatest number of absences at Newton and Seawell occurred in the summer months of June and July (see Figure 6.2). It is not clear whether these higher numbers of absences were connected to food scarcity on these plantations. The Newton logs show consistent corn rations for the slaves throughout the year, but there is evidence of starvation in some skeletons in Newton's slave cemetery (see Chapter 4). It is possible that the rations were not of the same quality throughout the year. The corn, yams, and millet allotted to slaves in June and July, for example, might have been rotten. Food scarcity or poor-quality rations could have driven some of the Newton slaves to abscond during the summer months, but it could also be that absences rose during these months because of less pressing labor demands after the completion of the harvest. Supervision was more lax. Managers were more tolerant of runaways. There may have been a combination of factors at work. The Newton manager, for example, may have even turned a blind eye to let a few slaves run away to forage for food during these months.

A closer examination of who the typical absent slave was offers frustratingly little insight into slaves' motivations. Many "unmarried" slaves probably had spouses on other estates, which would seem to give them cause to spend more time absent while they were visiting. The Newton and Seawell manager noted in the plantation census that "all Women whose husband's names are not mentioned, having children, their Husbands are men who do not belong to the Estate."[98] Although much of the other evidence points toward a link between absences and visiting kin on surrounding estates, a statistical analysis of the thirty-seven absent Newton and Seawell slaves who can be identified offers some surprising evidence. Overall, no tradesman was ever absent, and, among the field workers,

---

Gad Heuman, ed. *Out of the House of Bondage: Runaways, Resistance and Maroonage in Africa and the New World* (London: Frank Cass, 1986), 47.
[96] William Dickson, *Mitigation of Slavery, In Two Parts* (Miami, FL: Mnemosyne Pub. Inc., [1814] 1969), 308–309.
[97] Heuman, "Runaway Slaves in Nineteenth-Century Barbados," 102.
[98] "Report on the [Newton] Negroes," MS 523/288, Newton Family Papers.

women were more likely than men to run away. The absent slaves were, surprisingly, slightly more likely to be living with their spouses, and the women who were absent had fewer children than the average woman in the field. It is not clear why married slaves or slaves with fewer children were more likely to be absent, but one could surmise that the higher rate of absence among women in the field is a testament to the brutal demands of field work for women. The proportion of men and women was the key difference between absent slaves and the runaway slaves advertised in newspapers. Whereas men were disproportionately represented among slaves in runaway advertisements, the record of absences at Newton and Seawell makes it clear that women were just as likely as men – if not more so – to leave an estate for a short period of time.[99] Women, because they needed to care for their children and because they were not skilled at a marketable trade, may have been less likely to be able to runaway for long enough to merit a runaway advertisement.

Petit maroonage appears to have been less common at Prospect than it was at Newton and Seawell. Beginning in 1787, the Prospect work logs were printed pro-forma, and their pages included a column for runaways, suggesting that the managers anticipated short-term absences and that they continued to include these slaves in the total on the estate because they expected them to return. The runaway attempts at Prospect were longer in duration than they were at Newton, and they never involved more than two slaves missing at the same time. The missing slaves' names, genders, and gang affiliations were not recorded and thus analysis has to be speculative. It is possible that the managers recording the number of runaways failed to note absences of only a day or two in duration, differentiating conceptually between a longer term runaway and an absent slave. It is also possible that the slave listed as runaway changed frequently, although there was never more than two at any one time. If either or both were true, the difference in the pattern of flight from Newton/Seawell and Prospect might disappear.

As the creation of separate columns in the Prospect work log suggests, Caribbean managers did anticipate a significant amount of *petit maroonage*, and they tried to take it into account when they evaluated the total amount of potential labor that could be extracted from slaves. The Barbadian ameliorationist Dickson estimated that each individual slave would spend,

---

[99] "Report on the [Newton] Negroes," MS 523/288, Newton Family Papers; Justin Roberts, "Working Between the Lines: Labor and Agriculture on Two Barbadian Sugar Plantations, 1796–1797," *William and Mary Quarterly* 63.3 (2006), 551–586.

on average, nineteen days a year as a runaway. Dickson's estimate seems much too high and must have been a rhetorical exaggeration, intended to underscore the time lost to resistance when planters were too brutal with their bondsmen. Dickson's estimate was far higher than the average amount of time spent absent per field hand at Newton and Seawell. Although absences were common at Newton, Seawell, and Mount Vernon, they were short in duration. Furthermore, some slaves never fled the estate, so that each field worker on these estates spent, on average, less than a single day absent each year. Dickson's estimate was also much higher than the average amount of time Prospect slaves spent as runaways each year (0.9 days in 1787 and 3.5 days in 1791).[100]

Absences were far less common in Virginia than in Barbados or Jamaica. Like most Virginian planters, Washington contended with long-term runaways every few years, and he pursued them with great zeal even after he developed antislavery sentiments. He also punished them severely. He struggled, for example, to retrieve a runaway woman named Oney Judge until he died.[101] When a man named Abram ran away briefly in 1794, Washington insisted to his farm manager that the slave "get his deserts when taken, by way of example."[102] On a day-to-day basis, few Mount Vernon slaves were absent from their work. Washington's managers recorded the slaves who failed to report to their duties without being sick as both "absent" and as "ran away," but from January 1797 to May 1798, there were only five such incidents on all farms combined and none of them lasted longer than a full work week.[103]

Although the majority of Mount Vernon's short-term absences were not likely deliberate attempts at permanent escape, the exception was a slave named Caesar, who seems to have been trying his luck at a more permanent escape. Caesar, a field hand in his late forties, was absent twice in 1797. He actually ran away often from the estate in the 1790s. With no spouse on the estate and no children, Caesar had no direct family connections at Mount Vernon, which may have encouraged him to try a permanent escape. He also had the skills to evade capture and survive. After a six-day absence

---

[100] See Appendix B, Tables A6 to A9.
[101] Phillip D. Morgan and Michael L. Nicholls, "Slave Flight: Mount Vernon, Virginia, and the Wider Atlantic World," in Tamara Harvey and Greg O'Brian, eds., *George Washington's South* (Gainesville: University Press of Florida, 2004), 197–222.
[102] George Washington to William Pearce, March 30, 1794, in Fitzpatrick, ed., *Writings of Washington*, vol. 33, 309.
[103] Mount Vernon Farm Reports, 1797–1798.

in 1796, Washington speculated that Caesar might eventually "escape altogether, as he can read, if not write."[104]

Most of the Mount Vernon slaves were probably "runaways" without actually having run out of the bounds of the massive plantation. When Gunner missed work at the Mansion House farm in December 1797, he was almost certainly visiting his wife Judy, who lived at River Farm. Judy was in her fifties, a few years younger than Gunner. He was described as being in his nineties in 1799 but he was probably closer to about sixty-five at that time.[105] Washington bought Judy and her first child in 1764 from Garvin Corbin, during an aggressively expansionist phase of Mount Vernon's history. She worked at the mill plantation for many years but, by 1786 at the latest, she was at River Farm working as a field hand. She was still known as "Mill Judy."[106] Gunner was forced to travel to see her on Sundays and holidays. Yet, the overseers appear to have taken into account his family connections when they assigned tasks. Gunner was sometimes chosen to make whatever deliveries were necessary to and from River Farm, where he might have stayed part of the night, rising early to return to work at the Mansion House quarter. In the winter of 1793, he was sent to deliver tools at River Farm. The weather became bad, and he was stuck there for four days.[107] On at least one occasion, in July 1797, he was allowed to spend the entire week working at River Farm.[108] He could always hope for more. Gunner and Judy's son Will, born in 1773, lived with her at River Farm, working alongside her as a field hand.[109] Will died a young man, at some point in the 1790s. In 1799, when their master Washington died, Judy, now known as "River Farm Judy," was

---

[104] Mount Vernon Farm Reports, 1797; George Washington to Pearce, February 21, 1796, in Fitzpatrick, ed., *Writings of Washington*, vol. 34, 476.

[105] Mount Vernon Slave Inventory, June 1799; Fitzpatrick, ed., *Writings of Washington*, vol. 22, 14n.

[106] For tithables listing, Judy at Mill Farm, see Abbot, ed., *The Papers of George Washington: Colonial Series* vol. 6, September 1758–December 1760 (Charlottesville: University of Virginia Press, 1988), 217, 282, 428; Abbot and Twohig, eds., *The Papers of George Washington: Colonial Series* vol. 7, January 1761–June 1767 (Charlottesville: University of Virginia Press, 1990), 45, 139, 227–228, 313, 376–377, 442–443, 515–516; Abbot and Twohig, eds., *The Papers of George Washington: Colonial Series* vol. 8, June 1767–December 1771 (Charlottesville: University of Virginia Press, 1993), 104, 220–221; Mount Vernon Slave List, 1786.

[107] Weekly Farm Reports, February 1793, Mount Vernon Ladies Association Archives.

[108] Mount Vernon Farm Reports, 1797–1798.

[109] Will, thirteen in 1786, did not appear in the 1799 inventory. See Mount Vernon Slave List, 1786; Mount Vernon Slave Inventory, 1799.

in her mid-fifties, still married to Gunner and living alone.[110] Despite his advancing age and his inability to work, Gunner was never allowed to move to River Farm to work with her. Instead, he stole or took advantage of what time he could when he felt it absolutely necessary, as he did for a week in mid-December 1797. Although the evidence does not indicate when in the 1790s his son died, his absence in December or the week allowed him in July could have been related to him or his wife grieving his only son's death.

Compared to sugar plantations, there were few absences at Mount Vernon. Rather than be absent, Mount Vernon slaves were more likely to feign illness when they wanted to miss work. In such cases, they used their nights for travel and claimed sickness the next day. Washington was convinced that many of his people reported sick because of "night walking."[111] Most of the slaves had family members living on other farm quarters on the 10,000-acre expanse of Mount Vernon, and they undoubtedly used nights to visit their families. Using the night to travel and visit and claiming sickness in order to rest the next day was not as enticing an option for slaves on sugar plantations, where the detriments of the plantation hot house, a manifestation of the severe labor discipline on sugar estates, dissuaded slaves from trying to feign illness.

If they were gone for more than a couple of days, the vast majority of plantation runaways stayed hidden near the estate, in the surrounding neighborhood, or even on the estate fields among maturing crops, in thickets or woodlands, or hidden in the slave quarters.[112] In one rare incident, a forty-five-year-old Barbadian man named Johnny Beckles was discovered in 1805 after more than twenty-five years as a runaway. He was found living in the slave quarters of a nearby plantation.[113] Slaves, whether runaway or not, sought community, companionship, and familiar or predictable worlds. In Jamaica, for example, at the Vineyard pen, in 1751, a slave named Robin went missing. With nowhere to go, the runaway did what the Turner's Hall watchman had done. He hid in the woods close around Vineyard and snuck onto the pen to steal food and supplies.[114] Hidden in the woods beyond the bounds of the pen, he was free but alone and with no means of support. The farther he strayed from the bounds of the livestock

---

[110] Mount Vernon Slave Inventory, June 1799.
[111] Washington to William Pearce, May 18, 1794, in Fitzpatrick, ed., *Writings of Washington*, vol. 33, 369.
[112] Philip D. Morgan, "Colonial South Carolina Runaways," 57.
[113] Heuman, "Runaway Slaves in Nineteenth-Century Barbados," 104.
[114] July 17, 1751, Thistlewood Diary, Monson 31/2, Thomas Thistlewood Papers.

farm, the more likely it would be that he could maintain his autonomy but the less familiar his world became, the lonelier he would get, and the harder it would be to find food.

Allegiances, loyalties, and personal interests among the slaves at Vineyard were complicated. Several slaves in the community helped to catch Robin. Two slave girls came upon Robin and let out a cry. He ran off, but an enslaved man named Simon and the colored driver Dick "having ye doggs att hand ... seized him" and there was a great scuffle. Significantly, "Simon and Dick were first att him in ye Struggles." The overseer soon arrived to find that Robin had been wounded in "ye belly" during the fight. Three more slaves from a neighboring plantation were grinding corn at a mill nearby. They heard the cries and came to help hold the struggling Robin down "yet all Could Scarce hold him." Robin was finally secured, and Simon was rewarded for his efforts with a bottle of rum from his new overseer.[115] Robin was whipped and sent back to work the next day.[116]

Why were the Vineyard slaves so intent on helping to catch Robin? Clearly, there were individual rewards to be had for helping the new overseer, and if the slaves were caught sympathizing and aiding the runaway, they would be punished. Robin confessed that another slave, Titus, had sat at nights eating by his fire, indicating, again, that Robin, despite being a runaway, sought the companionship of the slaves he lived with on the estate to alleviate his loneliness. Titus was whipped.[117] To understand the motivations of the slaves who sought to capture Robin, it is also important to recognize that the runaway had been stealing from the stored provisions at Vineyard while he was in hiding.[118] Some of the slaves may have felt that they would all suffer as a community by the loss of provisions. Robin's individual act of resistance might have been understood as making the lives of the rest of the slaves in the community more difficult. Rather than posing a united front against the master, the Vineyard slaves helped their master catch a slave in order to help themselves.

Community connections and kinships ties, when they extended beyond the bounds of an individual estate, probably encouraged short-term runaways or absences. Yet, at the same time, community connections and ties to an estate, as well as a strong sense of belonging to a place – developed over decades of living and working on one plantation – undoubtedly

[115] July 31, 1751, Thistlewood Diary, Monson 31/2.
[116] August 1, 1751, Thistlewood Diary, Monson 31/2.
[117] July 31, 1751, Thistlewood Diary Monson 31/2; August 1, 1751, Thistlewood Diary, Monson 31/2.
[118] July 17, 1751, Thistlewood Diary, Monson 31/2.

worked to discourage long-term runaways. A fugitive was not always a subaltern resisting the oppressing class and seeking permanent escape. The lives of most slaves were embedded in a place and within a community network. Their range of options were both more limited and more complicated than has been allowed for in much of the literature on resistance and runaways. Even after the old watchman at Turner's Hall shot at the overseer, he stayed in the woods nearby. Although his skills were not as marketable in an urban setting as a carpenter's or mason's would be, he could have tried to reach Bridgetown and attempted to blend into the urban environment, or he could have gained passage aboard a ship and become a sailor, a maritime runaway.[119] Instead, he stayed. Perhaps he stayed until it was certain that the people and world he knew and the job he held – along with the identity and community position that stemmed from it – were no longer an option.

CONCLUSION

Work logs often depict slaves as nameless and, for the most part, interchangeable resources, but each laborer had a unique individual identity and place within a constantly evolving, dynamic, and multifaceted slave community. This is not to say that the slave created a life completely independent of the working world or even that the slave's world and the master's world paralleled each other. Instead, it is to recognize that the slave's world and the world of plantation production were inseparably entangled. The work slaves performed during the master's time did not simply overlap with the lives slaves built for themselves. Work and the identities drawn from that work were interwoven through all aspects of slave life. Masters were forced to acknowledge and take into account that human particularity and the intricate community networks and hierarchies on a plantation.

There were well-developed networks and hierarchies within the slave community, and the nature of that community was a product, in part, of the work slaves did and the occupational structure on an estate, especially on sugar plantations. Privileged slaves who held skilled and supervisory positions tended to sit atop the community hierarchy, and elite families came to control many of these privileged positions. This community hierarchy may have been more pronounced on sugar plantations than it was on large Chesapeake estates because the community on a sugar estate,

[119] Heuman, "Runaway Slaves," 100–101.

in terms of slaves per acre, was more concentrated and because the occupational structure was more extensive and multi-tiered, a product of both the many specialty roles for slaves in sugar production and of the labor discipline on sugar estates. The difference in status between privileged slaves and common laborers was also more pronounced on sugar plantations because field labor was so much more demanding on sugar estates. Proximity to the master's house played a significant role in shaping both occupational hierarchies and community hierarchies. Being a domestic or a sick nurse may not have improved a woman's chance of marrying, but it often gave her the opportunity to secure better occupations for her family members. Parents with positions as tradesmen or supervisors were more likely to be able to secure such spots for their children. Skilled and supervisory occupations gave slaves privileges and additional provisions, which gave them the opportunity to accumulate property. Inequality existed even within a slave community. Although community bonds and ties could offer individual slaves a sense of belonging and identity, economic inequities and social differentiation could sometimes produce oppressive community dynamics. Masters understood the hierarchies and family connections within the slave community – if only to an imperfect degree – and they helped to create hierarchies with their occupational assignments. But, in what was a continual feedback loop, they may have also acknowledged existing plantation hierarchies and aligned occupations to those hierarchies. Slaves developed ties to their community and to the place they lived: the plantation and its immediate neighborhood. Community and kinship networks, be they consanguinal or fictive, extended beyond the bounds of the estate, and these networks encouraged slaves to leave the estate at night on Sundays and even during some work days, taking the time they needed to visit friends and family. Yet, at the same time, the ties that bound a slave to a place and to a community – such as kinship, a sense of belonging to a place, and the possession of property – discouraged them from running away permanently.

Work shaped the lives slaves led, but the reverse was also true. Community and kinship shaped the work done on a large plantation in both the Chesapeake and the Caribbean. The knowledge and skills necessary to become a tradesmen or a driver were shared among family groups and passed down from one generation to the next. Slaves living on a plantation for decades came to understand more about estate lands, the weather, local conditions, and the work done on an estate than did the white managerial staff, who, because of constant turnover, were never able to acquire the same knowledge and experience. The process of creolization in the slave community further encouraged this tendency. Late eighteenth-century Jamaican plantations included large numbers of African imports and thus there was less shared experience of plantation production among the slaves than there was at the same time in Barbados, which was becoming predominantly creole or Virginia, which had become an almost entirely creole slave society. This shared knowledge and experience was beneficial to both masters and slaves. It made plantation production run more smoothly and efficiently, but it also gave slaves bargaining power and some leverage in master-slave relations and in labor negotiation.

Conclusion

The spirit of improvement swept through the plantation Americas in the late eighteenth century. It was born of broader Atlantic discourses about progress, humanitarianism, and civility, and it changed the working environment of the plantation and the lives of the enslaved workers. Overall, planters in Barbados, Jamaica, and Virginia successfully increased productivity levels, cut costs, reduced the risks in production, and, to a limited extent, improved the material conditions of slaves' lives and their health. They called it "improvement" and celebrated the mutually compatible nature of moral and economic progress. Productivity and improvement meant, foremost, an increase in the amount of time slaves spent working. Planters introduced a variety of new coercive instruments to their plantations, such as the clock, the plantation hospital, and the work log, and, in Jamaica in particular, a few sugar planters introduced drivers on Sundays to better regulate the slaves' provision work on their own grounds and their own time. These measures were all designed to foster greater labor discipline and increase the hours of labor.

With improvement, planters coerced and squeezed every last ounce of sweat from their slaves, but they also stressed ameliorative and benevolent management schemes and increasingly adopted paternalistic rhetoric. For most planters, the path to greater humanity and benevolence would be found through greater discipline and restrictions on the slaves' freedom and autonomy. They offered an alternative vision of modernity that embraced hierarchy and restrictions on autonomy as the key to civility and moral and economic progress. For slaves, who spent the vast majority of their waking hours laboring, the "improvements" of this era were debatable. The numbers of hours they worked and the constancy of their labors increased, and they were forced to grow more of their own food. The reproductive levels in the slave community improved with ameliorationist and pronatalist policies, but most field slaves – who constituted a majority on any plantation – lost some of the little time they had to themselves and they lost autonomy. At the same time, there was a small but growing cadre of elite male slaves on most large plantations because planters were training more of their slaves to work as craftsmen. This development gave a few slaves greater privileges and more negotiating power in the labor relationship, but even these slaves continued to be subjected to field labor, especially during the harvest.

There was significant economic incentive driving the improvement movement. The plantation complex was expanding rapidly in the last quarter of the eighteenth century. Not even the American Revolution could check the rapid growth of slave societies, largely by importation of slaves in the British Caribbean and by natural reproduction in the Chesapeake. Economic competition among plantation zones drove down the prices planters received for cash crops while increasing the cost of supplies. In the last half of the eighteenth century, planters in Barbados, Jamaica, and Virginia increasingly diversified production and experimented with a variety of crops and production schemes to improve profits and reduce the risks that came with relying on a single staple crop. They also hoped to cut costs and become more self-sufficient. The amelioration movement, rooted in agricultural improvement, was born in this context. It was, at its heart, an effort to reduce costs and risks.

The plantation complex came under attack by abolitionists and antislavery activists at its height in the 1780s and 1790s, when the numbers of new African slaves disembarking in the Americas had risen to the highest levels ever, more than 100,000 a year. Surging abolitionism in Britain, however, forced planters to consider different ways of managing their laborers, putting greater external pressures on an ameliorative project that had already begun in the Americas as part of a broader agricultural improvement scheme. Pressure from abolitionists transformed the ameliorationist discourse into a discussion centered on the masters' humanitarian duty to their bondsmen. The rising price of slaves and a growing Atlantic-wide concern with humanitarian reforms from mid-century onward had created a context in which Caribbean planters were more receptive to abolitionist pressure for amelioration, and the Enlightenment faith in the compatibility of moral and economic progress had given planters hope that amelioration and productivity could be mutually reinforcing goals.

As much as these three regions – Barbados, Jamaica, and Virginia – were all shaped by movements to improve agriculture and ameliorate the conditions of slavery, they differed in significant ways. Chesapeake planters had an easier time than their Caribbean counterparts applying the principles being preached by English agricultural improvers because the landscape and climate were more like England than were the torrid zones of the Caribbean. This may explain, in part, why Caribbean planters developed their own agricultural improvement literature, translating the principles of the agricultural improvers into something more appropriate for sugar cultivators. The rhetoric of amelioration and humanitarianism was more pervasive on the islands than on the mainland, but it influenced plantation management throughout the plantation Americas. The movement toward paternalist rhetoric in plantation management in the colonial and antebellum United States was the mainland equivalent of Caribbean amelioration schemes. Duty, humanitarianism, and benevolence were common themes in paternalist and ameliorationist discourses, but discipline and obedience were also central principles in these new ways of articulating the master-slave relationship. The amelioration and abolitionist movements were not only much stronger in the Caribbean than in the Chesapeake because Caribbean planters were subject to metropolitan standards more than their mainland counterparts. The amelioration and abolition movements were also more pronounced and had more of an impact on reproductive rates in Barbados than in Jamaica. In Barbados, the combination of the creolization of the slave population, a healthier climate, lands that were easier for slaves to work, and planters' more active efforts at amelioration brought about a naturally reproducing slave population at the turn of the nineteenth century – a unique development in the sugar islands.

The improvement movement fostered more thorough systems of plantation accounting. The managerial staff of large plantations throughout the plantation Americas began to use work logs to track slave labor, especially from the 1770s onward. Planters used these logs to ensure that no potential labor was lost from their bondsmen. The logs allowed planters to compel greater productivity, but they were also a kind of statistical fantasy, reducing people to individual and flexible units of production, assuming that all slaves were equal and interchangeable in their skills and abilities. Planters turned to labor statistics as a way of better managing and conceptualizing their slave populations. At the same time, the increasing concern that planters expressed with maintaining their slave populations – a result of the humanitarian reform movement – was manifest in another new kind of plantation record on Caribbean estates called an increase and decrease of stock account. Increase and decrease of stock accounts were also statistical in their approach to conceptualizing a population. Planters strove to improve natural reproduction or better control and understand it by recording it in these accounts. Some plantation managers insisted that these increase and decrease of stock accounts were the best indicator of whether slaves were well treated, regarding natural reproduction as the true test of the impact of amelioration. They were a way of quantifying progress in amelioration.

During this improving era, slaves worked the vast majority of the year on a wide variety of crops, and their hours of labor were increasing in the late eighteenth century. In Virginia, slaves were made to work an increasingly large number of crops, eliminating downtime in the seasonal rhythms of labor. In Jamaica, slaves were forced to work through many of their Sundays as planters began to use drivers to compel their slaves to grow food. Sugar planters also ran their mills during the harvest through early Sunday mornings and started them up again on many Sunday nights. They redefined the length of a day in order to have slaves mill and grow provisions on Sundays while still recording this day's labor as the slaves' day off. Barbadian and Jamaican slaves worked more hours during a good harvest year than their Virginian counterparts, but these long hours of labor probably did not have as significant an impact on the health of sugar slaves as one might expect. Sugar slaves worked more hours during the harvest season than at any other time of the year and, although they were not as healthy during this season as some planters insisted, death and sickness rates were also lower during that season than during the rainy cane holing and dunging months, and conception rates for women were high during the sugar harvest. The physical intensity of certain chores had a greater impact on slave health and reproduction than did the total hours of work. Cane holing and manuring were by far the most demanding of any agricultural tasks in Barbados and Jamaica, and many contemporaries acknowledged that the demands of cane holing had the greatest impact on the natural decrease of slaves in the islands. The rugged terrain made working conditions, particularly cane holing and dunging, more severe in Jamaica than in Barbados.

Diversification of production was common on all late eighteenth-century estates. Large planters in the Chesapeake added wheat, corn, and other grains to their tobacco production. They added fruit orchards, and those along the river started fishing. By diversifying production, they took advantage of a surplus in slave labor. Many Chesapeake estates, like

Mount Vernon, switched from being plantations relying on the production of the single staple – tobacco – to mixed farming units, growing a variety of crops while raising livestock and even fishing. At Mount Vernon, the slaves stopped growing tobacco altogether in the 1760s. Barbadian sugar planters diversified by growing provision crops among their canes to cut costs, especially during and after the American Revolution. They also experimented with cotton as both a primary and secondary cash crop. Many Jamaican sugar planters, particularly in the mountains, switched to coffee as a primary cash crop, or even grew a mixture of both sugar and coffee on the same estate. At the same time, some sugar planters continued to rely on a monocropping system of cane production. In multicropping systems of production, Caribbean planters grew extensive provisions or secondary cash crops alongside their sugar, and Chesapeake planters switched to mixed farming and grew a variety of grains. In contrast, in monocropping systems of production, planters relied almost exclusively on the production of a single staple, such as canes at Prospect plantation. Both multicropping and monocropping systems could be viable and profitable systems of sugar agriculture. For slaves, diversification and multicropping meant less highs and lows in the seasonal labor demands, more constant exertion but less monotony in daily tasks.

The nature of labor organization was among the most significant differences between sugar plantations and mixed farming in the Chesapeake. Gangs in the Caribbean were larger, more closely supervised, and more disciplined than gangs in the Chesapeake. Most Chesapeake slaves on large estates were divided into smaller working groups and spread across several farm quarters. On these quarters, there tended to be a single gang, led by a foreman who acted as a work supervisor more than a driver. On sugar plantations, there were multiple gangs divided hierarchically on the basis of physical ability and multiple drivers who were more severe than Chesapeake work leaders in their discipline and in their attention to maintaining a particular pace and rhythm. Slaves working in a gang obtained a kind of collective skill that contributed to their efficiency and production, but gang work was so psychologically oppressive that it has never been used successfully with free workers. Slaves became more efficient laborers in the Caribbean by working their way through the gangs – a kind of apprenticeship to field labor.

Masters strove to coerce as much labor as possible from their slaves, and sickness was one of the greatest impediments for planters trying to achieve maximum productivity. Slaves, even in an age of amelioration, were rarely given days off for sickness or for pregnancy. Most individual slaves worked more than 300 days a year. In the Caribbean, the hospital became a manifestation of the tension between the amelioration movement and the desire to extract the maximum potential from land and labor. Conditions in the hospital were so intolerable that these buildings became tools of labor coercion. Slaves were forcibly confined there when they were ill, and the planters maintained that this was in their best interest. Environmental theories of disease led planters to often blame rainy weather for deaths and illness, even though the high death rates in the rainy season seem to have been caused more by work than weather, but they rarely kept their slaves from the rain. Sickness rates in the Chesapeake rose during the winter months when the work was least demanding, suggesting that illness in the Chesapeake was more closely connected to weather and climate. Women were sick more often than men on sugar plantations, and their death rates were particularly high during holing and manuring seasons. The labor was particularly severe for most women. Men and women were sick for the same amount of average days on Chesapeake plantations, and old slaves were sick more often than young slaves – as one would expect. In contrast, in Barbados, it was the youngest slaves in the first gang who were sick most often, suggesting that they had some difficulty adapting to the pace of labor in this gang. Pregnant women were given more time off in the Caribbean than in the Chesapeake but only because the tasks on Chesapeake estates were much less arduous than the tasks on sugar plantations. Sugar planters were forced to allow women a little more time for pregnancy but, even in an era of pronatalist policies, they gave them far too little time for good health.

Slave labor was flexible and adaptable and, in the last half of the eighteenth century, as the creolization of the slave population continued, planters strove to cut the costs of plantation production by becoming self-sufficient. An increasing number of predominantly creolized plantation slaves were taught a variety of skills and crafts. Planters often differentiated between skilled slaves and common field laborers. They gave skilled slaves extra privileges and threatened to punish tradesmen and domestics by making them common field hands. Skilled slaves performed a significant amount of menial and common labor, particularly in the Caribbean. Although, compared to the Caribbean, production was more diversified on large Chesapeake plantations, some of the skilled slaves on large Virginian estates (particularly the carpenters, masons, and coopers) were more specialized than their island counterparts. At the same time, Chesapeake planters with an ever-growing laboring population were forced to find work other than agricultural labor for their slaves, and slaves in that region learned a wide

Conclusion 285

variety of crafts and skills over the course of their lifetimes. The boundary that planters drew between skilled and unskilled labor was not only porous, it was to some extent artificial. Planters associated women with common field work and men with skilled labor. Gender ideals encouraged them to exaggerate the division between skilled and unskilled work.

What set skilled slaves apart from field hands were the privileges they received for their work and their status in the plantation hierarchy. There was a strong connection between the working world and slaves' occupations and the formation of slave families, communities, and hierarchies. Skilled slaves, domestics, and supervisors tended to have a better quality of life with better housing and more food, time, and access to land. They were more likely to be married on the estate, and they had larger family units and larger numbers of children. The inequality in living conditions and in privileges led to hierarchical plantation communities in which, at least occasionally, the more privileged slaves oppressed the more common slaves, and where established creole slaves may have taken advantage of new African arrivals. Elite family units formed on estates because tradesmen often passed on their skills to their children and because elite slaves were often able to secure better occupations or privileges for their children or for other family members. Plantation communities extended beyond the boundaries of a single plantation. Extra-plantation networks fostered the creation of neighborhoods, particularly where the terrain and the conditions of labor allowed for slaves to visit other estates easily. In Jamaica, the demands of Sunday labor and the terrain made these extra-plantation networks more common than in Virginia. The establishment of these plantation communities reduced the likelihood that slaves, especially creole slaves, would run away permanently but extra-plantation community networks may have also encouraged slaves to be absent from work for a day or two at a time in order to visit other plantations.

Although Caribbean planters were more vocal in their insistence on amelioration, the conditions of slave life and the health and reproductive capacities of the slave community continued in this period to be much better on the mainland than in the islands. There were some improvements in reproductive rates on sugar plantations, especially in Barbados, but they came nowhere close to the reproduction rates of the Virginian slave population. Slaves there reproduced at a faster rate than anywhere in the British Americas. In large part, the difference between sugar plantations and the Chesapeake plantations was a product of the backbreaking labor on sugar plantations – particularly cane holing and the intensive amount of manuring per acre. The regimented gang labor system enabled sugar planters to drive their slaves even harder on tasks that were already arduous. The working conditions for slaves were better in Barbados than in Jamaica, in part because planters were more attentive to ameliorating those conditions in order to reduce the cost of importing new slaves in a market where the demand for slaves was continually outstripping the supply. Barbadian planters were smaller and the lands they were working were older, making it difficult for them to compete with Jamaicans for newly imported Africans. Compared to Jamaica, the flatter terrain, the shorter harvest season, the cleared lands, the trade winds, and the cooler weather made Barbados a healthier working environment. As an older sugar island where most lands had been continuously cultivated for over a century, Barbados may have also been an easier place for slaves to dig cane holes – the most demanding of plantation tasks. Wheat, corn, and tobacco production in Virginia was much less backbreaking for slaves than sugar production in the islands, and the climate was healthier. The working conditions for slaves in this era were more demanding in Jamaica than in Barbados and more demanding in Barbados than in Virginia. Slaves also had far less autonomy in the sugar islands and less hours to themselves than they did in Virginia. At the same time, all three areas continued to be influenced, even in the postwar era, by humanitarian reform and agricultural improvement movements, and by late Enlightenment thinking more generally.

Although scholars have tended to group Jamaica and Barbados as part of a Caribbean world distinctly different from the U.S. mainland, especially after 1783, in the years between the American Revolution and the abolition of the slave trade, the slave societies of the British Americas continued to operate as part of a larger British Atlantic system that needs to be understood as a whole. Thus, it is more difficult to draw clear distinctions in this era between colonial and antebellum slavery or between U.S. and Caribbean slave systems. Rather than the American Revolution, the abolition of the slave trade in 1807 was the point at which the histories of the Caribbean and mainland slave societies began to diverge. Before that point, they shared a common history. There were certainly vast differences between the working environment on sugar plantations and the working environment at the massive estates of Mount Vernon in Virginia, but the differences were almost as great as the differences among sugar plantations. The working world at Newton, an old and established Barbadian plantation in the dry, flat southeast of the island, looked very different from the working world at Prospect, a new Jamaican plantation in the wet and rugged area of northeastern Jamaica. The staple crop was not the sole factor dictating the working environment. Overall, scholars have tended to overlook the similarities between Caribbean sugar plantations such as Newton, Seawell, and Prospect, and large Chesapeake plantations, such as Mount Vernon, especially the similarities in plantation management strategies. They have also tended to collapse the separate histories of Barbados and Jamaica into one common history of the sugar islands.

In the nineteenth century, the slave societies of the American South began to develop very differently from slave societies in the Caribbean. The Caribbean continued to be influenced by metropolitan concerns and by antislavery protests to a much greater extent than was the American South. After 1807, the abolition of the slave trade, combined with a natural decrease in the population in Jamaica and limited land in Barbados, made the expansion of slavery in these islands difficult if not impossible. Without a consistent fresh labor supply, the slave populations grew older and smaller, and the sugar plantation complex began to decline. The naturally reproducing slave population of the U.S. South, the growth in cotton production, the opening up of new areas of slave settlement, and the movement of slaves from the Chesapeake to the Deep South meant that the slave societies of the U.S. South continued to flourish and expand. Whereas plantation slavery began a decline in the British Caribbean in 1807, it grew in the U.S. South until a civil war and the Emancipation Proclamation of 1863 put an end to the "peculiar institution."[1]

Not only were the working lives of enslaved laborers in Barbados, Jamaica, and Virginia being shaped by similar forces in the late eighteenth century, but there are also striking parallels between enslaved workers on large plantations and factory workers in the early stages of industrialization. These parallels suggest the extent to which scholars need to reincorporate the study of slavery into larger histories of laborers in the early modern Atlantic. The agricultural setting for plantation slavery and the ways in which slavery has been cast as a fundamentally distinct labor system have led scholars of slavery and of industrialization to overlook the similarities between plantation slaves and industrializing workers in Europe. However, by privileging the role of work culture and labor management over mechanization as a driving force in the process of early industrialization, or even by giving these elements equal weight, one can see significant parallels between Jamaican, Barbadian, or even Virginian

---

[1] Stanley L. Engerman, *Slavery, Emancipation and Freedom: Comparative Perspectives* (Baton Rouge: Louisiana State University Press, 2007), 1–3.

plantations and early factory settings. The English agricultural labor force began a slow transition toward factory labor in the 1780s, in the midst of the improvement ethos that was sweeping through the plantation Americas. Although factory labor was free labor and plantation slavery was unfree labor, the work environment of the plantation and the factory were becoming more alike at the end of the eighteenth century, which is not surprising because they were both being shaped by managerial theories that drew on Enlightenment discourses about the rational use of time, labor maximization, and progress. A comparison of the two labor systems and working environments shows which developments in the plantation Americas during the era of improvement were part of broader Atlantic trends in labor history and which were unique.

New kinds of labor discipline and systems of accounting for and tracking workers were used on both slave plantations and in the early stages of industrialization. Both planters and factory owners began to use clock time to regulate and track their laborers work.[2] During good harvest years, slaves worked almost as many hours each year on sugar plantations as workers in the early factories. Virginian slaves worked far less than either sugar plantation laborers or factory workers, but the diversification of production on Virginian plantations made the slaves' work efforts more constant, much like factory work, even if the variety of productive activities made the agricultural setting in Virginia quite different from factory labor. Barbadian and Jamaican planters – and, to a lesser extent, Virginian planters – used gang labor to standardize labor outputs and to keep slaves working at one consistent and rhythmic pace, like factory workers. The cultivation cycle throughout the Americas was divided into many smaller tasks to facilitate repetition of movement, specialization, and synchronized laborers among the slaves in each gang. Perhaps most significantly, the productivity increases per worker in industrialization and in late eighteenth-century plantation slavery were caused in large part by increasing labor discipline and the rising number of hours of labor.[3]

---

[2] E.P. Thompson, "Time, Work Discipline and Industrial Capitalism," *Past and Present* 38 (December 1967), 56–97; Leonard Rosenband, Merritt Roe Smith, and Jeff Horn, "Introduction," in Rosenband, Smith, and Horn, eds., *Reconceptualizing the Industrial Revolution* (Cambridge, MA: MIT Press, 2010), 17; G.N. von Tunzelman, "Technological and Organizational Change in Industry During the Early Industrial Revolution" in Patrick O'Brien and Ronald Quinlet, eds., *Industrial Revolution and British Society* (New York: Cambridge University Press, 1993), 258; Joel Mokyr, *The Enlightened Economy: An Economic History of Britain, 1700–1850* (New Haven: Yale University Press, 2009), 340–344.

[3] Joachim Voth, *Time and Work in England, 1750–1830* (New York: Oxford University Press, 2000).

By the end of the eighteenth century, there were several significant parallels in the lived experience of early factory work and plantation slavery, and there were similarities in the composition of the work force. Enslaved plantation workers toiled for more hours each year without exacerbating their health problems or lowering their reproductive rates, and this was partly because of improved provisioning. Slaves were being forced to grow more of their own foods, and more food was grown on the plantations during regular work days. Likewise, some scholars suggest that English laborers were able to work longer hours in factories at the end of the eighteenth century than they had a hundred years earlier in nonindustrial labor because there was more food available.[4] The sickness rates on most slave plantations, with the possible exception of some Jamaican plantations undergoing seasoning, were only slighter higher on average than sickness rates among early factory labor forces in England. Most plantation slaves in Virginia and Barbados were sick for less than three weeks per year. Likewise, early modern factory records show that the average worker on those sites reported sick from work for a half week to nearly four weeks per year depending on the factory, although the standard was one to two weeks.[5] The same range in sickness rates can be found on various slave plantations. Like early factory settings, the slaves on sugar plantations were the victims of horrific industrial accidents, such as having their hands ground off in sugar mills. Virginian slaves were never subject to such accidents, and they lived much healthier lives than early factory laborers or sugar plantation workers. Women and children had prominent roles in early factory labor forces. This kind of full labor force utilization helped increase productivity during industrialization. Likewise, female-majority field gangs were the norm in the plantations, and young children feeding the sugar mills was a common sight during the harvest on sugar plantations.[6] In fact, the creolization of enslaved populations throughout the Americas created more balanced sex ratios. Combined with the increasing number of men being trained as craftsmen, this meant that the proportion of women in the field gangs was growing.

As workers subject to increasing levels of worksite discipline, slaves and factory workers both found ways to collectively protest their conditions.

---

[4] Herman Freudenberger and Gaylord Cummins, "Health, Work and Leisure Before the Industrial Revolution." *Explorations in Economic History* 13.1 (1976), 1–12.

[5] Herman Freudenberger, Frances J. Mather, and Clark Nardinelli, "A New Look at the Early Factory Labor Force," *The Journal of Economic History* 44.4 (December 1984), 1089.

[6] Ibid., 1087.

Slaves sometimes sent a group of representatives to a local attorney or to the plantation owner to entreat him to address their working conditions or dismiss an overseer for ill treatment. About 5–10 percent of British factory workers belonged to unions designed to improve their working conditions and wages. Collective slave protests continued throughout the eighteenth century, and they appeared more often in the business correspondence of plantations as the century progressed. Likewise, union activity grew alongside the factories in Britain, but such combinations of workers were harshly suppressed in a series of acts between 1750 and 1799, and especially with the conservative reaction to radical French Jacobins.[7]

As similar as factories and plantations became during the improvement era, there were also critical differences between the two. There was a spectrum in plantations systems; Virginian plantations seemed to share less in common with factories than did Barbadian or Jamaican plantations. The agricultural settings for plantations and the outdoor nature of most of the work made plantation work routines more seasonal and variable than the work in early factories. Slaves were subject to harsh weather conditions and exposure to the elements to a degree that early factory laborers never had to experience. The slaves' knowledge of how to produce crops was always more important to the master than the unskilled factory laborers knowledge of production was to the factory owner, and this may have given slaves more leverage in master-slave relations, even if it was largely mitigated by the coercive force and violence that masters wielded. Finally, whereas the status and bargaining power of many craftsmen were eroding during the early stages of industrialization in England, there were an increasing number of creole slaves in the plantation Americas being taught craft skills, and this allowed them to improve material conditions for themselves and their families and gain bargaining power in labor negotiations with their masters.

Plantation slavery was one of a range of early modern labor systems, and it needs to be examined in that context, but it was also fundamentally distinct. Race was a key marker of difference between the plantation owners and their enslaved workers in the plantation Americas. Slaves, because of the chattel principle in slavery, were subject to much greater physical abuse than, for example, early factory laborers. Unlike free laborers, slaves also faced the threat of being sold away from their community or having their family members sold. In daily practice, the severity of the physical punishments slaves endured and their frequency was

---

[7] Mokyr, *Enlightened Economy*, 354–355.

decreasing by the end of the eighteenth century. Being sold away or having family members sold from large plantations in Barbados, Jamaica, and Virginia was also becoming less common for slaves in the late eighteenth century, particularly as reproductive rates improved. Increasingly, the vast majority of plantation slaves in Barbados, Jamaica, and Virginia lived their entire lives on one plantation. However, as the reproductive rates in Virginia continued to rise in the early nineteenth century and the African slave trade ended and new slave frontiers opened in the southwest of the United States, a massive internal slave trade began. Thus, the high reproductive rates in Virginia actually increased the threat that slaves would be separated from their families and their homes. Virginia, with a surplus labor force, became a labor supplier for the new slave frontiers after the closing of the slave trade. To a certain extent, the key difference between slaves and free laborers was not dependent on the working environment or the frequency with which they were subject to physical abuse or forced migration and dislocation. Instead, the key difference between slaves and free laborers was that slaves lived under the constant threat of being sold or having their families separated from them or being beaten and tortured. The threat and not the frequency of abuse was a critical element in the lived experience of slavery. Free workers in the early factories faced a different set of concerns (such as maintaining employment and feeding their families), but they were largely spared the threats of physical abuse that slaves faced daily.

The literature on plantation slavery is being reinvigorated as scholars have started to situate plantations within broader Atlantic frameworks and move beyond moribund debates about the degree to which slaves were able to resist domination or about the degree to which slavery was consistent with capitalism. Slavery was, foremost, a labor system, and work was central to slaves' lives. To humanize the study of plantation slavery, we need to move beyond stale depictions of evil oppressors and the heroically resisting oppressed. We need to understand the experiences of plantation slaves as workers both in the field and away from it, and we need to think about the cultural and intellectual forces, as well as the economic conditions, that shaped their working lives.

Appendix A: Note on Sources

To tally the tasks in the logs used in this study, I have been forced at a few points to make some estimates to fill gaps or produce comparable sets of figures. The overseers or drivers who recorded the logs did sometimes make errors. On a few days in the Newton log, for example, there are discrepancies and errors in the overseer's tally of the total number of slaves in the gang and the number of slaves at work on each task. In many cases, the reason for the error is obvious, such as the number of slaves in various work assignments being consistent for several days in a row and then a new slave joining the sick list while the number working on each task remained the same. In such cases, I have been forced to make an educated guess based on the patterns seen to that point about which chore the sick slave had been assigned until that day. Occasionally, the number of slaves at work in a gang or at a specific chore was not recorded, but these numbers can be derived through addition or subtraction or by internal evidence in the log. In total, however, my speculations do not amount to more than a 1 percent margin of error in determining the amount of annual labor planters allocated to each task.

The Prospect logs required the most significant amount of estimating. Although the total number of field hands was recorded often, the proportion in the first gang and the proportion in the second gang normally went unrecorded. However, there were points in the year in which the logs indicate how many slaves were at work in the first gang on a key chore such as cane holing or harvesting. I have assumed that this was approximately the number of able-bodied slaves in the gang and that the number of able-bodied slaves in the first gang, aside from sick slaves or runaways, remained constant throughout the year.

For all work logs, when multiple tasks were done in a single entry with no indication as to how much time was spent on each, I have normally divided the amount of time spent on each task equally so that, for example, three tasks done by a slave or by a gang in a given day or week were assigned a value in my calculations of a third of a day or week each. Occasionally, based on internal evidence in the logs, I have estimated that an unequal amount of time was spent on the multiple tasks being done in a single day or week. Some cultivations tasks were not linked to a crop, and I have occasionally been forced to guess at the crop, based on which crops were being cultivated in that period.

The most difficult part of a project aimed at gathering the data from plantation work logs is trying to understand the wide array of agricultural terms – often recorded in shorthand – being used on different plantations with an array of different provision and cash crops. Not only did each crop have its own specific cultivation techniques but those cultivation techniques changed over time, and each region employed slightly different terminology in describing these techniques. It was never easy for me to determine what work was being done when a chore was listed only as "cross-holing" or as "knocking out sugar." Contemporary agricultural manuals and the often descriptive letters among the plantation's managerial staff allowed me to decipher almost all of these agricultural terms. When it came to skilled work, I was sometimes forced to consult the staff at Colonial Williamsburg and at the Barbados Museum and Historical Society to help me determine what was meant by some of the tasks recorded in work logs. The process of interpretation here was extensive, but I have not attempted to cite each time I have uncovered what was meant by a shorthand reference to a chore. The field hands on all of the plantations at the core of this study did hundreds of tasks over the course of the year. To collapse these hundreds of tasks into smaller tables with approximately twenty to thirty categories, I was forced to sometimes simplify and generalize about the nature of chores.

The evidence in work logs must not be taken uncritically. Beyond the small errors in addition or tallying, overseers and managers may have been presenting a record of work that served their own agenda. They may have wanted to gain the favor of the owner, or they may have wanted to hide bad management decisions or a misuse of labor. In most cases, the accuracy of the data in the logs can be verified by using other sources, such as records of crop sales, milling and boiling house books, or the other financial and correspondence records of an estate. The plausibility test is also important in determining whether these sources are accurate. By checking multiple logs, plantation manuals, and contemporary estimates of how much time tasks took, I have determined whether the amount of time slaves were recorded as spending on various chores seemed plausible and whether it could be explained. In most cases, the logs appear to have been reporting an accurate picture of the work being done on an estate. The logs are still problematic as representative sources in that they tended to be produced for absentee owners, thus showing a bias in my evidence toward absentee estates. Most of these absentee estates were, however, managed by capable attorneys and managers living near or on the plantation. They were often resident planters themselves.

Appendix B

TABLE A1. *Most-Labor-Intensive Tasks Performed by Field Workers Each Month on Barbadian Plantations*

	Barbados	
	Newton (1796–1797)	Seawell (1796–1797)
January	Watching (Guard Duty)	Picking Cotton
	Molding Cattle Pens	Watching (Guard Duty)
	Mending Paths	Watering Young Canes
February	Digging Cane Holes	Picking Cotton
	Breaking Guinea Corn	Cutting Canes
	Cutting Canes	Breaking Indian Corn
March	Cutting Canes	Picking Cotton
	Molding Cattle Pens	Cutting Canes
	Employed about the Works	Employed about the Works
April	Holing for Yams	Digging Indian Corn Holes
	Molding Cattle Pens	Heaping Trash
	Heaping up Moldy Plants	Cutting Canes
May	Digging Cane Holes	Digging Yam Holes
	Weeding Canes	Molding Cattle Pens
	Holing for Guinea Corn	Holing for Guinea Corn
June	Molding Cattle Pens	Planting Indian Corn
	Digging Guinea Corn Holes	Heaping up Corn Stalks
	Weeding Indian Corn	Weeding Cotton
July	Molding Cattle Pens	Weeding Indian Corn
	Weeding Guinea Corn	Cross-Holing Canes
	Weeding Indian Corn	Digging Cane Holes
August	Cross-Holing Canes	Winnowing Guinea Corn
	Weeding Cane Holes	Weeding Cotton
	Weeding Guinea Corn	Weeding Canes

TABLE A1. (cont.)

	Barbados	
	Newton (1796–1797)	Seawell (1796–1797)
September	Weeding Guinea Corn	Molding Guinea Corn
	Molding Guinea Corn	Breaking Indian Corn
	Breaking Indian Corn	Cross-Holing Canes
October	Cross-Holing	Throwing out Dung
	Molding Guinea Corn	Weeding Cotton
	Throwing out Dung	Molding Cattle Pens
November	Throwing out Dung	Throwing out Dung
	Cross-Holing	Weeding Cotton
	Weeding Cane Holes	Tying up Trash
December	Throwing out Dung	Digging Cane Holes
	Weeding Canes	Planting Cane
	Watching (Guard Duty)	Bringing Home Marl

Sources: Newton and Seawell Work Logs, 1796–1797, MS 523/110 and MS 523/111, Newton Family Papers

TABLE A2. *Most-Labor-Intensive Tasks Performed by Field Workers Each Month on Jamaican Plantations, Part 1*

	Jamaica			
	Somerset Vale (1776–1777)	Prospect (1785)	Prospect (1787)	Prospect (1791)
January	Billing Coffee	Cleaning Canes	Building Livestock Pens	Cutting Canes
	Cleaning Canes	Carrying Home Copperwood	Cleaning Canes	Cutting and Carving Bush
	Breaking Corn	Digging Cane Holes	Digging Cane Holes	Banking Canes
February	Billing and Picking Coffee	Cutting Canes	Cutting Canes	Cutting Canes
	Picking Green Coffee	Cleaning Canes	Cleaning Provisions	Carrying Canes to Mill
	Cleaning Canes	Working on the Road	Tying Canes	Banking Canes
March	Cleaning Canes	Cleaning Canes	Cutting Canes	Cutting Canes
	Billing and Picking Coffee	Cutting Canes	Planting Canes	Banking Canes
	Molding Young Canes	Employed about the Works	Cleaning Canes	Tying Rum Canes

TABLE A2. (cont.)

	Jamaica			
	Somerset Vale (1776–1777)	Prospect (1785)	Prospect (1787)	Prospect (1791)
April	Cutting Canes	Cutting Canes	Cutting Canes	Cutting Canes
	Cleaning Corn	Cleaning Canes	Cleaning Canes	Molding Canes
	Stripping Canes	Planting Canes	Carrying Field Trash	Supplying Canes
May	Cutting Canes	Cleaning Canes	Cutting Canes	Cutting Canes
	Planting Corn	Cutting Canes	Cleaning Canes	Molding Canes
	Planting Peas	Digging Cane Holes	Carrying Field Trash	Carrying Canes to Mill
June	Cleaning Canes	Cleaning Canes	Cutting Canes	Molding Canes
	Digging Cane Holes	Cutting Canes	Hoeing Grass	Hoeing Canes
	Cutting Canes to Plant	Digging Cane Holes	Carrying Field Trash	Banking Canes

Sources: Somerset Vale Work Logs, 1776–1777, Codex Eng 180; Prospect Plantation Journal, 1785, 0627-0017; Prospect Plantation Journal, 1787–1793, 0627-0019

TABLE A3. *Most-Labor-Intensive Tasks Performed by Field Workers Each Month on Jamaican Plantations, Part 2*

	Jamaica			
	Somerset Vale (1776–1777)	Prospect (1785)	Prospect (1787)	Prospect (1791)
July	Cleaning Canes	Cleaning Canes	Cleaning Canes	Digging Cane Holes
	Billing Plantain Walk	Digging Cane Holes	Cutting Canes	Cutting Canes
	Stripping Canes	Cutting Canes	Hoeing Grass	Molding Canes
August	Digging Cane Holes	Trashing Canes	Cleaning Canes	Cutting Canes
	Planting Canes	Digging Cane Holes	Cutting Canes	Digging Cane Holes
	Cleaning Ground to Prepare for Canes	Trenching	Digging Cane Holes	Tying Cane Plants

TABLE A3. (cont.)

	Jamaica			
	Somerset Vale (1776–1777)	Prospect (1785)	Prospect (1787)	Prospect (1791)
September	Digging Cane Holes	Cutting Canes	Digging Cane Holes	Cutting Canes
	Cleaning Canes	Billing the Plantain Walk	Planting Canes	Molding Canes
	Stripping Canes	Trashing Canes	Trashing Canes	Hoeing Canes
October	Digging Cane Holes	Planting Canes	Cutting Canes	Cutting Canes
	Cleaning Canes	Cleaning Canes	Planting Canes	Molding Canes
	Supplying Canes	Cutting Canes	Digging Cane Holes	Digging Cane Holes
November	Cleaning Canes	Cutting Canes	Cutting Canes	Trashing Canes
	Cleaning Corn	Cleaning Canes	Digging Cane Holes	Hoeing Canes
	Cleaning Plantain Walk	Planting Canes	Supplying Canes	Planting Canes
December	Cleaning Canes	Planting Canes	Planting Canes	Cutting Canes
	Supplying Canes	Cutting Canes	Digging Cane Holes	Digging Cane Holes
	Making Shingles for Trash House	Cleaning Canes	Cleaning Canes	Making a Lime Kiln

TABLE A4. *Most-Labor-Intensive Tasks Performed by Field Workers Each Month of the Year at Mount Vernon (Combined Totals), 1797, Part 1*

	Mount Vernon (Combined Totals)
January	Cutting and Grubbing on the New Road
	Cutting and Mauling Rails
	Making Fences
February	Making and Repairing Fences
	Grubbing and Burning Brush
	Plowing (Unspecified Crops)
March	Plowing Corn
	Making Fences
	Grubbing and Burning Brush

TABLE A4. (cont.)

	Mount Vernon (Combined Totals)
April	Plowing Corn
	Planting Corn
	Fishing with the Seine
May	Plowing Corn
	Replanting Corn
	Plowing (Unspecified Crops)
June	Cutting Wheat
	Plowing Corn
	Harrowing and Raking Corn

Source: Mount Vernon Farm Reports, 1797

TABLE A5. *Most-Labor-Intensive Tasks Performed by Field Workers Each Month of the Year at Mount Vernon (Combined Totals), 1797, Part 2*

	Mount Vernon (Combined Totals)
July	Hoeing Corn
	Plowing Corn
	Cutting and Securing Wheat
August	Hoeing Corn
	Plowing Corn
	Plowing (Unspecified)
September	Plowing and Harrowing Wheat
	Plowing and Harrowing Rye
	Pulling Blades
October	Plowing and Harrowing Rye
	Digging up Potatoes
	Carrying Fodder out of the Field
November	Gathering and Husking Corn
	Hauling and Lofting Corn
	Threshing and Cleaning Wheat
December	Threshing and Cleaning Wheat
	Cutting and Grubbing on New Ground
	Hauling and Lofting Corn

Source: Mount Vernon Farm Reports, 1797

TABLE A6. *Average Number of Annual Working and Nonworking Days per Field Worker at Mount Vernon, 1797*

	Dogue Run	River	Muddy Hole	Union	Mansion	Mount Vernon Total
Days Worked	279.7	280.4	283.1	285.5	287.5	283
Nonworking Days	85.3	84.6	81.9	79.5	77.5	82
Sundays and Holidays	57.2	56.2	57.2	56.2	56.2	56.5
Stopped by Weather	0.3	9.6	1	0	1.8	3.4
Absent	0	0	0	0.7	0.8	0.2
Sick	26.7	14.9	17.3	19.6	14.9	18.6
In Child Bed (Giving Birth)	1.1	3.9	6.4	3	3.8	3.3
Annual Total	365	365	365	365	365	365

Source: Mount Vernon Farm Reports, 1797.

TABLE A7. *Average Number of Annual Working and Nonworking Days per Slave at Newton and Seawell, 1796 to 1798*

	Newton						Seawell			
	1796–1797				1797–1798		1796–1797			
	1st Gang	2nd Gang	3rd Gang	C	1st Gang	2nd Gang	1st gang	2nd Gang	3rd Gang	C
Days Worked	281.6	286	307	285	294	297.1	279.4	280.1	305.2	293.1
Nonworking Days	83.4	79	58	80	71	67.9	85.6	84.9	59.8	71.9
Sundays and Holidays	57.3	57.3	57.3	57.3	54	54	58.3	58.3	59.8	59.8
Given Days (Individual Slaves)	0	0	0	0.2	0	0	0.4	0.1	0	0.5
Absent	0.5	0.6	0	0	0.1	0.2	0.2	1	0	0
Sick	23.1	21.1	0.8	22.6	14.3	13.7	24.1	25.1	0	11.5
Locked-Up (In the Dungeon)	0.2	0	0	0	0	0	0.1	0.3	0	0
Lying-In (Giving Birth)	2.3 (3.9)	0	0	0	2.6 (4.3)	0	2.2 (3.6)	0	0	0
Miscarried	0	0	0	0	0	0	0.4 (0.7)	0	0	0
Annual Total	365	365	365	365	365	365	365	365	365	365

C = Craftsmen

The numbers in brackets represent the average days per female slave.

Because there are 357 days in the Newton work log and 366 in the Seawell work log (363 for the third gang and craftsmen), the averages per slave have been calculated and adjusted to show an average based on the exact number of days in a year (365).

Sources: Newton Work Logs, 1796–1798, Seawell Work Log, 1796–1797, MS 523/110, 111, 123, Newton Family Papers

TABLE A8. *Average Number of Annual Working and Nonworking Days per Slave at Prospect in 1787 and 1791*

Year	1787	1791
Days Worked	261.3	282.2
Nonworking Days	103.7	82.8
Sundays, Given Days and Holidays	59.6	61.0
Stopped by Weather	2.1	4.5
Sick	41.1	13.8
Runaway	0.9	3.5
Annual Total	365	365

The evidence does not allow for averages per field hand or for slaves in each gang. These averages are for all slaves in the workforce, Because there were only 355 days recorded in the 1787 log, the numbers for that year have been adjusted to show the exact number of days in a year (365). There were no women recorded as missing work while "lying-in" in 1787 or in 1791, despite the six births in those years. Lying-in women were probably included at Prospect among the sick slaves.

Source: Prospect Work Logs, 1787 and 1791, Prospect Plantation Journals 1787–1793, 0627-0019

TABLE A9. *Labor Activities of Field Workers on the Outlying Mount Vernon Farms in 1797, Part 1*

	Dogue Run		Union Farm		River Farm	
	Days	%	Days	%	Days	%
Corn	796	17.4	2,267.3	33.8	1,799.3	23.4
Wheat	683	14.9	1,059	15.8	1,059	13.8
Oats	76	1.7	136.3	2.0	241	3.1
Hay	15	0.3	8	0.1	4	0.1
Timothy	32	0.7	31	0.5	6	0.1
Flax	90	2.0	45.5	0.7	119.5	1.6
Rye	79	1.7	216	3.2	322	4.2
Potatoes	49	1.1	196	2.9	167.8	2.2
Peas	89	1.9	214.3	3.2	333	4.3
Turnip	27	0.6	52	0.8	48	0.6
Buckwheat	24	0.5	37	0.6	56.5	0.7
Clover	18	0.4	6	0.1	12	0.2
Barley	0	0.0	5.5	0.1	55	0.7
Locust	29	0.6	0	0.0	0	0.0
Fruit Orchards	2	0.0	0	0.0	30	0.4
Unspecified Plowing and Harrowing	623	13.6	232	3.5	827	10.8
Unspecified Grubbing	322	7.0	359.5	5.4	202.8	2.6
Cutting and Burning Brush, Bushes, and Briars	63	1.4	131.5	2.0	57.8	0.8
Miscellaneous Field Tasks	22	0.5	230.5	3.4	162.3	2.1
Cleaning, Clearing, and Plowing New Ground	118	2.6	20	0.3	0	0.0
Cleaning, Clearing, and Plowing Meadow Ground	203	4.4	109	1.6	31	0.4
Cutting, Carting, and Hauling Wood	43.5	1.0	156.5	2.3	85	1.1
Fencing and Making Fences	567.5	12.4	409	6.1	733	9.6
Fishing	26	0.6	44	0.7	50	0.7
Working at the Mill, the Mill Race, or the Distillery	85	1.9	207	3.1	64	0.8
Heaping, Carting, Hauling, and Spreading Manure	130	2.8	205.5	3.1	221	2.9
Livestock Work	96	2.1	162.5	2.4	638	8.3
Working at Other Farms on Unspecified Tasks	156	3.4	26	0.4	129	1.7
Nursing	21	0.5	26	0.4	17	0.2
Brickmaking	4	0.1	11	0.2	27	0.4
Working on Roads, Bridges, and Paths	15	0.3	51	0.8	47	0.6
Miscellaneous Non-Field Tasks	72	1.6	46	0.7	130	1.7
Total Work Days	4,576	100	6,701	100	7,675	100

Source: Mount Vernon Farm Reports, 1797

TABLE A10. *Labor Activities of Field Workers on the Outlying Mount Vernon Farms in 1797, Part 2*

	Muddy Hole		Total	
	Days	%	Days	%
Corn	1,041	26.1	5,903.6	25.7
Wheat	386.5	9.7	3,187.5	13.9
Oats	42	1.1	495.3	2.2
Hay	0	0.0	27	0.1
Timothy	0	0.0	69	0.3
Flax	33	0.8	288	1.3
Rye	313.5	7.9	930.5	4.1
Potatoes	19.5	0.5	432.3	1.9
Peas	0	0.0	636.3	2.8
Turnip	25	0.6	174	0.8
Buckwheat	0	0.0	117.5	0.5
Clover	8	0.2	44	0.2
Barley	12.5	0.3	73	0.3
Locust	0	0.0	29	0.1
Fruit Orchards	5	0.1	37	0.2
Unspecified Plowing and Harrowing	752	18.9	2434	10.6
Unspecified Grubbing	75	1.9	959.3	4.2
Cutting and Burning Brush, Bushes, and Briars	66	1.7	318.3	1.4
Miscellaneous Field Tasks	2	0.1	416.8	1.8
Cleaning, Clearing, and Plowing New Ground	307	7.7	445	1.9
Cleaning, Clearing, and Plowing Meadow Ground	74	1.9	395	1.7
Cutting, Carting, and Hauling Wood	20	0.5	305	1.3
Fencing and Making Fences	256	6.4	1,965.5	8.6
Fishing	18	0.5	138	0.6
Working at the Mill, the Mill Race, or the Distillery	96.5	2.4	452.5	2.0
Heaping, Carting, Hauling, and Spreading Manure	83.5	2.1	640	2.8
Livestock Work	58	1.5	954.5	4.2
Working at Other Farms on Unspecified Tasks	0	0.0	311	1.4
Nursing	0	0.0	64	0.3
Brickmaking	10	0.3	52	0.2
Working on Roads, Bridges and Paths	235	5.9	348	1.5
Miscellaneous Non-Field Tasks	43	1.1	291	1.3
Total Work Days	**3,982**	**100**	**22,934**	**100**

Source: Mount Vernon Farm Reports, 1797

TABLE A11. *Labor Activities of Field Workers at Prospect Estate in 1785*

	Work Days	%
Cane Cultivation	18,089	65
Trenching	700.5	2.5
Holing	1,870.5	6.7
Planting	1,992.5	7.2
Banking	559.5	2.0
Hoeing	336	1.2
Cleaning Canes and Cane Fields	5,978.25	21.5
Molding Canes	148	0.5
Trashing Canes	876	3.1
Supplying Canes	79.75	0.3
Carrying Dung	314	1.1
Cutting Canes	4,949	17.8
Gathering and Tying Cane Tops	285	1.0
Sugar Processing	1,753	6.3
Employed in and about the Sugar Works	1372	4.9
In the Still House	381	1.4
Mule Men	1,260	4.5
Waining Sugar to Ship	2	0.0
Provisions	315	1.1
Cocos	100	0.4
Potatoes	45	0.2
Corn	11	0.0
Cleaning the Plantain Walk	159	0.6
Livestock	142	0.5
Driving Home Steers	82	0.3
Gathering Feed for Stock	60	0.2
Logging	517	1.9
Planting Logwood	6	0.0
Cutting Logwood, Copperwood, and Cottonwood	167	0.6
Carrying and Carting Wood	344	1.2
Plantation Maintenance	920	3.3
Plantation Buildings	150	0.5
Slave Houses	370	1.3
Making Fences	73	0.3
Working on the Roads	327	1.2
Cutting, Tying, and Carrying Brush	251	0.9
Making Ropes and Baskets	24	0.1
Working at Lime Kiln	71	0.3
Total Recorded Tasks	23,332	83.9
"Different Jobs" and Unspecified Tasks	4,489	16.1
Total Field Labor	27,821	100.0

Source: Prospect Plantation Journals 1785, 0627-0017

TABLE A12. *Total Labor Activities of First Two Gangs at Prospect in 1787 and 1791, Part 1*

Task	Gangs 1 Work Days	%	2 Work Days	%	Total Work Days	%
Canes	27,372	86.8	2,886.5	93.2	30,258.5	87.4
Burning Land to Plant	58	0.2	0	0.0	58	0.2
Holing	2,518	8.0	0	0.0	2,518	7.3
Trenching	245.5	0.8	60	1.9	305.5	0.9
Planting	2,046	6.5	35	1.1	2,081	6.0
Banking	707	2.2	360	11.6	1,067	3.1
Drawing	59	0.2	142	4.6	201	0.6
Molding	1,788.5	5.7	300	9.7	2,088.5	6.0
Cleaning, Hoeing, and Weeding	3,101.5	9.8	1,282.5	41.4	4,384	12.7
Supplying	3,76.5	1.2	0	0.0	376.5	1.1
Carrying Dung to the Canes	0	0.0	42	1.4	42	0.1
Trashing	1,147.5	3.6	354	11.4	1,501.5	4.3
Cutting	14,428.25	45.8	34	1.1	14,462.25	41.8
Tying up and Carrying Canes and Tops	681.5	2.2	217	7.0	898.5	2.6
Stocking up Canes	38	0.1	60	1.9	98	0.3
Burning Canes	37	0.1	0	0.0	37	0.1
Shipping Sugar	139.5	0.4	0	0.0	139.5	0.4
Sugar Processing	157	0.5	0	0.0	157	0.5
Employed about the Works	91	0.3	0	0.0	91	0.3
Working in the Still House	66	0.2	0	0.0	66	0.2
Mule Men	366	1.2	0	0.0	366	1.1
Coffee	0	0.0	20	0.6	20	0.1
Hoeing and Cleaning Ground to Plant	0	0.0	20	0.6	20	0.1

Source: Prospect Plantation Journals, 1787–1793, 0627-0019

TABLE A13. *Total Labor Activities of First Two Gangs at Prospect in 1787 and 1791, Part 2*

	Gangs					
	1		2		Total	
Task	Work Days	%	Work Days	%	Work Days	%
Provisions	501	1.6	38	1.2	539	1.6
Cleaning Provisions	120	0.4	0	0.0	120	0.3
Cleaning the Plantain Walk	232	0.7	0	0.0	232	0.7
Potatoes	59	0.2	0	0.0	59	0.2
Corn	30	0.1	0	0.0	30	0.1
Digging Out Stores	60	0.2	38	1.2	98	0.3
General Trash Work	713.25	2.3	20	0.6	733.25	2.1
Livestock Work	1,284	4.1	60	1.9	1,344	3.9
Planting Guinea Grass	0	0.0	60	1.9	60	0.2
Hoeing Grass	601	1.9	0	0.0	601	1.7
Cutting and Cleaning Pasture	203	0.6	0	0.0	203	0.6
Building Livestock Pens	459	1.5	0	0.0	459	1.3
Carrying Trash to the Sheep Pen	21	0.1	0	0.0	21	0.1
Plantation Maintenance	321.5	1.0	40	1.3	361.5	1.0
Mending the Roads	113.5	0.4	0	0.0	113.5	0.3
Repairing Plantation Works	89	0.3	0	0.0	89	0.3
Carrying Thatch for Buildings	99	0.3	0	0.0	99	0.3
Cleaning about the Works	20	0.1	40	1.3	60	0.2
Lime Kiln	332.5	1.1	0	0.0	332.5	1.0
Building a Lime Kiln	252.5	0.8	0	0.0	252.5	0.7
Bringing Home Lime	80	0.3	0	0.0	80	0.2
Cutting Brush	455.5	1.4	0	0.0	455.5	1.3
Miscellaneous Work	27	0.1	31	1.0	58	0.2
Total	31,529.5	100	3,095.5	100	34,625	100

Source: Prospect Plantation Journals, 1787–1793, 0627-0019

TABLE A14. *Labor Activities of First Two Gangs at Newton, 1796–1798, Part 1*

	1		2		Total	
	Work Days	%	Work Days	%	Work Days	%
Cash Crops	20,136.5	37.5	5,389	37.1	25,525.5	37.4
Canes	17,204.2	32.1	3,880.5	26.7	21,084.7	30.9
Cane Field Preparation	509	0.9	0	0.0	509	0.7
Cane Holing Activities	7,301	13.6	853	5.9	8,154	12.0
Supplying and Planting Canes	1,947	3.6	368	2.5	2,315	3.4
Tending the Growing Canes	2,597.8	4.8	1,890.5	13.0	4,488.3	6.6
Harvesting Canes and Clearing Field	4,849.3	9.0	769	5.3	5,618.3	8.2
Sugar and Rum Refining	2,932	5.5	1,508.5	10.4	4,440.5	6.5
Milling	935	1.7	834	5.7	1,769	2.6
Boiling	1,508	2.8	585	4.0	2,093	3.1
Distilling	488	0.9	54.5	0.4	542.5	0.8
Curing	1	0.0	35	0.2	36	0.1
Provision Crops	12,420.3	23.1	4,865	33.5	17,285.3	25.4
Guinea Corn (Millet)	5,361.8	10.0	933.7	6.4	6,295.5	9.2
Indian Corn (Maize)	1,579.5	2.9	682.7	4.7	2,262.2	3.3
Corn (Unspecified)	1,838.5	3.4	1,845	12.7	3,683.5	5.4
Yams	1,967.5	3.7	474.5	3.3	2,442	3.6
Potatoes	1,080.5	2.0	418.5	2.9	1,499	2.2
Peas	338	0.6	172.7	1.2	510.7	0.7
Eddoes	187	0.3	132.5	0.9	319.5	0.5
Arrowroot	39.5	0.1	137	0.9	176.5	0.3
Bonavist	0	0.0	48.5	0.3	48.5	0.1
"Other Grains"	28	0.1	20	0.1	48	0.1
Livestock Labors	7,741	14.4	450.5	3.1	8,191.5	12.0
Molding, Razeing, and Cutting Around Pens	5,407	10.1	0	0.0	5,407	7.9
Gathering Food and Feeding Stock	0	0.0	106.5	0.7	106.5	0.2
Minding Stock	1,628	3.0	340	2.3	1,968	2.9
At the Horse Stable	344	0.6	0	0.0	344	0.5
Other	362	0.7	4	0.0	366	0.5

Source: Newton Work Logs, 1796–1798, MS 523, 110, 123, Newton Family Papers

TABLE A15. *Labor Activities of First Two Gangs at Newton, 1796–1798, Part 2*

	1		2		Total	
	Work Days	%	Work Days	%	Work Days	%
Soil Management	5,470	10.2	1,411	9.7	6,881	10.1
Spreading, Turning, Throwing, Carrying Dung	5,438	10.1	1,102.5	7.6	6,540.5	9.6
Digging and Bringing Home Marl and Sand	9	0.0	176	1.2	185	0.3
"Pecking" and Clearing Rocks	23	0.0	38	0.3	61	0.1
Loading Carts with Marl and Rocks	0	0.0	60.5	0.4	60.5	0.1
Other	0	0.0	34	0.2	34	0.0
General Crop Trash Work	893	1.7	1,371.5	9.4	2,264.5	3.3
Plantation Maintenance	1,260	2.3	627	4.3	1,887	2.8
Attending the Plumbers and Masons	90	0.2	476.5	3.3	566.5	0.8
Paths, Roads, and Highways	483.5	0.9	32.5	0.2	516	0.8
Fetching Bricks	231	0.4	27	0.2	258	0.4
Molding and Cleaning Ponds	220	0.4	0	0.0	220	0.3
Cleaning and Leveling the Yard	168	0.3	24	0.2	192	0.3
Painting and Repairing Buildings and Houses	42	0.1	31	0.2	73	0.1
Filling up an Old Well	66	0.1	9	0.1	75	0.1
Yard Work	0	0.0	10	0.1	10	0.0
Other	88	0.2	17	0.1	105	0.2
"Watching" (Guard Duty)	4,654	8.7	0	0.0	4,654	6.8
"With Carts" (Transport Work)	464	0.9	311	2.1	775	1.1
Nursing	460	0.9	0	0.0	460	0.7
Caring for Pregnant Slaves	227	0.4	0	0.0	227	0.3
Caring for Children	129	0.2	0	0.0	129	0.2
Caring for Sick Slaves	103	0.2	0	0.0	103	0.2
Other	1	0.0	0	0.0	1	0.0
Miscellaneous	93	0.2	104	0.7	197	0.3
Totals	53,654	100	14,529	100	68,183	100

Source: Newton Work Logs, 1796–1798, MS 523/110, 123, Newton Family Papers

TABLE A16. *Labor Activities of First Two Gangs at Seawell, 1796–1797, Part 1*

	Gangs					
	1		2		Total	
	Work Days	%	Work Days	%	Work Days	%
Cash Crops	6,418.5	39.4	3,115.5	47.3	9,534	41.7
Canes	4,124	25.3	1,266	19.2	5,390	23.6
Cane Field Preparation	119	0.7	97	1.5	216	0.9
Cane Holing Activities	1,778	10.9	40	0.6	1,818	7.9
Supplying and Planting Canes	522.5	3.2	178	2.7	700.5	3.1
Tending the Growing Canes	569.5	3.5	540	8.2	1,109.5	4.8
Harvesting Canes and Clearing Field	1,135	7.0	411	6.2	1,546	6.8
Sugar and Rum Refining	492.5	3.0	249.5	3.8	742	3.2
Milling	139	0.9	124	1.9	263	1.1
Boiling	217	1.3	97	1.5	314	1.4
Distilling	136.5	0.8	28.5	0.4	165	0.7
Curing	0	0.0	0	0.0	0	0.0
Cotton	1,802	11.1	1,600	24.3	3,402	14.9
Provision Crops	4,711.5	28.9	2,232	33.9	6,943.5	30.3
Guinea Corn (Millet)	1,981	12.2	540	8.2	2,521	11.0
Indian Corn (Maize)	1,296.5	8.0	458	7.0	1,754.5	7.7
Corn (Unspecified)	357	2.2	235	3.6	592	2.6
Potatoes	425	2.6	322	4.9	747	3.3
Yams	452	2.8	271	4.1	723	3.2
Eddoes	144	0.9	96	1.5	240	1.0
Peas	44	0.3	113	1.7	157	0.7
"Other Grains"	0	0.0	0	0.0	0	0.0
Bonavist	0	0.0	153	2.3	153	0.7
Arrowroot	12	0.1	44	0.7	56	0.2
Livestock Labors	1,693.5	10.4	112.5	1.7	1,806	7.9
Molding Pens	1,243	7.6	0	0.0	1,243	5.4
Gathering Food and Feeding Stock	0	0.0	62	0.9	62	0.3
Minding Stock	368.5	2.3	50.5	0.8	419	1.8
Other	82	0.5	0	0.0	82	0.4

Source: Seawell Work Log, 1796–1797, MS 523/111, Newton Family Papers

TABLE A17. *Labor Activities of First Two Gangs at Seawell, 1796–1797, Part 2*

	Gangs					
	1		2		Total	
	Work Days	%	Work Days	%	Work Days	%
Soil Management	1,211	7.4	434	6.6	1,645	7.2
Spreading, Turning, Throwing, Carrying Dung	1,150	7.1	214	3.2	1,364	6.0
"Pecking" and Clearing Rocks	20	0.1	0	0.0	20	0.1
Bringing Home Marl and Sand	41	0.3	179	2.7	220	1.0
Other	0	0.0	0	0.0	0	0.0
General Trash Work	229	1.4	258	3.9	487	2.1
Plantation Maintenance	214	1.3	79	1.2	293	1.3
Paths, Roads, and Highways	48	0.3	14	0.2	62	0.3
Molding and Cleaning Ponds	97	0.6	0	0.0	97	0.4
Painting and Repairing Buildings and Houses	9	0.1	47	0.7	56	0.2
Yard Work	0	0.0	18	0.3	18	0.1
Other	60	0.4	0	0.0	60	0.3
"Watching" (Guard Duty)	1,594.5	9.8	0	0.0	1,594.5	7.0
"With Carts" (Transport Work)	21	0.1	130	2.0	151	0.7
Nursing	101	0.6	0	0.0	101	0.4
Caring for Sick Slaves	28	0.2	0	0.0	28	0.1
Caring for Pregnant Slaves	57	0.3	0	0.0	57	0.2
Other	16	0.1	0	0.0	16	0.1
Lime Kiln	0	0.0	118	1.8	118	0.5
Miscellaneous	104	0.6	106	1.6	210	0.9
Totals	16,298	100	6,585	100	22,883	100

Source: Seawell Work Log, 1796–1797, MS 523/111, Newton Family Papers

TABLE A18. *Frequency Distribution of Sick Days for Newton Field Workers, 1796–1797*

Sick Days	Number of First-Gang Slaves
0–9	32
10–19	22
20–29	9
30–39	8
40–49	7
50–59	5
60–69	1
70–79	1
80–89	2
90–99	2
100+	1

Ninety individuals who were recorded as sick with the first gang in 1796–1797 can be identified by using the July 1796 list of slaves. However, the gang ranged in size from eighty-nine to ninety-two slaves, so at least two others were drawn from the plantation population to work in the gang at certain points in the year. Some of the slaves who worked in the first gang also worked in the second gang. The totals for these slaves include days spent sick with either gang.
Sources: Newton Work Log, 1796–1797 and "Report on the [Newton] Negroes," MS 523/110, 288, Newton Family Papers

TABLE A19. *Frequency Distribution of Sick Days for Mount Vernon Field Hands, 1797*

Sick Days	Number of Slaves
0–9	36
10–19	20
20–29	13
30–39	10
40–49	3
50–59	3
60–69	1
70–79	1
80–89	1
90–99	1
100+	0

Sources: Mount Vernon Farm Reports, 1797–1798; Mount Vernon Slave List, 1786; Mount Vernon Inventory, 1799; various George Washington papers

TABLE A20. *Labor Activities of Ditchers at Mount Vernon in 1797*

Task	Work Days	%
Field Work and Common Labor	**475.5**	**42.0**
Curing, Cutting, Tending, Making, and Stacking Hay	225.5	19.9
Cutting Wood	130	11.5
Cutting Ice	32	2.8
Cutting and Shocking Wheat	28	2.5
Cutting and Tending Grass	16	1.4
Cleaning and Weeding Cotton	14	1.2
Planting, Cleaning, and Picking Potatoes	12.5	1.1
Other	17.5	1.5
Working at the Mill and Distillery	**167**	**14.8**
Fencing	**127.5**	**11.3**
Ditching	**99.5**	**8.8**
Fishing	**84**	**7.4**
Working at the Brick Yard	**45**	**4.0**
Mending Roads	**40**	**3.5**
Planting Hedges and Trees	**36**	**3.2**
Miscellaneous	**19.5**	**1.7**
Working Outside Mount Vernon	**14**	**1.2**
Livestock	**9**	**0.8**
Loading and Unloading Corn and Flour	**8**	**0.7**
Setting a Lime Kiln	**7**	**0.6**
Total	**1,132**	**100**

Source: Mount Vernon Farm Reports, 1797

TABLE A21. *Labor Activities of Spinners and Knitters at Mount Vernon, 1797*

Task	Total for Group		Alse	
	Work Days	%	Work Days	%
Spinning	2,144	56.0	140	47.5
Knitting	784	20.5	0	0
Working in the House	411	10.7	58	19.7
Sewing	207	5.4	95	32.2
Winding and Reeling	100	2.6	0	0
Unspecified	87	2.3	0	0
Doing "Nothing" or "Had No Yarn"	50	1.3	0	0
Washing	40	1.0	0	0
Nursing	2	0.1	2	0.7
Cutting Shirts	1	0	0	0
Total	3,826	100	295	100

Source: Mount Vernon Farm Reports, 1797

TABLE A22. *Combined Work Days of Craftsmen at Newton and Seawell, 1796–1798*

Task	Masons Work Days	%	Coopers Work Days	%	Carpenter Work Days	%
Skilled Labors and Craft Work						
Sugar and Rum Processing	76	4.1	685.5	30.5	1	0.3
Making and Filling Hogsheads, Casks, and Pots	14	0.8	604.5	26.9	1	0.3
Other	62	3.4	81	3.6	0	0.0
Building and Repairing Plantation Works	236	12.9	204	9.1	62	20.7
Constructing Tents and Houses	252	13.8	218	9.7	16	5.3
Whitewashing and Painting Buildings	121	6.6	25	1.1	0	0.0
Maintaining and Repairing the Well	9	0.5	30	1.3	9	3.0
Making and Mending Miscellaneous Items	261	14.1	279.5	12.4	28	9.3
Fences, Walls, and Railings	220	11.9	123	5.5	15	5.0
Pails and Other Containers	0	0.0	38	1.7	2	0.7
Tables and Chairs	0	0.0	65	2.9	6	2.0
Coffins	0	0.0	5	0.2	5	1.7
Other	41	2.2	48.5	2.2	0	0.0
Total Skilled and Craft Labors	955	52.6	1,442	64.1	116	38.7
Field Work and Common Labor						
Ginning and Packing Cotton	29	1.5	11	0.5	0	0.0
Field Labor	178	9.7	327	14.5	56	18.7
Pecking Rocks	73	4.0	96	4.3	9	3.0
Cutting Down Trees and Bushes	31	1.7	120	5.3	20	6.7
Cutting Canes	17	0.9	32	1.4	5	1.7
Other	57	3.1	79	3.5	22	7.3
Weighing and Storing Corn	8	0.4	20	0.9	0	0.0
Livestock Labors	133	7.3	185	8.2	36	12.0
Molding Pens	77	4.2	104.5	4.6	12	4.0
Other	56	3.1	79.5	3.5	24	8.0
Lime Kiln	35	1.9	33	1.5	17	5.7
Cutting Up Fuel to Burn Lime	27	1.5	27	1.9	14	4.7
Other	8	0.4	6	0.4	3	1.0
Total Field and Common Work	383	20.9	576	25.6	109	36.3

TABLE A22. (cont.)

Task	Masons Work Days	%	Coopers Work Days	%	Carpenter Work Days	%
Working Outside the Plantation						
Sent Out or Sent on Errands	43	2.4	65	2.9	13	4.3
Hired Out	389	21.2	95	4.2	55	18.3
Total Work Outside the Plantation	212	16.8	62	4.4	68	22.7
Miscellaneous						
Working at the Dwelling House	27	1.5	25	1.1	0	0.0
At Home	9	0.5	34	1.5	0	0.0
Other	26	1.4	13	0.6	7	2.3
Total Miscellaneous	62	3.4	72	3.2	7	2.3
Total Annual Labor	1,832	100	2,250	100	300	100

Source: Newton Work Logs, 1796–1798; Seawell Work Log, 1796–1797, MS 523/110, 111, 123, Newton Family Papers

TABLE A23. *Carpenter Activities at Mount Vernon in 1797*

Task	Work Days	%
Craft Work		
Building and Repairing Estate Buildings and Works	739	39.2
Barns	312	16.7
Distillery	268	14.2
Mill and Mill Race	62.5	3.2
Mansion House	27.5	1.5
Fish House	23	1.2
Other	46	2.4
Making and Mending Carts, Plows, and Other Tools	564.5	29.9
Wheat Machines	235	12.5
Carts and Cart Wheels	169	9.0
Plows	102.5	5.4
Field Tools and Carpentry Tools	47	2.5
Other	11	0.6
Other Craft Work	125.5	6.7
Making Shingles	88	4.7
Working in the Shop	30	1.6
Joining Planks	14.5	0.8
Making Fences	42	2.2
Working in the Cooper Shop	32	1.7

TABLE A23. *(cont.)*

Task	Work Days	%
Making and Mending Miscellaneous Small Items	22.5	1.2
Making Coffins	10	0.5
Others	12.5	0.7
Repairing and Building Boats	22.5	1.2
Fixing or Building Hay Ricks and Floors	15	0.8
Total Craft Work	1563	82.9
Field Work and Common Labor		
Hauling and Sawing Wood	151	8.0
Field Work	83	4.4
Livestock Work	7	0.4
Total Field Work and Common Labor	241	12.8
Working Outside of the Estate		
In Town/Traveling on Errands	32	1.7
Total Working Outside of the Estate	32	1.7
Miscellaneous		
Domestic Work	14	0.7
Fishing	7	0.4
Working as a Wagoner	6	0.3
Other	22	1.2
Total Miscellaneous	49	2.6
Total Annual Labor	1,885	100

Source: Mount Vernon Farm Reports, 1797

TABLE A24. *Labor Activities of Coopers at Mount Vernon in 1797*

Task	Work Days	%
Craft Work		
Coopering	434	69.1
Making and Trimming Barrels, Casks, Hogsheads, Tubs, and Pails	384.5	61.2
Working in the Coopers Shop on Various Tasks	50.5	8.0
Cutting Hoop Poles	42	6.7
Making Flour Bands	22	3.5
Working on the Mill and the Mill Race	18	2.9
Working in the Distillery (Small Jobs)	16	2.5
Making Items for the Dairy	12	1.9
Other Craft Work	21.5	3.4
Total Craft Work	565.5	90.0

TABLE A24. (cont.)

Task	Work Days	%
Field Work and Common Labor		
Working in the Harvest Field	30	4.8
Other Field Work	26	4.1
Cutting Trees and Piling Wood	4	0.6
Making a Half Bushel for Muddy Hole	1	0.2
Cutting Ice	0.5	0.1
Total Field Work and Common Labor	61.5	9.8
Miscellaneous		
Domestic Work	1	0.2
Total Miscellaneous Work	1	0.2
Total Annual Labor	628	100

Source: Mount Vernon Farm Reports, 1797

TABLE A25. *Labor Activities of Masons (Brick Layers) at Mount Vernon, 1797*

Task	Work Days	%
Craft Work		
Constructing and Maintaining Estate Buildings and Works	64	11.5
Barns and Shades	25	4.5
Distillery	15	2.7
Brick Wall	12	2.1
Other	12	2.1
Brickmaking	182.5	32.7
Preparing and Cleaning a Brick Yard	9	1.6
Preparing and Burning a Brick Kiln	41	7.3
Digging Brick Dust, Earth, and Clay	55.5	9.9
Making Bricks	77	13.8
Other Craft Work	13	2.3
Dressing Shingles	6	1.1
Rounding Fellows	4	0.7
Working in the Shop	2	0.4
Dressing Stone for Cheese Press	1	0.2
Total Craft Work	259.5	46.5
Field Work and Common Labor		
Carrying Stones to the Mill and the Distillery	90	16.1
Field Work	65	11.6
Cutting Ice and Filling the Ice House	8	1.4

TABLE A25. (cont.)

Task	Work Days	%
Gathering Timber	4	0.7
Butchering Hogs	4	0.7
Total Field Work and Common Labor	171	30.6
Working Outside of the Estate		
In Town/Traveling on Errands	22	3.9
Total Work Outside of Estate	22	3.9
Miscellaneous		
Fishing	61.5	11.0
Mending Fishing Seines	36.5	6.5
Other	8	1.4
Total Miscellaneous Labor	106	19.0
Total Annual Labor	558.5	100

Source: Mount Vernon Farm Reports, 1797

TABLE A26. *Duration of Absences at Newton and Seawell, 1796–1798*

Consecutive Work Days Missed	Absences
1	37
2	10
3	6
4	1
5	2
6	0
7	0
8	0
9	1
Total	57

Absences of longer than one day in which the slave went unnamed on one day but named on the others were assumed to be for the same slave. Absences of one day in duration were included whether the slave was named or not.

Sources: Newton Work Logs, 1796–1798; Seawell Work Log, 1796–1797; Seawell Work Log, 1798, MS 523/110, 111, 122, 123, Newton Family Papers

TABLE A27. *Number of Slaves Away during Each Absence at Newton and Seawell, 1796–1798*

Number of Slaves Absent	Absences
1	34
2	10
3	1
4	0
5	0
6	1
Total	46

The only absences included are those in which the names of slaves are given or in which it is clear how many slaves were absent together. Absences in which more than one slave was absent were counted as a single event.

Sources: Newton Work Logs, 1796–1798; Seawell Work Log, 1796–1797; Seawell Work Log, 1798, MS 523/110, 111, 122, 123, Newton Family Papers

Bibliography

Primary Sources

Manuscripts

Barclays Group Archive, Manchester
  Records of the Jamaican Prospect Estate
Barbados Department of Archives
  Fitzherbert Papers
  Drax Hall Plantation Records
Shilstone Library, Barbados Museum and Historical Society
  Hannays Plantation Accounts
British Library
  Lowther Estate Records, Papers of the Duke of Cleveland
  Martin Papers
Cambridge University Library
  Vanneck-Arcedeckne Papers
Earl Greg Swem Library, College of William and Mary
  Jerdone Family Papers
Historical Society of Pennsylvania
  Powell Family Papers
Huntington Library
  Stowe Papers
Institute for Commonwealth Studies
  J. F. Alleyne Letterbook
  Taylor Family Papers
John Carter Brown Library
  An Account of Duckensfield Hall Estate Negroes
  Dovaston, John, "Agricultura Americana or Improvements in West India Husbandry Considered Wherein the Present System of Husbandry used in England is Applied to the Cultivation or Growing of Sugar Canes to Advantage...wrote in the year 1774."

    Somerset Vale Work Logs and Slave Lists
    William Dickson's Personal Copy of *Mitigation of Slavery* and Notes
    Bryan Edwards "Notes on Long's History of Jamaica"
Library of Congress
    Skipwith Family Papers
    Mount Vernon Weekly Farm Reports
Lincoln County Record Office
    Thomas Thistlewood Papers
Mount Vernon Ladies' Association Archives
    George Washington's Correspondence with Managers
    Mount Vernon Weekly Farm Reports
National Archives
    "Journal of Twenty Years Spent in the West Indies, from 1768," Pottinger Papers
National Library of Wales
    Jamaican Materials in the Slebech Papers
Somerset Record Office
    Heylar Manuscripts
United Society for the Propagation of the Gospel Archives
    Codrington Papers, C Series
University of Exeter Library
    The Gale-Morant Papers
University of Miami Libraries
    Typescript of Charles Ruddach Letters, Jamaica Manuscripts collection, 1774–1950
Senate House Library, University of London Archives
    Newton Family Papers
Virginia Historical Society
    Cabell, William commonplace books for 1769–1795
    Cabell, William commonplace books for 1791–1822
    Custis Family Papers
    Fleet, William letter, 1798
    Hite, Isaac commonplace book for 1776–1859
    Keane, Michael Letterbook 1787–1790
    Lee Family Papers
    Martha Randolph Jefferson, 1826 Letter
    Mason Family papers
    Mercer Family papers
    Mount Airy Work Log
Wilberforce House Museum
    Various Jamaican Plantation Accounts, 1779

Printed Material

Abbot, W. W. et al., eds., *The Papers of George Washington*, 57 vols. Charlottesville: University of Virginia Press, 1976.

"African Institution," *Edinburgh Review or the Critical Journal*, 2nd ed., vol. 15 (October 1809–January 1810): 485–503.
Art of Making Sugar, The. London, 1752.
Baker, I. P. *An Essay on the Art of Making Muscovado Sugar Wherein a New Process is Proposed*. Kingston, Jamaica: Joseph Weatherby, 1775.
Barclay, Alexander. *A Practical View of the Present State of Slavery in the West Indies*. London: Smith, Elder & Company, 1827.
Barclay, David. *An Account of the Emancipation of the Slaves of Unity Valley Pen in Jamaica*. London: W. Phillips, 1801.
Beckford, William. *A Descriptive Account of the Island of Jamaica: With Remarks Upon the Cultivation of the Sugar-Cane*, 2 vols. London: T & J, Egerton, 1790.
 Remarks upon the Situation of Negroes in Jamaica. London: T & J Egerton, 1788.
Belgrove, William. *A Treatise upon Husbandry or Planting*. Boston: D. Fowle, 1755.
Binns, John Alexander. *A Treatise on Practical Farming: embracing particularly the following subjects, viz.: the use of plaister of Paris, with directions for using it and general observations on the use of other manures: on deep ploughing, thick sowing of grain, method of preventing fruit trees from decaying, and farming in general*. Frederick-town, Maryland: Printed by John B. Colvin, 1803.
Blake, Sir Patrick. "Culture of Sugar in the West Indies," in Arthur Young, ed., *Annals of Agriculture* 31 (London, 1798): 360–370.
Bordley, J. B. *Husbandry and Rural Affairs*. Philadelphia: Budd and Bartram, 1799.
Bowring, John, ed. *The Works of Jeremy Bentham*, vol. X. New York: Russell & Russell, 1962.
Boyle, Robert, "Essay Containing a Requisite Digression Concerning Those that Would Exclude the Deity From Intermeddling with Matter," in M. A. Stewart, ed., *Selected Philosophical Papers of Robert Boyle*. Indianapolis: Indiana University Press, 1991.
Campbell, Tony. *The Printed Maps of Barbados: From the Earliest Times to 1873*. London: Map Collector's Circle, 1965.
Caines, Clement. *Letters on the Cultivation of the Otaheite cane: the manufacture of sugar and rum; the saving of melasses; the care and preservation of stock; with the attention and anxiety which is due to Negroes: To these topics are added, a few other particulars analogous to the subject of the letters; and also a speech on the slave trade, the most important feature in West Indian cultivation*. London: Messrs. Robinson, 1801.
Carman, Harry J. *American Husbandry*. New York: Columbia University Press, 1939 [1775].
Clark, William. *Ten Views in the Island of Antigua*. London: T. Clay, 1823.
Collins, David. *Practical Rules for the Management and Medical Treatment of Negro Slaves in the Sugar Colonies*. London: J. Barfield, 1803.
Craton, Michael, James Walvin, and David Wright, eds. *Slavery, Abolition and Emancipation: Black Slaves and the British Empire*. London: Longman, 1976.
Cully, George. *An Essay on the Breeding of Stock: viz Horses, Black Cattle, Sheep, and Swine*. Kingston, Jamaica: His Majesty's Printing Office, 1796.

"The Cultivation and Manufacture of Sugar in America," *The London Magazine: The Gentleman's Monthly Intelligencer* 38 (June 1769): 319–320.

Cresswell, Nicholas. *The Journal of Nicholas Cresswell, 1774–1777.* New York: L. MacVeagh, the Dial Press, 1924.

Dallas, Robert Charles. *A Short Journey in the West Indies: in which are Interspersed, Curious Anecdotes and Characters*, 2 vols. London: J. Murray, Fleet-Street, and J. Forbes, Covent-Garden, 1790.

Dancer, Thomas. *The Medical assistant; or Jamaica Practice of Physic: Designed Chiefly for the use of Families and Plantations.* Kingston, Jamaica: Alexander Aikman, 1801.

De La Beche, H. T. *Notes on the Present Condition of the Negroes in Jamaica.* London: T. Cadell in the Strand, 1825.

Dickson, William. *Letters on Slavery: To which are added, addresses to the whites, and to the free Negroes of Barbadoes; and accounts of some Negroes eminent for their virtues and abilities.* Westport: Negro Universities Press, 1970 [1789].

    Mitigation of Slavery, In Two Parts. Miami, FL: Mnemosyne Publishers, 1969 [1814].

Edwards, Bryan. *The History Civil and Commercial of the British Colonies in the West Indies*, 2 vols. Dublin: Luke White, 1793.

Fitzpatrick, John Clement, ed. *The Writings of George Washington: From the Original Manuscript Sources, 1745–1799*, 39 vols. Washington, DC: Government Printing Office, 1931.

Franklin, Benjamin. *The Interest of Great Britain Considered with Regard to Her Colonies And the Acquisitions of Canada and Guadeloupe.* Reprinted. London: B. Mecom, 1760.

Frere, George. *A Short History of Barbados from its First Discovery and Settlement to the Present Time.* London: J. Dodsley, 1768.

Gibbes, Philip. *Instructions for the Treatment of Negroes, etc., etc., etc.* London: Shepperson and Reynold's, 1786.

    Instructions for the Treatment of Negroes, etc., etc., etc., 2nd edition with additions. London: Shepperson and Reynold's, 1788.

    Instructions for the Treatment of Negroes, etc., etc., etc. Reprinted with additions. London: Shepperson and Reynold's, 1797.

Grainger, James. "Sugar-Cane: A Poem, In Four Books [1764]," in Thomas W. Krise, ed., *Caribbeana: An Anthology of English Literature of the West Indies.* Chicago: The University of Chicago Press, 1999: 166–261.

    On the Treatment and Management of the More Common West- India Diseases (1750–1802). J. Edward Hutson, ed., Kingston, Jamaica: University of the West Indies Press, 2005.

Greene, Jack P., ed. *The Diary of Landon Carter of Sabine Hall, 1752–1778*, 2 vols. Charlottesville: University Press of Virginia, 1965.

Hilary, William. *Observations on the Changes of the Air and the Concomitant Epidemical Diseases, In the Island of Barbadoes.* London: L. Hawes, W. Clarke, and R. Collins, 1759.

Hughes, Griffith. *The Natural History of Barbados.* New York: Arno Press, 1972 [1750].

Kein, Patrick. *An Essay upon Pen-Keeping and Plantership.* Kingston, Jamaica: His Majesty's Printing Office, 1796.
Kerr, Thomas. *A Practical Treatise on the Cultivation of the Sugar Cane and the Manufacture of Sugar.* London: JJ Griffin & Co., 1851.
"Landon Carter's Crop Book, Letters to Washington, October 27, 1796," *William and Mary Quarterly,* 1st ser., 21 (1912): 11–21.
Lascelles, Edwin, et al. *Instructions for the Management of a Plantation in Barbadoes. And for the Treatment of Negroes, etc., etc., etc.* London: [s.n.], 1786.
Lewis, Matthew. *Journal of a West India Proprietor: Kept During a Residence in the Island of Jamaica.* London, J. Murray, 1834.
Locke, John. "Essay on the Poor Law," in Mark Goldie, ed., *Locke: Political Essays.* Cambridge Texts in the History of Political Thought. New York: Cambridge University Press, 1997.
Long, Edward. *The History of Jamaica,* 3 vols. Montreal: McGill-Queen's University Press, 2003 [1774].
Mair, John. *Book-Keeping Methodiz'd: or, a Methodical Treatise of Merchant-Accompts, According to the Italian form,* 2nd ed. Edinburgh: Sands, Brymer, Murray and Cochran, 1741.
 Book-Keeping Methodiz'd: or, a Methodical Treatise of Merchant-Accompts, According to the Italian form, 5th ed. Edinburgh: Sands, Brymer, Murray and Cochran, 1757.
 Book-Keeping Methodiz'd or a Methodical Treatise of Merchant-Acompts, according to the Italian form, 7th ed. Edinburgh: Sands, Donaldson, Murray, and Cochran, 1763.
Marsden, Peter. *An Account of the Island of Jamaica.* Newcastle: S. Hodgson, 1788.
Martin, Samuel. *An Essay upon Plantership,* 2nd ed. London: T. Smith, 1750.
 An Essay upon Plantership, 4th ed. London: Samuel Chapman, 1765.
 A Short Treatise on the Slavery of Negroes in the British Colonies. Antigua: Robert Mearns, 1775.
Mathison, Gilbert Farquhar. *Notices Respecting Jamaica in 1808, 1809, 1810.* London: J. Stockdale, 1811.
Minutes of the Society for the Improvement of Plantership in the Island of Barbados. Liverpool: Thomas Kaye, 1811.
Moreton, J. B. *West India Customs and Manners: Strictures on the Soil, Cultivation, Produce, Trade, Officers and Inhabitants with the Method of Establishing and Conducting a Sugar Plantation to which is Added the Practice of Training New Slaves,* rev. ed. London: J. Parsons, W. Richardson, H. Gardner, and J. Walter, 1793.
Moseley, Benjamin. *A Treatise on Tropical Diseases and the Climate of the West Indies.* London: T. Cadell, 1787.
 A Treatise on Sugar. London: G. G. & J. Robinson, 1799.
 A Treatise on Sugar: With Miscellaneous Medical Observations, 2nd ed. London: John Nichols, 1800.
"Natural History of the Sugar Cane from a Paper to the Royal Society." *Gentleman's Magazine,* December 1799.

Northup, Solomon. *Twelve Years a Slave*. Baton Rouge: Louisiana State University Press, 1968 [1855].
"Oxen in Barbadoes," *Annals of Agriculture*, 32 (1799).
Poyer, John. *The History of Barbadoes...Till...1801*. London: Frank Cass, 1808.
Pinckard, George. *Notes on the West Indies*. London: Longman, Hurst, Rees, and Orme, 1806.
Ramsay, James. *An Essay on the Treatment and Conversion of African Slaves in the British Sugar Colonies*. Dublin: T. Walker, C. Jenkin, R. Marchbank, L. White, R. Burton, P. Byrne, 1784.
Remarks on the evidence delivered on the petition presented by the West-India Planters and Merchants, to the Hon. the House of Commons. London: J. Bew, 1777.
"Review of American Husbandry," *The Monthly Review*, LIV. [London, 1776], Art. VII. in Carmen, ed. *American Husbandry*. New York: Columbia University Press, 1939: xvi–xxx.
"Review of Letters to a Young Planter," in *The Monthly Review or Literary Journal* 74 (January–June 1786): 65.
Robson, Nicholas. *Hints for a General View of the Agricultural State of St. James in the Island of Jamaica*. London: John Stockdale, 1796.
Roughley, Thomas. *The Jamaica Planters' Guide; or, a System for Planting and Managing a Sugar Estate or Other Plantation in that Island and throughout the British West Indies in General*. London: Longman, Hurst, Rees, Orme, & Brown, 1823.
Sheridan, R. B., ed. "Letters from a Sugar Plantation in Antigua, 1739–1758," *Agricultural History*, 31 (July, 1957): 3–23.
Smith, Adam. *An Inquiry Into the Nature and Causes of the Wealth of Nations*. New York: The Modern Library, 1937 [1776].
Stewart, John. *An Account of Jamaica and Its Inhabitants*. London: Longman, Hurst, Rees and Orme, 1808.
Strickland, William. *Observations on the Agriculture of the United States of America*. London: W. Bulwer and Co., 1801.
Taylor, Clare, ed. *West Indian Planter Attitudes to the American and French Revolution*. Aberystwyth: University College of Wales, Department of History, 1978.
Thomson, James. *A Treatise on the Diseases of Negroes, As they Occur in the Island of Jamaica: With Observations on the Country Remedies*. Jamaica: Alex. Aikman, 1820.
Three Original Practical Treatises on the Cultivation and Manufacture of Coffee, Cotton, and Indigo. Kingston, Jamaica: [s.n.], 1787.
Tull, Jethro. *The Horse-Hoeing Husbandry*. Dublin: A. Rhames, 1733.
Turnbull, Gordon. *Letters to a Young Planter; Or Observations on the Management of a Sugar Plantation*. London: Stuart and Stevenson, 1785.
Vibæk, Jens. "Dansk Vestindien 1755–1848," in Johannes Brøndsted, ed., *Vore Gamle Tropekolonier*, 2nd ed., vol. 2. Copenhagen: Fremad, 1966–1968 [1952–1953]: 110–111.
"West Indian Agriculture," *Annals of Agriculture* 9 (1788).

Weston, William. *The Complete Merchant's clerk: or, British and American Compting-House.* London: Charles Rivington, 1754.
Williamson, John. *Medical and Miscellaneous Observations, Relative to the West India Islands.* Edinburgh: Smellie, 1817.
Wright, Philip, ed. *Lady Nugent's Journal of her Residence in Jamaica from 1801–1805.* Kingston, Jamaica: University of the West Indies Press, 2002.
Young, Arthur. *A Course of Experimental Agriculture.* London: J. Dodsley, 1770.
  Political Essays Concerning the Present State of the British Empire. London: Strahan and T. Cadell in the Strand, 1772.

Secondary Sources

Anderson, Virginia DeJohn. *Creatures of Empire: How Domestic Animals Transformed Early America.* New York: Oxford University Press, 2004.
Anstey, Roger. *The Atlantic Slave Trade and British Abolition, 1760–1810.* Atlantic Highlands, NJ: Humanities Press, 1975.
Armstrong, Douglas V., et al. *The Old Village and the Great House: An Archaeological and Historical Examination of Drax Hall Plantation, St. Ann's Bay, Jamaica.* Urbana: University of Illinois Press, 1990.
Ashton, T. S. *The Economic History of England: The Eighteenth Century.* Reprinted. New York: Routledge, 2006 [1955].
Ashworth, John. "The Relationship between Capitalism and Humanitarianism," *American Historical Review* 92.4 (1987): 813–828.
Aufhauser, R. Keith. "Slavery and Technological Change," *The Journal of Economic History*, 34.1 (1974): 36–50.
  "Slavery and Scientific Management," *Journal of Economic History* 33 (1973): 811–824.
Beckles, Hilary. "Creolisation in Action: The Slave Labour Elite and Anti-Slavery in Barbados," *Caribbean Quarterly* 44.1-2 (1998): 108–128.
  "Crop Fetes and Festivals in Caribbean Slavery," in Alvin O. Thompson, ed. *In The Shadow of the Plantation: Caribbean, History and Legacy.* Kingston, Jamaica: Ian Randle Publishers, 2002: 246–265.
Beier, A. L. "'A New Serfdom:' Labor Laws, Vagrancy Statutes and Labor Discipline in England, 1350–1800," in A. L. Beier and Paul Ocobock, eds., *Cast Out: Vagrancy and Homelessness in Global and Historical Perspective.* Athens: Ohio University Press, 2008: 35–64.
Bennett, J. Harry. *Bondsmen and Bishops: Slavery and Apprenticeship on the Codrington Plantations of Barbados, 1710–1838.* Berkeley: University of California Press, 1958.
  "Cary Heylar, Merchant and Planter of Seventeenth Century Jamaica," *William and Mary Quarterly*, 3rd ser. 21.1 (January 1964): 53–76.
Berg, Maxine. "Women's Work, Mechanisation and the Early Phases of Industrialisation in England," in Patrick Joyce, ed., *The Historical Meanings of Work.* New York: Cambridge University Press, 1987: 64–98.
Berlin, Ira. *Many Thousands Gone: The First Two Centuries of Slavery in North America.* Cambridge: Belknap Press of Harvard University Press, 1998.

Berlin, Ira, and Philip D. Morgan, eds., *Cultivation and Culture: Labor and the Shaping of Slave Life in the Americas*. Charlottesville: University of Virginia Press, 1993.

Bezis-Selfa, John. "A Tale of Two Ironworks: Slavery, Free Labor, Work and Resistance in the Early Republic," *William and Mary Quarterly* 56.4 (1999): 677–700.

Blackburn, Robin. *The Overthrow of Colonial Slavery, 1776–1848*. London: Verso, 1988.

Blassingame, John. *The Slave Community: Plantation Life in the Antebellum South*. New York: Oxford University Press, 1979.

Blight, David W. "The World the Slave Traders Made: Is There a Postrevisionism in Slavery Historiography?" *Reviews in American History* 19.1 (1991): 37–42.

Boomard, Peter, and Gert J. Oostindie, "Changing Sugar Technology and the Labour Nexus: The Caribbean, 1750–1900," *New West-Indian Guide* 63.1–2 (1989): 3–22.

Breen, T. H. *Tobacco Culture: The Mentality of the Great Tidewater Planters on the Eve of Revolution*. Princeton, NJ: Princeton University Press, 2001.

Bridenbaugh, Carl. *The Colonial Craftsmen*. New York: New York University Press, 1950.

Brown, Christopher L. *Moral Capital: Foundations of British Abolitionism*. Chapel Hill: University of North Carolina Press, 2006.

Burnard, Trevor. *Mastery, Tyranny and Desire: Thomas Thistlewood and his Slaves in the Anglo-Jamaican World*. Chapel Hill: University of North Carolina Press, 2004.

  "Et in Arcadia Ego: West Indian Planters in Glory, 674–1784," *Atlantic Studies* 9.1 (March 2012): 19–40.

Burstin, Haim. "Unskilled Labour in Paris at the End of the Eighteenth Century," in Thomas Max Safley and Leonard N. Rosenband, eds., *The Workplace Before the Factory: Artisans and Proletariats, 1500–1800*. Ithaca: Cornell University Press, 1993: 63–72.

Candow, James E. "A Reassessment of the Provision of Food to Enslaved Persons, with Special Reference to Salted Cod in Barbados," *Journal of Caribbean History* 43.2 (December 2009): 265–281.

Carrington, Selwyn. *The Sugar Industry and the Abolition of the Slave Trade, 1775–1810*. Gainesville: The University Press of Florida, 2002.

Cateau, Heather. "The New 'Negro' Business: Hiring in the British West Indies, 1750–1810," in Alvin O. Thompson, ed., *In the Shadow of the Plantation: Caribbean History & Legacy*. (Kingston, Jamaica: University of the West Indies Press, 2002): 100–120.

  "'A Question of Labor': British West Indian Plantations, 1750–1810," *Plantation Society in the Americas* 6.1 (1999): 65–94.

  "Conservatism and Change Implementation in the British West Indian Sugar Industry 1750–1810," *Journal of Caribbean History* 29.2 (1995): 1–36.

Christopher, Emma. *Slave Ship Sailors and Their Captive Cargoes, 1730–1807*. New York: Cambridge University Press, 2007.

Clark, Gregory. "Factory Discipline," *The Journal of Economic History* 54.1 (March, 1994): 128–163

Coclanis, Peter A. "Bookkeeping in the Eighteenth-Century South: Evidence from Newspaper Advertisements," *South Carolina Historical Magazine* 91.1 (1990): 21–33.
"The Captivity of a Generation," *William and Mary Quarterly* 61.3 (July 2004): 544–555.
Cohen, Patricia. *A Calculating People: The Spread of Numeracy in Early America*. Chicago: The University of Chicago Press, 1982.
Coelho, Philip R. P., and Robert A. McGuire, "An Exploratory Essay on the Impact of Diseases upon the Interpretation of American Slavery," in John Komlos and Joerg Baten, eds., *The Biological Standard of Living in Comparative Perspective*. Stuttgart: Franz Steiner, 1998: 181–189.
Cook, Margaret G. "Divine Artifice and Natural Mechanism: Robert Boyle's Mechanical Philosophy of Nature," *Osiris* 2nd ser. 16. Science in Theistic Contexts: Cognitive Dimensions (2001): 133–150.
Cooper, Dan, and Brian Grinder. "Probability, Gambling and the Origins of Risk Management," *Financial History* 93 (Winter 2009): 10–38.
Crader, Diana C. "Slave Diet at Monticello," *American Antiquity* 55.4 (October 1990): 690–717
Craton, Michael. *Searching for the Invisible Man: Slaves and Plantation Life in Jamaica*. Cambridge: Harvard University Press, 1978.
Sinews of Empire: A Short History of British Slavery. Garden City, NY: Anchor Press, 1974.
"Jamaican Slavery," in Stanley Engerman and Eugene Genovese, eds., *Race and Slavery in the Western Hemisphere: Quantitative Studies*. Princeton: Princeton University Press, 1975: 249–284.
"Hobbesian or Panglossian? The Two Extremes of Slave Conditions in the British Caribbean, 1783–1834." *William and Mary Quarterly* 35.2 (1978): 324–356.
Craven, Avery. *Soil Exhaustion as a Factor in the Agricultural History of Virginia and Maryland, 1608–1840* Gloucester, MA: P. Smith, 1965[1926].
Crothers, Glenn A. "Agricultural Improvement and Technological Innovation in a Slave Society: The Case of Early National Northern Virginia," *Agricultural History* 75.2 (Spring 2001), 135–161.
De Vries, Jan. "The Industrial Revolution and the Industrious Revolution," *The Journal of Economic History* 54.2 (June 1994): 249–270.
Daston, Lorraine. "Afterword: The Ethos of the Enlightenment," in Jan Golinski, William Clark, and Simon Schaffer, eds., *The Sciences in Enlightened Europe*. Chicago: University of Chicago Press, 1999: 495–504.
Davis, David Brion. *The Problem of Slavery in the Age of Revolution, 1770–1823*. New York: Oxford University Press, 1975.
Inhuman Bondage: The Rise and Fall of Slavery in the New World. New York: Oxford University Press, 2006.
Delbourgo, James. *A Most Amazing Science of Wonders: Electricity and Enlightenment in Early America*. Cambridge: Harvard University Press, 2006.
Donoghue, John. "'Out of the Land of Bondage:' The English Revolution and the Atlantic Origins of Abolition," *The American Historical Review* 115.4 (2010): 943–974.

Douglas, Robert L. "Myth or True: A White and Black View of Slavery," *Journal of Black Studies* 19.3 (1989): 343–360.
Drescher, Seymour. *Econocide: British Slavery in the Era of Abolition*. Pittsburgh: University of Pittsburgh Press, 1977.
  The Mighty Experiment: Free Labor Versus Slavery in British Emancipation. New York: Oxford University Press, 2002.
Dubois, Laurent. *Avengers of the New World: The Story of the Haitian Revolution*. Cambridge: Belknap Press of Harvard University Press, 2004.
Dunn, Richard. "Sugar Production and Slave Women in Jamaica," in I. Berlin and P. D. Morgan, eds., *Cultivation and Culture: Labor and the Shaping of Slave Life in the Americas*. Richmond: University Press of Virginia, 1993: 49–72.
  "Servants and Slaves: the Recruitment and Employment of Labor," in Jack P. Greene and J. R. Pole, eds., *Colonial British America: Essays in the New History of the Early Modern Era*. Baltimore: Johns Hopkins University Press, 1984: 157–194.
  "After Tobacco: The Slave Labour Pattern on a Large Chesapeake Grain-and-Livestock Plantation in the Early Nineteenth Century," in Kenneth Morgan and John J. McCusker, eds., *The Early Modern Atlantic Economy*. New York: Cambridge University Press, 2000: 344–363.
  "A Tale of Two Plantations: Slave Life at Mesopotamia in Jamaica and Mount Airy in Virginia," *William and Mary Quarterly* 34.1 (1977): 32–65.
  "'Dreadful Idlers' in the Cane Fields: The Slave Labor pattern on a Jamaican Sugar Estate," *Journal of Interdisciplinary History* 17.4 (1987): 795–822.
Dusinberre, William. *Them Dark Days: Slavery in the American Rice Swamps*. New York: Oxford University Press, 1996.
Earle, Carville, and Ronald Hoffman, "The Ecological Consequences of Agrarian Reform in the Chesapeake, 1730–1840," in P. D. Curtin et al., *Discovering the Chesapeake: The History of an Ecosystem*. Baltimore: Johns Hopkins University Press, 2001.
Eckenrode, H. J. "Negroes in Richmond in 1864," *Virginia Magazine of History and Biography* 46.3 (July 1938): 193–200.
Edelson, S. Max. *Plantation Enterprise in Colonial South Carolina*. Cambridge: Harvard University Press, 2006.
Elkins, Stanley. *Slavery: A Problem in American Institutional and Intellectual Life*. Chicago: University of Chicago Press, 1959.
Eltis, David. *The Rise of African Slavery in the Americas*. New York: Cambridge University Press, 2000.
Ely, Melvin Patrick. *Israel on the Appomattox: A Southern Experiment in Black Freedom from the 1790s through the Civil War*. New York: Knopf, 2004.
Engels, Freidrich. *The Condition of the Working Class in England*. New York: Oxford University Press, 1993.
Engerman, Stanley L. *Slavery, Emancipation and Freedom: Comparative Perspectives*. Baton Rouge: Louisiana State University Press, 2007.
  "France, Britain and the Economic Growth of Colonial North America," in John J. McCusker and Kenneth Morgan, eds., *The Early Modern Atlantic Economy*. New York: Cambridge University Press, 2000: 227–249.

"Slavery at Different Times and Places," *American Historical Review* 105.2 (2000): 480–484.
Evans, C. "Work and Workloads During Industrialization: The Experience of Forgemen in the British Iron Industry 1750–1850," *International Review of Social History* 44.2 (August 1999): 197–215.
Faust, Drew Gilpin. *James Henry Hammond and the Old South: A Design for Mastery*. Baton Rouge: Louisiana State University Press, 1982.
Fleischman, Richard K., and Thomas N. Tyson, "Cost Accounting during the Industrial Revolution: The Present State of Historical Knowledge," *Economic History Review* 46.3 (August 1993): 503–517.
Fogel, Robert William. *Without Consent or Contract: The Rise and Fall of American Slavery*. New York: Norton, 1989.
  The Slavery Debates: A Retrospective, 1952–1990. Baton Rouge: Louisiana State University Press, 2003.
Fogel, Robert William, and Stanley L. Engerman. *Time on the Cross: The Economics of American Negro Slavery*. Boston: Little & Brown, 1974.
  "Changing Views of Slavery in the United States South: The Role of Eugene D. Genovese," in Robert Louis Paquette and Louis A Ferleger, eds., *Slavery, Secession and Southern History*. Charlottesville: University Press of Virginia Press, 2000: 1–16.
Foucault, Michel. *Discipline and Punish: The Birth of the Prison*. New York: Vintage Books, 1995 [1977].
Frängsmyr, Tore, John L. Heilbron, and Robin E. Rider. *The Quantifying Spirit in the Eighteenth Century*. Berkeley: University of California Press, 1990.
Freudenberger, Herman, and Gaylord Cummins. "Health, Work and Leisure Before the Industrial Revolution," *Explorations in Economic History* 13.1 (1976): 1–12.
Freudenberger, Herman, Frances J. Mather, and Clark Nardinelli. "A New Look at the Early Factory Labor Force," *The Journal of Economic History* 44.4 (1984): 1085–1090.
Gallman, Robert E., and Ralph V. Anderson. "Slaves as Fixed Capital: Slave Labor and Southern Economic Development," *Journal of American History* 64. 1 (June 1977): 24–46.
Galloway, J. H. *Sugar Cane Industry: An Historical Geography from its Origins to 1914*. New York: Cambridge University Press, 1989.
Gaspar, Barry David. *Bondsmen and Rebels: A Study of Master-Slave Relations in Antigua*. Durham, NC: Duke University Press, 1993.
Genovese, Eugene D. *Roll Jordan Roll: The World the Slaves Made*. New York: Vintage Books, 1974.
Glennie, Paul, and Nigel Thrift. "Revolutions in the Times: Clocks and the Temporal Structures of Everyday Life," in David N. Livingstone and Charles W. J. Withers, eds., *Geography and Revolution*. Chicago: University of Chicago Press, 2005: 160–198.
Goddard, Richard B., ed. *George Washington's Visit to Barbados, 1751*. Wildey, St. Michael, Barbados: Cole's Printery Ltd, 1997.
Golinski, Jan. *British Weather and the Climate of Enlightenment*. Chicago: University of Chicago Press, 2007.

Goveia, E. V. *The West Indian Slave Laws of the Eighteenth Century.* Bridgetown: Caribbean Universities Press, 1970.
Gray, Lewis C. *History of Agriculture in the Southern United States to 1860.* Washington, DC: The Carnegie Institution of Washington, 1933.
Green, William A. "The Planter Class and British West Indian Sugar Production, before and after Emancipation," *Economic History Review* 26.3 (August 1973): 448–463.
Grove, Richard. *Green Imperialism: Colonial Expansion, Tropical Island Edens, and the Origins of Environmentalism, 1600–1860.* New York: Cambridge University Press, 1995.
Hafter, Daryl. *Women at Work in Preindustrial France.* University Park: Pennsylvania State University, 2007.
Hall, Douglas. "Absentee Proprietorship in the British West Indies, to about 1850," *Jamaican Historical Review* 4 (1964): 15–35.
Halttunen, Karen. "Humanitarianism and the Pornography of Pain in Anglo-American Culture," *The American Historical Review* 100.2 (April 1995): 303–334.
Handler, Jerome S. "The History of Arrowroot and the Origin of Peasantries in the British West Indies," *Journal of Caribbean History* 2 (1971): 46–93.
 "Plantation Slave Settlements in Barbados, 1650s to 1834," in Alvin O. Thompson, ed., *In the Shadow of the Plantation: Caribbean History and Legacy.* Kingston, Jamaica: Ian Randle, 2002: 121–158.
Handler, Jerome S., and Frederick W. Lange, *Plantation Slavery in Barbados: An Historical and Archaeological Investigation.* Cambridge: Harvard University Press, 1978.
Harrison, Mark. *Medicine in an Age of Commerce and Empire: Britain and Its Tropical Colonies, 1660–1830.* New York: Oxford University Press, 2010.
Haskell, Thomas L. "Capitalism and the Origins of the Humanitarian Sensibility, Part 1," *American Historical Review* 90.2 (1985): 331–362.
 "Capitalism and the Origins of the Humanitarian Sensibility, Part 2," *American Historical Review* 90.3 (1985): 547–566.
Hawke, Gary. "Reinterpretations of the Industrial Revolution," in Patrick O'Brien and Ronald Quinlet, eds., *The Industrial Revolution and British Society.* New York: Cambridge University Press, 1993: 54–78.
Heuman, Gad. "Runaway Slaves in Nineteenth-Century Barbados," in Gad Heuman, ed., *Out of the House of Bondage: Runaways, Resistance and Maroonage in Africa and the New World.* London: Frank Cass, 1986: 95–111.
Higman, B. W. *Slave Populations of the British Caribbean, 1807–1834.* Baltimore: Johns Hopkins University Press, 1984.
 Slave Population and Economy in Jamaica, 1807–1834. New York: Cambridge University Press, 1977.
 Jamaica Surveyed: Plantation Maps and Plans of the Eighteenth and Nineteenth Centuries. Kingston, Jamaica: Institute of Jamaica Publications, 1988.
 Montpelier: A Plantation Community in Slavery and Freedom, 1739–1912. Kingston, Jamaica: The Press University of the West Indies, 1998.
 Plantation Jamaica, 1750–1850: Capital and Control in a Colonial Economy. Kingston, Jamaica: University of the West Indies Press, 2005.

"Physical and Economic Environments," in Verene Shepherd and Hilary Beckles, eds., *Caribbean Slavery in the Atlantic World: A Student Reader.* Kingston, Jamaica: Ian Randle Publishers, 2000.

"Economic and Social Development of the British West Indies From Settlement to ca. 1850," in Stanley L. Engerman and Robert E. Gallman, eds. *The Cambridge Economic History of the United States.* New York: Cambridge University Press 1996: 297–336.

"The Slave Family and the Household in the British West Indies, 1800–1834," *Journal of Interdisciplinary History* 6.2 (1975): 261–287.

"The Sugar Revolution," *Economic History Review* 53.2 (2000): 213–236.

Hudson, Larry. *To Have and to Hold: Slave Work and Family Life in Antebellum South Carolina.* Athens: University of Georgia Press, 1997.

Huggins, Nathan. "The Deforming Mirror of Truth: Slavery and the Master Narrative of American History," *Radical History Review* 49 (1991): 25–46.

Hunt, Lynn Avery. *Inventing Human Rights: A History.* New York: Norton, 2007.

Hunter, Brooke. "Wheat, War and the American Economy during the Age of Revolution," *William and Mary Quarterly* 62.3 (2005): 505–526.

Horn, Pamela. "The Contribution of the Propagandist to Eighteenth-Century Agricultural Improvement," *Historical Journal* 25.2 (June 1982): 313–329.

Innes, Stephen, ed. *Work and Labor in Early America.* Chapel Hill: The University of North Carolina Press, 1988.

Innis, Donald Q. *Intercropping and the Scientific Basis of Traditional Agriculture.* London: Intermediate Technology Publishing, 1997.

Irwin, James R. "Slave Agriculture and Staple Crops in the Virginia Piedmont," PhD. Dissertation, University of Rochester, 1986.

Isaac, Rhys. *Landon Carter' Uneasy Kingdom: Revolution and Rebellion on a Virginia Plantation.* Oxford: Oxford University Press, 2004.

Jekyll, Walter. *Jamaican Song and Story.* London: D. Nutt, 1907.

Johnson, Michael P. "Work, Culture and the Slave Community: Slave Occupations in the Cotton Belt in 1860," *Labor History* 27.3 (1986): 325–355.

Johnson, Walter. "On Agency," *Journal of Social History* 37.1 (Fall 2003): 113–124.

Kamoie, Laura Croghan. *Irons in the Fire: The Business History of the Tayloe Family and Virginia's Gentry, 1700–1860.* Charlottesville: University of Virginia Press, 2007.

Kay, Marvin, L. Michael, and Lorin Lee Cary, "'They are Indeed the Constant Plague of Their Tyrants': Slave Defence of a Moral Economy in Colonial North Carolina, 1748–1772," in Gad Heuman, ed., *Out of the House of Bondage: Runaways, Resistance and Maroonage in Africa and the New World.* London: Frank Cass, 1986: 37–78.

Kiple, Kenneth. *The Caribbean Slave: A Biological History.* New York: Cambridge University Press, 1984.

Knight, Frederick C. *Working the Diaspora: The Impact of African Labor on the Anglo-American World, 1650–1850.* New York: New York University Press, 2010.

Kulikoff, Alan. *Tobacco and Slaves: The Development of Southern Cultures in the Chesapeake, 1680–1800.* Chapel Hill: University of North Carolina Press, 1986.

Liebman, Matt, and Elizabeth Dyck. "Crop Rotation and Intercropping Strategies for Weed Management," *Ecological Applications* 3.1 (1993): 92–122.
Lee, Jean B. "Mount Vernon: A Model for the Republic," in Philip J. Schwarz, ed., *Slavery at the Home of George Washington*. Mount Vernon: Mount Vernon Ladies Association, 2001: 13–46.
Levy, Andrew. *The First Emancipator: The Forgotten Story of Robert Carter, the Founding Father Who Freed His Slaves*. New York: Random House, 2005.
Loftfield, Thomas C. "Creolization in Seventeenth-Century Barbados: Two Case Studies," in P. Farnsworth, ed., *Island Lives: Historical Archaeologies of the Caribbean*. Tuscaloosa: University of Alabama Press, 2001: 207–233
Lyson, Thomas A., and Rick Welsh. "The Production Function, Crop Diversity, and the Debate between Conventional and Sustainable Agriculture," *Rural Sociology* 58.3 (1993): 424–439.
Macdonald, Fiona A. "The Infirmary of the Glasgow Town's Hospital Patient Care, 1733–1800," in Paul Wood, ed., *The Scottish Enlightenment: Essays in Reinterpretation*. Rochester, NY: University of Rochester Press, 2000.
Mair, Lucille Mathurin. "Women Field Workers in Jamaica during Slavery," in Brian L. Moore, ed., *Slavery, Freedom and Gender: The Dynamics of Caribbean Society*. Kingston, Jamaica: The University of the West Indies Press, 2001: 183–196.
Manning, Susan, and Frances D. Cogliano. "The Enlightenment and the Atlantic," in S. Manning and F. D. Cogliano, eds., *Atlantic Enlightenments*. Burlington, VT: Ashgate, 2008: 1–18
Marzio, Peter C. "Carpentry in the Southern Colonies during the Eighteenth Century with Emphasis on Maryland and Virginia," *Winterthur Portfolio* 7 (1972): 229–250.
McClelland, Peter D. *Sowing Modernity: America's First Agricultural Revolution*. Ithaca, NY: Cornell University Press, 1992.
McCusker, John. "The Economy of the British West Indies, 1763–1790: Growth, Stagnation or Decline," in J. McCusker, ed., *Essays in the Economic History of the Atlantic World*. London: Routledge, 1997: 310–330.
McCusker, John, and Russell Menard. *The Economy of British America, 1607–1789*. Chapel Hill, NC: University of North Carolina Press, 1985.
McDonald, Roderick A. *The Economy and Material Culture of Slaves: Goods and Chattels on the Sugar Plantations of Jamaica and Louisiana*. Baton Rouge: Louisiana State University Press, 1993.
McGowen, Randall. "The Well-Ordered Prison: England, 1780–1865," in Norvall Morris and David J. Rothman, eds., *The Oxford History of the Prison: The Practice of Punishment in Western Society*. New York: Oxford University Press, 1998: 71–99.
McMenemy, H. "The Hospital Movement of the Eighteenth Century and Its Development," in Frederick N. L. Poynter, ed., *The Evolution of Hospitals in Britain*. London: Pitman, 1964: 43–69.
McNeill, John Robert. *Mosquito Empires: Ecology and War in the Greater Caribbean*. New York: Cambridge University Press, 2010.
Meitzner, Laura S., and Martin L. Price. *Amaranth to Zai Holes: Ideas for Growing Food under Difficult Conditions*. North Fort Myers, FL: ECHO, 1996.

Menard, Russell R. *Sweet Negotiations: Sugar, Slavery and Plantation Agriculture in Early Barbados*. Charlottesville: University of Virginia Press, 2006.
"Colonial America's Mestizo Agriculture," in Cathy Matson, ed., *The Economy of Early America: Historical Perspectives and New Directions*. University Park: Pennsylvania State University Press, 2006: 107–123.
Mepham, M. J. "The Scottish Enlightenment and the Development of Accounting," in R. H. Parker and B. S. Yamey, eds., *Accounting History: Some British Contributions*. Oxford: Clarendon Press, 1994: 268–293.
Metzer, Jacob. "Rational Management: Modern Business Practices and Economies of Scale in the Ante-Bellum Southern Plantations," *Explorations in Economic History* 12.1 (1975): 123–150.
Mintz, Sidney. *Sweetness and Power: The Place of Sugar in Modern History*. New York: Penguin Books, 1985.
"Slave Life on Caribbean Sugar Plantations: Some Unanswered Questions," in Stephen Palmie, ed., *Slave Cultures and the Cultures of Slavery*. Knoxville: University of Tennessee Press, 1995: 12–22.
Mokyr, Joel. *The Enlightened Economy: An Economic History of Britain, 1700–1850*. New Haven: Yale University Press, 2009.
"Technological Change, 1700–1830," in Roderick Floud and Donald McCloskey, eds., *The Economic History of Britain since 1700. Vol. 1: 1700–1860*, 2nd ed. New York: Cambridge University Press, 1994.
"The European Enlightenment and the Origins of Economic Growth," in Jeff Horn et al., eds., *Reconceptualizing the Industrial Revolution*. Cambridge, MA: MIT Press, 2010: 65–86.
Morgan, Jennifer. *Laboring Women: Reproduction and Gender in New World Slavery*. Philadelphia: University of Pennsylvania Press, 2004.
Morgan, Kenneth. *Slavery and Servitude in Colonial North America: A Short History*. New York: New York University Press, 2001.
"Slave Women and Reproduction in Jamaica, c1776–1834," *History* 91 (2006): 231–253.
Morgan, Philip D. *Slave Counterpoint: Black Culture in the Eighteenth-Century Chesapeake and Lowcountry*. Chapel Hill: University of North Carolina Press, 1998.
"Colonial South Carolina Runaways: Their Significance for Slave Culture," in Gad Heuman, ed. *Out of the House of Bondage: Runaways, Resistance and Maroonage in Africa and the New World*. Totowa, NJ: Frank Cass & Co. Ltd., 1986: 57–78.
"Slaves and Livestock in Eighteenth-Century Jamaica, Vineyard Pen, 1750–1751," *William and Mary Quarterly* 52.1 (1995): 47–76.
"Task and Gang Systems: The Organization of Labor on New World Plantations," in Stephen Innes, ed., *Work and Labor in Early America*. Chapel Hill: University of North Carolina Press, 1988: 189–220.
Morgan, Phillip D., and Michael L. Nicholls. "Slave Flight: Mount Vernon, Virginia, and the Wider Atlantic World," in Tamara Harvey and Greg O'Brian, eds., *George Washington's South*. Gainesville: University Press of Florida, 2004: 197–222.

Mullin, Michael. *Africa in America: Slave Acculturation and Resistance in the American South and the British Caribbean, 1736–1831.* Chicago: University of Illinois Press, 1992.
Oakes, James. *Slavery and Freedom: An Interpretation of the Old South.* New York: W. W. Norton & Company, 1990.
Oldenziel, Ruth. *Making Technology Masculine: Men, Women and Modern Machines in America, 1870–1945.* Amsterdam: Amsterdam University Press, 1999.
Olsen, Kirsten. *Daily Life in Eighteenth-Century England.* Westport, CT: Greenwood Press, 1999.
O'Malley, Greg. "Final Passages: The Intercolonial Slave Trade, 1619–1807," Ph.D. Dissertation, Johns Hopkins University, 2006.
Ormrod, Richard K. "The Evolution of Soil Management Practices in Early Jamaican Sugar Planting," *Journal of Historical Geography* 5.2 (1979): 157–170.
Outram, Dorinda. *The Enlightenment,* 2nd ed. New York: Cambridge University Press, 2006.
Overton, Mark. *Agricultural Revolution in England: The Transformation of the Agrarian Economy.* New York: Cambridge University Press, 1996.
Paquette, Robert L. "The Drivers Shall Lead Them: Image and Reality in Slave Resistance," in Paquette and Louis A. Ferleger, eds., *Slavery, Secession and Southern History* Charlottesville, 2000: 31–58.
  "Social History Update: Slave Resistance and Social History," *Journal of Social History* 24.3 (Spring 1991): 681–685.
Penningroth, Dylan. *Claims of Kinfolk: African-American Property and Community in the Nineteenth-Century South.* Chapel Hill: University of North Carolina Press, 2003.
Phillips, David, "Crime, Law and Punishment in the Industrial Revolution," in Patrick O'Brien and Ronald Quinlet, eds., *The Industrial Revolution and British Society.* New York: Cambridge University Press, 1993: 156–182.
Phillips, Ulrich Bonnel. *American Negro Slavery: A Survey of the Supply, Employment and Control of Negro Labor as Determined by the Plantation Regime.* New York: D. Appleton & Company, 1952 [1918].
Porter, Roy. *The Enlightenment.* New York: Palgrave Macmillan, 2001.
  The Creation of the Modern World: The Untold Story of the British Enlightenment. New York: W. W. Norton & Company, 2000.
Prude, Jonathan. "To Look upon the 'Lower Sort': Runaway Ads and the Appearance of Unfree Laborers in America, 1750–1800," *Journal of American History* 78.1 (1991): 124–159.
Puckrein, Gary. "Climate, Health and Black Labor in the English Americas," *Journal of American Studies* 13.2 (August 1979): 179–193.
Pursell, Matthew C. "Changing Conceptions of Servitude in the British Atlantic, 1640–1780," Ph.D. Dissertation, Brown University, May 2005.
Quattrone, Paolo. "Is Time Spent, Passed or Counted? The Missing Link between Time and Accounting History," *Accounting Historians Journal* 32.1 (2005): 185–208.
Ragatz, Lowell J. *The Fall of the Planter Class in the British Caribbean, 1763–1833.* New York: Octagon Books, 1977 [1928].

Rockman, Seth. *Scraping By: Wage Labor, Slavery, and Survival in Early Baltimore.* Baltimore: Johns Hopkins University Press, 2009.

Roberts, Justin. "Working Between the Lines: Labor and Agriculture on Two Barbadian Sugar Plantations, 1796–1797," *William and Mary Quarterly* 63.3 (2006): 551–586.

"Uncertain Business: A Case Study of Barbadian Plantation Management, 1770–1793," *Slavery & Abolition* 32.2 (June 2011): 247–268.

Roberts, Michael. "Sickles and Scythes: Women's and Men's Work at Harvest Time," *History Workshop Journal* 7.1 (1979): 3–28.

Rosenband, Leonard N. "Productivity and Labor Discipline in the Montgolfier Paper Mill, 1780–1805," *Journal of Economic History* 45.2 (June 1985): 435–443.

"Hiring and Firing at the Montgolfier Paper Mill," in L. N. Rosenband and M. Safley, eds., *The Workplace before the Factory: Artisans and Proletarians, 1500–1800.* Ithaca: Cornell University Press, 1993: 225–240.

Rosenband, Leonard, Merritt Roe Smith, and Jeff Horn. "Introduction," in Rosenband, Smith, and Horn, eds. *Reconceptualizing the Industrial Revolution.* Cambridge, MA: MIT Press, 2010: 1–20.

Rule, John. "The Property of Skill in the Period of Manufacture," in Patrick Joyce, ed., *The Historical Meanings of Work.* New York: Cambridge University Press, 1987: 99–118.

Russo, Jean B. *Free Workers in a Plantation Economy: Talbot County, Maryland, 1690–1750.* New York: Garland Publishing Inc., 1989.

Rusnock, Andrea A. *Vital Accounts: Quantifying Health and Population in Eighteenth-Century England and France.* New York: Cambridge University Press, 2002.

"Biopolitics: Political Arithmetic in the Enlightenment," in William Clark, Simon Schaffer, and Jan Golinski, eds., *The Sciences in Enlightened Europe.* Chicago: University of Chicago Press, 1999: 49–68.

Rutman, Darrett B., Charles Whetherell, and Anita Rutman. "Rhythms of Life: Black and White Seasonality in the Early Chesapeake," *Journal of Interdisciplinary History* 11.1 (Summer 1980): 29–53.

Ryden, David Beck. *West Indian Slavery and British Abolition, 1783–1907.* Cambridge: New York University Press, 2009.

"Does Decline Make Sense? The West Indian Economy and the Abolition of the British Slave Trade," *Journal of Interdisciplinary History* 31.3 (2001): 347–374.

"Planters, Slaves and Decline," in Heather Cateau and S. H. H. Carrington, eds., *Capitalism and Slavery: Fifty Years Later.* New York: Peter Lang Publishing Inc., 2000: 155–170.

Sargent, Frederick II. *Hippocratic Heritage: A History of Ideas about Weather and Human Health.* New York: Pergamon Press, 1982.

Schwartz, Stuart. *Sugar Plantations in the Formation of Brazilian Society, Bahia, 1550–1835.* Cambridge: Cambridge University Press, 1985.

Slaves, Peasants and Rebels: Reconsidering Brazilian Slavery. Urbana: University of Chicago Press, 1992.

Schweninger, Loren. "Counting the Costs: Southern Planters and the Problem of Runaway Slaves, 1790–1860," *Business and Economic History* 28.2 (1999): 267–275.
Scott, Daryl Michael. *Contempt and Pity: Social Policy and the Image of the Damaged Black Psyche, 1880–1996*. Chapel Hill: University of North Carolina Press, 1997.
Scott, Rebecca J. *Slave Emancipation in Cuba: The Transition to Free Labour, 1860–1899*. Pittsburgh, PA: University of Pittsburgh Press, 2000.
Sensbach, Jon F. "Charting a Course in Early African-American History," *William and Mary Quarterly* 50.2 (1993): 394–405.
Shapin, Steven. *The Scientific Revolution*. Chicago: University of Chicago Press, 1996.
Shepherd, Verene A. *Livestock, Sugar and Slavery: Contested Terrain in Colonial Jamaica*. Kingston, Jamaica: Ian Randle Publishers, 2009.
  "Livestock and Sugar: Aspects of Jamaica's Agricultural Development from the Late Seventeenth to the Early Nineteenth Century," *The Historical Journal* 34.3 (September 1991): 627–643.
  "Diversity in Caribbean Economy and Society from the Seventeenth to the Nineteenth Centuries," *Plantation Society in the Americas* 5.2–3 (1998): 175–187.
Sheridan, Richard B. *Sugar and Slavery: The Economic History of the British West Indies*. Baltimore: Johns Hopkins University Press, 1974.
  Doctors and Slaves: A Medical and Demographic History of Slavery in the British West Indies, 1680–1834. New York: Cambridge University Press, 1985.
  "Strategies of Slave Subsistence: The Jamaican Case Reconsidered," in Mary Turner, ed., *From Chattel Slaves to Wage Slaves; The Dynamics of Labour Bargaining in the Americas*. Bloomington: Indiana University Press, 1995: 48–67.
  "Why the Condition of the Slaves Was 'less intolerable in Barbadoes than in the other sugar colonies,'" in Hilary Beckles, ed., *Inside Slavery: Process and Legacy in the Caribbean Experience*. Kingston, Jamaica: University of the West Indies Press, 1996: 31–50.
  "Changing Sugar Technology and the Labour Nexus in the British Caribbean, 1750–1900, with Special Reference to Barbados and Jamaica," *New West Indian Guide* 63.1–2 (1989): 60–92.
  "The Formation of Caribbean Plantation Society, 1689–1748," in P. J. Marshall, ed., *The Oxford History of the British Empire: The Eighteenth Century*, vol. II. New York: Oxford University Press, 2001: 394–414.
  "The Crisis of Slave Subsistence in the British West Indies During and After the American Revolution," *William and Mary Quarterly* 33.4 (1976): 615–641.
  "Samuel Martin, Innovating Planter of Antigua, 1750–1776," *Agricultural History* 34.3 (1960): 126–139.
Sherman, Sherman. *Telling Time: Clocks, Diaries and the English Diurnal Form, 1660–1785* Chicago: University of Chicago Press, 1996.
Shuler, Kristrina. "Health, History, and Sugar: A Bioarchaeological Study of Enslaved Africans from Newton Plantation, Barbados, West Indies," Ph.D. Dissertation, Southern Illinois University, Carbondale, 2005.

Sidbury, James. "Slave Artisans in Richmond, Virginia, 1780–1810," in Howard B. Rock, Paul A. Gilje, and Robert Asher, eds., *American Artisans: Crafting Social Identity, 1750–1850*. Baltimore: Johns Hopkins University Press, 1995.
Smith, Mark. *Mastered by the Clock: Time, Slavery and Freedom in the American South*. Chapel Hill: University of North Carolina Press, 1997.
Smith, Simon David. *Slavery, Family and Gentry Capitalism in the British Atlantic: The World of the Lascelles, 1648–1834*. New York: Cambridge University Press, 2006.
"Sugar's Poor Relation: Coffee Planting in the British West Indies, 1720–1833," *Slavery & Abolition* 19.3 (December 1998): 68–89.
"An Introduction to the Plantation Journals of the Prospect Sugar Estate," in Records of the Jamaican Prospect Estate *[microform]*, Wakefield, England: Microform Academic Publishers, 2003: 1–29.
Spierenberg, Peter. "The Body and the State: Early Modern Europe," in Norvall Morris and David J. Rothman, eds., *The Oxford History of the Prison: The Practice of Punishment in Western Society*. New York: Oxford University Press, 1998: 44–70.
Starkey, Otis P. *The Economic Geography of Barbados: A Study of the Relationships between Environmental Variations and Economic Development*. New York: Columbia University Press, 1939.
Stead, David R. "Risk and Risk Management in English Agriculture, c1750–1850," *Economic History Review* 57.2 (2004): 334–361.
Steinfeld, Robert J. *Coercion, Contract and Free Labor in the Nineteenth Century*. New York: Cambridge University Press, 2001.
The Invention of Free Labor The Employment Relation in English and American Law and Culture, 1350–1870. Chapel Hill: University of North Carolina Press, 1991.
"Changing Legal Conceptions of Free Labor," in Stanley Engerman, ed., *Terms of Labor: Slavery, Serfdom, and Free Labor*. Stanford, CA: Stanford University Press, 1999: 137–167.
Steinfeld, Robert J., and Stanley L. Engerman. "Labor- Free or Coerced? A Historical Reassessment of Differences and Similarities," in Tom Brass and Marcel van der Linden, eds., *Free and Unfree Labor: The Debate Continues*. New York: Peter Lang, 1997: 107–126.
Stone, Lawrence. *The Family, Sex and Marriage in England: 1500–1800*. London: Weidenfield & Nicolson, 1977.
Sweet, James H. *Recreating Africa: Culture, Kinship, and Religion in the African-Portuguese World, 1441–1770*. Chapel Hill: University of North Carolina Press, 2003.
Tadman, Michael. "The Demographic Cost of Sugar: Debates on Slave Societies and Natural Increase in the Americas," *American Historical Review* 105.5 (2000): 1534–1575.
Tarlow, Sarah. *The Archaeology of Improvement in Britain, 1750–1850*. Leiden: Cambridge University Press, 2007.
Taylor, Eric Robert. *If We Must Die: Shipboard Insurrections in the Era of the Atlantic Slave Trade*. New Orleans: Louisiana State University Press, 2006.

Thirsk, Joan. *Alternative Agriculture: A History from the Black Death to the Present Day*. New York: Oxford University Press, 2000.

Thompson, Alvin O. *Flight to Freedom: African Runaways and Maroons in the Americas* Kingston, Jamaica: University of the West Indies Press, 2006.

Thompson, E. P. "Time, Work Discipline and Industrial Capitalism," *Past and Present* 38 (December 1967): 56–97.

Thompson, Mary. "'They Appear to Live Comfortable Together': Private Lives of the Mount Vernon Slaves," in Philip J. Schwarz, ed., *Slavery at the Home of George Washington*. Mount Vernon: Mount Vernon Ladies Association, 2001.

Thompson, Peter. "Henry Drax's Instructions on the Management of a Seventeenth-Century Barbadian Plantation," *William and Mary Quarterly* 3rd ser. 86.3 (2009): 565–604.

Thornton, Amanda. "Coerced Care: Thomas Thistlewood's Account of Medical Practice on Enslaved Populations in Colonial Jamaica, 1751–1786," *Slavery & Abolition* 32.4 (Fall 2011): 535–559.

Thornton, John. *Africa and Africans in the Making of the Atlantic World, 1400–1800*. New York: Cambridge University Press, 1992.

Turner, Mary. "Planter Profits and Slave Rewards: Amelioration Reconsidered," in Roderick A. McDonald, ed., *West Indies Accounts: Essays on the History of the British Caribbean and the Atlantic Economy in Honour of Richard Sheridan*. Kingston, Jamaica: University of the West Indies Press, 1996, 232–252.

"Chattel Slaves into Wage Slaves: A Jamaican Case Study," in Mary Turner, ed. *From Chattel Slaves to Wage Slaves: The Dynamics of Labour Bargaining in the Americas*. Bloomington: Indiana University Press, 1995.

van der Linden, Marcel. "The Origins, Spread and Normalization of Free Wage Labour," in Tom Brass and Marcel van der Linden, eds., *Free and Unfree Labor: The Debate Continues*. New York: Peter Lang, 1997: 501–524.

Vandermeer, John. *The Ecology of Intercropping*. Cambridge: Cambridge University Press, 1992.

van Stipriann, Alex. "The Suriname Rat Race: Labor and Technology on Sugar Plantations, 1750–1900," *New West Indian Guide* 63.1–2 (1989): 94–117.

von Tunzelman, G. N. "Technological and Organizational Change in Industry During the Early Industrial Revolution," in Patrick O'Brien and Ronald Quinlet, eds., *The Industrial Revolution and British Society*. New York: Cambridge University Press, 1993: 254–282.

Voth, Joachim. *Time and Work in England, 1750–1830*. New York: Oxford University Press, 2000.

Walsh, Lorena S. *Motives of Honor, Pleasure and Profit: Plantation Management in the Colonial Chesapeake, 1607–1763*. Chapel Hill: University of North Carolina Press, 2010.

"Slave Life, Slave Society, and Tobacco Production in the Tidewater Chesapeake, 1620–1820," in Ira Berlin and Philip D. Morgan, ed., *Cultivation and Culture: Labor and the Shaping of Slave Life in the Americas*. Charlottesville: University Press of Virginia 1993: 170–202.

"Land Use, Settlement Patterns and the Impact of European Agriculture, 1620–1820," in Philip D. Curtin et al., eds., *Discovering the Chesapeake: The History of an Ecosystem*. Baltimore: Johns Hopkins University Press, 2001.

"Plantation Management in the Chesapeake, 1620–1820," *The Journal of Economic History* 49.2 (June 1989): 393–406.

"Slavery and Agriculture at Mount Vernon," in Philip J. Schwarz, ed., *Slavery at the Home of George Washington*. Mount Vernon: Mount Vernon Ladies Association, 2002: 47–77.

"Work and the Slave Economy," in Gad Heuman and Trevor Burnard, eds., *The Routledge History of Slavery*. New York: Routledge, 2011: 101–118.

Ward, J. R. *British West Indian Slavery, 1750–1834: The Process of Amelioration*. New York: Oxford University Press, 1988.

"The Amelioration of British West Indian Slavery, 1750–1834: Technical Change and the Plow," *New West-Indian Guide* 63.1–2 (1989).

"The Profitability of Sugar Planting in the British West Indies, 1650–1834," *Economic History Review* 31.2 (May 1978): 197–213.

Watson, Karl. *A Kind of Right to be Idle: Old Doll, Matriarch of Newton Plantation*. Cave Hill: University of the West Indies Press, 2000.

The Civilised Island, Barbados: A Social History, 1750–1816. Ellerton, Barbados: Graphic Production, 1979.

Watts, David. *The West Indies: Patterns of Development, Culture, and Environmental Change since 1492*. Cambridge: Cambridge University Press, 1987.

"Origins of Barbadian Cane Hole Agriculture," *Journal of the Barbados Museum and Historical Society* 32.3 (May 1968): 143–151.

Weiss, Robert. "Humanitarianism, Labour Exploitation, or Social Control? A Critical Survey of Theory and Research on the Origin and Development of Prisons," *Social History* 12.3 (1987): 331–350.

White, Shane, and Graham White. *The Sounds of Slavery: Discovering African-American History Through Songs, Sermons, and Speech*. Boston: Beacon Press, 2005.

Wiencek, Henry. *An Imperfect God: George Washington, His Slaves and the Creation of America*. New York: Farrar, Straus and Giroux, 2003.

Wikinson, Alec. *Big Sugar: Seasons in the Cane Fields of Florida*. New York: Knopf, 1989.

Wilmot, Sarah. *"The Business of Improvement": Agriculture and Scientific Culture in Britain, c. 1770–c. 1870*. Bristol, England: Historical Geography Research Group, 1990.

Woodward, Donald. "An Essay on Manures: Changing Attitudes to Fertilization in England, 1500–1800," in John Chartes and David Hays, eds., *English Rural Society, 1500–1800: Essays in Honour of Joan Thirsk*. New York: Cambridge University Press, 1990.

Wolf, Eva Sheppard. "Early Free Labor Thought and the Contest over Slavery in the Early Republic," in John Craig Hammond and Matthew Mason, eds., *Contesting Slavery: The Politics of Bondage and Freedom in the New American Nation*. Charlottesville: University of Virginia Press, 2011: 32–48.

Yamey, B. S. "Scientific Bookkeeping and the Rise of Capitalism," *Economic History Review* 1.2–3 (1949): 99–113.

Index

abolition, British and US slave trade, 186
abolitionism, 19, 44–5, 48, 52, 78, 280
accounting practices, 38
   and absenteeism, 57
   plantation managers use of, 56, 58, 68–9
   Scottish influence on, 23, 57
   technology of, 40–1, 87
accounts
   boiling house records, 26, 57, 72, 75, 77, 79
   increase and decrease, 60–1, 176, 282
   slave inventories, 249–50
   statistics in, 32, 42, 56, 68
accounts, work log, 61–8, 281
   calculation of labor days, 83–5
   definitions of time in, 74–7
   depersonalization in, 239, 275
   design of, 57
   and economic diversification, 79
   George Washington's use of, 164
   in improvement movement, 32, 85–6
   recording techniques of, 159
   slave resistance in, 270
   weather recording in, 195
Africans, *see* slaves, African
agriculture, English, 102
agriculture, experiments, 37, 40–1, 79, 280
agriculture, sustainable, 114
agriculture, techniques of
   cross holing, 24, 106–7, 107
   historical development of, 20, 102, 112
   intercropping, 99, 101–2, 108
   weeding, 111–13, 121, 132, 143, 155–7
Alexandria, Virginia, 22

Alleyne, Elizabeth, 45
Alleyne, John Forster, 98–100
Alleyne, John Gay, 262
amelioration, 164, 200–1
amelioration, growth of, 44, 47–8
amelioration, ideas about
   agricultural improvement, 48, 52, 59, 78–9, 128–9, 280
   antislavery movements, 52–3, 78
   discipline, 52–3, 163–7
   division of labor, 137, 151–2, 158
   housing, 193–4
   paternalism, 53, 279
   pronatalist policies, 181, 186
   proslavery movements, 49
   self-sufficiency, 40, 43, 79
   slave families, 250
   tools, 108
   total work days, 70, 83
   work speed, 109, 120, 137, 286
   see also humanitarianism
amelioration, laws of, 23, 25, 54
American exceptionalism, 7
American Revolution, 13–14, 280, 286
   cost of provisions during, 91, 103, 283
   effects of, 25, 31, 39, 129
Anderson, James, 33
animal husbandry, 40, 46–7, 59–60, 113, 117–19, 141
   growth of, 16–17
   improvements in, 38
Antigua, 46
   sugar production of, 10, 107
   work logs of, 61, 67

Atlantic World, historiography of, 7, 25, 286–7
attorneys, plantation, 6, 42, 59, 206, 262, 290
see also planters

Bacon, Francis, 34, 67
Baker, IP, 231
Barbadian Society for the Improvement of Plantership, 20, 33–4
  estimates of total work days, 74, 83, 96, 107
    on cultivation of sugar and cotton, 99, 101
Barbados, economy of, 12, 14, 41
Barbados, geography of, 8, 13, 20, 45, 56, 286
Barbados, slave population of, 13–14
Barritt, Thomas, 60, 109–10
Beckford, William, 216, 248
Belgrove, William, 42–3, 56, 70, 80
  use of Henry Drax's management instructions, 61, 135–6, 153
Bentham, Jeremy, 50, 61
Blake, Patrick, 214
Blue Mountain Plantation, 248
boilers, enslaved, 230–3
  bargaining powers of, 230
  experiential skills of, 231–2
bookkeepers, 7, 57–8
Boyle, Robert, 35
Braco Plantation, 140, 146
Bridgetown, Barbados, 19
Burstin, Haim, 218
Bybrooke Plantation, 72

Cabell, William, 52, 197
Caines, Clement, 61, 67
cane holes, digging of, 105–6, 175
  cost of, 149–50
  effects of on health, 106, 110, 128, 176–8, 282
  labor requirements of, 105–10, 121, 123–8, 143–4, 161
capitalism, 5, 38
Carter, Landon, 40–1, 72–3
Ceded Islands, 12, 14, 46
children, slave
  adolescents, 187, 264–5
  health of, 142
  height of, 142, 187

work allocation of, 140–3, 257, 262
Christ Church, Barbados, 20–2, 98
Clarendon, Jamaica, 140
Clark, William, 156
clocks
  during harvest, 69
  horological revolution, 34
  time discipline, 70, 72–3, 75, 78, 288
  use of in accounts, 26, 69
  use of in boiling houses, 69, 72, 75, 233
  use of in mills, 72
  see also time
Codrington Plantation, 20, 52, 91, 141
coffee, 12–13, 101, 143–4
Collins, David, 115, 191, 193–5
  ideas about gang labor, 137, 151–2
  ideas about sickness, 161
  ideas about women, 154
community, definition of, 241
coopers, enslaved, 203–4, 207–9, 214, 222–4, 228–9, 245–6
  families of, 258
corn
  beginnings of cultivation in Virginia, 16, 22, 41, 91
  harvest of, 92–3
  labor requirements of, 92
Coromantee, 211
  see also slaves, African
cotton, 21, 91, 98–101
  cultivation after hurricanes, 98–100
  growth of in United States, 97–8
  harvest of, 13, 124
  labor requirements of, 90, 143–4
creolization
  effect of on community, 240, 276, 277
  effect of on work productivity, 30, 213
  increase of, 30, 256, 284, 289
Cresswell, Nicholas, 199
criminals, 50–1, 200
Cromwell, Oliver, 11
cultivation, seasons of
  comparative, 23, 24, 128–9
  effect on diet, 171–3
  effect on health, 24, 128
  harvesting, 122, 128
  historiography of, 39, 80–1
  importance in agriculture, 38–9
  total work time, 87–9
  work organization, 24, 120
  see also work; weather

Danish Caribbean, 61
Daston, Lorraine, 49
deforestation, 10, 13
Dickson, William, 114, 175, 183, 203, 223, 270–1
  description of gang labor, 148, 151
  estimates of work days, 83–5
diversification, economic
  drawbacks of, 118
  effects on skill development, 41
  effects on technology, 38–9
  effects on work routines, 81–2, 120, 129
  influence of amelioration on, 81
  reduction of risks in, 81, 90
doctors, 7, 115
domestics, enslaved, 210–11, 243, 250, 252–7, 276, 284–5
Dovaston, John, 48, 52, 77, 211
Drax Hall Plantation, 141
Drax, Henry, 42–3, 61, 102, 135–6, 141, 153
drivers, enslaved, 75, 77–8, 131, 139, 143, 150
  skilled work of, 213–14, 261
  value of, 214
Duckensfield Hall Plantation, 20, 127, 146, 224
dyewood, 101

Edwards, Bryan, 78, 136, 142, 171, 202, 214
Egypt Plantation, 71
Ellis, William, 80
empiricism, Baconian, 6, 32
energy, economy of, 244–6
Engels, Friedrich, 228
England, 50
Enlightenment
  concepts of race, 206
  concepts of work, 6–7, 25, 27–8, 30, 50, 59
  and liberty, 6
  moral reform of, 44, 49–52, 51–2, 61, 79
  and natural rights, 27–8
  philanthropic projects of, 23, 49
  stage-based theories of development, 204–5
  views of discipline, 30, 49–50
  views of progress, 27, 36, 132–3, 171, 205, 280
  weather recording of, 195

Enlightenment, science, 23, 27, 31–2, 40–1, 232
  see also Newtonian universalism
Enlightenment, Scottish, 23

Fairfax County, Virginia, 22
festivals, 120
fevers, 191
Franklin, Benjamin, 37, 60
free blacks, 235
freedom, concepts of, 3, 5

gang labor, 131, 142–3, 145, 187, 212
  collective skill of, 149–50
  connections to cane holing, 105, 123, 135–6, 139, 144–5, 149–50
  experiments with, 132, 150–3
  inefficiencies of, 151
  interdependence of, 127, 131, 136, 138, 144–6, 148
  monotony of, 149, 152, 235
  origins of, 135–6, 153, 158
  provision work of, 101, 105, 143–4, 155–7
  on secondary crops, 143–4
  synchronization of work efforts in, 115, 131, 144–6, 148–9
  work hours of, 37, 75, 77, 82
gangs
  crop determinism of, 158
  depersonalization of, 133–5, 150–1
  economies of scale in, 145
  formation of, 131–2, 135, 150–1, 283
  planters' concept of, 133–5, 153
  quantification of, 151
  size of, 108, 123, 136–41
  spatial dimensions if, 146
  subdivisions of, 137–40, 144–5, 152
  supervision cost of, 138, 145–8, 152
gangs, infirm, 137–8, 155–7, 187–8
gangs, jobbing, 105, 109–10, 116, 136, 141, 149
  rising costs of, 99
  see also gang labor; gangs
Gibbes, Philip, 137, 143, 151–2, 192, 244, 248
Gildert, Francis, 213
Gill, Russell, 49
Gold Coast, 211
Grainger, James, 113, 192

grains, 31, 37, 41–3, 47, 110–11, 118
  harvest of, 127–8, 148, 226–7
  share of revenues, 22
  see also wheat

Haitian Revolution, 12, 100
  effect on British sugar production, 53
healers, enslaved, 253–4
Higman, B W, 223
Hilary, William, 190
Holder, H.E., 135
hospitals, plantation, 40, 50, 164–7, 171, 284
  beginnings of, 166
  gender divisions in, 182
  lack of in Virginia, 166
  punishment of, 166–7
  size of, 165–6
Howard, John, 50
humanitarianism, 28, 31, 44–7, 52–3, 78, 281
  see also amelioration, ideas about
hurricanes, 13–14, 18, 58, 135, 198
  effects of on amelioration laws, 54
  effects, on cotton production, 98–9
  effects of on shipping, 69, 81, 89, 121, 123
  effects on work routines, 196
  provisioning after, 248

Ibo, 250
  see also slaves, African
improvement, agricultural
  British improvers in, 35, 40, 42, 281
  correspondence networks of, 40
  crop rotation of, 17, 39, 41, 79, 102
  role of manure in, 36, 40–1, 79, 114, 119
  use of the plow, 17, 40–1, 129
Industrial Revolution, 25, 89, 205
  effects on deskilling of labor, 209, 218, 235
  industrious revolution, 29
  work culture of, 207
insurance, 123

Jamaica, economy of, 15
Jamaica, geography of, 10, 15, 21, 285
Jamaica, slave population of, 14–15
Jefferson, Thomas, 40, 43, 53

Keane, Michael, 43, 234

Kein, Patrick, 52, 216
Kingston, Jamaica, 11, 19

labor, divisions of, 131, 145
  sexual divisions of, 127, 138, 141, 153–7
labor, early modern systems of, 30, 33–4, 37–8, 69
labor, free, 36–7, 39, 75, 78, 133, 152
labor, *see* work
Lancaster County, Virginia, 20
Lane, John, 20
Lane, Thomas, 20
Leeward Islands, 10, 20
Lee, William, 118, 210, 213–14
Lesser Antilles, 114
Lewis, Matthew, 171
Locke, John, 48–9
logging, 85, 101
Long, Edward, 193
Louisiana, 232
Lowcountry, United States, 8, 131
Lowther Plantation, 98, 153

Mair, John, 58
malaria, 177, 179
manuals, plantation, 56, 60, 70, 74, 77
manumission, 53
manure, 128, 200, 282
  effects on health, 177, 180, 191, 223
  planters' measuring of, 57
  and plowing, 111
  role in work routines, 113–20, 145
  slave resistance to, 268
  use of in amelioration, 47
  during wet weather, 197
marriage, slave, 250–3
Martin, Samuel, 34–5, 43, 46–9, 51, 70
masons, enslaved, 203–4, 208, 211, 222–4, 228–9, 284
Mathison, Gilbert, 181
mechanistic philosophy, 34
Mercer, James Francis, 198
miasmas, theory of, 190, 194
Mintz, Sidney, 2
Monticello Plantation, 41
mortality
  effects of work on, 176–8
  rates of among whites, 177
  rates of in summer, 174
  in winter, 178–9
Moseley, Benjamin, 171

mosquitos, 177, 179
Mount Airy Plantation, 20, 41
Mount Vernon Plantation, 22–3, 86–7, 129, 165, 286
    cash crop production of, 104, 126, 128
    economic diversification of, 91, 97
    experiments at, 41
    families of, 251–3, 255, 257–9
    labor organization of, 147, 169, 283
    labor patterns of, 87–8, 92–3, 110–13, 116–17, 132, 198
    resistance at, 271–3
    sickness patterns of, 170, 178–9, 182, 184, 186, 188–9
    skilled work at, 208, 217–21, 225–30, 236
    total annual work hours of, 86
mulattos, 210, 236, 244, 255, 259, 260

neighborhoods, plantation, 266–7
Newtonian universalism, 6, 32
    see also Enlightenment, science
Newton Plantation, 19–22
    census of, 249–50
    dungeon of, 51
    families of, 249–55, 258, 260–1
    harvest of, 124–9
    hospital of, 165–6
    impact of weather on, 196
    labor organization of, 139, 141–4, 146, 155–6
    labor patterns of, 88–9, 93–7, 101–2, 104–7, 109, 115–20
    provision grounds at, 245
    runaways at, 264–71
    sickness rates of, 169–70, 172–6, 180–2, 186–8
    skilled work at, 204, 213, 223–6, 228, 233, 236
    total annual work hours of, 86
    total work days of, 85
North Carolina, 268
Northern Neck, Virginia, 20

overseers
    reputation of, 41
    see also planters

Parnassus Plantation, 140
pasturage, 40–1, 48, 79, 118
Penitentiary Act, 51

pests, 18, 98
Phillipsfield Plantation, 20, 187
    hospital of, 165–6
    labor organization of, 157
    mill work of, 26
    sickness rates of, 168–9
    work reductions of during cane holing, 110
piracy, 11
plantations
    historiography of, 72
    compared to factories, 69, 81, 207, 288, 290
planters, 6, 20, 118
    definition of, 7
    displacement of guilt, 249
    historiography of, 48, 50–1, 53, 57, 79
    responsiveness to external factors, 99–100, 103
    see also attorneys, plantation; overseers
Pleasant Hill Plantation, 20, 187
    accounts of, 60
    harvest of, 122, 126, 128–9
    hospital of, 166
    labor organization of, 157
    mill work of, 26
    overseers' comments on slaves' disposition, 54
    sickness rates of, 168
    work reductions of during cane holing, 110
political economy, 204–7
Portland, Jamaica, 21–2, 193, 196
Potomac River, 97
pregnancy, 181–2, 284
    see also women, slaves
Prospect Plantation, 19, 21–2, 85–6, 283, 286–7
    harvest of, 122–4, 126, 128–9, 171
    impact of weather on, 193, 196–7
    labor organization of, 137, 142–3, 146, 155–6, 159
    labor patterns of, 93–4, 101, 103–4, 108–9, 112, 116–18
    runaways at, 270–1
    sickness rates of, 167–8, 170–1, 173–7, 185
    total annual work hours of, 86
    total work days of, 84
provision grounds, 85, 87, 103, 242, 245, 283

provisions, 73, 78, 90, 101–3, 105
  during harvest, 171
  provisioning systems of, 102, 269, 289
punishment, 45–6, 51–2, 54, 78, 221, 265–6
  for theft, 256
  threat of the field, 234–5

race, 190, 206, 210–11
rain
  in Barbados, 191
  effects of on harvest, 197–8
  effects of on health, 194, 284
  in Jamaica, 191
  mortality rates in, 191
  planters' ideas about, 190–1, 200, 284
  protections from slaves, 194–5, 199
  and sugar cultivation, 69, 121, 194
rangers, enslaved, 243
resistance
  feigning illness, 163–4, 167, 169–70, 199, 272
  historiography of, 2, 3, 42, 240–2
  protest of working conditions, 290
  refusal to change occupations, 234, 238–9
  runaways, 85, 266–73
  work absences, 263–5, 269, 271
rice, 8, 84, 212
Richmond County, Virginia, 20
Richmond, Virginia, 20
Robson, Nicholas, 216
Rollstone, Samuel, 238–9
Rosenband, Leonard, 230
rum, 13, 40, 58, 96, 103, 171
  given to slaves, 194–5, 274
  stolen, 254

Sabine Hall Plantation, 20
Safley, Thomas, 230
Salt River, Jamaica, 71
sawyers, enslaved, 224
Scotland District, Barbados, 20
scurvy, 179
Seawell Plantation, 19–21, 26, 129, 287
  cotton at, 99–101
  creole slaves on, 213
  families of, 249, 251–9
  harvest of, 121, 124, 126–8
  hospital of, 166
  impact of weather on, 196

labor organization of, 141, 144, 157
labor patterns of, 95–7, 102–4, 107–9, 112, 116, 118
runaways at, 264–71
sickness rates of, 169–70, 172–6, 185–6
skilled work at, 202–4, 222–3, 225–8, 236
total work days of, 84
Seven Years' War, 13
shipping, 122–3
sickness, 167–70
  of adolescents, 187–9
  in Barbados, 169–70
  definition of, 162
  of elderly, 186–9
  during harvest, 171–3
  in Jamaica, 167–9
  master-slave negotiation of, 161, 163–4, 284
  and provisioning, 171–5
  and seasoning, 24
  and total labor days, 83–5
  in Virginia, 170
  in winter, 178–9
skill, 211–12, 236
  Aristotelian traditions of, 210
  of Barbadian planters, 39
  and drivers, 217–18
  experiential learning of, 149, 157
  and field work, 127, 212
  and plowmen, 214–15
  and slaves' knowledge of plantation soils, 213
  see also slaves, skilled
skill, gendering of, 154–5, 204, 215, 218–19, 225, 236
slave productivity, 30–1, 74–5, 124–5, 129
slavery, definition of, 37–8
slavery, efficiency of, 30, 49, 76–8
slavery, historiography of, 2–6
slavery, profitability of, 37, 42
slaves
  fertility of, 29, 54, 86, 282
  price of, 47, 53, 99
  see also women, slaves; children, slaves
slaves, African, 21–2, 85, 137, 212–13, 232–3
  and field labor, 256
  see also Coromantee; Ibo
slaves, communities of
  leadership of, 244
  and occupations, 24

Index

plantation size effect on, 240, 242
resistance of, 2, 24, 53, 274
spatial dynamics of, 240, 242
unequal wealth distribution of, 24, 276, 285
slaves, creole, 22, 30, 236
   sickness rates of, 170, 199
   value of, 212–13, 290
   wealth accumulation of, 247
slaves, discipline of, 26–30, 32, 45–9, 51–2, 73, 131
slaves, elite, 243, 244, 252–8
slaves, families of, 24, 247, 250, 252–9
slaves, hierarchies of, 53, 121, 226–7, 241, 248–50, 275–6
slaves, hired, 225–6
slaves, natural reproduction of, 31–2, 47–8, 78–9, 162–3, 252–3, 280–2
slaves, property of, 247
slaves, skilled, 24, 68, 75, 255–8
   health of, 34
   privileges of, 202, 223–4, 235, 239, 259–61
   proportion of, 207–9
   selection of, 210–11, 236–7
   value of, 223
   women, 259–61
   work routines of, 73, 75, 202–4, 222–30, 260
   compared to free tradesmen, 229–30
   see also skill
slave trade, transatlantic, 17, 110, 286
Smith, Adam, 145, 205, 218
Smith, Mark, 69
societies, agricultural, 20
   see also Barbadian Society for the Improvement of Pkantership
soils erosion of, 107–8, 111, 116, 129, 135, 146
soils, quality of, 22, 40–1, 47, 107–8, 129, 147
Somerset Vale Plantation, 20, 91, 101–2
   gender divisions at, 224–5
   harvest at, 121–2, 126, 128–9, 227
   labor organization at, 140, 144, 155
   labor patterns at, 108
   mixed cropping patterns at, 91, 101–2, 104–5, 112
songs, work, 149
   see also gang, labor; gangs
South Carolina, 8, 212

St. Domingue, revolt of, *see* Haitian Revolution
St. John, Barbados, 20
St. Kitts, 56, 61, 133, 137, 139, 214
St. Thomas, Jamaica, 20
St. Vincent, 43, 161
Steele, Joshua, 83
Steuart, James, 205
sugar, 12, 39, 57, 69, 101, 128
   agricultural cycle of, 69, 105, 268
   effects on health, 58, 70, 282
   expansion of in Caribbean, 97
   growing conditions of, 21
   harvest of, 37, 87–9, 110, 117, 120–8
   labor requirements of, 93–6
   prices of, 98, 121
   rationing of, 96, 107–8
   seasons of production, 81, 90, 93, 95, 121
sugar, boiling of, 230–2
sugar mills, 21, 125
   industrial accidents in, 72, 172, 289
   night labor of, 87, 89, 121, 124–7, 173
   repairs of, 99
   use of clocks in, 34–6, 69, 72, 76
   women's labor in, 156
sugar, Otaheite, 40
sugar revolution, 10–11, 53
Suggs, Theodorick, 52
Sunday labor, 124–7, 246, 251
Sutherland, William, 248
systems, concept of, 31–5, 42, 47, 56, 78

task labor, 131, 133, 152–3, 158, 245
Taylor, Simon, 20, 60, 229, 248, 250
technology, 17, 30, 32, 34–40, 205–7
   in agriculture, 41–2, 54
   compatibility of with slavery, 205–7
   and mechanization, 37–8
Temple, William, 50
Thistlewood, Thomas, 138, 262, 267
   notations of time in diary, 70–3
Thomson, James, 182
time, measurements of, 26–9, 30, 32, 67–70
time, motion studies of, 26–7, 75
time, *see* clocks
tobacco, 17, 37, 43
   in early Virginian agriculture, 16, 91
   seasons of production, 81, 90
   soil exhaustion of, 111, 146
   work gangs, 132
Tobago, 54–5

tools, 37–8, 154, 205–7, 212, 215–16, 222
total work days of, 84
  work logs of, 61, 67, 75
  work routines of, 92–3, 112–13, 116–17, 119, 198
Trelawny, Jamaica, 140
Tulldeph, Walter, 61
Turnbull, Gordon, 32, 77, 194
Turner, Mary, 248
Turner's Hall Plantation, 20, 45–6
  during American Revolution, 103
  community of, 273–5
  families of, 251, 253, 257, 259
  protest of slaves at, 262
  woods of, 238–9

universe, clockwork, 70

Vere Plantation, 140
Virginia, economy of, 17, 41, 79, 129, 282–3
Virginia, geography of, 16, 22–3
Virginia, slave population of, 17–18

Ward, JR, 175
Washington, George, 22–3, 40–2, 43, 198–9, 208
  on agricultural machinery, 215
  on amelioration, 47
  attempts at self-sufficiency, 92
  experiments of, 97
  management of tradesmen, 226–8
  manumission of slaves, 53
  punishments of slaves, 202, 233–5
  on sick slaves, 164, 189
  on systems, 33
  use of clock, 26
  use of work logs, 61, 67–9
  visit to Barbados, 117
Washington, Martha, 220
watchmen, enslaved, 238–9
weather
  effects of on health, 105, 179, 284
  effects of on provisions, 192
  effects of on work, 85, 121–2, 124, 163, 191–2, 195–9
  planters' ideas about, 35, 190–3, 200, 284
  slaves' ideas about, 193, 195

Westmoreland, Jamaica, 12
Weston, Wiliam, 58
wheat, 16, 22, 91
  harvest of, 159
  labor requirements of, 92, 163
  seasons of production, 81, 90, 127, 154
  see also grains
Windward Islands, 9, 11
women, slave, 154, 178, 243–4, 270
  effects of field work on, 180–1, 200
  fertility of, 182, 282
  mortality of, 177–8
  planters' conception of, 154, 158, 215–16
  sickness of, 24, 180–1
  weeding work of, 156–7
  working as drivers, 155–7
Wood, Sampson, 20, 182, 233, 249, 254, 264
  accounting practices of, 26, 58, 249
  on amelioration of work conditions, 115
  methods of discipline, 51
  on slaves' health, 163–4
  on slaves' rest days, 77
work
  concepts of, 205, 236
  effects of Barbadian terrain on, 118, 138–9, 200
  effects of on health, 34, 83, 114–15, 119–20, 199–200
  effects of Jamaica terrain on, 85, 138–9, 146, 200
  effects of Virginian terrain on, 22
  moral redemption of, 50–1
  and seasoning, 110, 167
  specialization of, 136, 144–5, 150, 158, 218–19, 224–5
workers, free, 36–7, 49, 75, 79, 206, 288
workhouses, 50, 166
work, industrial, 30, 32, 45, 49, 87, 288
work, total days of
  per year, 81–5
work, total hours of
  per month, 87, 128
  per year, 86–7

York Plantation, 124
Young, Arthur, 32, 80, 214